A BLEEDING SLAUGHTERHOUSE

The outrageous true story of the Alexandra Hospital Massacres, Singapore, February 1942

Stuart Lloyd

CatMatDog Storytelling

'I congratulate you on your research and writing.'
Brigadier Henry Wilson.

'Excellent! I really hope you get your deserved reward for this monumental work.' Stephen Mackenzie, ex-Royal Australian Air Force.

'Fascinating to get more insight into the story of Dad's experiences. We are amazed and pleased to discover all this new information so many years on.' Maureen Lane, daughter of survivor Pte Bert Gurd, RAMC.

Also by Stuart Lloyd

Bamboozled – The Lighter Side of Expat Life in Asia.

The Depths of December – The Sinking of the HMS *Prince of Wales, Repulse,* and *The British Empire, 1941.*

The Grubby Little Men Who Raped Hong Kong – The True Story of the St Stephen's College Massacre, December 1941.

The Malay Experiment – The Colourful Story of How Capt George Bruce Made the Malay Regiment Fit to Fight, 1933-1942.

The Missing Years – A PoW's Story from Changi to Hellfire Pass.

The Nightmare of Nanking – Selected Stories from The Nanking Massacres of 1937-38.

Tales from the Tiger's Den – An Oral History of Foreigners in the Far East from 1920 to 2020.

Published by: CatMatDog Publishers, Australia.
ABN: 85312594003
CatMatDog.com

Contact the author: stulloyd.worldsmith@gmail.com

ISBN: 978-0-6453280-4-2
Available in paperback and eBook.

Cover design and maps: Stuart Lloyd
Interior typesetting: Shahid Aziz

'The hunter shall cradle the wounded bird to his breast.'

窮鳥懐に入れば猟師も殺さず

– Japanese proverb –

'Man's inhumanity to man makes countless thousands mourn.'

– Robert Burns –

CONTENTS

Foreword By Col (Ret'd) M A Slade L/RAMC iii
Introduction by Stuart Lloyd vii
The Cast/ Dramatis Personae xv
List Of Maps and Illustrations xix
Prologue 1

Part 1 - The Build Up

Curtain-Raiser in China 7
Meanwhile in Singapore 13
Beer, Biscuits and Bushido 21
The Indians Pad Up 29
Steaming Towards Singapore 41
Gold Rush and Greed 59
Running Repairs 77
Swinging Singapore 83
Open for Business 91

Part 2 - The Main Act

Rising Sun, Sinking Empire 115
A Mauling in Malaya 129
The Battle for Singapore 151
West Coast Warpath 177
Singapore's Dunkirk Day 193
Heading for the Harbour 209
The Perfect Storm 221
Ceasefire and Silence 299

Mopping up the Mess 313
Scattered in all Directions 339
Rolling on to Rangoon 353
Could Things Get Any Worse? 357
The Victors Become Vanquished 369
A Deadly Diaspora 385

Part 3 - Post War

The Beginning of the End 397
The Sugamo Showdown 429
The Case that Crash-Landed 435
Trial and Errors 445
A Belated Bombshell 465
Making Sense of that Senseless Thing 481

Acknowledgments 525
Bibliography and Sources 529
About Stuart Lloyd 537

FOREWORD

By Colonel (Retired) M A Slade L/RAMC

There are some books, which once read, you cannot get completely out of your mind. This is one of them. Whether you are just curious, a scholar, military historian or, like me, have a personal connection to this story, you will at once be absorbed. At the end you will be compelled to reflect with very mixed and conflicting emotions upon what you have read.

I joined the Royal Army Medical Corps (RAMC) as a boy soldier in 1972, retiring in 2011. I have been involved in many conflicts and humanitarian activities over the intervening 40-year period. I have witnessed much. However, I volunteered to join this fine Corps and never regretted a moment of it. My experiences have, however, exposed me to the fragility of civilised behaviours which it seems – far from being deep-rooted in our cultures and psychology – are in fact only a very thin veneer deep. What one apparently civilised human will do to another under differing circumstances has always both shocked and fascinated me. I have to some extent become conditioned to the base levels of human behaviours and the subsequent effect upon individuals and communities. But this story places individuals and events under the microscope in order to highlight what motivated the aggressors and to remind the reader of the bravery of the recipients.

The motto of the RAMC is '*In Arduis Fidelis*'. Translated, this means Faithful in Adversity. Although not formally established as the RAMC until 1898, the Corps can trace its proud history back to 1660. This book demonstrates that the soldiers and officers of the Corps were, even when tested to the bitter end, true to their motto.

In contrast to today's professional soldiers and officers of the British armed forces medical services, it should be remembered that many of the medical personnel caught up in this appalling event were effectively conscripts who were propelled into active service with the minimum of preparation and just vague expectations of what was to come, bar to just treat the sick and injured. Nobody could have foreseen what nightmarish and monstrous acts would be perpetrated in a perfectly nice hospital in an exotic posting such as Singapore.

This book offers first-hand testimony regarding the behaviour of many elements of the Imperial Japanese Army which confirms that, far from being actions of last resort in personal survival terms, these horrific acts were organised, deliberate and ruthlessly applied and – when considered in the context of slaughtering unarmed medical and other hospital personnel and their patients – simply unforgivable. The armed forces of Japan were (and remain) signatories to the Geneva Conventions (the 'rules of war'). However they were not ratified by Japan until 1953. This is important because, despite not ratifying these Conventions at the time of the war, Japan promised to abide by and respect them. Had this been the case, then clearly, they would have not illegally attacked a marked medical facility, and engaged in the subsequent wholesale murder of medical staff. Likewise, any survivors falling into their hands should have been defined not as Prisoners of War, but rather Retained Personnel.

The difference is that Retained Personnel must be allowed to continue discharging their medical duties to all (including injured enemy) with priority of treatment based upon clinical need alone. What greater contrast to this internationally agreed approach to the treatment of medical staff has there ever been?

Many years ago, I discovered that my wife's grandfather (Pte Frank Hill, RAMC) had apparently been killed at the fall of the Alexandra Hospital on 14-15 February 1942. My father-in-law, Brian Hill, knew next to nothing regarding his father's service and demise as, at the time of his reported death, Brian was only three years old. His family didn't seem to know much beyond this headline. Subsequent enquiries and research over many years has now filled in many gaps. He was a member of 198th Field Ambulance which, owing to the imminent fall of Singapore, had withdrawn from previous locations and, unusually, become co-located with the hospital.

He miraculously survived the massacre and, following a

period in Changi Camp, was sent on a 'hell ship' via Rabaul on the island of Papua New Guinea and then on to Balalea island in the Western Solomon Islands where, with nearly 600 others (mainly Royal Artillery), they were tasked to construct an airstrip. However, the American Airforce spotted this activity and began to regularly bomb the island, killing many Allied prisoners who were given no shelter. The Japanese eventually believing that they were about to be overrun, murdered all of the remaining prisoners including, it is believed, Frank Hill. He was just 23 years old.

It was during this long journey of discovery in respect of Brian's father that we came into contact with the author of this engrossing and important book.

Stuart Lloyd has been gracious enough to mention this event within these pages, where, along with stories from many others, a real feel for the individual actors can be gleaned. In masterfully drawing together the strategic, operational and individual components of this horror story it highlights in stark terms how – at all levels – just a few individuals can massively shape events and outcomes and not necessarily either be held either accountable or to be rewarded. Indeed, there is more than a suggestion of a conspiracy of silence and dissonance contained here which, along with questionable coincidences, casts a long shadow over this most shocking of war crimes.

October 2021,
United Kingdom.

INTRODUCTION

I love a perfect mystery. And the Alexandra Hospital Massacres have captured my imagination like no other, being made up of several previously unsolved mysteries within the mystery, as you shall soon see.

This book is really about humanity and inhumanity. My intention in researching this book was to be as forensic as possible, but my aim as a storyteller was to express the amazing humanity that shone through. As award-winning author Neil Gaiman said: 'The greatest triumphs and the greatest tragedies of the human race are nothing to do with people being basically good or people being basically evil, they're all to do with people being basically people.'

What I want to get across with this investigation into these egregious events is an understanding of The Alexandra Hospital Massacres as a perfect storm. A chaotic confluence. Who were all those fateful figures who ended up in this western corner of an equatorial island – an island many had never heard of before disembarking there – at that particular time? Patients, doctors, nurses, orderlies, officers and soldiers from both sides. What decisions had they made, or were made for them, to be there? What events had brought them together face-to-face or side-by-side? And why the context created that convergent situation with its horrifically unfortunate outcomes.

It is a wildly undulating story trajectory: at once, a 'Whodunnit?' and a psycho-thriller, because after all the years it was still not known who actually committed these most heinous of actions in all of World War 2. So that was my main challenge and jumping off point.

The deeper I dived into the story, the more I saw it as a continuum. Not just what happened on the weekend of 14-15 February 1942, but the preparation and lead-up for our protagonists, and what became of those who were lucky enough to survive?

Delving further into this rabbit-hole, I realized there was an amazing collection of individuals under the hospital's Red-Crossed roof. People with incredibly eccentric, colourful and fascinating back-stories, and some who went on to achieve great eminence post-war.

Getting to know and understand the central characters was exciting – tracking down them or their next of kin was utterly adrenaline-inducing, and to wake up to a positive response in my email inbox was an unadulterated thrill, an addictive dopamine shot. One of the reasons is that it has enabled me to meet and correspond with some fantastic folks who didn't seem to mind my parachuting intrusively into the most personal aspects of their lives and family memories.

I want to put you, dear reader, into the army-issued boots of the Allied and Japanese cast members. So you come along right beside me on this fascinating, often-forensic, journey of discovery.

The understory of this book is the competitiveness between the Japanese divisional commanders and their charges. Who would be the first into Singapore to capture that prized Union Jack flag fluttering atop Fort Canning?

The major geo-politics of the Malayan campaign have been well and oft told, and I will assume a certain amount of that background knowledge in you. Rather than being bogged by dry military detail about mega-movements of divisions, regiments, etc I was far more interested in getting to know the key characters of the story – getting into their heads, their lives, their emotional space as far as possible. My style is more 'history from below' as noted military historian Antony Beevor calls it. More concerned with the fear, the chaos, the human frailty, than the macro-movements and geo-politics. Because even the mightiest conquering division is made up of thousands of individuals with hopes and dreams and possibly a blister on their big toe which is ruining their otherwise victorious day. So we can get emotionally invested in them and feel their life abruptly changing as fate dictates their fortune for better or worse.

For example, one poor chap was sent to The Alex (this being my preferred nomenclature for the British Military Hospital Singapore, based on common usage of the day) with hemorrhoids, which consigned him to events far worse than he could ever have imagined. A far greater pain in the arse, you could say.

It was George MacDonald Fraser – famous for his *Flashman* series, but who also served in the Burma campaign – whom I must thank for opening my eyes to the 'Minutiae of the Moment'. His book *Quartered Safe Out Here* captured exactly that, all the more powerful for being his own astute battlefield observations.

And so in my research I started paying greater attention to the moments between the major events. Especially the human frailties, more especially of the Japanese infantry who are widely perceived as, and written about, as unquestioning automatons. The pioneering work of Henry Frei in interviewing Japanese soldiers, in Japanese language, changed the game for me here. For here were soldiers who called each other 'idiot' or 'arsehole', just as the Allies playfully or maliciously did, stubbed their toes in clumsy moments, questioned their very involvement in the war, missed their families back home, and even at times humorously mimicked their officers.

To that end, I was fortunate to tap into the generous perspective of passionate Japanese military historian and author, Hajime Marutani. When I first approached him regarding this project he ended his reply with: 'By the way, I have never heard of the massacres of Alexandra Hospital.' To have him locate specific handwritten documents, unpublished in Japanese let alone English, shed voluble light on incidents where previously only stereotypical speculation may have taken place.

I lived in Singapore for 10 wonderful years and remember a lop-sided pillbox concrete pillbox on the roadside near my apartment on Pasir Panjang Road on the west coast, in the shadows of Kent Ridge, which loomed behind. I was living within four kilometres of the Alexandra Hospital yet, as I recall, my first knowledge of the Alexandra Hospital Massacres came many years later through Noel Barber's brilliantly emotive fiction, *Tanah Merah*. (He was equally adept at non-fictional journalism, too, of course, and I rate his *Sinister Twilight* on the fall of Singapore as a must-read.)

Thereafter, it was Paul Pilkington who fanned the flames of my curiosity, when he told me his father, Capt Hugh Pilkington of the 6th Royal Norfolks, had survived the massacre. 'Would you like to read his diaries?' he asked one day, somewhat redundantly. That innocent question changed the shape of my life, leading to writing my first war book, *The Missing Years*, and leading military history tours through Southeast Asia. (Indeed I was flattered to be asked by NRMA Travel to design and lead tours for veterans' families and other enthusiasts, taking several groups on immersive narrative journeys through Singapore, Malaysia and Thailand. Perhaps the most fulfilling work I've ever done, and something I would still love to do more of.)

Paul and I soon visited the hospital together, and were given a copy of Jeff Partridge's comprehensive overview of the hospital, *Alexandra Hospital: From British Military to Civilian Institution 1938-1998.* Which in turn pointed me towards the rigorous research of Peter Bruton, whose own uncle – the wide-smiled, gap-toothed John Bruton – was caught up in this barbaric melee, encapsulated in Peter's paper *The Matter of a Massacre.*

It was an eerie moment that resonated greatly when I found out that the first victim at the hospital, RAMC orderly Pte Hugh Lloyd, shared my family name but was not related.

There have been a few other key catalysts towards a better understanding of that murderous weekend, none perhaps more so than Col William Irwin, RAMC, who was CO of The Alex from 1967-70. He praised Capt Tom Smiley and team for continuing to operate 'in what surely must have been the most difficult and dangerous conditions in which surgery has ever been performed'.

I was lucky enough to have several correspondences with Fiona Smiley, his daughter, who shared with me the intimate love letters of her then newly engaged parents, and shed much light on pre-war life at the hospital and Singapore expat life in general. This really fleshed out the surgeon way beyond being just 'a rugby-playing Northern Irelander.' And knowing these details helps us to understand the personal stakes each participant had in this episode.

Perhaps the greatest thrill I had in piecing together this puzzle literally happened at the 11th hour, 11:59 to be precise, when relatives of two survivors of the Sisters' Quarters massacre revealed their fathers had penned memoirs of that God-awful time they were incarcerated in the outhouse. The recollections were raw and emotive – one even too powerful for survivor Norman Bryer's daughter Lyn to read from cover to cover, so the handwritten manuscript had been kept locked away in a safe. The other stunning memoir was penned by Bert Gurd. I trembled as I read them because this was the first time those viewpoints had ever been aired (and they went miles beyond the matter-of-fact affidavits that have been the sole source of information available thus far). You will see what I mean!

In 1968 Irwin published a letter in *Soldier* magazine which flushed out survivors' and relatives of survivors' accounts from all corners of the Commonwealth, helping to triangulate reports, and establish greater certainty in what did or did not happen in the lead-up, duration, and aftermath of the period, clouded as it was by such chaos in the final hours before Singapore fell.

Indeed there has been a lot of myth created around the massacres. For a start, that there were only a handful of survivors. Incorrect. There were about 900 patients in the hospital. The vast majority survived the Saturday slaughter. But of the Sunday Sisters' Quarters episode, the survival rate was less than three percent from around 200 starters. These were two very distinct events, and that is why I choose to refer to them as 'massacres' in the plural. Both very different in cause and culpability, as you will see.

'It is part of the human condition that individual accounts of happenings, especially those involving death and disaster, will vary,' Irwin wrote. 'Some men will remember one thing and some another; an incident that is highlighted for one man will be blotted out from another's brain, and when an individual's own safety is in danger as it is in battle, then the eye-witness accounts must be increasingly at variance.'

This is at the heart of the investigative writer's job. To corroborate versions that tally, but not to automatically dismiss one person's experience or perception simply because it seems to be an outlier. Perhaps that is the *only* accurate unfiltered version of all? Because even in tape-recorded oral histories I've come across veterans contradicting themselves. So at some point the writer must draw a reasonable line in the mud based on the 'evidence', much of it clouded by perception and psychological distance and dissonance.

Most of the research sources such as dispassionate affidavits were captured within a year or two of war's end. Many diaries were compiled – at pain of execution – during their PoW years or on the ship home immediately thereafter. Many of the oral histories were recorded in the 1970s and 80s. My primary research interviews with survivors were done in the 2000s. But even though I'd captured these latter accounts in person I still had to filter which parts were reliable and consistent, and which ones not.

If I compare my 2005 interview of Dr Bill Frankland with what appears in his 2018 biography, *From Hell Island to Hay Fever*, many of the details are wildly inconsistent. There again, he may be forgiven, for the 107-year-old is still practicing medicine in Harley Street, regarded as the 'Godfather of Allergy Treatment' and is – at the time of writing – the world's oldest expert witness.

In the course of researching and writing this book over the past 12 years (not continually – my bank manager couldn't possibly allow that) I've interviewed people in Australia, Singapore, England, Philippines, Thailand, Japan, Canada and Scotland.

In the latter case, I enjoyed my conversations with Dick Lee, who was completely frank and fully expressive about the atrocities he'd seen in the hospital and on the Death Railway, and saw the value in sharing them, and how those of his comrades who'd not spoken about them seemed to have passed away far younger, eaten up by their unspoken trauma. Shortly before his passing, he kindly sent me an autographed copy of *And the Dawn Came Up Like Thunder* by Leo Rawlings (his campmate, who famously catalogued his experiences on the Railway in ink sketches) plus copies of all his cards, photos, letters, and memorabilia from Changi.

During one conversation on The Alex he'd said: 'Can you imagine the state of people in that bleedin' place? People with legs off, arms off, backs blown out. So many wounded, like a bleedin' slaughterhouse.' *Boom!* That was it – I knew I had the title of my book. He repeated the phrase a few more times, and it has also been uttered by other survivors in passing, thus cementing it as the title.

I've ransacked the Australian War Memorial in Canberra, the International War Memorial in London, and the National Archives and the National Library, both in Singapore.

These were all amazing and fascinating adventures. But it was my first visit to the Yasukuni Shine in Tokyo in 2017 that truly put things in perspective for me. For it was here that I really saw the big picture, literally, on a massive mural display of the Asia Pacific theatre. It became instantly clear: The sheer size of the front they were operating along was insuperable for the small nation. No wonder supply lines were stretched thin, and strategic chinks appeared. The Japanese were brilliant in the battle, less so in the war.

As I pieced together my own research for this story, a few other things became clear. One was the surprising connectedness of events that happened far apart in time and geography, yet shared characters or characteristics. There were some surprisingly familiar faces that cropped up again in unexpected places at various different points of the continuum.

The Alex was not the only hospital outrage or massacre to be carried out by the Japanese, with similar examples in China, Hong Kong and Burma, but the British were not completely devoid of blood on their hands either and the Japanese by no means had a monopoly on atrocity.

Chief among things that became clear was that there seemed to be an official cover-up with regards to this incident. There is eerily scant documentation of the British Military Hospital Alexandra. Ominously, these episodes, which became known as the Alexandra Hospital Massacres, do not rate a single word in *History of the Second World War: The War Against Japan* by S. Woodburn Kirby, the official British history. Its Australian counterpart, *Australia in the War of 1939–1945: The Japanese Thrust*, by Lionel Wigmore, affords the episodes just six lines. The progress and outcomes of the War Crimes trials also plays strongly to this thesis.

Was there something to hide? If so, what, why and by whom? This adds a tantalizing frisson – not that any extra is needed – to this story to me as a storyteller. And one to which I've devoted an inordinate amount of time and effort chasing down to help my own empathetic understanding of what it would be like to be in those boots, and to help bring some illumination and closure to families of veterans and victims who suffered in those dismally dark and distant days in that chaotic corner of that British outpost on the equator: Singapore.

Stuart Lloyd.
Orange, NSW
November, 2021.

THE CAST/ DRAMATIS PERSONAE

The main characters in this dreadful drama, in order of appearance ...

Pte Francis 'Bert' Gurd, 35, 198th Field Ambulance, RAMC. A farm boy from Hampshire, Gurd attended training at Watford, where he met and wanted to marry the daughter, Rosa, of the family he was billetted with. She'd said no.

Capt Richard 'Dick' Waller, 25, Royal Artillery. The son of an RA officer in the British Indian Army, and born in India. Shipped to Hong Kong in 1936 before his posting to Malaya. Wounded in a strafing run, then hospitalized in The Alex.

Lt Gen Mutaguchi Renya, 53, commander of 18th Division, IJA. A hardened veteran and committed practitioner of the *bushido* warrior code, he was driven by lofty ambitions matched only by his desire for *sake* and feminine company.

Robert Loveday, 45, had been working at Fort Canning as Chief Surveyor of Works in the Chief Engineers Office, Malaya Command. Responsible for military construction tenders, including some aspects of the Alexandra Hospital.

Col Tsuji Masonobu, 53, 25th Army HQ. Tsuji was the strategic mastermind behind the Malayan campaign, armed with recent experience in the Sino-Japanese war, a maverick mindset and deep disdain for America and the West.

Maj Denis Mulvany, 38, RAMC. Born in Calcutta. A surgeon at The Alex, and son of an Indian Army doctor. Married to **Ethel**, 37, a Canadian who became a Red Cross Ambulance driver at 1st Malayan General Hospital and a VAD at The Alex.

Capt Constantine Petrovsky, 28, RAMC. A Russian-born exile who lived in Manchuria, China, and Japan then went to study medicine in Hong Kong. His aim was to get to the Eastern Front but he never made it past Singapore.

Sgt Norman Bryer, 32, RAF. A coconut planter and reservist in Malaya pre-war, this keen sportsman and pilot developed blood clotting that led to his long hospitalization at The Alex right at the outbreak of the war with Japan.

Capt Yoshiaki Iwasaki, pilot with Imperial Japanese Naval Air Service. Took part in the first bombing raid of Singapore, and would cover most bases in the Asia Pacific. Put full faith in what his fortune-teller would tell him.

Sapper Daniel 'Danny' Fraser, 25, 36th Fortress Company, Royal Engineers. Joined the Army due to lack of other work in Scotland at the time, and posted to Singapore in 1938 constructing pillboxes and other coastal defences.

Capt Cyril Wild, 34, 3rd Indian Corp HQ. Son of a religious minister. Worked for an oil company in Japan pre-war, learning the language and customs. Became an intelligence officer at Fort Canning. Famous for carrying the 'white flag'.

Sister Edith 'Woodie' Stevenson, 30. British midwife and missionary who arrived in Singapore in 1939. Moved to work at The Alex at end of December 1941, only to endure the most intense six-week period of the hospital's history.

Gunner Fergus Anckorn, 23, Royal Artillery. A keen amateur athlete and budding magician who'd leave his fellow gunners spellbound. He signed up imagining plenty of exotic travel in foreign climes. He was half right.

Gunner Richard 'Dick' Lee, 21, Royal Artillery and HQ 11th Division Indian Army. Dick was a keen motorcyclist, enjoying rides in the country with his girlfriend on the back. Became a dispatch rider for his Division's commander.

Capt Hugh 'Pilk' Pilkington, 37, 6th Royal Norfolks. Born in India and became a rubber planter in Malaya for several years pre-war. Ironically, returned to England only to be posted back to fight near his previous rubber estate.

Col Joseph Craven, MC, 53, RAMC. Decorated for gallantry as a stretcher-bearer in WW1 and practiced medicine before emigrating to New Zealand and becoming hospital superintendent. Appointed as Commanding Officer at The Alex.

Lim Bo Seng, 32. A China-born Singapore-based entrepreneur who had interests in biscuit and brickmaking factories in the Alexandra area. Married with seven children he was a true patriot with strong anti-Japanese sentiment.

Cpl George Johnson, 24, RAMC. From Durham, George was assigned to 32 Company, and initially shipped out to the BMH Shanghai. When the situation became too tenuous there, they transferred to The Alex in Singapore.

Pte Sydney Hoskins, 22, RAMC. From Surrey, also part of the 32 Company cohort having enlisted at the end of 1939, former printer's engraver Sydney would end up working as a medical orderly in various parts of The Alex.

Capt Tom Smiley, 24, RAMC. Strongly religious Irishman from a family of pharmacists. He was a keen rugby player and had got engaged just before shipping out for the Far East and starting work at the Tanglin Barracks Hospital.

Capt Roylance Parkinson, 30, RAMC. With his red hair and ready smile, many liked this Mancunian doctor. But beneath the surface he was a conscientious objector to the war, his drafting into the service, and posting to the Far East.

Principal Matron Violet Jones, 51, QAIMNS. The rather spinsterly and strict matron was universally liked and respected for the example and high standards she set to her team that sailed out with her to nurse at The Alex when it opened.

Sister Brenda Macduff, 28. English nurse who had a boyfriend and, when she was posted out to Malaya, he asked his friend, lawyer (and FMS Volunteer) **Pte Ken Macduff**, to keep an eye on her. Brenda and Ken soon married!

Cpl Robert Veitch, 28, Federated Malay States Volunteer Force. A Scottish mining engineer, he came out to Malaya in 1937 to join his friends for some adventure out East. Served in the Armoured Cars unit in Malaya/ Singapore.

Col Ito Kojiro, 40, commanding officer of 2/55th Regiment 18th Division, IJA which was active down the west coast of Singapore, and especially around the Alexandra and Keppel Barracks area.

Warrant Officer Arai Mitsuo, 114th Regiment 18th Division, IJA. Had seen action in southern China before shipping down to Malaya just three weeks before the capitulation. His regiment was fighting extremely close to the hospital.

***All ages and ranks as at 14 February 1942.**

LIST OF MAPS AND ILLUSTRATIONS

1 Pre-War Places of Interest. Singapore.... 18

2 Buildings and Sites, Alexandra District 1941.... 19

3 Alexandra Hospital, Main Buildings 1942.... 173

4 IJA Division Movements, Feb 1942.... 174

5 Hills used for IJA HQ & Target Objectives.... 175

6 Advance of 18th Div IJA Troops, 14 Feb 1942.... 220

7 Three Attack Waves, 14 Feb 1942.... 286

8 Paths Taken to Sister's Quarters Outhouses : 2 Groups.... 287

9 Sister's Quarters Outhouses, 14-15 Feb 1942.... 288

10 Sister's Quarters Toolshed.... 289

11 Sister's Quarters Servant Quarters.... 290

12 Sister's Quarters Pantry.... 291

13 Escape Route: Sydney Hoskins 15 Feb 1942.... 292

14 Escape Route: Norman Bryer 15 Feb 1942.... 293

15 Escape Route: Bert Gurd 15 Feb 1942.... 294

16 Escape Route: George Johnson 15 Feb 1942.... 295

17 Escape Route: Richard Waller 15 Feb 1942.... 296

18 Position of 18th Div IJA Troops Evening, 15 Feb 1942.... 297

PROLOGUE

Sisters' Quarters Outhouse, 14-15 February 1942.

'About 57 of us are put into the end room,' says stocky farmer-turned-medical orderly, Pte Bert Gurd, referring to a ramshackle space probably used as a toolshed. He estimates it to be about 12-15 feet square, with double-doors and a window opposite. 'The only ventilation is a small lattice arrangement high up, plus one broken tile. The door and window are boarded up by the Japanese. There was just sufficient room to stand up.'

He sees his great pals Pte Frank Onslow, 30 and married, Pte Stanley Pearce, and Pte Kenneth Butler – all of 198th Field Ambulance, RAMC – are sardined into the same spartan, suffocating space. Plus a pyjama-clad mish-mash of walking wounded Indian Army commissioned officers and soldiers, and a British artillery officer, Capt Richard Waller, who was hospitalized after his gun unit was strafed. The hands of some are so tightly bound with rope the scarring will leave visible reminders for the rest of their lives (which, sadly for most here, is merely hours away).

'Capt John Brown, a very young officer of the Dental Corps, tries to maintain some kind of discipline without success. We cannot get any co-operation at all from the Asiatics – several Indian patients, one or two Malays. They lie down and stay down, moaning and grumbling, causing our guards to thump on the doors threatening us. Our thoughts and feelings can be better imagined than described during that awful night.'

The battle for Singapore rages and thunders around them, the death rattle of an Empire making a desperate last stand.

'As the night drags on, our humiliation increases and the extreme heat and thirst make some of us delirious. Some talk of suicide, some talk of trying to break through the roof. In turn we fan one another with our handkerchiefs. I tie my shirt to the lamp flex and, with a string, take turns to work it to and fro. We are all utterly miserable – our lips sore and tongues swollen.'

With water promised for 6am, and thinking it to be around 4am by then, he asks for the time. 'Twenty to two,' comes the heart-breaking response. 'This night seems like twenty years.' Those whose watches had not been plundered by the guards might have heard their young lives ticking by, second by painstaking second.

Around 4am someone from the servants' room adjacent calls out saying they have 70 occupants. 'At least they do until four die.' A devout young Roman Catholic – who will one day join the local choir and sing – Bert looks up towards heaven. 'The broken tile is directly over me and I pray more intensely than I have ever prayed before for it to rain and quench our thirst.'

The unsettling wails and shouts of delirium rise. And Rise. AND RISE.

'In our party, those who were the loudest in their talk of the necessity of keeping our spirits up are the first ones to break down. By this time most of us are delirious.' Reduced to farm animals. Or worse.

Six o'clock ticks by with not a drop of the promised water. 'Our officer suggests trying to bribe our guards, and a number of wristwatches and rings are handed to Brown.'

Hopes rise when they hear an Allied officer – with a small smattering of Japanese words – in a neighbouring room is said to be negotiating for water. Then nothing. Then hope. Reports that buckets of water will be brought. Still nothing. Nothing but fading hope as the sun rises on another sultry, steamy Singapore day.

'We are now told by occupants of the next room, that seven of the inmates have died during the night. Suddenly I realize that today is my birthday – it also looks like being the day of my death.' A hell of a way to spend your 36th birthday. Shells burst. Nearer. More often. 'Our surroundings shake with two explosions, and a host of tiles fall from the roof on to our heads. We dress a few scalp wounds with field dressings. The ventilation is now better, but the blazing sun adds to our terror.'

Allied shellfire seems to be zeroing in, concentrated in the immediate vicinity of their huts. Closer and closer until the toolshed receives a hit. Dust. Debris. Doors and shutters splinter and crack. They can see sentries posted all around the hutment building, Japanese machine gunners lying tensed and poised beside their lethal weapons.

Suddenly, a movement of a different sort. Shuffling and shouting outside. The noise of boards being removed. 'Are we being taken out or is it another false alarm?' Bert wonders. 'Our boards are now being taken down amidst terrific explosions.' But Bert is now worried that they are all going to die on the receiving end of British artillery as the 'considerable noise of battle firing' deafens them.

'I see through a crack in the door that the Japanese are taking prisoners away from other rooms. They take them in groups of six or eight with their hands tied behind them, and each group tied together.' Perhaps 100 shuffle by. Then they start to wonder why none of these water parties are being returned. 'Like wildfire the idea spreads – it appears to be a one-way trip. I remark: "Well, if it's curtains, let's meet it with a smile".

'Our doors are now wide open and I see L/Cpl Jack Jones with a group manacled and roped together being marched away with several sentries. Jones looks 20 years older since last night.'

This process continues for around twenty minutes until noon.

As another manacled group passes out of sight, yet another shell thuds in dangerously close to the toolshed. 'The Jap guards race across the courtyard and shelter in a kind of porch outside. Someone behind me suggests making a break for it: "Better be shot taking a chance than butchered in cold blood".'

'Now's our chance,' someone responds.

'Come on then!' Bert says. 'Two of us turn left – I am one – two turn right. We race around the building to the rear. I glimpse some Japs huddled in a trench. All is confusion but I run – run as I never ran before – down the slope. The Japs shout and I expect to be rubbed out every second. How can they miss me, shirtless as I am?'

Part 1

THE BUILD-UP

(Detail of letter by Lt Walter Salmon)

CURTAIN-RAISER IN CHINA

'Then the Japanese reverted to their usual cunning.'

Peiping, China, July 1937. China was bearing the brunt of Japan's encroachment on her territory and sovereignty, starting with their invasion of agriculture-rich Manchuria. This had been going on for six years by this point, and tensions were building. China was wearying of rolling over and appeasing them, and one of the loudest voices was that of Wong Lang-Tsai.

Wong was a magistrate in the Wanping district of Peiping (as Beijing was called), which included the brick-walled Wanping Fortress dating back to 1640. It was surrounded by lush parkland and, to the west, the Yongding River was crossable by the ornately decorated brick-and-stone Luguo Bridge. Many also called it the Marco Polo Bridge.

The Peiping-Hankow Railway ran through this area, with a station at Fengtai, which was on the Peiping-Pukow line. A rather strategic crossroads.

The Japanese China Garrison Army (JCGA) were stationed in Peiping, and – having taken Fengtai in September 1936 – were now at serious loggerheads with the Wanping City, because they desperately wanted to purchase 6000 acres of land to build a barracks and aerodrome. 'I was approached more than twenty times by the Japanese regarding purchase of the land, which I always refused,' said Wong. 'Then the Japanese reverted to their usual cunning.'

First the Japanese started conducting day exercises, then on 7 July 1937, around 7pm, night manoeuvres were carried out by a battalion of the 1st Infantry Regiment without prior notice. 'I had previously warned my soldiers to take the strictest precautions against starting any incident and on this particular occasion I took the added precaution of closing the gates of the city because we had reason to believe the field exercises were being carried out with live ammunition,' recalled Wong.

Then things stepped up a notch, alarming the Chinese force guarding the Marco Polo Bridge, the 219th Infantry Regiment.

The regimental commanding officer, Col Ji Xingwen, received a telephone message from the Japanese claiming that Pte Shimura Kikujiro was missing, suspected abducted by the Chinese. Wong ordered a search of Wanping but the private was not found. The Japanese troops demanded permission to enter the walled city to investigate for themselves. Not wanting to panic his citizens, Col Ji refused.

'When I refused their demands, they fired a few shots at the city,' said Wong. The Japanese then called for negotiations at midnight. But the answer was still 'No Entry' to Wanping.

The Japanese insisted on a joint investigation, and Wong and colleagues were invited to meet the Japanese commander at Wanping at dawn. That physically robust commander – with his prominent forehead, bulbous nose and bushy eyebrows – turned up, looking and acting impatient. He was Col Mutaguchi Renya. Mutaguchi was enjoying a rather meteoric rise through the ranks of the Imperial Japanese Army (IJA) since graduating from its Academy in 1910. He'd served in Siberia against the Bolsheviks, been a military attaché in Paris, and served in the General Affairs Section of the Army in Tokyo. Now, in Peiping, the 48-year-old from Saga, on the southern island of Kyushu, had the chance to really prove himself again as commander of the JCGA.

He was driven by an interrupted childhood in Saga prefecture – chiefly, being adopted, then the early death of his government official father – to restore the family name, a family that had given rise to numerous high officers of state over the years, but not in most recent generations. There was no grey-scale: he saw the world in starkly uncompromising black-and-white terms.

'Mutaguchi voiced his extreme disapproval of an investigation committee,' said Wong, 'and demanded that I should take immediate measures against any person responsible for the Japanese soldier's disappearance. When I made it clear I would not comply with his demands, Col Mutaguchi ordered eight lorries of soldiers to Wanping and he told me he planned to take matters into his own hands.'

Wong and his team departed immediately but, heading back, they were halted by a Japanese officer at Salang, on the right flank of a railway bridge less than a mile northeast of Wanping. 'Behind him I saw a Japanese detachment drawn up in formation with machine guns and trench mortars trained on the little city. The officer told me the situation had become so critical that they had decided to resort to military action if the incident was not settled satisfactorily.'

Mutaguchi was pushing for complete evacuation of Chinese troops from Wanping, and access for Japanese through the eastern gate, plus negotiations for a final settlement.

'When I insisted that the investigation committee had been appointed to negotiate a satisfactory settlement, the Japanese officer angrily declared that the gates of Wanping must be opened and that my own life was in danger if I did not comply.' No sooner had Wong arrived in the Walled City than the trench mortars started raining down, and the machine guns opened fire. 'It was clear to me that the Japanese wanted to take the city. So I ordered my handful of soldiery to reply to the Japanese fire. The incident almost ended in comedy when word came that the missing Japanese had been found,' said Wong. Turned out the 'lost' soldier had been on his way back from the exercise, dived off for an emergency toilet stop, lost his way and found his way back to his unit hours later.

But it was too late. The Second Sino-Japanese War was on.

The battle raged for 25 days, trapping civilians – who could not possibly evacuate – in the crossfire. Wanping was reduced to a shambles.

'A month after the Peiping/Wanping incident, my unit entered Beijing,' said Mutaguchi. 'There I visited a Chinese army hospital and made a statement toward 900 wounded Chinese soldiers as I wanted to show my respect to the enemy. I conveyed that the Emperor of Japan told us to make sure we must treat wounded enemy with thoughtful care … and paid my deep respect for their sacrifice and loyal attitude for their nation by fighting so great.'

Almost immediately the Japanese Shanghai Expeditionary Force moved on Shanghai, tackling the National Revolutionary Army (NRA). On 13 August 1937, the Battle for Shanghai began in earnest.

The Japanese were frustrated by their inability to take Shanghai quickly because they were outnumbered 10:1. But their mountain guns roared away from rooftops to devastating effect. Overall it took them nearly 3.5 months, ending up with beach landings in Jiangsu and Hangzhou, and a series of flanking manoeuvres to finally capture it, before the NRA retreated – every man for themselves – in the chilly driving rains of November. The Japanese were stinging, angry, revengeful. Because China was not even supposed to be their biggest threat. That was Russia.

So with Shanghai in the bag, the southern capital of Nanjing – 300km northwest of Shanghai – now became the next important target.

**

Mutaguchi, having triggered all of this, had already shipped back north to Peiping by this stage. But now, enter the IJA 18th Division under Lt Gen Ushijima to bolster Matsui's forces. The 23rd, 35th, 55th, 56th Infantry brigades, plus the 114th and 124th Infantry regiments were part of the battle order from October 1937. Raised in September 1937 the 'Chrysanthemum Division' (as the 18th was nicknamed) from Kyushu was fresh legs for the central China campaign and rushed into action.

Most of these 18th Division recruits were sturdy and strong young men from northern Kyushu, who'd just completed their basic military training in 1937. The area is known for coal mining, where conditions were notoriously tough and physically demanding. So these were the toughest of the tough, the hardest of the hard. Just the sort of soldiers a commander would want to lead into battle.

Takayuki Shiraishi, who works for an international food science company in Tokyo, explained: 'Kyushu people are taller, bigger and stronger than other Japanese.' His explanation is partly because there are two origins of Japanese people – those whose ancestors came from northern China and went to north of Japan, and those from southern China who settled in Kyushu. 'Their diet is also much more potatoes and meat protein,' Takayuki explained. 'Not rice and fish. Also even their *sujo* (wine) is made from potato, not rice.'

Just three days later, on 13 December the Japanese had captured the city's five main gates, trapping a large number of Chinese officers and soldiers within its 20-metre high, nine-metre wide ancient walls. The 18th Division's 114th Regiment – sourced from Fukuoka – was at Nanking to celebrate the falling of the gates, but then shipped south immediately. The balance of the 18th Division was now on its way to securing Hangzhou en route to Canton in the south.

**

The final generally accepted tally during the occupation of Nanking was 50,000 raped, and 300,000 killed.

'The Rape of Nanking was not the kind of isolated incident common to all wars,' said Arnold Brackman, the young United Press reporter who covered the IMFTE. 'It was deliberate. It was policy. It was known in Tokyo.' A state-endorsed pervasive code of field service, in other words.

So Mutaguchi had kicked this thing off. And from this horrendous episode, we can see the diametrically opposite preparations the two sides – the Japanese and the Allies – had in the years that would finally lead to their brutal meeting on the west coast of Singapore in February 1942.

MEANWHILE IN SINGAPORE

'But one thing was troubling Loveday ...'

Singapore 1937. You can imagine the post-prandial glee. It's a Saturday night. A dinner party with good friends was in full swing. The empty bowls of spicy lamb curry have been spirited away by the houseboy, many cold Tiger beers have done their job of refreshment, and now the men of the party were possibly moving onto port and cigars, or possibly still on the gins and tonic.

Starched white shirts were showing sweat marks because this is near enough to being on the equator, and the doors and windows of the double-storied 'black and white' house are thrown wide open to the night. A ceiling fan is whirring away trying its best to keep up. All are gathered around as a lady, Mrs Dobb, tinkles away on the piano, skillfully accompanied by a very tall man on the viola, covering the party tunes and singalong showpieces of the day: *Home Sweet Home, My Lucky Day,* and possibly a Noel Coward showtune, *Someday I'll Find You*. There were probably requests for something by Jack Hylton, the hot swinging big band star of the day, but that's a little tricky for this duo to muster or master.

You see, the towering 6'4" viola player – who also took turns on the piano – was really an Army man, a captain in the Royal Engineers to be precise. Robert Loveday was just on 41, and had arrived in Singapore recently just in time to celebrate New Year's eve. He'd passed out from Brompton Barracks in Chatham in July 1914, just as his country needed him to serve in Macedonia and Egypt. He was supremely proud to be part of the Royal Engineers, who could trace their lineage back through every conflict Britain had been involved in since William the Conqueror's Military Engineers in 1066. He'd ended the war as a corporal with the Great War medal and Victory medal pinned to his chest, and a 20-year-old bride, Alice, by his side.

Around that time, Loveday was promoted to lieutenant, and based at Larkhill, a garrison town near Salisbury, Wiltshire. He knuckled down, building up his qualifications within the RE Corp. Becoming a Professional Associate of the Charted Surveyors Institute (PASI) was a long way from toiling as a humble clerk when he was just 15. Two children were added, Dorothy then Donald.

Their Christmas in 1930 was all the merrier with his recent promotion to captain, and another daughter, Pamela, was on the way. His personal medal collection also expanded, adding a Jubilee Medal, and most recently the Coronation medal to commemorate the coronation of King George VI and Queen Elizabeth.

The duo struck up another tune, *Mad Dogs and Englishmen*. It drew guffaws of ironic resonance because this group was living that very life. This was *their* song!

In tropical climes there are certain times of day
When all the citizens retire
To tear their clothes off and perspire
It's one of those rules that the greatest fools obey
Because the sun is much too sultry
And one must avoid its ultra violet ray

'Everybody!'

Papalaka papalaka papalaka boo
Papalaka papalaka papalaka boo
Digariga digariga digariga doo
Digariga digariga digariga doo
© *Noel* Coward, 1931.

From the back verandah, Alice looked across at Robert admiringly, happy to be settling fast into their new life in the exotic East. Why, certainly their airy double-storey house at 1 Sherwood Road would be the envy of all the wives back home. And certainly nothing like Robert – who was born in Battersea, in the shadows of a power station and Wandsworth prison – could've ever imagined living in himself. Their children were being raised in a completely different and better world here in Singapore.

Loveday's father Charles was a hotel butler but, within a few years, his mother, Fanny – born in Dublin where her father, a sergeant major with the 10th Hussars was posted – had moved herself and the kids out to Bishopsthorpe Rd in York, Yorkshire. It was a street peopled by railway firemen, porters and stokers, bicycle mechanics, and postmen. Soon another move nearby, and Robert grew up in his grandmother, May Chapman's, house in Thorpe Street, with his older sister Lilian and younger sister Hilda. Charles was working in London, and living in a boarding house provided by his employer. He would soon move to New York working as a steward, and start a new family there.

But the rigours and privations of his childhood and that 'War to End All Wars' were the last thing on Robert's mind now.

'Everybody!'

Bolyboly bolyboly bolyboly baa
Bolyboly bolyboly bolyboly baa
Habaninny habaninny habaninny haa
Habaninny habaninny habaninny haa

**

On Monday morning, Loveday hopped into his squat second-hand Morris Ten and headed for the office, passing through the pleasant Tanglin Barracks district with its many colonial-style military buildings, and church, whitewashed and gleaming in the sun.

Most of the houses set on this former nutmeg plantation date back to the 1920s and, as an engineer, he would have quietly admired the pioneering work of Capt George Collyer who'd originally overseen the construction of this barracks way back in 1861. The astronomical construction cost of £20,000 was a source of controversy back in the day, until the Government of India stepped in to cover it, due to the hard-learned lessons of the Sepoy Mutiny.

The Tanglin Barracks hospital was particularly interesting, looking at once colonial yet incorporating local design features such as the wide eaves to facilitate better shade and ventilation.

Before long he'd reached Fort Canning. As the Chief Surveyor of Works in the Chief Engineer's Office, Malaya Command, Loveday worked in this newly developed HQ precinct reporting to the Chief Engineer, Webster. 'The Battlebox' had just been completed the previous year, an imposing command centre built atop Fort Canning Hill, with the city of Singapore spread out below. A gothic archway hinted at the history of what was also known previously as Government Hill and Bukit Bendera (Flag Hill). A flag mast was prominently visible, from which a large Union Jack hung limply in the still morning air.

Fort Canning had originally been sited here because of its commanding views over the harbour, allowing for its eight-inch cannons to repel any unwanted forces. Forces which never arrived. It would also serve as a protective redoubt should the European residents need to seek shelter from local civil uprisings (another lesson painfully learned in India, after which the Fort started construction in 1859).

Colonial governors had also chosen this as their preferred place of residence over the years, and even Raffles had built his first home among the shady trees on this same hill.

It was amid this setting that Loveday sat down to tackle his rapidly growing to-do list. The garrison in Singapore was being rapidly expanded. Apart from some projects in Tanglin and Tyersall, the big-ticket item was the forthcoming construction of a new hospital to the west at Alexandra. He and Lt Frederic Croft, born in South Africa, met with the Chief Superintendent Draughtsman, Warrant Officer JW Colbran to discuss the designs, specifications and requirements of the sprawling precinct.

But one thing was troubling Loveday ...

He'd done his best to play catch-up based on a rather hurried 12-day handover transition with his predecessor. It was clear that contract work was going to be a big part of his new work scope. But everything seemed too frantically urgent here. In reviewing existing contracts he noticed only six tenders by invitation had been issued – the rest were lump sum contracts. 'This was absolutely against office regulations for Engineer service,' he said. 'The regulation provides for bills for quantities in all contracts above £750.'

He had taken this irregularity up with his predecessor. 'I learned that this unusual procedure for local contracts had been approved by the War Office because of a want of necessary staff to deal with the work,' the earnest Loveday said. 'The construction work was vitally urgent, the normal regulations relaxed in order that no delay should occur in the building program.'

So the typical process had become for the Chief Engineer's Office to accept the lowest tender, so long as this was below the War Office estimate. Maj Butler, DCRE, would make the final call on everything but it was up to Loveday to make the recommendation for acceptance or otherwise. He was the gatekeeper. He alone could decide who to invite to tender for jobs. And he was the only one who knew who had been invited.

So, on this insignificantly small tropical island, a major military master-plan was in place and slowly taking physical shape, although few believed it would ever be needed nor would it face a serious challenge. After all, this was just ... Singapore.

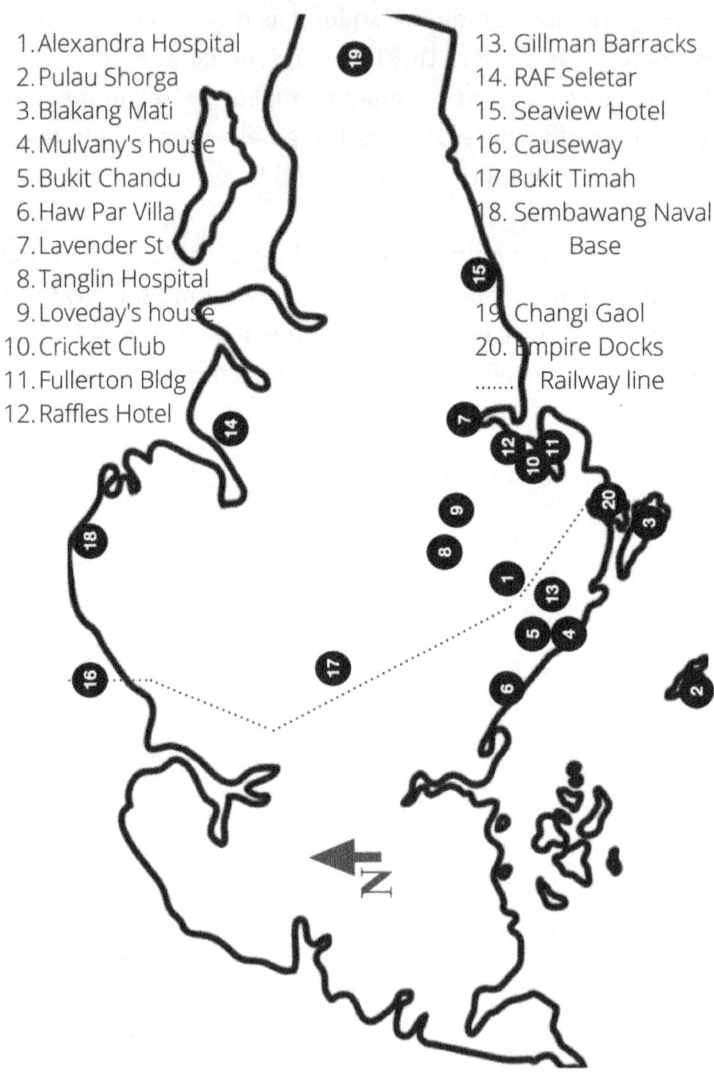
PRE-WAR PLACES OF INTEREST, SINGAPORE
1. Alexandra Hospital
2. Pulau Shorga
3. Blakang Mati
4. Mulvany's house
5. Bukit Chandu
6. Haw Par Villa
7. Lavender St
8. Tanglin Hospital
9. Loveday's house
10. Cricket Club
11. Fullerton Bldg
12. Raffles Hotel
13. Gillman Barracks
14. RAF Seletar
15. Seaview Hotel
16. Causeway
17 Bukit Timah
18. Sembawang Naval Base
19. Changi Gaol
20. Empire Docks
.... Railway line
N

BUILDINGS & SITES IN ALEXANDRA DISTRICT, 1941

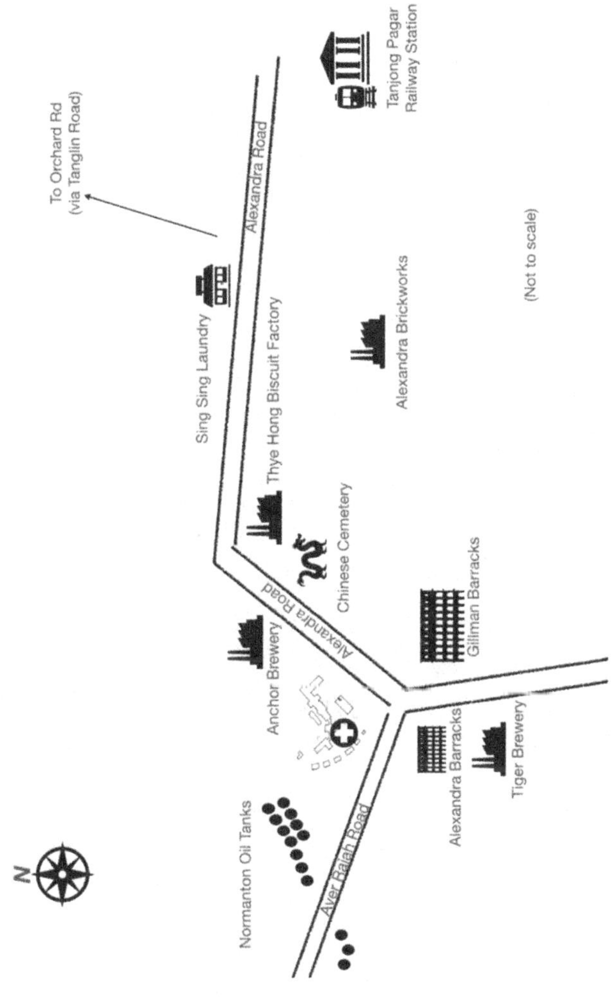

BEER, BISCUITS AND BUSHIDO

'The Army set aside 32 acres near the railway line.'

Way back in 1864, the British had constructed a road that connected River Valley Road to Pasir Panjang on the west coast of Singapore. Although the locals gave it a nickname, *Chui bo Lai* (Hokkien for 'within the rice mill') its official name was Alexandra Road, named for Alexandra of Denmark who had just married King Edward VII the previous year and so became the Queen Consort of the United Kingdom.

It was still largely a rural area of plantations and farms when the Alexandra Brickworks took five acres of slightly hilly land at the intersection of Tanjong Pagar Road and Alexandra Road, and set about making red clay bricks in 1899. Their timing was impeccable because the British chose this newly accessible area outside of the city as the site for its Alexandra Barracks in the early 1900s. 'Home' was strongly represented in the street names such as Canterbury, Cornwall, Winchester and York Streets, although initially the troops garrisoned here were Indian troops including the 99th Daccan and 3rd Brahmans. The commanding officer was accommodated in the stately Bukit Damai ('Peaceful Hill'), a double-storey colonnaded home that afforded sweeping views over the Straits of Singapore. The expansive grounds also included a tennis court.

The hill proved not so peaceful for Lt Col Edward Martin, commanding officer of the 5th Bengal Light Infantry, when the local Sepoy Mutiny arose 15 February 1915. Half of his regiment stormed Bukit Damai when word got around that they might be posted to Europe where they'd need to fight against fellow Muslims. The action spread to Tanglin Barracks where the Sepoys invaded the Tanglin Hospital, turfing out doctors and German patients. The siege lasted a week, and involved a killing spree of locals and British officers, soldiers, and civilians, and was put down when one Russian and, ironically, two Japanese warships arrived.

Among the reinforcing party were 75 Japanese sailors who helped in tracking down the mutineers in jungle at the north of Singapore, and finally suppressing them. This was the only action Singapore saw in WW1.

The original Alexandra Barracks also included a hospital, with a rectangular ward block around 200-feet in length and perhaps 40-feet wide, with a main office block opposite. (These were located on the same site, where the sports field of The Alex Hospital today is.) Swampy pools to the west, fed by water from Sungei Alexandra, toward Ayer Rajah Road were an inescapable feature.

In 1906 the Alexandra Barracks were extended to an adjacent area, just north, called Normanton. Its main feature was two rectangular parallel red-roofed brick buildings, about 40 metres apart. A long rifle range, over the road to the west, was a big feature of this barracks. The Normanton Oil Depot – a cluster of 35 oil tanks – straddled Ayer Rajah Road, with work completed by 1922. These would serve mainly as fuel reserves for the admiralty's Eastern Fleet.

A further study of the island's defences was commissioned in 1927, the exercise being led by Gen Webb Gillman, a decorated Boer War and World War 1 veteran.

As tastes changed and demand for sand-faced bricks and flooring tiles grew, the brickworks joined forces with the Borneo Company in 1928, who brought in modern machinery and techniques allowing them to expand on a larger scale. Around that time, too, the far-sighted government was pushing initiatives to create local employment and industries, thus reducing Singapore's reliance as a trans-shipment port. The 750-acre Alexandra Industrial Estate was one of two such estates constructed, as the Singapore Improvement Trust also launched a grand plan to provide subsidized public housing for residents.

So it was happy days at the brickworks, which was readily visible for miles round with its chimney stack soaring skyward from the *lalang*-roofed open-sided huts of the factory. (*Lalang* is a long reedy grass, common in Southeast Asia.) And the toughness of their product was well-reputed – and independently tested – to have a crush-strength higher than concrete bricks.

With the Industrial Estate established, the construction of the marble-statued art deco Tanjong Pagar Railway Station nearby in 1932 made it even more attractive, becoming easier for manufacturers to get their products to market. This line serviced Singapore to Kuala Lumpur and many points in northern Malaya beyond.

Malayan Breweries had set up shop west of Alexandra Road the year before, with Heineken joining forces with local company Fraser & Neave to create a model brewery for tropical conditions. German brew-masters were employed, and Tiger Beer was launched in 1932.

Sniffing an opportunity, Beck's, the German brewer, set up the Archipelago Brewery Company the following year by establishing a brewery capable of bottling and canning 450,000 gallons of beer each year. The building, designed by Swiss architect Heinrich Rudolf Arbenz, became known as 'The Anchor Brewery' after its signature product. It was perhaps no coincidence that both these breweries were also strategically close to a major potential customer: the British forces situated nearby in Normanton, Alexandra Park and Tanglin. Alexandra Park was a colonial residential estate that mushroomed on the back of other military developments in the area to house officers and their families.

The next significant structure along Alexandra Road was the Thye Hong Biscuit and Confectionary Factory, at the corner of Tiong Bahru Road, which used modern conveyor belts and automatic cookie stamping machines, and started dishing out its delicacies in 1935.

Further military expansion was called for, sandwiching another new barracks, Gillman, into the area between Telok Blangah Road and the most prominent topological feature of the lower west coast, Mount Faber. It grew organically with the area to later include an eight-lane swimming pool (with stepped sun terraces at one end and a few palm trees for full tropical effect) and a school, Alexandra School, which catered for students of both military and civilian families. The first occupants of Gillman were the Middlesex Regiment, the second battalion to be stationed on Singapore Island at that time, who moved in early 1936.

Another little business which set up at #11 was the Sing Sing Laundry, owned and run by Mr KS Tan, who soon set about securing contracts from all the nearby military establishments.

And the army set aside 32 acres of that 750-acre plot near the railway line in Alexandra for a new British Military Hospital. Their first one had been built in 1909 on Pulau Blakang Mati (meaning literally, 'Island of Death Behind', probably not where you'd want a hospital sited). This was closed when the new Tanglin Barracks hospital opened in 1912.

**

Meanwhile, Japan was in the midst of its own urgent development of her forces too, and conscription notices were being mailed out to all able-bodied specimens. Not that the standards were particularly high. Or tall. Infantrymen had to be 150cm or taller, with a chest measurement more than half their height, minimum weight to be 100 pounds. And so the recruits entered a world of brutal training, regimentation and preparation.

'The slightest misstep was rewarded with a slap or a boxing of the ears, or a flurry of fists,' according to Henry Frei, a Japanese-speaking academic and military historian. 'One Sgt Oichi counted more than 3000 slaps in his first month from his corporal.' That's an average of 100 per day! The IJA was trying to inculcate survival and dependability. 'The army needed, if not inhumans, at least efficient cogs for the military machine. "You are nothing but wretched one-cent men!" their officers would shout, quoting the price of a stamp on the conscription postcard.'

Much has been written about *bushido*, the code of the Samurai warriors. This had been abolished with the ending of the Tokugawa shogunate in 1867, nearly three quarters of a century prior. The essence had over the years become: 'Your aim is to die – killing as many of the enemy as you can first, but to die.' More particularly in the Kyushu area, where the 18th Division was raised, the *Hagakure* code was internalized thus: 'Let it be realized that to die is the most necessary act of a Samurai.'

The *bushido* code was fomented in times when great poverty was normal and not much value was therefore placed on life itself. A Samurai gratefully traded his life for food, housing, and other essentials, from his feudal lord. But it still lived on in the mythology of the great Japanese warriors of yore, and – while it was not officially incorporated into the Army regulations – it remained as a high-level ideal. More than that, the *bushido* code was still being taught to the officer corps at Military Preparatory School and many of the rising officers, such as Lt Col Tsuji and Col Mutaguchi, openly embraced and evangelized the *bushido* code.

'Most of us weren't *bushido*,' said infantryman, Susumu Miyashita, 'but the practice of it and the pressure to go and fight honourably began to work its way into our consciousness. Once you had been drafted and were inside that culture, it was everywhere and you forgot the outside world.'

Tsuji stood just over 5'2' in his army boots with his perfectly round specs echoing the shape of his sparsely-haired head. He was fanatical about the art of sword-fighting known as *kendo*, and had graduated top of his year at the Military Staff College. He was also an ardent proponent of *gekokujo*, which translates as 'leading from below' or – in practical application – 'loyal insubordination'. Meaning a selective adherence to discipline and orders. Insolent some might call it. He was quirky, but tolerated because, though he was a mere colonel, he had political clout in his corner in the form of former minister of war, Itagaki Seishiro, and future wartime premier, Tojo Hideki.

Tsuji's own lifestyle was diagonally different to that of Mutaguchi though, the former actively renouncing and avoiding the wine, women and song usually available to an officer of his class, until he did eventually marry, to someone from outside of military family circles and he fathered five children. Tsuji was a hardliner, known for his temper tantrums, often verging on madness. In 1936 he had proclaimed it was prohibited to offer an injured soldier a drink, and served as a staff officer in the Kwantung Army, China, for two years from 1937. Here he stirred up provocative border incidents with the Russians, and even forced officers taken prisoner by the Russians at Nomonhan to commit suicide *after* they'd been repatriated. The result was that Itagaki had him transferred to the Research Unit on Formosa (Taiwan) where he helped set up the IJA Jungle Warfare School. Thus his brutal attitude to surrender was etched deep into the army's psyche.

**

Training was gruelling for would-be officers. All cadets in the 1920s had to pass through the Military Academy at Ichigaya, likened more to an overcrowded prison than a school. Failure in exams often led to suicide. Everything in the curriculum – estimated as being about four times as time-intensive as at a Western military academy – the focus was on perfection and triumph, inculcating a *seishin* mindset of 'a will which knows no defeat' especially in the face of superior enemy forces with superior materiel. Complete annihilation was preached as the objective, and especially the idea that no enemy member should be able to escape to fight another day. It taught high-ranking officers to lead from the front, with command posts situated further forward than Western doctrine would entertain or allow.

'When the Japan-Russo war occurred, such moments came up often,' Mutaguchi wrote in his memoir, of how hard-fought battles should end with both sides shaking hands and 'cry for each other's hardship with deep emotion. So I was determined that I would have to act the same way based on *bushido* when I encounter enemy in the future.'

The War Ministry Manual and the *Military Training Regulations* were their sacred texts. To quote the *War Ministry Manual*: 'The essence of military discipline is obedience. There it is necessary that the officers and men of the whole army should form a habit of sacrificing their lives for their Emperor's country, obeying their superiors with full sincerity and executing their superior's orders faithfully.' And to quote the *Military Training Regulations*: 'Subordinates should obey immediately the orders of their superior, irrespective of their nature. Such orders are irresistible.' To junior soldiers, second-year soldiers relatively were men of great authority and they had to treat third-year soldiers almost as deities.

As they went to sleep exhausted each night, four words reverberated through their minds: *'Yell! Stick! Turn! Retract!'* It was the four-step bayonet drill they'd practiced thousands of times over. Body and mind working together.

This burgeoning *bushido*-ism in turn was overlaid on the 'Five Words' Imperial Rescript which had entered the Army in 1873:

1. A soldier must do his duty to his country.
2. A soldier must be courteous.
3. A soldier must show courage in war.
4. A soldier must keep his word.
5. A soldier must live simply.

So the training was drumming these edicts into their heads, with Spartan simplicity possibly becoming the most important of them. Japanese soldiers would have a big advantage operating in the tropics with the bare minimum of pack to carry and a reliance on picking up rations and abandoned 'Churchill supplies' en route.

'Roughly speaking, 10kg loss of sweat over the course of a day is not rare for active soldiers stationed in the tropics,' found Yas Kuno, Professor of Physiology, Nagoya University School of Medicine. 'Carrying a pack of just 15 pounds causes soldiers to sweat an additional half pound of fluid per hour,' found military science researcher, Mary Roach. So travelling light packed many benefits.

The Imperial Japanese Navy operated along a similar line of exhortation. Training leaflets for naval pilots were unambiguous: 'With a tenacious and tireless spirit we are striving to reach a superhuman degree of skill and perfect fighting efficiency.' Which made sense because the Japanese engineers, in close consultation with their German counterparts, were working tirelessly to create the ultimate flying machines.

**

1 June 1937 saw a young man Iwasaki Yoshiaki register for basic training at the Yokusuka Naval Base, south of Yokohama at the entrance of Tokyo Bay. Ringed by green hills, the snow-capped Mt Fuji towered gloriously in the summer sun behind. 'After five months of basic training, I was transferred to the 40cm main cannon division

of the battleship *Mutsu*,' Iwasaki told me. The *Mutsu* was a dreadnought battleship that dated back to the end of WW1. It had recently been revamped, now sporting an imposing pagoda-style mast and anti-torpedo bulges.

Many of these practice exercises were held in the extreme icy waters far north of Japan so as to escape prying eyes. 'The duty was so tough where young sailors had no time to take rest all day long, and some of my friends jumped into the ocean and killed themselves,' said Iwasaki. Such practice exercises alone could incredulously account for up to 100 deaths by suicide or accident.

Mutsu had four hydro-reconnaissance planes. 'I loved to go up to the deck and see the airplanes taking off from the catapult. At the same time, I envied airplane engineers who all wore very white and clean uniforms, while mine and other gunnery sailors' white clothes were dirty because of too much oil.'

Iwasaki plotted to improve his lot. Ironically this was the same strategy many British and colonial officers were taking to upgrade their life and lifestyles, too. But it often involved moving to India.

THE INDIANS PAD UP

'It was pretty boring in England and better pay in India.'

India, 1933. A most incredible shipboard romance had blossomed into a marriage between a former schoolteacher and an RAMC doctor. Ethel Rogers was a vivacious and ambitious Canadian – whose mother had died during childbirth – sent on an all-expenses first-class educational tour of the Far East by the newly formed Canadian Society for Literature and the Arts. Ports of call were to be Japan, China, Singapore and India. Even the Canadian prime minister, RB Bennett, had met with the 29-year-old go-getter before she headed off to join the yellow-funnelled *Empress of Japan*.

She changed her ticket from first-class to tourist-class, figuring the refund would help purchase some art and craft items for the Society.

On arrival in Japan, she watched as a large white limousine, flying the Canadian ensign, pulled up alongside the docks, intrigued to see who warranted such VIP treatment. Only when the official party came up and asked for 'Miss Rogers, please,' she realized it was *her*. The prime minister had really laid on everything for her here: she got to stay with the Canadian ambassador, and was invited by the black pearl king, Mr Mikimoto, to his islands. She was even presented to Emperor Hirohito and Empress Kojun of Japan, in a 'very informal affair that took place in the palace garden.'

Next stop was China, where a sumptuous lunch, including caviar, was laid on by the Canadian ambassador. She insisted her ship-board friends join her, and they returned to the boat in very high spirits, singing *O Canada*, *The Maple Leaf Forever*, and more, with garrulous gusto.

But back on board, she soon began to feel as green as the water in that dirty river, as food poisoning gripped her. She tried to ride it out, but by midnight it was clear a doctor was needed. As the ship's doctor was rather fond of his drink he was unable to be roused. But, there were two young British doctors as passengers on the boat. Capt Denis Mulvany, on his way back to his post in India, was the same age as Ethel, and joined the RAMC after graduating in 1930 and was promoted to captain and posted to the Indian hill station of Ranikhet within three years. He made his way down immediately to her tourist-class cabin, and – as shocked as he was to see her condition – was immediately smitten by her fair brown hair, blue eyes, smooth skin.

'Why didn't you call me before?' he said, as he sat in his pyjamas and bathrobe at the end of her bed. She misheard his plummy English tones as, 'What did you call me for?'

'Well, 'tisn't for your looks,' the feisty Canadian shot back, dismissing his tight curls of black hair and Clark Gable-styled moustache. 'If that's what you're thinking, you can just get out of here!' (She'd admit later that he looked rather chic in his nightgown.)

Denis considered this reply before his own return of serve: 'You're not going to die – you'll be alright with a temper like that!' He had some 'grog' sent down to her to knock the tee-totaller out for the night.

Bumping into her on deck the next day he cautiously enquired about her health, noting she was nearly the same height as he (she stood 5'7'). He advised she get some exercise, quickly adding, 'I'll assist you,' and they walked the deck.

Berthing in Hong Kong the quiet doctor boldly took the opportunity to invite her off the boat. 'Come into the city with me,' he said. 'We could have tea at the Victoria Hotel and then look in the shops.' This afforded the luxury of time to discover each other more deeply, in terms of where they came from and where they were individually heading in life. 'When I get off in Singapore,' continued the effervescent Ethel, 'I'm going to Bangkok to meet the King of Siam.' Capt Watson-Armstrong, the Siamese consul in Japan, had fixed this introduction. Denis wondered why such a connected woman moving in such high circles was travelling tourist-class, not realizing the back-story of how she'd traded her ticket to support her fund-raising activities.

Next stop: Singapore. And she was due to leave for Siam the next day. Denis didn't want this magnetic lady to slip through his fingers. He once again invited her ashore, summoning a rickshaw to take them to the Singapore Swimming Club. Along the road was an archway with the sign reading 'Kiss Your Girl Here!' He probably felt like it, but restrained himself, which only made her more keen for it.

The pool, the first in Malaya and one of the social epicentres for colonials on the island, featured a dozen lanes, high-dive boards, palm trees and an impressive three-storey clubhouse. On the terrace, she sipped an Orangeade, while he nursed a *chota* (whisky and soda), all the while chatting and enjoying the cooling breezes coming off the Malacca Strait.

Back on board, he invited her for a walk on the deck. As they strolled slowly, he stopped. 'Miss Rogers,' he said in his quiet, confident tone, 'I would like to marry you.' She was taken off-balance.

'My goodness I don't even know you.' A slightly awkward long silence ensued before she blurted out: 'What is your full name?'

'Denis Paul Francis Mulvany.'

'Well, I'm Ethel Wilhelmine Rogers.'

'And where do you live?'

'Lucknow, India.'

Silence. 'I think I'd like to marry you,' she finally replied. This was a moment that would change her life forever. Initially for the better, later for the worse.

They retired to their respective cabins, abuzz with excited emotions. But she woke up early, packed her trunk, walked the streets of Singapore alone, and decided to call it off, returning to continue on to Siam as planned. Denis spotted her walking up the gangplank.

'So you changed your mind?'

'And so you were drunk,' she said, blaming the whisky *chota* for his irrational rush of emotion. He quickly explained how little alcohol was in his one drink and that he'd consumed the night before. This appeased her and they went to breakfast to smooth things over. Here Denis sealed it by announcing to all in earshot that they were engaged. She agreed to cancel her Siam sojourn, and was surprised to find out he'd already cancelled her ticket. By the time they put into Colombo she had an engagement ring on her finger.

**

And so they arrived in Cawnpore (today's Kanpur), a historical East India Company city near Lucknow, which had played a starring role in the 1857 Sepoy Mutiny. Denis' father John had also been a doctor in the British Indian Army, so there was much tradition running in the family. Denis had been born in Calcutta in 1904 then sent, as was the practice, to boarding school in England.

With her Red Cross experience in Canada, Ethel wanted to work, to contribute, by helping out the nurses at a nearby hospital bathing and feeding local infants. Denis put his foot down firmly: 'It is beneath you as the future wife of a doctor, to do this work.'

'Well, let me tell you,' she retorted, 'I'm not going to put up with this. I'm not going to be under anybody's orders. I'm going straight to Bombay and take a ship home.' Once again, they smoothed things over.

Within a couple of months, Mulvany's colonel staged their grand wedding, replete with a guard of honour, four horses pulling their white carriage, and the 10th Hussars' band gracing the ensuing reception. Champagne flowed freely.

'Well, this is the life!' the new Mrs Mulvany might've found herself saying, as she settled into the rather fabulous life of being a British Army officer's wife in India. With no fewer than 22 servants (if you count the four stable-hands) attending to their needs at home, there was barely a finger for her to lift. So she took to horse riding, her favourite mount called Ginger.

Then one day came a rude wake-up call from this reverie. The village she'd ridden through just the day before had disappeared, washed away in epic floods. She watched villagers with nothing left try and pick up their lives, and felt suddenly pathetic for her indulgent lifestyle. 'You, Ethel Mulvany, who led a useful life in Canada, can do something.'

What she did was set about promoting the art and craft of these Purdah women to Canada. She leveraged her contact, the prime minister, to secure funding and set up a large exhibit as part of the Canadian National Exhibition in 1935. The expo was wildly successful, selling over half a million dollars of local arts and crafts, with even more unfulfilled orders on the books. And the exotic baby animals proved a real draw card, too – tigers, elephants and mongeese. But one star attraction didn't make it: a cigar-smoking panda. Sadly, the crew on the ship took it on deck for a photo opportunity, when it had lost its balance and fell overboard.

As a result of this great trade promotion, Ethel was awarded the King's Silver Jubilee Medal – one of only 50 to be awarded in the United Provinces of India – by Sir Harry Haig, the governor. She was now very much part of the fabric in Cawnpore, and the Mulvanys planned to spend a further 20 years – effectively till his retirement – there.

Cue some serious 'curveballs' as they might call them in softball which Ethel loved playing as a student. Because this success came at a price to her physical and mental health. She was exhausted. She also miscarried, a devastating mental blow. But typically selflessly, she dealt with the matter herself, burying the foetus in the backyard, and waiting till Denis had had his dinner that night before informing him. This led to some ongoing bleeding complications for her. Denis himself came down with appendicitis, necessitating an operation, plus several transfusions.

Then at home in her Cawnpore garden one day, she was bitten by a large cobra. A bite that can often kill within 15 minutes. But her quick-thinking bearer, Ran Bharose, grabbed a razor blade and deftly cut-away the poison-infected flesh around the bite, packing the wound with permanganate crystals. He then put his madam on his bicycle and got her to the British hospital where Denis worked, within nine minutes. The captain, who Ethel described as 'the calmest and coolest man in the world,' set about saving his wife's life over the next few days. She was presented a sacred monkey by a Hindu priest to protect her from further snakebites.

In the spring of 1939 Ethel's adoptive mother was taken gravely ill, and Ethel wanted to spend some valuable time with her. Denis would accompany her as far as England, where they'd spend time with his family, before she'd continue on to Canada, and he'd return to India. Ethel buried her mother, and took some time to regain her emotional strength among family and friends.

Then came the shock news that Denis was to be posted to that new British Military Hospital in Singapore. 'When will I see him again?' she fretted, as she boarded the SS *Ascania* from Montreal to Liverpool. The day she arrived the SS *Athenia*, heading in the reverse direction, was torpedoed by a German U-boat off the coast of Ireland.

Could she ever make it back to India, and would Denis still be there?

**

Poona, India, had been under British rule for over 120 years, and a large military cantonment had been established in the east of the small but important city. It is difficult to underestimate the cultural effect of the British Indian Army. For a start, without it, the Brits might still be wearing red coats instead of *khaki*, an Indian word, fabric and colour which was adopted and used firstly in 1868. Then other words such as *gymkhana* and *jodphurs* migrated into English, and of course curry (from *kari*) has become not just a staple of the English diet, but chicken tikka masala has been recently voted the most popular dish in Britain.

A major camp and army staff college was at Doolally, 100 miles north of Mumbai. Those who'd spent too long in-camp or under the hot tropical sun, were said to have gone '*doolally*', another expression that was widely imported into English slang. This cultural interchange and appropriation was about to ramp up exponentially from the late 1930s. 'In the Indian Army, apart from the regular Indian Army there were many many states with agreements with the British, over 500 in fact, and some of these states would maintain in peacetime a military unit – it might be an infantry unit, it might be cavalry, it might be a camel unit, mules, gunner,' Maj Roy Hudson explained to me. The articled civil engineer had joined the Territorial Army the day Chamberlain went to see Hitler because it was felt a war was imminent. He completed sapper training and became 2nd Lt Hudson. 'I went to headquarters of Royal Engineers for a course on building bridges, and was called up in August 1939 to our war station on Isle of Wight and war started on 3 September.'

**

In Poona, the 44th Indian Infantry Brigade was formed in June 1940, assigned to the 17th Indian Infantry Division. Brig George Ballentine, 48, was an old India hand, having been seconded to the Punjab regiment post-war after recovering from his injuries shortly after landing at Gallipoli in 1915. He was a good-looking rugby player and keen rower, while his younger brother, also with the Indian Army, enjoyed his *chukkas* of polo. If any reminders were needed of the perils of a frontier posting, George's three-year-old daughter died after contracting polio in the Punjab. His wife hastily left India, taking their older daughter with her.

Soon came a life-changing clarion call for Sapper Hudson and others. 'They announced that volunteers were required to go out to India because they were expanding the Indian Army and wanted more officers. I did it for two reasons: it was pretty boring in England for what they called the 'phony' war, and also there was better pay in the Indian Army.'

In the Hudson bloodline were a long line of adventurers: 'I had a good number of aunts and uncles and they were all travelled, they'd been out to India and that sort of thing. One of my ancestors was in the East India Company. And he was a sailor, eventually captain of a ship. He used to go out to China and Calcutta and those places in the 18th century.' So Roy was in with both boots. 'My draft, 50 of us, left Scotland aboard the *Highland Chieftain*.' Roy revelled in the 'absolutely luxurious' shipboard conditions. 'We were in first-class accommodation, perhaps two to a cabin, and England was in rationing. Food was excellent, bottle of wine with every meal.'

Roy had chosen the Royal Bombay Sappers and Miners out of three Engineers choices, all of whom shared the Sanskrit motto, '*Sarvatra*' (everywhere). 'You can join Madras Sappers and Miners, but they all speak Tamil – only a few NCOs speak Urdu the common Army language. And I'd been trying to learn Urdu all the time I'd been on board ship, so I crossed them out. Then the other were the Bengal Sappers and Miners, you had to get on a train for three or four days going north before you get to the depot.'

Typically units were headed by British officers only, with Indian other ranks (*sepoys*) under their command. (The Indian Army had its own separate nomenclature for ranks). Indian officers only had command over other Indians, even though they might outrank a British officer. 'All of the Indian Army was recruited really from the northwest from Punjab,' said Hudson. 'Sikhs, Mussamans, Hindus.'

One major exception was the Madras Sappers and Miners. 'They consisted of people from south India who were not normally considered martial tribes. But the only unit in the army that used Madrassers were the S & M because they were better educated and for an engineer you need education.' This seemingly trivial cultural nuance would play a crucial role in later events at the Alexandra Hospital.

**

Things were hotting up in Poona around July 1941 with more battalions being raised to bolster the 44th Indian Brigade, and a more intense pre-deployment training regime which stretched them and their weaponry thin. Most germane to our story are the 1/6th Punjabs, 8/7th Punjabs, and 14/6th Punjabs because, as part of the 44th Indians, they were ultimately diverted to Malaya despite all their training being geared to conditions in the Middle East, Iraq specifically.

Col James Sainter, MC, had earned his medal in the Somme in 1916 when he led a flanking party in a raid which killed upto 50 enemy. Prior to this he had placed a mine in the wire within 25 metres of the enemy's trenches, and accounted for three enemy with his service revolver. With such a daring style it wasn't long before his luck ran out, he was injured, and invalided back to England. Now here he was, aged 45, as the commanding officer of the 1/6th Battalion.

Most of the British officers in India were either English or Scottish, and Capt Robert Brown, just 22, was the latter. He admired the loyalty his Indian other ranks displayed. 'They do become very attached to the British officer as long as one is good to them,' he said. 'They stood by him.' Would that claim remain standing in the heat of battle? He would soon find out. Also serving alongside Brown and Sainter was a Kiwi, 2nd Lt John Wilson, an aspiring lawyer who'd answered the call for volunteers in India, and had freshly arrived in-country with around a dozen others. A two-month training program was his first obligation, which was 'mainly learning the language,' which proved challenging for new arrivals and would present cross-cultural communication issues in peacetime as in war.

The 8th Punjab was a proud regiment, mustering 10 battalions by 1941, with the 7th Battalion under command of Lt Col Willis Southern, formerly of the Lancashire Fusiliers and a resident of India (and officer in its army) for 22 years already to date.

The Indian Mutiny of 1857 was the catalyst for the formation of several new battalions across the country to put down the rebellion. The 14th Punjabs was a clear beneficiary of this expansion policy, and now Lt Col Louis Sobaux Ingle, an MC recipient in his early forties, was leading its 6th Battalion. Another WW1 veteran, Ingle had led a company of the Punjabi infantry in the North-West Frontier and Persia with distinction. His medal citation referenced how he 'continually led his platoon forward under heavy fire,' and highlighted his inspiring 'cool courage.'

So generally these leaders seemed like they had the right credentials and were made of stern stuff when it counted. Much like Maj George Bruce who founded the Malay Regiment to test the Malay temperament for combat suitability. Except this was no experiment: the British Indian Army was a much-proven outfit with a longstanding proud military and martial heritage. But one can't help thinking whether life at the top was just a tad too cushy.

On arrival in early 1941 Roy had wasted no time in setting himself up for the good life as a *nabob*. He immediately joined the Poona Club. 'It was a sort of up-noise thing. Evenings, dances, that sort of thing. They had a very nice officers' mess, we each had a bearer, a servant who looked after you the whole time from morning to night, and when you went in to have your meal he'd be standing behind your chair, properly dressed with a turban and everything. It was an easy life.'

Meanwhile the British Indian Army was expanding rapidly and during the war would reach 2.5 million, the largest volunteer force in history. As new units were created, so others were stripped of their experienced VCOs, denuding them of depth and stretching the talent thinly across the officer classes.

Any feeling of the war coming to India? 'Nothing, nothing at all.' Hudson spent most of his time over the next year there horse-riding.

Around 70,000 Indian troops, mainly the more martial-minded Sikhs, would be sent to Malaya. And meanwhile thousands more soldiers from the British Army were steaming towards Singapore, too.

A classic shipboard romance blossomed between Capt Denis Mulvany and Ethel, when she was taken ill on board and they called for a doctor. She had just visited Japan and China and he talked her into stopping in India -- and getting married with great ceremony.

Col Mutaguchi Renya (left) and Col Tsuji Masonobu were both keen proponents of the *bushido* code, although it was not part of the Army's official regulations. Below, Mutaguchi in action, Marco Polo Bridge, China 1937.

STEAMING TOWARDS SINGAPORE

'I joined the Army to be fed and have a bed.'

Sailing eastward on the smart white steamship *SS Dilwara* in 1936 was a tall 17-year-old from Lancashire, Pte Jack 'Stan' Sharpley. He'd signed on for the Army the previous year. 'Seven years on the Regulars, and five on the Reserves,' said Stan. He was assigned to the Loyal North Lancashire Regiment, which had been posted to Shanghai. 'Oh yeah, brilliant! I'm going to see the world!' He knew nothing about the Far East then, and perhaps his only preconception was that everything would be cheap. They were barracked in Great Western Road, running out to the western suburbs of the International Settlement, where estates of the elite nestled among the trees, and a small aerodrome was constructed.

They were earning a mere 10 shillings a week, but it was ample 'because everything in Shanghai was so cheap.' However, what they'd not factored in was competition from the newly arrived Americans. 'They had about 10 times as much money as us, so the nightclubs and pubs used to put up signs "Out of Bounds to British Soldiers" because they had the money and we didn't. We used to get a rickshaw and race one another back to the barracks,' remembered Sharpley. 'We'd say *"Chop chop! Da Xi Lu*!" (Hurry, hurry, Great Western Road.)'

Mid-1938 saw the arrival of more British forces to act as peacekeepers between the various international concessions and the local population. Among these was George Britton (junior) of the East Surrey Regiment. His father was a veteran of WW1 who suffered a mustard gas attack, leading to unemployment and his sudden premature death when George junior was just 12. 'He was a happy kid, one of the cleverest boys in his class,' according to his sister, Elsie, but the world suddenly became harder for the family. 'One day in woodworking class, the teacher hit him on the back of his neck,' recalled Elsie, 'George swung around with a mallet still in his hand, and was accused of threatening the teacher.' He was duly expelled at the age of 15, so went off and found a job with Makepeace Printers. But within a few weeks he decided he wanted to join the Army.

'Mother would not sign the papers, so he tried himself,' recalled Elsie. The recruitment officer asked how old he was. Seventeen, he lied, giving a false birth year, which didn't add up. 'He was told to go home and grow up.' His real birth date was ironically Armistice Day, 11 November. A few short months later he got a neighbour, Mr Mann, to sign for him and successfully enlisted in the South Wales Borderers, aged 15 years and three months. And within a few months he found himself shipped off to those wooden barracks at Great Western Road, Shanghai.

'His mother and sister never forgave Mr Mann,' said his daughter Beth Steiner Jones. 'But George wrote to them and asked them not to try to get him discharged because he was earning a good wage and as a cadet he would earn much less but be doing the same work.' With some of his salary, he bought exotic gifts for his family. 'George sent me a silk handkerchief from Shanghai,' recalled Elsie. 'I still have it. Also a pink embroidered article.'

When and if they needed any medical attention, George, Stan and cohort would head to the British Military Hospital Shanghai, on Central Road closer in towards the Bund. Here, Matron Ruddock and her team of QA sisters, including Sisters Yvonne Ninnis, Ethne Butterworth, and Helen Kilroe, would nurse them back to good cheer again.

**

These QA sisters were a very select band. By 1939 there were just 640 QAIMNS nurses, supplemented by Territorial Army Nursing Service (TANS). They were nicknamed 'Girls in Grey' because of their dresses, a 'demure shade of mid-grey' that Florence Nightingale believed signalled restraint and calm – just what any wounded soldier would want. But 'tropical whites' were their garb for the Far East.

After four years of training, most went directly into the Forces, although some preferred to join the Colonial Nursing Service in various exotic outposts. Those that chose the Army soon found a difficult adjustment period, because of the military penchant for paperwork and process. 'The patients' towels must lie thrice folded,' was one such example.

Although an onlooker might be deceived watching them shipping out from Millbank Military Hospital on the banks of the Thames. 'Their luggage spilled over the pavements: golf clubs, tennis racquets, favourite Persian rugs, even a sewing machine and a bird in a cage,' is how an observer described one batch's departure. Garden party outfits and tropical white were de rigeur for those sailing east. Others made sure to dash across to Harrod's perhaps for some special undergarments and such. From there they'd boarded a train to Glasgow – a 24-hour ride – to ship out on the handsome single-masted double-funneled *Dominion Monarch.*

**

At this point, another interesting character entered the frame, too. Constantine Petrovsky was just 11 when Sakhalin (which was occupied by Japan from 1905 to 1924) was handed back to Russia. As his Czarist family was in exile, and wealthy from mining interests, they were targetted by the Communists. Hence scars from a sabre on his scalp, from a foiled home invasion by Communists, during which one of their party guests – a Japanese general – was also shot in the jaw. They had to leave, fast, and – like many 'White Russians' – fled to the nearest places: China or Japan.

'The Japanese were very sympathetic,' Constantine's future wife, Dr Kathleen Petrovsky, would tell me. 'An icebreaker came and rescued them and took them to Japan.' The whole family would be there a year, before moving to Harbin in northern China. Wanting to study medicine, he headed to Hong Kong, the nearest place a European-recognized medical degree was available. He spent time in Shanghai first, studying English. But then the Japanese took Harbin. 'When I was in Hong Kong I knew what was going on in China. After all, they're brutal, cruel, but they could fight us.'

'These poor students were cut off from home, funding and everything,' Kathleen would say. 'The White Russian community in

Hong Kong took in funds.' Despite his poor English and other disruptions, Constantine graduated with the university's gold medal in 1938. The tall, dark-haired young man with thick round black spectacle frames took on jobs in Kowloon Medical Centre and Queen Mary's hospital, a 'newly built, beautiful hospital'. But being entrepreneurial, he wanted to set up his own practice, and became a Port health officer while doing that on the side. With war approaching, he wanted to get to the Eastern front. 'He went to speak to the British Army who promised him everything, thinking he'd get to Russia proper.'

He joined the RAMC in Hong Kong in 1939 but, on the way to Europe, he was offloaded in Singapore 'much to his disgust'. He was ordered to meet with Brig Charles Stringer, Deputy Director Medical Services (DDMS), Malaya Command. 'He said, "Look here, Petrovsky, you're not going to Europe – we've not enough doctors for the armed services here. So you're going to stay".' He was assigned to The Alex at lieutenant level 'to get used to military way of life.' That included a month of studying military law, changing guards, being an orderly, and socializing at the many nightspots popular with the troops.' Then he was assigned to Malaya Field Ambulance No 4. But getting used to the army way would be relatively easy for the man described as 'black and white, disciplined, ordered,' by his son, Nikolai.

'He attracted trouble, or trouble attracted him, but he wasn't pleased,' said Dr Kathleen Petrovsky

Similarly, Irish QA nurse Sister Ruth Dickson, around 49 by then, seemed to have shuttled around China since 1923, working variously as a missionary and nurse, and shipping out again to work in Newchang, China on an evangelistic mission from 1936 onwards.

But the interesting turn of events with Japanese aggression in Shanghai would push all these characters toward Singapore and into the Alexandra Hospital's orbit.

**

Cedric 'Norman' Bryer from Middlesex had been in Malaya, working the Telok Bahru coconut estate in the central northwest area near Perak since 1934. One of his parents' contacts, Ceylonese Harris

Andre, had a father who was a big noise in Malayan plantations, and the necessary introductions were made, hence his move out here. Bryer was one of seven kids born to a jeweller, who also refined gold and silver, in historic Clerkenwell, central London. Norman's father taught his older sister Vera to box so she could stand up to her taller brothers (she went on to become quite famous in the West End, as did her daughter Denise Bryer at the BBC who would marry game-show host, Nicholas Parsons).

Norman might've done some boxing too, but tennis was his thing. His father Claude's business was successful enough to send Norman to Highgate School, a 450-year-old institution which counted notables such as TS Eliot, Gen Sir Edward Leach, VC, and Rev John Venn (inventor of the eponymous diagram) among its alumni. Given the lingering post-war recession, another family contact, Arthur Pritchard, suggested Australia might represent more opportunities for him so he sailed off to work on a farm near Melbourne. And, oh, take your 15-year-old brother, Clifford, because he'd recently been expelled from school.

'Norman was always considered a strong, reserved, sensible elder brother,' his daughter Denise would say. 'Clifford was a handful and a bit wild, with the looks of Errol Flynn.' Clifford would return from Australia with a broad Aussie accent and a broken nose, and signed up with the RAF, going on to become a rear-gunner. Norman diligently signed on as a reservist with the RAF when he arrived in Malaya, flying Tiger Moths at the Perak Flying Club, and squeezing in these duties between games of tennis at the Lower Perak Tennis Club and rounds of golf at the Ipoh Golf Club, one of the oldest clubs in the world, and the Selangor Club. 'I had been ordered to report to RAF Station Seletar in Singapore a few days before war had been declared with Germany in September 1939 and had to leave my job on the coconut estate without delay.'

He went into training as a torpedo bomber pilot there for two years.

**

Already based in Singapore were Royal Engineers Fortress

Companies: the 30th and 34th on anti-aircraft duties, the 35th, 36th, and 41st on coastal defences. These all fell under the command of Lt Col HM Taylor. Part of the 36th Company was a young Scottish sapper by the name of Daniel Fraser, who set to work building pillboxes around the coast.

Fraser candidly admitted he signed on at the depot in Hamilton, Scotland, in 1935 (aged just 19) 'because there was very little work. So I joined the Army to be fed and have a bed. I was sent to Chatham and taught drill and demolitions for 10 weeks. Then sent to Porton, the chemical defense unit.' He worked there until his company's July 1938 posting to Singapore. He remembered 'all these big amusement places, the Gay World, we used to come down, the United Servicemen's Club was like a hostelry and we used to go to the dance halls in our free time off.'

At this time, another corps of the Royal Engineers were busy laying the solid concrete foundations for the Alexandra Hospital. It was to have 356 beds – double the size of the existing Tanglin Barracks Hospital – split among medical, surgical and officers wards, laboratories, and a mortuary.

After about one year in Changi, Fraser and his 36th Coy shipped up to Batu Muang Fort which guarded the southeastern sector of Penang Island with its massive guns. They were the first British soldiers on that island, and now came under the command of Lt Col DA Rendle, another World War 1 veteran.

**

Stan Sharpley and his rickshaw-racing 2nd Loyals were transferred after two years in Shanghai down to Singapore in 1938, a move that would effectively double the size of the British garrison in Singapore. You could imagine raucous roars of appreciation as their trucks passed the Tiger Breweries just over the road from Gillman Barracks. 'Aye, the Tiger Breweries was just a way off from our football field, across Alexandra Road,' he said. The ads of the day exhorted: 'Drink Tiger Beer. Gets rid of boredom and any frustration.'

Stan was allocated a barrack room in D Block, 365 steep steps up from the guard room. 'Every day of the year, there was a step for it.'

Immediately they fell into a new routine, which included a little boredom and only the odd frustration. 'We used to have to get up at six, out for PT maybe half past six or seven, breakfast at 7:30 to 8:30, then the usual square-bashing and then afternoon siesta, mosquito net down, too hot to do anything.' Relatively mild exertion compared to what their Japanese counterparts were doing. Sunburn was a major issue for the new arrivals. 'In peacetime, sunburn was a crime in Singapore. One Sunday I got burnt from head to foot. Ooh! Terrible sunburn. Awful!' You could be put on a charge for getting about, even a short distance, without your hat, cap or solar *topee*.

But once the stinging heat and humidity had lessened, it was time for sports. 'Football matches, tennis tournaments, cricket matches.' Stan played hockey for the battalion and football for one of the companies. Opposing teams might come from the RAF, Fort Canning, RAMC, or even further up-country in Malaya.

'We used to go to the NAAFI on Alexandra Road, but 10 o'clock was closing time and we had to be back in barracks by 10.' If they ventured out locally, casual clothing was acceptable, but venturing further out into town required army dress. And of course, these young men were keen to explore Singapore town. But they were in for a rude shock: 'Expensive!'

Their 10 shillings would not stretch as far as it did in Shanghai. 'We were very limited in going out because we were on very, very small wages,' Stan explained. 'From Gillman Barracks we used to go to the Union Jack Club, across the road from the Cathay picture house. If anyone won house at Bingo or something, they were practically millionaires!' The Union Jack Club had opened in 1924 to cater for British sailors and soldiers.

The art-deco Cathay was still under construction, destined to be the tallest building when it opened in 1941. At 16 storeys, it was Singapore's first concrete skyscraper. Around town, Stan noted that 'Chinatown was just a shantytown in those days, covered in litter and takeaway basket things' and Orchard Road was definitely the main street. 'It was mainly pubs and a few hotels. There was one huge supermarket, it had a lift outside the building.' The locals still dressed in more traditional garb – 'If you saw a Malay he'd have a *sarong* on' – and he found Singaporeans generally hospitable, social. 'They were very, *very* kind to us.'

The Army marched on its proverbial stomach, and Stan and friends, probably including Lancashire lad, Titch Crosston, often frequented a little café in Orchard Road for local food. 'There's one Chinese dish that I'll never forget – nobody back home can make a tomato soup like the Chinese. Beautiful, *beautiful*.'

The Cricket Club was occasionally visited, and the Tanglin Club later extended its membership facilities, but to officers only. Similarly, the Raffles Hotel was out of bounds for other ranks. 'We were barred from going anywhere near the Raffles because it was high-brow,' recalled Stan. 'The Red Caps if they saw you would say, "What are you doing here? Get away or we'll book ya".' But, boys being boys, Stan and friends would occasionally sneak into the Long Bar. 'It was huge!'

The Red Caps were also on duty at another favourite haunt of the forces. 'We knew Singapore in them days as Lavender Street,' Stan laughed and rolled his eyes. Lavender Street was the red light district, where the White House was a popular drinking spot. The street came into being in 1858, linking Rochor Bridge with Serangoon Road, and was a name suggested very much tongue-in-cheek by local residents because of the pungent pong from the 'night-soil' used to fertilize the Chinese market gardens in the area.

The area developed on the back of the 1930s rubber boom, where wealth was best demonstrated by how ornately elaborate the facades of the two-storey shop-houses could be made. Art deco was also on show at The New World, the entertainment theme park which was a big draw in the area.

Less salubrious again was the area around Sungei Road which everyone knew as 'Thieves Market'. The flea market peddled second-hand goods, contraband, you name it. Even British Army surplus, which may not have actually been surplus in the strictest sense.

And amid all of this, a red light district flourished. 'Very, very cosmopolitan,' said Sharpley. 'They'd say to you, "You want nice girl?

German, Japanese, Chinese, English, American?" We probably paid a fiver or ten pound sterling.' But Singapore was known as something of a 'Last Chance Saloon' for many of the world's working girls at the tail-end of their careers, squeezing a few last dollars from plying their trade. If the Red Caps happened along, there was trouble. 'They'd go to the door and say "Out now and report to the Medical Inspection room" and you'd head back to barracks.' A short-arm inspection would ensue. Generally the men would have to pass a weekly inspection in order to get their paychecks, anyway.

Just five kilometres from barracks to the west coast, another popular weekend outing became the Haw Par Villa gardens, which had just opened in 1937. Also known as 'Tiger Balm Gardens' after its owner's therapeutic product, the photogenic gardens were full of papier-mache animals, figurines and pagodas. 'We used to get a boat and go out there.' Sometimes his company would also play some golf – probably at the Keppel Club near Labrador – always a recipe for sunburn and an admonition from the doctor. 'This is the life,' Stan thought. 'When you're in the forces you always look forward to seeing different places. So I joined up for 21 years.'

**

Another long-termer was Brig Charles Stringer, DDMS. Fifty two by now, the Irishman had been educated at Queens College, Belfast, having studied medicine. The following year, 1910, he joined the RAMC. He showed uncommon nerve in WW1, garnering a DSO for 'conspicuous gallantry under fire in saving wounded from falling into the hands of the enemy,' and was also mentioned in dispatches in France 1918. Further stints in exotic Waziristan earned him the OBE. Now he was here in Singapore with his nurse wife Olga, and they operated as a very close team personally and professionally.

**

Dr Geoffrey Rogers had moved out from London to Miri in Sarawak to a position at the Shell Company's hospital. Shell had struck oil here back in 1910 and were well established. It wasn't his first preference, though. 'My father was a doctor, and his father was a doctor,' explained his son, Hector, born in London in 1934, soon after his parents' marriage. 'They were all either medical men or men of the church. They came from contrasting worlds. Mum got into nursing, possibly to catch a doctor for a husband, I suspect that. The objective was to earn enough money to return to the UK, buy a practice, and become a GP.'

Still, life in Sarawak in 1938 was something of a paradise playground. 'Terrific! We had a rather nice colonial life,' remembered Hector. 'It was a privileged life, we had a Chinese *amah* (maid). One just accepted that. I learned to swim, high diving.' When they reached school age, the boys tended to be sent away to boarding school, mostly in the Cameron Highlands, a tea-growing area, around 200km due north from Kuala Lumpur. Leave with the family usually involved a steamer headed to Singapore, KL, or Penang.

**

Yoshiaki Iwasaki resolved to join the Naval Air Force ground engineering crew, and sat for his exam in December 1938. He nailed it and entered the Flight Engineering School in Kasumigaseki, Ibaraki. An air base had just been opened there the previous year, 85km north of Tokyo on farming land claimed on the personal orders of Emperor Hirohito. After an intense six-month program, he graduated in June 1939, and was assigned to a newly established squadron called Chichi Jima Air Squadron, a naval unit with hydro-reconnaissance planes, the type he used to love seeing catapulting off the *Mutsu*'s deck. The small island of Chichi Jima, about 250km north of Iwo Jima, was bristling with naval craft, long-range radio equipment, heavy artillery, and the seaplane base. Altogether thousands of personnel were stationed on this strategic island.

So he'd improved his lot, but Iwasaki was still not satisfied because – as he spent more time fixing the planes on Chichi Jima – he came to learn that pilots looked down on ground crews. So his problems were not over. In fact, things were about to get a lot worse. 'One of my duties was to carry pilots from the water to the beach in order not to make them wet after they came back from a mission,' he said. 'However, one day, while I was carrying a pilot, I slipped on some seaweed and fell into the water. I hit my head hard, going unconscious. Of course the pilot got wet completely. That night I was beaten up by the pilot so badly at the Navy hospital.' That very same night Iwasaki decided to become a pilot, in order to be better than the men he was currently serving.

Naturally the NCOs and instructors didn't like such a request from this upstart, and he came in for a lot of flak at the squadron. But he studied late into every night, finally passing his pilot's exam. Soon after, he visited a fortune-teller. 'The fortune-teller said that I shall be a navy personnel and a mechanical expert, and I shall never be seriously wounded even though my airplane crashes.' He hoped that to be true as he soon shipped off to China to run bombing raids on Chengdu and Chongqing, against rapidly improving Chinese pilots trained under an agreement with Chiang Kai Shek for Claire Lee Chenault and Russian air aces to be 'air advisers' to his air force.

**

While the Japanese were battling hard in China, a British Oxford scholar was already hard at work in Japan. Cyril Wild was the beak-nosed son of the Bishop of Newcastle, and had gone to join Shell near Liverpool St, London. But after a year he was posted to their subsidiary, the Rising Sun Petroleum Company in Yokohama, not far from where Iwasaki had started his oil-soaked naval career. Just before he left Britain, the 23-year-old announced his engagement to Celia, the daughter of close family friends. So it would have been a mixed bag of emotions as he sailed alone in mid-1931 for his new life in the East.

The culture shock and homesickness hit him immediately. The company had laid on a house for him in Nagoya, but 'why there's been nothing worse than two cases of diphtheria during the last six months, passes my comprehension,' he wrote to his beloved brother, David. 'There are no drains at all – each house has a box opening onto the street,' he wrote of the sub-standard sanitary arrangements. But he did find mirth in the sign of a local tailor shop: 'We give ladies fits upstairs.'

Thankfully a transfer to Yokohama soon came. To kill the lonely hours outside of work, he resorted to reading, the classics of Virgil and Homer being favourites, and then set about learning the local language as a way to fast-track his career prospects. A teacher came to his office every lunch hour. He and Celia married on his first home leave after four years, and she returned to Japan with him. Eschewing the endless expat cocktail circuit, they spent evenings at home playing the piano and singing together.

Cyril ended up in Yokohama General Hospital for an operation to remove the septum from his rather large nose. 'My op went off extremely well. The Japanese who performed was absolutely first-rate,' he told his brother. Meantime his Japanese ('a peculiarly complicated tongue') had improved to the point where the company recognized his potential as an asset, and gave him a full year off, on full pay, in order to study and become fluent.

Celia and he moved up to Tokyo, and soon they made friends in the British Embassy circuit, and started enjoying sailing weekends in rented cottages on Lake Chuzenji – a stunning natural paradise nearly 200km north of Tokyo. He was spending four hours at school, and Celia was relishing the weather and views of the sun on the pine trees outside their house, plus the tennis and swimming. 'It is great fun living in Tokyo. We are incredibly happy and don't in the least mind life being a picnic.' She also found the people 'all very friendly disposed' in Tokyo.

But then odd things started to happen around 1938-39. They had felt for some time that their servants were paid to spy on them as foreigners. They also had evidence on at least one occasion that the police had come around and questioned their cook while they were out, and even rummaged through Cyril's papers and things upstairs. Xenophobia seemed always simmering, and there were 'rabid' anti-British articles in the daily press, and articles warning residents of spying by foreign residents and tourists. 'See a foreigner and recognize a spy,' was the watchword. This seemed to peak at the end of 1937, with 'Chastise Outrageous England' rallies all over Japan. These often threatened to spill over violently, and Cyril considered sending Celia home, especially as his business had dropped off by about 30 percent as the war with China deepened.

The Anti-Britain thing was most likely a political ploy to divert the citizens' attention away from the slower-than-expected progress in China.

Still, Prince Chichibu and his princess were leaving for England and planning to visit Oxford. Cyril was invited to a tea party in their honour because he was the Hon Sec of the Cambridge & Oxford Society in Tokyo, of which half the members were Japanese, including the prince.

Cyril was then posted down to Osaka, as imports were drying up, and the cost of living rising. 'One has to admire the fortitude and unity of the Japanese people, whatever one's opinion may be of the terrible goings-on in China.'

He became friendly at this point with an Irish doctor, 37-year-old Ransome Allardyce, who had been commissioned as a lieutenant in the RAMC in 1934 after attending Trinity College, Dublin. He was the youngest of four children born to their tailor father, of which three ended up practicing medicine but sadly two had been lost in WW1. He was superintendent of the International Hospital in nearby Kobe-Honshu. At the outbreak of war in 1939 he evacuated his wife Madeleine and three young kids – George, Jean and Anne – to Australia. Before leaving Japan, Allardyce gave most of his possessions to his servants, destroyed his car, and headed to see his family in Australia.

By mid-September 1939, Cyril had virtually no work to do, and also felt the call of his country intensely. Since university days he'd been in the Ox and Bucks Light Infantry, and was considered a reserve. 'I suppose the battalion is doing intensive training right now and I wish that I was in it with you,' he wrote to his brother. But he'd just been informed that he was to stay on with his job in Japan 'in the best interests of the country which has ample supplies of men nearer home.' He then made a strong if ill-directed prediction based on Hitler's alliance with Russia, then seen as Japan's real threat: 'This place is definitely going to stay neutral, otherwise with my knowledge of the lingo I'd have been shot out of this country, probably to ... Hong Kong. There is now not the slightest risk that Japan will join forces with Germany.' Further, he enjoyed the fact that the anti-British feeling dried up overnight, 'and we English out here had a really good laugh after all those months of tension.'

Nevertheless he sent Celia home due to the uncertain future, and started campaigning with the flamboyantly named Maj Gen Francis Stewart Gilderoy Piggott, the military attaché at the Tokyo embassy, for his own release from the oil company. In June 1940 he was finally able to rejoin his regiment in Oxford.

**

Tsuji transferred from Formosa to the operations section of the General Staff, where he wasted no time propounding his contemptuous views of the west and westerners, and his pro-Pan-Asian stance. 'The most determined single protagonist for war with the United States' is how Military Service Bureau chief, Tanaka Ryukichi, described him.

**

In Singapore itself, 27-year-old Edith Stevenson – an elegant raven-haired beauty with thin arching eyebrows and a fine straight nose – arrived in September 1939 after training in midwifery and as a missionary in Birmingham, and started work at St Andrew's Hospital for women. A year later she was promoted to Matron of St Andrew's Orthopedic Hospital on the east coast at Siglap.

**

Back in the UK, a rather cheeky 20-year-old, Fergus Anckorn, went from being the youngest member of Britain's Magic Circle to being Gunner Anckorn when he signed up for the Royal Artillery at Woolwich Barracks in October 1939. He'd seen a poster for a travel agency advertising, 'Come to Sunny Siam'. 'If only I could wave a magic wand and spend the war there, away from it all,' he idly thought of the deteriorating situation at home. At first he was nervous at the idea of all that discipline and people swearing at him. But, he rationalized, the 118th Field Regiment was a Territorial Unit, 'so it wasn't like I was a real soldier, or going into proper war or anything.' He soon got in the swing of things, especially athletics where he excelled at the half-mile race, winning the brigade medal at sports day. In his spare time, he'd practice his shifty card tricks on his fellow gunners to their amazement and amusement.

Oswald Griffin signed up for the Territorial Army because it was a good way to get out of unemployment, and the TA gave them a little bit of money to get on with. As one of seven brothers and sisters, all tightly grouped age-wise, this was an important consideration. Despite being from rural Norfolk he was not a farm worker, nor cut out to work for the Norwich Union Insurance company. Which meant that lads like him ended up working for the Coleman's mustard factory or in canning factories if they were lucky. He landed a job at the latter, and soon after married a 'town girl', Alice. Ossie was just 22, she a trifle older. Ossie followed his father's footsteps by serving in the 5th Royal Norfolks, as did his friend from school, Jack Rysborough, and his other good buddy, Horace Seaman. This was exciting stuff for Ossie.

Nearly 19 at this stage, Dick Lee was having a ball. 'I used to have a bike ... that was my sport, motorbiking with my girlfriend on the pillion, myself along with another couple of chaps who had bikes. That's why dispatch rider was priority number one when I went into the Army. ' He signed up and was assigned to the 3rd Field Training Regiment. 'Even in the Artillery you do your training with your guns and all that lark, but I was always a driver. I used to like that, hooking up the gun and pulling it around the field.'

Another who'd landed back into this global political scrum was former rubber planter Hugh Pilkington. He was described in the 1927 Malaya Cup rugby program as being a doughnut-loving 'baby elephant' who always put in his best game for his adopted home state, Seremban. He'd also undergone 10 years of diligent weekend training with the Malay States Volunteer Rifles in Malaya, before returning to live in Norfolk with wife Phyllis. Soon after they returned to what they hoped would be an easier and quieter lifestyle, the order was given to double the size of the Territorial Army.

1 September 1939 saw the 6th Royal Norfolks mobilized as a battalion in Norwich. 'Pilk' signed on as an HO (Hostilities Only) non-regular, gazetted as Lt Hugh Pilkington, the day German troops reached Warsaw. Also in the 6th Royal Norfolks was driver Frederick

Bales, who was just 20. Maj FL Cubitt from east Norfolk, who'd had experience in the Territorial Army, was in command.

**

September 1939 was a pivotal month for the world, with far reaching implications for even its farthest corners, including New Zealand. Without hesitation, the medical superintendent of Auckland Hospital, Joseph Craven – a reserve officer in the Territorials – let it be known he was keen to lend his experience where it was required. There had been plenty of experience since he was born in Northumberland 51 years earlier. He'd worked in the Royal Victoria Infirmary in Newcastle upon Tyne, before taking to the sea as a ship's surgeon for the prominent Peninsular and Oriental (P&O) Steam Navigation Company, which had a colourful past including shipping hundreds of thousands of chests of opium during the later 1800s.

With the outbreak of WW1, Craven had joined the RAMC, being rapidly promoted to command the 1st Northumberland Field Ambulance as a lieutenant colonel despite being just 26. The action took him and his medico colleagues to the frontlines in France, Belgium and Germany, and Craven showed he was a true leader one day when removing the wounded as part of a stretcher-bearer party. He discovered an officer and six wounded men in an old enemy pillbox. He went off to find bearers, and returned with them, all the while weaving hither and thither among severe machine gun fire and dodging shrapnel. For this, he was awarded the Military Cross, and on other occasions earned mentions in dispatches, and was made a Chevalier of the Legion of Honour.

In 1925, he and his northern English wife Nora moved to New Zealand where he practiced medicine in the northern harbour-side suburb of Birkenhead, before being tapped for the superintendent job at the Auckland Hospital, an Italianate-style building to the east of the city, separated enough should there be an epidemic breakout of sorts. Turns out there was: polio. Craven consulted on and supervised the hospital's engineer, Fred Jacobs, who was building the first iron lung machines to be used in New Zealand.

While his colleagues knew him as having a 'bright, cheerful disposition and radiated happiness all round,' Craven did suffer a serious setback in 1936 with regards to treatment of children, and visitation rights by parents, at the hospital. A Mrs Rawson had lost her five-year-old daughter after a head injury and internal bleeding had put her in hospital for five weeks. She wrote a stinging letter to the board about her perceived harsh treatment. Mrs Rawson complained that she'd went to Dr Craven to get a visitation pass, but was refused it, without her seeing the superintendent. The child underwent another serious operation with the mother only allowed to visit and sit bedside for an hour each day. 'She rapidly got worse and died while being operated on,' according to a news report at the time.

The heat was on Craven because the board were tired of such complaints, which did the board and hospital no good. One board member called for a full enquiry, while another rallied to Craven's aid saying, 'I refuse to believe that he is a hard-hearted man,' referring to other letters of grateful appreciation from parents and patients.

His overall cheerful disposition would soon further change, and be forever changed, when he too found himself deeply embroiled across the seas in the catastrophic rabbit-hole of The Alex. The hospital was well under construction by this stage, but it was enmeshed in a major controversy that had Singapore society transfixed.

Life in Malaya was not all hard work on rubber plantations for Hugh Pilkington (left). Apart from rugby and parties, Volunteers learned warcraft on weekends.

GOLD RUSH AND GREED

'I felt like blowing out my brains.'

Singapore 1938. There was something of a gold rush happening if you were in the construction business. The recent opening of the somewhat controversial Singapore Naval Base with its massive 1000-foot graving dock made big global headlines. 130,000 tons of British Portland cement was used in that project alone. Approved in 1921, many saw it as an expensive folly while those on the other side of the political divide saw it as a strategic necessity. Singapore itself was viewed as 'one of the five strategic keys that lock up the world'.

And now word was getting around that the War Office had a once-in-a-generation-sized cheque book for developments and improvements around Singapore. The Gillman Barracks – a series of three-storey rectangular white barrack blocks – had already gone up to house the Middlesex Regiment, but there was more housing for officers and others required. And that area on the west coast was slated for a lot more development.

An important part of the music-making Engineer Loveday's job was to meet and know potential suppliers. British and British-related interests were muscling in. Guthrie's (who operated out of a relatively lofty three-storey modern office building among the shophouses at Boat Quay), Bousteads, Stewarts & Lloyds, United Engineers, Fogden Brisbane, Beavis and Co, and Gammon Malaya were all trying to sniff out the lucrative spoils. Gammon's was founded in India by John C Gammon back in 1919, and their man on the ground here was Henry Cowling. Cowling was eager to safeguard European interests, because he was feeling the increased interest and pressure from locals who were also wanting a piece of this British-baked pie.

Key among the local players were Soh Hun Swee and Lim Bo Seng. Hun Swee and his wife were both well educated, both Christians, both musical, and his wife did a lot for the Chinese poor.

Hun Swee saw locals as having an advantage over Europeans, especially Johnny-come-lately new market entrants, because he believed they would have trouble securing suitable labour forces and competitive building material supplies compared to a native son like himself.

Lim Boh Seng was just touching 30, with refined rather pointy features, a proud mane of slicked back hair, round glass frames, and usually well-dressed in a smart shirt and tie. Lim had inherited his father's business 10 years earlier and had since started running two businesses: one was the Hock Ann Brickworks, another was biscuits. And now he and his brothers had teamed up to seek their fortune in construction.

Like Soh, Lim was also very active in the Chinese community in Singapore. He was already the Chairman of the Singapore Building Industry Association. But, more pointedly, Lim and other Chinese in Singapore were increasingly active in propagating and participating in anti-Japanese activities – whatever they could do to boycott Japanese goods and raise funds to support the war effort in China, they would do.

Into this mix flooded the new opportunists. ES Macmillan of Malayan Wire and Mesh, Mr Wong of Ah Hong and Mr Tong of Union Construction all arrived from Shanghai at the same time in 1937.

Macmillan was particularly enterprising because, apart from Malayan Wire and Mesh, he was also a director of Standard Engineering. Then he bumped into a newly arrived chap named Ferguson, who was staying at the popular Seaview Hotel near where Macmillan lived at 500B East Coast Road.

Also in that neighbourhood was the Coconut Grove Club, run by American actress Gene Bales and her husband, Dale (who renamed himself Bill Bailey), a saloon-keeper and opportunistic vaudevillian who was wiped out by the stock market crash of the 1930s, leaving them with nothing but the sack of cash he had stashed under his mattress. Outside of the fancy hotels, it was the rave of the day, and regarded as one of the wildest nightspots in all of Asia.

Ferguson and Macmillan immediately decided to go into a joint venture together offering consulting and importing. So Sino-British was soon incorporated and set up office in Meyer Chambers at Raffles Place. They dealt in steel and building materials, plus tiles from Hong Kong, China and Japan. Ferguson met Capt Loveday sometime in September 1938 at Fort Canning, and they had a productive discussion on tiles.

Despite the prospects and potential, business was proving difficult for Sino-British and they made no inroads with the RAF nor the Public Works Department. Was it because the company represented Japanese brands and flew in the face of the strong anti-Japanese boycott? Partially, possibly, yes. But what they didn't know is that they were coming up head-to-head against Soh on various projects, and he was doing his best to run these interlopers out of town.

Around this time, Soh called Loveday to ask to visit him at his house. Loveday asked if it was official business. 'Partly,' was his cryptic response. Loveday told him all official business should be done at his office. And that seemed to be the end of that.

Ferguson also met Soh, who liked to drop the names of British military officers liberally into conversations and give the impression that he was tapped in, and more of a mover and shaker with greater influence than he probably was. Still, Ferguson was impressed and suggested an introduction to Macmillan. Nothing concrete came of it immediately, but their understanding of how the market worked increased.

**

For the main Alexandra Hospital construction contract, Loveday decided this should go to a European contractor. Finally, good news! Sino-British won a contract for the Alexandra Hospital. There was some suggestion that Macmillan had told Ferguson to ask Loveday to persuade the chief medical officer of Alexandra to change the colour of tiles so they could get the order, but the important thing is they were off to the races now.

More good fortune followed. Macmillan got acceptance of some Hong Kong tiles from the War Department which placed another order for 100,000 tiles for Tanglin Barracks. But, as the project commenced, the Chinese workers went on strike because the tiles were 'from Japan'.' Japan? Why would they think that?

One can't help seeing images of a seething and jealous Hun Swee sniping from the shadows. Hun Swee went to Loveday's house first regarding the windows and tiles for the hospital contract. Hun Swee was trying to push German floor tiles and Reliance metal windows. 'I told him he was wasting his time as Mr Bennett, the European salesman of Guthrie's had already informed me that Maj Butler, the deputy commander in charge of the work, had already inspected Guthrie's tiles and windows and condemned them,' said Loveday. 'Hun Swee asked me not to say anything to Bennett about him coming to see me, as he, Hun Swee, was definitely employed by Guthrie's to deal with Chinese contractors only.'

He'd got into Loveday's ear and told him the Sino-British 'Hong Kong tiles' actually came from Japan. Well, this was a hiccup. Macmillan removed those offending tiles shipped from Tianjin (which was now considered Japanese territory due to their military territorial gains), and delivered Hong Kong tiles. But not before the chief surveyor in Hong Kong had visited the factory to check.

It was a strong leverage tool that local Chinese operators had, to get Chinese labourers on side and get them to strike to enforce the boycott. But Cowling continued his own efforts to try and push European interests. To that end, he asked another industry associate, AG Dobb, if he'd like to meet Loveday, because Dobb too was finding business tough even though they'd previously worked on major jobs such as the fort at Blakang Mati and the Johor Battery. Dobb's self-named company had an ultimate parent company in the sprawling Borneo Company conglomerate, and his workers had been on strike already. He was reluctant because he'd been tendering endlessly for War Department contracts with not much success recently and in any case his relations with them were 'not altogether happy.'

'Come on,' urged Cowling. 'There's a new chap in place now. You should meet him.' Cowling made a call. Within 20 minutes Capt Robert Loveday and wife Alice arrived, drinks were served, and an amiable chat about contracting ensued between Dobb and Loveday.

Soon after New Year, Macmillan met Loveday at Fort Canning. It was a very agreeable chat, leading to further social meetings with Macmillan, Dobb and Loveday, all with their wives in tow. Things were gluing together very nicely now.

**

Meanwhile construction was continuing apace at The Alex. In May the main exoskeleton was well in place and the roof was completed. Interestingly to many was the fact that most of the labourers were female, Chinese *samsui* women to be exact. Samsui women, from the Cantonese province of Guangdong, were much in evidence, as a restriction had been placed on men emigrating through the mid- and late-30s. They toiled in traditional garb, coolie-style tunics, replete with oblong red headgear. Its purpose was chiefly to ward off evil spirits, but a secondary function was to stop their skin turning the same colour as their hats.

The contrast between them and their overseers – the sappers in their natty khaki tropical shorts and long socks with solar *topee* hats – could not have been more stark.

**

For all Loveday's busyness, apart from finding time to read books on China lent to him by Hun Swee, there were also the demands of a growing family with Dorothy now aged 18, Donald now 12, and Pamela, seven. So, coupled with the fact his old Morris was giving him lots of troubles, he sauntered off down Orchard Road to the Lyons Motors car showroom and kicked a few tyres.

'Shortly after, Hun Swee turned up at my house with a Wolsely 14-horsepower motor car,' said Loveday. 'He told me I could take it for a week to try it out and the price was $1200. I asked him how he knew I was looking for a motorcar and he told me someone from Lyons had told him. After a week had passed and I heard nothing from him, I went to his house on the East Coast to see about the car. I explained the car was too big and too expensive for me, and also I thought his price was too high.' Hun Swee insisted he try it for another week or so, and meantime he would consider if the price could be reduced.

'I called him about a week later and he said he'd not yet made up his mind,' said Loveday. 'At this stage I'd made up my mind that the car was beyond my means and too expensive to run, and there was also the difficulty of finding a buyer for my Morris 10. I asked Hun Swee to call at my house and take the car away.' But Hun Swee never did. 'So I drove the car to Raffles Place, left it in the carpark complete with ignition, and proceeded to take a taxi to Fort Canning. I telephoned Hun Swee and told him where the car was and that I did not want it.' Loveday was playing a very straight bat to Soh's sneaky ball game.

But then in the middle of 1939, a Chinese contractor, Chia Swee Teck, tendered for construction of messes at Nee Soon Village for $240,000. It was the lowest tender. A meeting with Chia was fixed at Lim's office. Loveday sat him down and explained his tender form had 'hundreds' of mistakes in his bill of quantities or summary of cost. 'But Loveday said he was prepared to overlook the mistakes if Swee Teck could pay him $3000,' recalled Lim. Swee Teck was taken aback, and did not agree to such payment. Instead the job went to the second lowest tender, Woh Hup, which had projects such as Clifford Pier and Changi Prison under its belt.

Worlds began colliding further when Macmillan learned that Hun Swee knew Loveday. In July 1939 Loveday invited Soh Hun Swee and Macmillan to his house, and after a few such meetings at his home, at Macmillan's home, and even at the Botanical Gardens, he finally got down to the sharp end of business. He had suggested the formation of a ring of contractors that would control the handing out of jobs for the War Department. The mechanics were to be this: contractors were to add 10% to their contract price and the successful tenderer was to add half of that back into The Ring. Half of this was to go to Loveday, the other half split between Hun Swee, Macmillan and other unsuccessful tenderers.

Loveday and Macmillan would handle all European contractors, Soh would handle the Chinese contractors. 'The contract work in Malaya was extremely urgent and I had to ginger up these Chinese contractors in order to get contracts settled quickly and enable the work to get started,' said Loveday. He saw himself as honourably pushing for and implementing a system to check prices better, and often fighting for price reductions 'even when the chief engineer thought fit to approve such high prices because of extreme emergency.'

'My business improved considerably,' reported a happier Macmillan. He soon contacted Dobb and told him that if he wanted to get work from the War Department, then he must join The Ring. What on earth? Macmillan spelt it out. A sort of collusion between all the European suppliers, helping each other out where possible, working together for common good especially on smaller projects adjacent to current jobs, whilst still ostensibly competing on major works. Dobb realized this was surely crossing some kind of moral/ethical line, but ... well ... I'm not sure ... oh, OK then. His company needed the work.

And soon, Dobb was awarded a contract to construct three miles of *atap* (straw-roofed) huts for camps springing up at Alexandra, Tyersall, and Tanglin. Suddenly The Ring seemed a splendid thing.

Whilst the collusion was proving fruitful, there were confusions and misunderstandings. For example, Dobb's sample huts were fitted with mesh windows by Macmillan's firm. But, as part of a work-in-progress inspection involving Loveday, the latter pointed out that not all huts were required to have mesh windows, only the annex buildings. 'Nonsense,' stammered Macmillan, who could see a huge potential order going up in smoke. They adjourned to Dobbs' site office, where a perusal of the contract confirmed that indeed only the annex buildings needed the mesh. He admonished Dobb for not including it in his budget.

Soh paid Loveday $2000 in connection with deviation orders on a hutted camps project, which was also to stop 23-year old QMS Cyril Lush 'making a nuisance of himself' on the construction site. 'He was giving a lot of trouble,' said Soh, referring merely to the fact that Lush was performing basic due diligence and quality control on the work done on site.

It is not clear whether the Alexandra nursing sisters' quarters was a Ring job or not: Soh believed it to be a competitive tender, but in any case received no money for it. Then it came time for the building inspection. The bricks had been supplied by Lim Boh

Seng. But on closer examination the concrete bricks used cost just $12 per 1000 compared to $29 for the hardier red clay bricks. The work was immediately condemned by Deputy Commander Butler. Lim tried to appeal to Loveday, seeking recourse, and these approaches often created awkward situations regarding rank, job scope responsibility, etc. 'I told him to get a civil engineers' report if he was right in his contention that the condemnation was unjust,' said Loveday.

**

Loveday continued in full flight, constantly visiting the homes and offices of Soh Hun Swee, Lim Boh Seng, Macmillan, Pascoe, Dobb and others. Many of these were also regular invitees to his small house parties. Macmillan dropped by freely uninvited any time he liked. Many more musical nights were enjoyed. Mrs Dobb was a pianist, and both Sohs were musical. So much merry music-making at the Lovedays' was enjoyed, probably adding new hits like *Run Rabbit Run* and *We'll Meet Again* to their repertoire. As a bonus, Alice's brother, RAF regular Flight Lieutenant John Burnett, in his late-thirties, was also luckily stationed in Singapore with his wife and their young daughter.

Life was good. Except for one small thing ...

Lt Croft was the keeper of measurements on most projects. And he was not divulging these. 'It would be so much better if I was also in charge of measurements,' argued Loveday. But continuing the chat with a concerned Macmillan it was indicated by Loveday that it should be 'easy to fix Croft so that the measurements would be on the good side.' Macmillan did indeed try to 'fix' him and Croft did not warn him off.

Big European companies like United Engineers, Fogden Brisbane, Beavis and Co, and Gammon were all allegedly co-opted into The Ring. But Loveday wanted even more contractors ... soon Union and Ah Hong both paid the standard $3000 joiners fee to get in. Mr Tong of Union paid the money directly to Loveday at Loveday's home one evening, and the following evening, Mr Wong of

Ah Hong surreptitiously left the cash on his chair when he left, which Loveday then pocketed.

It became quite a job to keep track of all the ins and outs and owings. Especially when trying to put things in code. Soh knew Loveday as 'Brown' and sometimes entered his name in the books as 'L' or 'Love'. Dobb referred to Loveday sometimes as 'Stevens'. If it was beginning to feel rather unseemly, things were about to get decidedly dodgier.

Loveday turned up to Macmillan's house, took $30,000 cash from the back of his car, and asked Macmillan to keep it for him. Macmillan put it in an attache case and locked it. Days later, Loveday asked Dobb if he could keep a safe at home for The Ring's ill-gotten gains. A safe was bought and the attache case put into it.

Dobb, a naturally cautious type and to whom the safe was inexplicably charged, asked that Loveday and Macmillan be the ones to operate the safe and only those two, together, could open it. Agreed.

**

That September the world woke up to headlines that large swathes of the world were at war with each other and with Germany. On 10 September 1939 the local newspaper headline trumpeted that the Alexandra Hospital was 'nearly ready'.
The main hospital construction was completed 'well into 1939,' according to Lloyd Hayes, the young RADC private from Bristol, but several months more were required to fit it out and make it operationally ready.

**

Hun Swee sold Macmillan 10,000 bags of Japanese cement, and – looking to divest out of the suddenly unsellable German agency products – Hun Swee suggested Macmillan and he go to Japan and secure some good Japanese agencies instead. Several such trips were made.

But something was amiss and in October 1939 Macmillan suddenly quit The Ring. 'I must say I was quite enthusiastic about

The Ring initially but then later got rather fed up with it,' said Macmillan. 'The Ring had got to such terrific proportions.' Obviously the more competitors in The Ring, the more the jobs were being divided around. Plus managing the payments became a headache. Some, such as Dobb were considered by some to be fast to receive Ring payments, but slow to make them when due. Other project payments were made confusing by variations and occasional suspension of the work. So when was payment into The Ring actually due and how much? Obviously there was no rulebook to govern this. And a large amount of mutual trust was needed.

'I got fed up with the whole business,' said Macmillan. He told Dobb and Mr Jackson of Borneo company so, too. Loveday was desperately trying to hold it all together. He couldn't afford, financially nor professionally, for The Ring to unravel. He told Macmillan there was no reason to leave.

Hun Swee offered Macmillan a share, even though he was no longer going to be connected with The Ring, or pay him a certain amount per month. 'I turned around and said I was not a blackmailer, I was very angry,' said Macmillan. 'Captain and Mrs Loveday said they would need to square me up but I told them I didn't want their money, and they could keep the money I had got from The Ring business.'

Loveday gave Dobb and Ferguson the combination code and permission to go and open the safe and take out the loot, of which Dobb was to keep $17,500 in bonds owing to him. The pair were amazed to find up to $80,000 cash inside. They stuffed it into Macmillan's attaché case best as they could but had to leave out $10-12,000 which simply could not fit into the bulging bag. 'The money inside was in various denominations, mostly in unbroken bundles,' according to Dobb. 'The $17,500 bonds covered the payment I'd made by check to Hun Swee through Loveday.'

Ferguson then went to his room at the Seaview and called Alice Loveday to say the case was safe with him. He then popped it into his own suitcase, which sat in his room, unlocked, for the next few weeks.

Loveday and Alice were in the car one day when they passed Ferguson and Macmillan going the other way. 'We've come to collect the parcel,' shouted Loveday to Ferguson. Ferguson returned to his room and handed it over to Mrs Loveday.

**

In January 1940 a clandestine mediation was required between Loveday and Hun Swee. At Hun Swee's house, Lim Bo Seng opened the door to the Lovedays. 'Is Hun Swee going to pay the money due to us?' demanded Loveday immediately. Lim summoned Soh.

'Are you going to pay us our money?' repeated Loveday angrily.

'Please, let's sit down and discuss this quietly,' asked Lim.

At the heart of the matter were some suspended projects, for which Soh didn't feel he should be handing over money.

'That's hardly fair,' Lim told the Lovedays.

Lim then spoke aside to Soh in Chinese.

'Since all of us speak English, it is very rude of you to speak in Chinese,' Alice admonished Lim.

'This is not a social call, Mrs Loveday, but a business visit,' Lim retorted.

Slowly the temperature of the room subsided, enough for Loveday to concede and agree that money on suspended contracts should be held by Soh. Therefore a balance of $40,000 would be payable according to Soh, referring to his coded account book and making some quick calculations. Soh went to his room and presently returned with a bundle of cash wrapped in newspaper. Each bundle of notes was neatly tied with string. He counted it out ... 17 ... 18 ... 19 ...

'I have only $19,000 on me tonight. The rest I can pay you tomorrow.'

Loveday took the money, and they left sharply.

The waters were now getting really murky. Hun Swee went directly to the 30-year-old Lt Croft. Hun Swee indicated he had 'the Army, Navy and Air Force in the palm of his hand,' according to Croft, and asked Croft to tell his superior Loveday to persuade the chief engineer to accept a contract without a bill of quantity. He offered

Croft $10,000 to make that happen. He paid Lt Croft $1000 down, with $9000 to follow if he could furnish the tender price that would be accepted and that only contractors in Hun Swee's Ring would be invited to tender. Further, he told Croft about The Ring, with Hun Swee and Loveday running it. He also sweetened the deal by telling Croft to go to a motor showroom in Orchard Road and pick out a car for himself.

Macmillan broke ranks and threatened to go to Webster, Loveday's superior officer. His partner Ferguson stepped in and arranged to meet Loveday and his wife at the Capitol cinema one evening. Mrs Loveday said if Ferguson met them the next day, he would be paid the $10,000 Macmillan claimed was owing to him. Ferguson did meet them the next day, but Loveday then claimed that Macmillan was not owed $10,000, rather $5000. He received the cash to pass to Macmillan.

The Ring had obviously reached breaking point. 'I specially went home to report it,' admitted Ferguson. 'I asked the police what I should do with the cash. They advised me to bank it into our Sino-British account, which I did.'

There was some thought that perhaps a competitor, probably Hon John 'Jiddy' Dawson, JP, the top man at Guthrie's Singapore – who had declined an offer to become a director at Malayan Wire & Mesh – had shopped them. No. 'I reported it myself,' Ferguson confirmed. Macmillan was then questioned and made a statement.

In March 1940 Hun Swee was arrested.

**

The others were now all rightly nervous. Macmillan met Loveday a couple more times, firstly at Siglap road. They agreed to close ranks and keep their mouths shut. The second meeting was with Loveday and Ferguson on a Sunday morning in Dairy Farm Rd. Macmillan said he was going to tell the truth. Loveday said that can't happen – he'd lose his job.

That same evening, Macmillan went around to the Dobb's house. The Lovedays were there. Alice Loveday was worried, crying with Mrs Dobbs on the back verandah. 'You worried me very much with what you said in the morning,' Loveday said to Macmillan. 'I've had a very hard day with Mrs Loveday, who is extremely worried you were going to speak the truth.' The weeping from outside was still audible.

'I think you misunderstood what I meant,' replied Macmillan.

'By Jove, what a relief that is!' said Loveday, noticeably relaxing. He called Alice in and asked Macmillan to repeat his statement. Phew! The attitude of the Lovedays immediately brightened, much like the sun in Singapore breaking through after a torrential afternoon downpour.

Loveday put his hand in his pocket: 'You know you had me worried. All day I've been carrying this around.' He produced a revolver and placed it on the table.

'What is that for?' Macmillan asked.

'Maybe for using on Croft or myself some time,' Loveday laughed nervously. 'I felt like blowing out my brains.'
Macmillan and Dobb shuffled uneasily. Alice then told him to put the weapon away.

Their collective chief worry was whether Hun Swee's book of The Ring was in police hands or not. They sweated on this.

Loveday and Macmillan kept meeting at Macmillan's house whenever the latter was home in between business trips to Bangkok or to visit principals in Japan. After some time, Loveday indicated that Hun Swee was going to Australia, after which the case would fall flat. Indeed Soh's case was discharged, although he was not fully nor formally acquitted. But on 9 May 1940, the police came to Dobb's house and took away his bonds. So obviously the investigation was still alive and active.

The Lovedays grew increasingly frantic. One of their family friends, accountant Charles Woodcock, was asked one evening – after he returned from taking their young daughter, Pamela, to the cinema – to keep a package for them. It was a locked tin box wrapped in paper. As a family friend he agreed to do so, no questions asked, because he had been present one evening when a burglar had come to their premises and helped them try to track him down. The Lovedays had also been burgled on another recent occasion. Unbeknown to him, so he claimed, the tin contained bearer bonds.

When Inspector Edmond Bunnens of the Anti-Vice Branch, and his colleague Mr Fowler, called at 1 Sherwood Road, the Lovedays were not home. They let themselves in and commenced a search of the property. They turned up no papers, no records nor relevant evidence. Just then, Alice Loveday returned home, no doubt somewhat shocked and surprised to find a search in progress. But she remained composed and assisted them without hesitation. They were particularly interested in the safe. She opened it ... and ... and there was nothing but $500 cash in it.

**

The Lovedays' good run and good times came crashing down like a multi-storey building with a load-bearing joist removed. Robert was arrested and set down for a court martial at Tanglin Barracks in August 1940. Barely over half a mile from their married quarters bungalow at Sherwood Road.

The irony is this: 'Loveday' is an ancient name whose history on English soil dates back to the Norman Conquest of England in 1066. Indeed, the same battle related to the commencement of the Military Engineers. This old English name, Loveday, was also a nickname for a day, according to medieval custom, set aside for reconciliation and settlement of disputes or feuds. Would there be any love to be found among this starched seriousness, especially with Dr Charles Herbert Withers-Payne, the judge advocate and widely published legal expert, presiding?

He faced 25 charges of conspiracy to defraud the War Department, and corruption, and with 'organising a wholesale system of corruption for his own benefit' in assisting contractors to secure War Department contracts. Charges related to The Alex included the Sisters' Quarters and other ancillary hospital buildings. The size of his personal benefit was estimated to be $169,000 (around $3,000,000 in today's money).

On the jury panel of his court martial were Brig Arthur Curtis, Commander, Fixed Defences of Singapore, Lt Col Clement Mead of the Royal Engineers, plus five other senior officers. The balding, bespectacled Curtis, 52, was highly experienced, having served in the Army since 1910.

Mr Francis Vaux, counsel for prosecution, was a keen chess player – indeed he would become the President of the Singapore Chess League, no less. A tall, wiry man, he had a high and wide forehead and a Chaplinesque moustache that made it look like his mouth was way too high in his face.

In his defence corner, Loveday had selected EM Tampoe-Philips. Tampoe-Philips was a heavy hitter in Malayan legal circles whose father was a well-renowned coconut planter in Jaffna, Ceylon. As a barrister, he'd secured his BA LLB from Cambridge, and had been admitted to the Supreme Court in Singapore in October 1919. Well experienced, well regarded.

This was set to be a serious face-off. And indeed it proved to be.

**

Vaux kicked off by referring to the endless furtive meetings between Loveday and certain witnesses: 'Such meetings call for an explanation by a man in the accused's position.'

Prosecution presented its case for 11 full days. The Singapore media was transfixed, with lengthy reports and updates each day in the Straits Times and other media as far afield as rural Australia. Charge #12 was 'Requesting 1% of the value of the job to construct Alexander (sic) Barracks.'

The prosecution witnesses bore names and faces very familiar to the accused: Soh Hun Swee and Macmillan were among the 20 European and Chinese witnesses called.

Soh flipped and flopped. Poacher turned gamekeeper. His own case had since been discharged but he'd not been acquitted: 'The sword of likelihood of a second prosecution is hanging over his head.' So he was naturally going all-out for self-interest and preservation at any cost to the truth. Macmillan ditto.

In response, Tampoe-Philips said: 'All I can say is I deny all those allegations tending to create suspicion. In this case the Crown is faced with the insuperable difficulty in that nearly every witness is what's called an accomplice.'

And so it went on for a few more days.

Finally, Loveday took to the stand, rising to his full 6'4". He had a thick sheaf of papers, 23 pages in all. 'I deny the whole of the allegations against my honour,' was his central message. But he also pointedly remarked that allegations against him only came after Hun Swee's arrest. He further challenged 'strange evidence' of some of his meetings with Chinese contractors. 'It is strange that Hun Swee and Robert Macmillan, both prosecution witnesses who were enemies at first, became thick as thieves.'

After 1.5 hours he'd spent all his bullets. He sat down. Were those beads of sweat on his ruddy brow?

In summary, Withers-Payne called the witnesses 'of both bad character and little if any reliability.' Loveday might have snuck a hopeful glance across to Tampoe-Philips at that point. Withers-Payne zeroed in on Soh: 'Having heard and seen Soh Hun Swee, the court may well come to the conclusion that nothing is beyond his ingenuity or his falsehood. Soh Hun Swee and Macmillan, particularly, the defence has said are men who will do anything, and there appears to be little exaggeration in that statement.'

Next, he turned to Loveday. 'As to the character of the accused there could be no doubt in the minds of the court that Loveday, by merit and hard work, had reached his present position and was an officer of ability and efficiency.' This was all to the good, and Loveday could be forgiven for allowing himself a moment of positivity. The panel of officers then adjourned and deliberated on the 700 typed pages of transcript from the preceding 16 days. And deliberated. And deliberated. For 7.5 hours.

Loveday was found not guilty on 17 of the 25 charges against him. Phew! But ... that meant he was still guilty on eight. He was to be cashiered, and would serve a 4.5 year sentence. The medal-wearing First World War veteran, at the height of his career, was busted.

On announcement of the verdict, Robert Loveday 'appeared affected' according to a court reporter, and when asked by Withers-Payne if he had anything to say, said: 'No, sir.'

**

Loveday was taken directly to E Block, Changi prison, where he would share a cell with notorious Japanese journalist-turned-spy Shinozaki Mamoru, who had also just been incarcerated to spend 3.5 years behind bars for 'collecting information that might be useful to a foreign power.' That might well have included updates on the construction of The Alex, as well as other key installations around the island, and of particular interest to Shinozaki's masters were the sitings of the island's big guns.

E Block housed the European and Eurasian prisoners, and the two prisoners shared a 6' x 10' cell. Cozy to say the least, especially given his towering height. But there was at least 'a mattress, very clean water, and a toilet.'

Their day here would start with a 5am wake-up call, cells would be opened at 6am for them to exercise before a breakfast of 'three small pieces of bread, jam and very thin tea.' Then it was off to the workshop to repair mailbags until a half-hour lunch break at noon, during which a pork chop would usually be served up with some bread or rice. Then it was back to the workshop till shower time at 5pm. An inspection at 6pm would be followed by issue of three cigarettes as 'salary' for the day's work, with three more small pieces of bread and cheese for dinner.

When lights went out at 9pm, one imagines Loveday would be left with thoughts of regret of the relatively lavish lifestyle he could be experiencing with his young family on the outside had he just played it straight. He launched an immediate appeal, which was unsuccessful. Alice and the children returned to England. At least here on Sundays he could visit the prison library and indulge in his enjoyment of reading.

Greed had finally grabbed him. Which is something that could never be said of the selfless altruistic types who typically gravitated towards signing up with the Royal Army Medical Corps and would soon also find themselves drawn inexorably into the orbit of that newly opened military hospital in Singapore.

LOVEDAY DENIES ALL ALLEGATIONS

Defence Counsel To Make Final Address To-day

THE closing stages of the Loveday case have been reached, and this morning, Mr. E. M. Tampoe-Philips, counsel for the accused, Captain R. C. Loveday, R.E.—who is being tried by court martial on 25 charges of conspiracy to defraud the War Department and corruption—will make his final address and deal at length with the evidence.

LOVEDAY SENTENCED BY COURT MARTIAL

To Be Cashiered & Receive 4½ Years' Penal Servitude

FINDINGS PROMULGATED AFTER LENGTHY TRIAL

Singapore society was transfixed by The Ring's corruption trial. Local entrepreneur, Lim Bo Seng, (right) went on to join Force 136 and became a national hero.

Capt Robert Loveday of the Royal Engineers would end up in Changi Gaol.

RUNNING REPAIRS

'Five months of misery.'

RAMC Crookham, December 1939. That winter was freezing by anyone's standards. A record low of -23 degrees was recorded in Wales, and the whole United Kingdom was similarly afflicted. Why, even the sea around parts of Britain froze that year.

And, against this backdrop, the newly constructed No 1 Training Depot RAMC – a large acreage of cottage-like wooden huts in bucolic Crookham, near Aldershot, Hampshire also known as Boyce Barracks – was drilling its men in the art of repairing those injured on the battlefield.

'No radiators or fire, and the walls damp as hell,' wrote 22-year-old shopkeeper turned medical orderly, Pte Len Knott from Room 13 in C Block. 'I only took off my trousers and coat to go to bed, everything else I kept on. Yes, and I had to wash and shave in cold water.' Still, he managed to keep his wavy hair lushly Brylcreemed, presenting as a rather dashing young man with a very pleasant face and strong features.

Many of the recruits were already familiar with basic medical repairs from their civilian jobs as doctors and orderlies, but training had to be repeatedly done by the book to the point of excruciating boredom for some. Stretchers. Bandages. Splints. Stretchers. Bandages. Splints. Stretchers. Bandages. Splints ...

RAMC recruits were required to be at least 5'2" inches in height, not a particularly tall order. They initially enlisted for seven years with the RAMC colours and a further five years with the Reserve, another option being three years and nine years respectively.

Coupled with the regulations of being in uniform, some found it rather repressive. Knott found himself sweeping a road one morning, perhaps regretting he'd given up his previous life, even though the monotony of that retail job 'drove me crackers.' Besides, his home life was not much to rave about either. He was one of seven children fathered by an alcoholic London City Council sewerage inspector, Philip, an East Ender who'd take out his frustrations on the kids by liberally lashing out at them.

There were lectures, on first aid as well as things like gas attacks. Plus field days. 'This means going through conditions which approximate actual war conditions and rescuing wounded whilst a fleet of tanks and squad of Bren gunners make things more amusing by doing similar antics.' These were held on a field around five miles distant from the camp.

Then there were also fire drills. 'Think of it,' said Knott. 'Stuck in barracks for a week and rushing out into the dark in the evening to wade through the mud and stand at the guardhouse when the bugle blows. What a bloody fizzle! Everything's done like that here.'

But naturally there was room for the odd playful prank and practical joke when not fully supervised. Some scallywags jokingly referred to the RAMC as the 'Rape and Murder Corp', and others as 'Run Away Matron's Coming.' And there was the odd 'vile' concert staged in the gym. 'I've always said we're treated worse than convicts,' he told his musician brother Phil. 'I wish your band was coming here to play.' Both he and his brother had inherited an unlikely love for classical music from their sewerage inspector father.

The RAMC had to instill in them the traditional peculiarities of the corps, some of which dated back to the unit's formation in 1898. For one, nomenclature. Rank is used, but never the prefix or suffix of 'Doctor'. Next they had to have weapons skills but, under the Geneva Convention, these may be used only in self-defence situations. This resulted in more peculiarities. For example, on parade other ranks never fix bayonets. And officers do not draw their swords, so that while they salute with their right hand, their left is holding their scabbard.

Realistically this meant in battle they relied fully on their surrounding army units for protection. Hopefully their prayers would be answered in those times of need. As insurance, each meal was prefaced by a special grace: 'God bless this food and wine to sustain the work of these thy servants in the Royal Army Medical Corps and keep us mindful that it is not for ourselves but for others that we strive. Through Jesus Christ Our Lord, Amen.'

For others that we strive would be repeatedly borne out in the years to come, complementing their motto 'Faithful in Adversity'.

**

A key component unit of the RAMC were the Field Ambulances. These comprised a medical officer, his batman, 13 officers and 225 other ranks (sergeants, corporals and privates). Each unit also had ambulances, but the driving of these was done by members of the Royal Army Service Corp (RASC), who were then attached to the unit.

These Field Ambulance units were stationed just behind the front lines, so any injured would be brought back by the regimental first aid team, and the Field Ambulance unit would then triage them through from advanced dressing station, main dressing station, casualty clearing station or, in worst case situations, a hospital. Each division had three such Field Ambulances.

**

Otherwise, the recruits who were being prepared for 32 Company RAMC (which ran the military hospitals in the Far East) came from all over and the near-cryogenic conditions gave them something extra to bond around. There was Cpl George Johnson from Durham, Pte Lloyd Hayes, a 22-year- from Bristol, and 39-year-old QMS Edward Lunt, from Bolton. From Surrey came 24-year-old Lt William Weston and 21-year-old Pte Sydney Hoskins, a short, brown-haired brown-eyed chap with a cherubic face and ready smile, who had until recently worked as an engraver in a printing company.

This 'five months of misery,' as medic Will Brand described his period at Crookham that winter, ensured that whatever or wherever followed it was bound to be a huge improvement. Or would it?

**

After the basic training at the Boyce Barracks, or at No 2 Training Depot in Edinburgh for others, they went off and did their trade specialist training elsewhere.

Cpl James Torbit became a dispenser, and Knott did pharmacy too, the latter little knowing that in the future this would become his livelihood and that of many of his relatives too. Medic Will Brand became particularly good friends with Lloyd Hayes, who joined the Dental Corp, and who in turn would become close friends with Pte John Willard from Brighton. The youngest of the unit was Cpl Hugh Mitchell from Surrey, who'd just turned 20 and was receiving specialist training in new fangled X-ray techniques. By contrast, Pte Harry Saye was nigh on 30, the maximum allowable RAMC recruitment age which was being relaxed as the situation demanded.

Despite the tawdry surroundings, nature of training, and prospect of war, the rather dashing-looking Knott had a spring in his step now because he'd just met a curly-haired beauty, Joan, on a blind date and had fallen hard for her. When he could secure leave, he'd take off to spend Sundays with her. Even when he couldn't get leave, he'd often get a Scottish mate to answer for him at roll call ('Do you think a Scotsman can pronounce "Knott" without giving the game away?'), or apply to attend a church parade and skive off to 'spend the day illegally' with Joan. 'What sheer bloody stupidity it is to be in the Army away from you,' he wrote to his sweetheart after one such blissful Sunday. He immediately set about getting engaged, and marrying her. But she was a minor, aged under 19, so her widowed mother, Alice, had to sign a consent form for the marriage to go ahead.

**

The 198th Field Ambulance was based at Macclesfield in Cheshire. One of the draftees into the 198th was Frank Onslow, aged around 28, a bookish-looking gent with small round specs, a few blonde curls atop his head, and a somewhat mischievous grin. He and wife Joan had married just five years prior, and already had three children – Pauline, Valerie and Michael – within that time. He left his employment at the Sun Engraving Company at Watford and duly answered his nation's call to carry the wounded out of further harm's way.

Watford also featured in another story, this one involving St John Ambulance volunteer and farmer from Downton, Bert Gurd. 'Before the war I was beginning to get fed up with farming, having lived all my life on a farm,' the 33-year-old said. Standing at 5'8" he was quite a big-boned, solid fellow with a generally quiet demeanour, having been a scholarship student at 400-year-old Gillingham Grammar School in Dorset. At the age of 14 he'd been presented with a prize by the governors for an essay he'd written on the Great War. In Watford he billetted with the Newman family while he attended his training, whereat the full-faced fellow – with quite large protruding ears and a winning smile –immediately fell for Rosa, the raven-haired daughter of the family, and a courtship ensued. 'I think dad wanted to get married before they went,' daughter Maureen would tell me. 'And she insisted they waited till after the war because they still might not be alive or anything else.'

21-year-old Pte Frank Hill, a spinning mill worker from Huddersfield, joined in March 1940. Young as he was, he'd already been married for two years to Nancy. They would soon add a son, Brian, to their family. Hailing from nearby Mexborough was George Lee, and he and Frank got to know each other, being in the same unit.

Others assigned to the 198th included Lance Corporals John 'Jack' Jones and William Steel, and Privates Stanley Pearce, Kenneth Butler, Harry Copperwheat, Arthur Bruce, Ken Adams, and Roy Temple.

Len Knott and his brother Phil, a keen French horn player with the Salvation Army band, were due to be posted wherever in the world the Army needed them most. But, because Phil was now married and expecting a child, he was let off the hook. Len was assigned to the 198th Field Ambulance. His wedding would have to wait.

**

As 1941 grew older, the pace at Crookham and outposts like Macclesfield grew more frantic. Final inoculations were administered, with much frenzied preparation to get as many as 450 stretcher-bearers at a time ready for overseas postings.

Pte Sydney Hoskins was given a choice: 'They gave him an option for the war,' his grand-daughter, nurse Selena Hoskins would tell me. 'Either go to Oxford and work in a hospital or go travelling. And he decided to go travelling.' Her cousin Jo Walker added: 'He became an orderly for an easy life ... he had to sign up but didn't want to be in any fighting, and he thought he could just sit it out in Singapore.'

The 196th, 197th and 198th Field Ambulances were attached to the British 18th Division. The 198th Field Ambulance was to be part of the 53rd Brigade formation. Destination: unknown, whispered to be the Middle East.

In late October, Nancy Hill held 18-month-old baby Brian in her arms at Macclesfield station, as the train – loaded with men of the 198th – pulled away from the station. How long would it be before this silly war nonsense was over and they'd see Frank again?

SWINGING SINGAPORE

'I'm afraid it is rather a bed of vice in many ways.'

Singapore 1940. The popular shops of the day speak of the oft-indulgent high-life being enjoyed here. French Palais des Modes was run by French woman, Helen Monier, at shop 12A in the Capitol Building, and she sold lingerie, hats and gowns to those wanting to be part of the trendy and sassy society of the day.

In Battery Road, an Australian called Mrs Howe ran GH's Cake Shop. She'd been around for many years, previously offering baking lessons at the YMCA. But now she'd created something really special. 'At marble-topped tables the clientele would recklessly ignore their waistlines in exchange of Mrs Howe's gateaux and home made ice-creams,' gushed one media report of the day.

Ice cream was also a crowd favourite at another shop along Hill Street, which was rated as 'in bounds' for Her Majesty's Forces (an important criteria if you didn't want to fall foul of the Red Cap MPs). Street food was a definite no-no.

Rental of a two-storey shophouse in town would cost about $20 per month, considered reasonable. Change Alley was just across the Anderson Bridge and here the crowd would be milling around, shopping, sightseeing, perhaps catching a movie such as *The Fighting 69th*. In it, James Cagney's character Jerry Plunkett is court-martialed and awaiting execution in a jail cell when a German shell hits it, and he finds himself suddenly free.

Sion Abraham enjoyed the cinemas because they were air-conditioned. But one of his favourite hangouts was The 10 Cent Store around Middle Road. 'It was a Japanese store and, before the war, the Japanese were so polite.' (The Japanese proprietor turned out to be 'a big shot' in the Sime Road internment camp Sion would sadly discover later.)

Another popular service was incredibly low prices for British servicemen to process their rolls of film taken on leave. Of course, there was much intelligence to be gleaned from these.

The Japanese community, numbering in the low thousands, had set up its own school, clubhouse, and cemetery. The Toyo Hotel stood on Queen Street, adjacent the post office. And to keep everyone in touch with all things Japanese, the *Nanyo Shimpo* newspaper. Most symbolically, the Japanese consulate-general had moved into an imposing 86,000 square foot house – which cost a whopping $22,000 in 1935 when purchased by a Mr Ikeda – at 11 Upper Wilkie Road, on Mt Emily above Middle Road. Not only was it close to 'Little Japan', but it sent a very clear signal of ambition to Government House nearby.

'In them days, there were more Japanese shops than there would be Chinese,' said Stan Sharpley. 'An awful lot of Japanese in Singapore in them days. And they used to know more about the island than we did.'

'Japanese goods flooded the market,' remembered Dr Yeoh Sang Aung. Being paid just $1.50-2.00 per day for his efforts, the price was attractive. 'Cheap and terrible. Their products lasted a day. A Japanese bike would cost one quarter of a Raleigh.'

**

Into this milieu, more British were arriving to bolster the defences and resources in the Far East. A 23-year-old Ulsterman, Tom Smiley, had just graduated with a medical degree from Queen's University in Belfast and had not long been in his first house surgeon position when he signed on to the RAMC and life suddenly kicked into fast-forward. His family were pharmacists, and Tom lived above Smiley's Chemist in the picturesque town square of Castlewellan in County Down. His father Samuel had married the local primary school teacher, and together they raised their family as staunch Methodists. Tom's strong character, sporting prowess, and Christian values saw him rise to head boy of Methodist College Belfast, one of the country's leading grammar schools.

He was one of those sort of boys: first XI cricket and captain of the first XV rugby team, too. A natural leader and all-rounder.

During his medical studies at Queens' University he fell in love with a beautiful Scottish lass, Elizabeth Mills, who was studying medicine in the year below him. But her parents were against this union, her mother constantly laying down the law: 'Medicine *or* matrimony but not the both!' However, they kept their relationship a secret from their parents and Tom would write to Elizabeth during the long summer breaks when she returned to Scotland. Such letter writing would produce some treasurable family memories in the future.

War was declared soon after Tom's graduation and he and his best friend, Humphrey Thomson – son of Sir and Lady William Thomson – went to the recruiting office straight away but were told that they needed to complete their six-month internship before they could be accepted into the RAMC. So off they hurried to the Royal Victoria Hospital in Belfast, during which time Tom and Elizabeth's love life intensified. Next, Tom and Humphrey were off to Leeds for their training in April 1940 and were told that they were being posted to the Far East, much to their disappointment.

With only a few days before embarkation it was time for some quick action. Now-captain Humphrey raced back to Belfast to marry his Mary, and Elizabeth and Tom announced their engagement that same day, 18 April 1940. Tom borrowed money for the ring from his brother. Elizabeth gave him a shiny silver cigarette case, elegantly hinged, with his initials 'TBS' and her signature engraved.

Smiley and Thomson sadly farewelled their loved ones at the Belfast docks, and set off on the long journey to Singapore.

'Such a lot has happened to me during the last month,' he wrote to Elizabeth from Paris to in May. 'I met your mother and father, I left the Royal (hospital), I spent my first holiday with you, you met my mother and father, I joined the army, I visited your home. I then got engaged to the only girl in the world and lastly I had to leave you, my dearest one. What a wonderful time we'll have when we are together again. I am certain that this war won't last long, and we'll be reunited soon and we will be able to start our life together. Always your very dearest, Tom.'

From Marseilles he and another six RAMC lieutenants boarded a ship for Singapore, arriving on 24 May. Immediately he noted the difference with Britain, with no black-outs enforced and cinemas, shops and entertainments all lit up and open for business. 'All of my travels and the arrival in Singapore has been the fullest experience I've ever had in my life. We got off the boat at 12 o'clock after some trouble with coolies getting the luggage off. A whole reception committee was there to welcome us! They were expecting several colonels and majors to staff the new hospital and I think they were very disappointed to see the six of us – only lowly inexperienced lieutenants!'

He soon wrote off another very lengthy letter to Elizabeth. 'Well, my darling, the sun is shining brightly and if you were here I would take you swimming. However Humphrey, Hugh, George, Lennox and myself went in the morning to the Cathedral. It was a wonderful sight – it was packed to overflowing, lots of people standing outside, and the grounds were just packed with cars. It was an impressive sight seeing so many air force, navy and army in their various uniforms and the ladies were all dressed in bright colours – the difference between our Methodist church at home struck me.'

He soon got in the swing of the colonial life with golf, cricket, rugby and swimming keeping his mind off Elizabeth. Fort Canning was his first posting where he was the doctor in charge of the army families in the mornings, and took the ENT clinics in the afternoon. Oddly he was put in charge of Singapore's fetid storm drains, a tropical phenomenon which he knew very little about.

'Tom finally got a job in surgery at the Tanglin hospital, which he was pleased about,' said daughter, Fiona. 'He was determined to make the most of his time in Singapore so that he could later specialize in surgery after the war.' He shared a house in Mount Elizabeth, half way along Orchard Road, with four other doctors, probably being 'Humphrey, Hugh, George, and Lennox' whom he mentioned in his first letter home.

**

The Tanglin Hospital was an airy building with wide over-hanging eaves as protection against tropical sun and rain. It had three main wards and had served as the main military hospital for nearly 30 years. Lt Col Cornelius was Smiley's commanding officer, having seen action in World War 1, and, although he'd reached retirement age, was kept on by the Army in what was obviously deemed to be a not-so-demanding position.

Smiley was shocked in the briefing to learn that one full ward, a third of the hospital, was given over to VD patients. 'Dearest,' he wrote to Elizabeth, 'I'm glad I've got you and God to help me in this place. I'm afraid it is rather a bed of vice in many ways. It seems that 80% of Europeans have VD! Isn't that terrible? These are official figures, and the drinking seems to be very heavy too.'

Smiley himself was a light social drinker, happy to have one or two, but not happy to be caught up in 'the curse' and cost of endless rounds. 'Everyone seems short of money and yet they go out every night and drink.' He was happy to switch to something like a grapefruit juice because he took his fitness quite seriously. He was 'a very good rugger player' according to Capt Bill Frankland, and was soon playing for the Army, and travelling all over Malaya to play against other club and provincial sides.

In writing to Elizabeth, he made sure to mention his precious engagement gift. 'My beautiful cigarette case that you gave me was admired last night and I felt very proud to say that it was given to me by my fiancee!'

One of his colleagues, Bill Frankland, another recent arrival, took Smiley to task over his one bad habit, though – smoking, entreating for him to give it up.

Frankland was born the same year the hospital had been built, 1912, and they enjoyed exploring the common ground, personally and professionally. 'My uncle who'd been to Oxford a long time before me said, 'The only advice I can give you is when you go to a Freshie's function they'll try to get you drunk. Get drunk and you'll never want to get drunk again". I followed that,' said the committed teetotaller. Frankland always wore the Sam Browne belt that his father, a chaplain, had worn in the First World War.

Both were very focused on their work, much of which involved curing those with gonorrhea and syphilis, a little below Smiley's aspirations as a surgeon. One rather awkward case was that of an officer who'd acquired a dose, and a cover-up by the authorities was in progress to keep it hushed up. It seems that most of these cases could be traced back to the ladies of Lavender Street. Brig Charles Stringer had declared the brothels of Singapore 'disgraceful' when he arrived to take up his posting here in 1938.

**

Capt Roylance Parkinson, RAMC, a 30-year-old Mancunian doctor with red hair and a ready smile who'd also come in on the *Dominion Monarch*, reported for duty at Tanglin, too. Smiley recalled him as being 'tall and slight.' He'd been with the Army less than two years and had just got married to Sheila, a First Aid Nursing Yeomanry officer he'd met at his last posting at Anglesea, before he got his shipping orders.

Unlike Frankland and Smiley, Parkinson was a draftee who very much conscientiously resented, if not fully objected to, the whole military thing and war as a way of solving problems. He wanted to forge on with a career as an obstetrician, so the sooner the war was over, the better. Frankland found the deeply-dimpled man to be self-centred.

Pte Len Knott and his 32 Coy RAMC cohort also gladly took up base here, happy to be in the warm tropics away from that freezing hellhole, Boyce Barracks at Crookham, and the perilous uncertainty of Shanghai.

Others were glad to escape the incessant heat of India, such as Cpl Joe Nutter, a wiry man standing just 5'4" in his army stockings. After training as an orderly the 25-year-old Yorkshireman spent a few years with the Indian Army working in the hygiene section of his unit (having left home with a simple note to his mum, 'Gone to join the Army').

**

The months passed by and Elizabeth qualified as a doctor and Tom Smiley desperately tried to persuade her to come out to Singapore to be married. Humphrey Thomson was sent to Penang Island and then Tom was sent to Port Dickson along the west coast of Malaya to be medical officer of the Federated Malay States Volunteer Force (FMSVF) for a month. 'This was the first time he experienced the beautiful beaches and the native life of Malaya and he went fishing with the locals and helped the Tamil families in the rubber plantations,' Fiona Smiley would tell me. But he quickly realized that the unfit and unprepared volunteers were not ready for any action ...

'They are nearly all rubber planters, tin miners, magistrates etc. and it is funny to see the chief magistrate of Negri Seremban going on a route march as he is rather large! The troop quarters are the funniest thing because all these chaps are just rolling in money and they don't like the idea of cleaning up the barrack rooms themselves so they employ their "boys" to get their hands dirty! Let's hope the Volunteer force will never be called on for active service!'

**

One day a senior officer, probably Cornelius or Maj Lewis Davies (a Rugby school alumnus and golf-playing Welshman) summoned Frankland and Smiley into a meeting. There were two openings and he gave them an option. 'And my great friend and I spun a coin, "Heads or tails?"' recalled Frankland. 'I won it: heads! I went to Tanglin. If I'd lost I would have gone to Alexandra.' And so Frankland stayed on at Tanglin and was able to exercise his interest in dermatology and allergies, whilst Smiley packed his bags for The Alex, there to be initially involved in anaesthetizing patients for minor surgery.

Smiley moved into hospital quarters because of the increased demand by incoming troops for other accommodations around the island.

Little did Frankland and Smiley know how significantly life-changing that flippant coin toss would turn out to be.

THE SUNDAY TIMES 17

BIG SINGAPORE MILITARY HOSPITAL

Will Have 356 Beds For Officers And Men

HEIR TO THRONE

THREE-STOREYED BLOCK GOING UP AT ALEXANDRA

Staff Of More Than 30 British Nurses

New Sultan

UP-TO-DATE EQUIPMENT

Man Leaps From 17th Storey; Had Spent 11 Hours On Ledge

The construction of the biggest military hospital outside of Britain was big news, eagerly followed. Below: the building nearing completion in mid-1940.

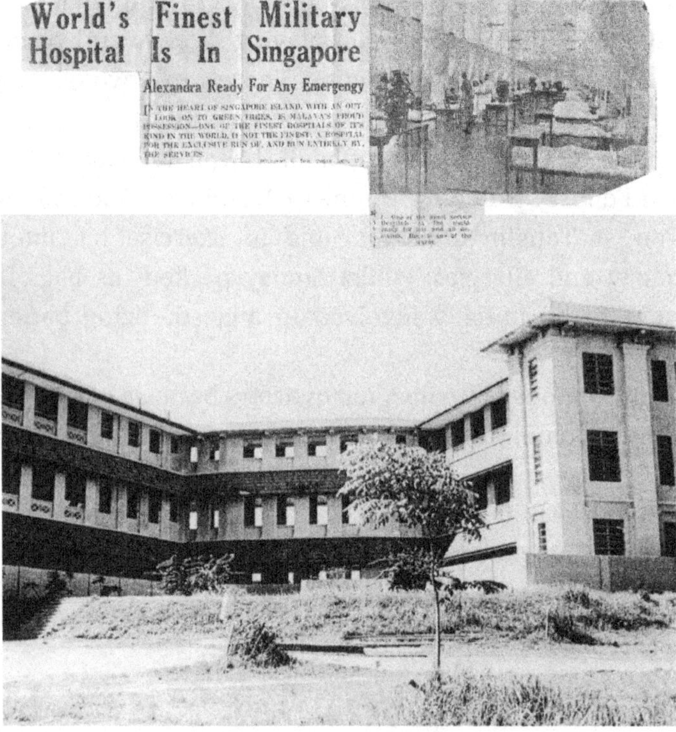

World's Finest Military Hospital Is In Singapore

Alexandra Ready For Any Emergengy

IN THE HEART OF SINGAPORE ISLAND, WITH AN OUTLOOK ON TO GREEN TREES, IS MALAYA'S PROUD POSSESSION—ONE OF THE FINEST HOSPITALS OF IT'S KIND IN THE WORLD, IF NOT THE FINEST: A HOSPITAL FOR THE EXCLUSIVE USE OF, AND RUN ENTIRELY BY, THE SERVICES.

OPEN FOR BUSINESS

'We had a very happy year doing a great deal of surgery.'

19 July 1940. The British Military Hospital Alexandra opened. *The Straits Times* turned up, and trumpeted this as part of Britain's military might: 'The most up to date and one of the largest military hospitals outside Great Britain.'

An added touch that went on just before opening was blast walls. 'Preparations for war generally included a little bit of wall, pavement, or walls five- or six-feet high put across passage ways so that they constituted a little bit of anti-blast or anti-splinter protection,' said Yeoh Sang Aum, a Malayan medical student at General Hospital. These went up around some of the bigger buildings in town, hospitals, such as the General where he worked.

At the end of July 1940, the War Office published its *Singapore Defences: 16th Edition of Works Services* document. The total budget for Singapore's defence infrastructure that year was £603,000 (almost £3.5 billion today). The Alexandra Hospital would chew up 265,900 of that (to be fair, spread over two years, but still a mountain of money). £172,100 was allocated for the main block, including the basement chapel. The balance was to Officers' Quarters (21,300), MS Quarters (15,400), RAMC Barrack Block (13,900), Externals, which included the football field, WO stores, etc, (21,200) and Nursing Sisters' Quarters.

The Sisters' Quarters – a contract issued under the bailiwick of Loveday – was allocated £22,000. Stringer's wife Olga, the nurse, showed a particular interest in the construction of these quarters, adding nuanced 'feminine touches' which were perhaps not sensed nor felt necessary by the laddish sappers who constructed it.

The chief medical officer was the vastly experienced 51-year-old Col Joseph Craven, a somewhat controversial appointment, who met with resistance from some quarters. 'He somehow got the command, to the consternation of Lt Col Bennett,' according to Smiley. The furrow-browed mustachioed Craven – who wore black round-framed spectacles – moved into a double-storey married quarters home with Nora, on the lawns immediately to the north of the main ward block.

The officer assisting him was Capt Ernest Smyth, OC Surgical Division, who in turn would have the smoking Irish rugby player, Capt Tom Smiley, as his offsider. 'The theatre suite had not been erected at that time and we modified some rooms to serve as theatre suite,' said Smiley. 'At the end of this jutting out portion is a longer room than the others – with an open corridor at both sides. This was our theatre.'

'He became surgical assistant and was able to gain some of the surgical experience that he craved,' Fiona Smiley would tell me. 'During that time he unexpectedly was put in charge of 20 mental patients being sent to Bombay, including Dr Peter Kerley, the famous radiologist who had suffered a nervous breakdown.' One of 14 children in his family, Sir Peter Kerley would go on to be one of the world's foremost radiologists, diagnosing King Charles V1's lung tumour and becoming an adviser to the Minister for Health.

Maj James Bull was a specialist radiologist from Buckinghamshire. Just on 30 himself, he was especially pleased with the assistant assigned to him, the youngster, Hugh Mitchell. 'He had an infectious enthusiasm for everything he undertook, whether it was in his work or recreation,' Bull recalled. 'A good brain, an easy manner, a great capacity for work, and a highly developed consciousness. I had complete confidence in him as an assistant and he never let me down. Everything he did he threw himself into it 100%.' And indeed Mitchell did a *lot* – not only playing just about all sports on offer, but running and organising many of the RAMC sports teams and activities.

An eclectic mix of personnel completed the opening team. 'Col Julian Taylor arrived sometime during that year. He was consultant surgeon to the forces in Malaya and had been senior surgeon at University College London before join up.' Bespectacled Taylor was 53, a WW1 veteran. Maj Lyndsey Webster, formerly with an oil company in Sarawak, took over when Capt Smyth was sent up-country for a secondment stint. Capt William Young was appointed general duties medical officer. Capt Eric Cruickshank, a 27-year old

Scotsman who was 'new professor of medicine in Trinidad' who was 'up for a challenge', according to Smiley. And Cyril Wild's doctor from Japan, Capt Allardyce, was on the opening team too. After a very quick reunion with his family in rural Armidale, Australia – and passing wife Madeleine some pearls he'd smuggled out of Japan – Allardyce took up a position at The Alex.

Those not qualified by rank or availability of officers' digs, were housed in the RAMC barrack block. This was a three-storey affair, with a dining room, sergeants' canteen, and large recreation room, on the ground floor. Each floor accommodated around 80 in sturdy iron beds, which were blow-lamped by Tamil servants against bed bugs weekly. Ah Chung, nicknamed 'Sew Sew Girl', dutifully stitched and made running repairs to their clothing as required.

'We had a very happy year doing a great deal of surgery,' was Smiley's memory of the period. Smiley continued to work and play golf, swim and played rugby for the Army. 'The war must have seemed another world away,' his daughter Fiona would tell me.

**

Meanwhile, all this time, the 18th Division IJA was in action in Southern China. Maj Gen Takeda Hisashi, 46, was appointed chief of staff in Canton. As part of the China Expeditionary Army, the 55th, 56th and 114th Regiments were heavily engaged in the battle for Guangzhou, the capital of Guangdong (Canton) province.

The Japanese seemed to underestimate the will and clout of the Chinese armies, especially the Kuo Min Tang, dissipating themselves too widely across many fronts simultaneously. After the collapse of France in June 1940 the Japanese became increasingly aggressive, and towards the end of that month occupied part of the Hong Kong peninsula in an attempt to blockade the colony.

British troops at Peking and Tientsin were withdrawn two months later, and the two battalions at Shanghai (which included the 2nd Bn East Surrey Regt) sent to Singapore. One wonders whether they sang the well-known song of the day (to the tune of the 1926 hit *Bye Bye Blackbird*) as they left:

Wrap up all my care and woe
Here I go, swinging low
Bye-Bye Shanghai
Won't somebody wait for me
Please get in a state for me
Bye-bye Shanghai

**

The destination of 32 Coy RAMC was kept something of a secret, but the band of doctors and nurses thawed out nicely as they passed through sun-drenched ports such as Aden, Colombo, Singapore, then headed north for Hong Kong, and finally around 20 disembarked at Shanghai. Their posting was the British Military Hospital, Shanghai.

Among this corps were Will Brand, the bookish-looking bespectacled Lloyd Hayes, Alf Sutton and George Johnson, the latter the youngest of six children of a coke-oven labourer in a local ironworks in Hartlepool. George worked as a shop assistant at Lipton's grocer before joining the RAMC in 1935 aged just 17.

**

In July, a trainload of 55 QA nurses was bound for Liverpool. Daphne van Wart, a vivacious 26-year-old brunette had used her two-day embarkation leave to visit her aunt, farewelling her with the assurance: 'Don't worry about me, I'm going to such a safe place.' Five, including her, were headed for Hong Kong. The balance were Singapore-bound. Also on that train was the very spinsterly Principal Matron Far East, Miss Violet Jones. 'She gave us a pep talk on how to behave with the officers and the need to avoid affairs with married men,' said Daphne, clearly not paying much attention, drawn ahead by dreams of sparkling gin fizzes and dashing young officers.

The *Empress of Australia* drifted out of Liverpool on a warm night, and Daphne soon got in the swing of the shipboard socializing. 'I had a boyfriend, a gunner, and he was married. Matron Jones was fairly strict but the liner was huge, and there were 55 of us. She couldn't be everywhere.'

**

In Shanghai, the stay of 32 Coy RAMC was cut short by the rapidly deteriorating situation. In early September 1940, they boarded the SS *Hosang* for Singapore.

What it lacked in comfort it made up for in stories. In 1934, Indian Customs had found eight pounds of cocaine valued at £1000 (£70 million today) secreted inside bamboo cages containing chickens and ducks on the vessel.

And so this company found themselves at Tanglin Military Hospital, which was now well in need of expansion and overhaul. But that would be the role of the brand new Alexandra.

In addition to doctors, dentists and medics of the 32 Coy RAMC, a boatload of 30 Queen Alexandra Imperial Military Nursing Service sisters arrived in Singapore aboard the *Dominion Monarch*, too. A further 20 had come from Shanghai and other outposts. Plus Matron Jones and her 50 QAs from the *Empress of Australia*. And Margot Turner, a stunning blue-eyed English beauty who'd worked two years in a garrison hospital in India before being transferred to Kuala Lumpur. Or so she thought. En route the destination was revealed to be Singapore and she initially ended up at 1st Malayan General Hospital, Johor. Lively and athletic, her love of swimming, golf and tennis meant she'd come to the right place. And her looks ensured her dance-card was always full on nights off at the Raffles.

'I remember very well about the nurses at the Alexandra,' said Stan Sharpley, handily garrisoned across the road, with a cheeky wink.

'We were pleased to see them,' confirmed Lloyd Hughes.

'Their mess was up on the hill to the right of the hospital as it faces,' according to Smiley. The team for the biggest military hospital outside of Britain was taking shape. They moved into the Nursing Sisters' Mess across the road and railway line from the hospital in Alexandra Park.

**

The long-serving man from Lucknow, India, Maj Denis Mulvany had been at The Alex for a few months already, and his hyper-active and capable wife, Ethel, now finally joined him. She'd caught a train from

France to Italy, boarding the luxurious liner SS *Conte Verde* to Bombay, as the noose tightened around Europe and seaways became increasingly unsafe. Next she was to cobble together, by whatever overland-and-sea means, the leg to Singapore. As she went to disembark, she was told her onward passage to Singapore had been secured. Later she would find out that one of Denis' patients, Brig Alec Wildey – the 51-year-old commanding officer of Anti-Aircraft Defences, Malaya – was so grateful for the emergency appendectomy he'd performed, he pulled some strings to ensure she made it quickly and safely to Singapore.

The *Conte Verde* docked in Singapore on 23 March 1940 – seven years after he'd proposed on deck to her – and Denis hardly recognized Ethel who'd chunked on 19 pounds in as many days of onboard gorging.

Her first priority was to find the couple accommodation, a difficult task given the influx of troops. She soon found a house with a room to rent at 112 Pasir Panjang Road, less than five minutes from Denis' workplace, and marched over one lunchtime to break the news to him: 'I got a house!'

Initially they were to share the four-bedroom double-storey colonial style bungalow, but the landlord moved out, unnerved by the military's requisitions in the area overlooking the west coast, just north of the Labrador battery with its newly-installed six-inch guns. She moved to join her son in Sumatra, leaving behind her two dogs, Bowby and Brutus.

And so the Mulvanys moved in. Ethel was most impressed that things seemed to work in Singapore. 'You could flick on the electric stove, turn the tap and know you'd get clear water, and in some parts use the flush toilet.'

The view out to the Straits was framed by frangipani, palm trees, and colourful canna lilies. Beyond lay islands, lots of tiny islands, spreading south towards the Dutch East Indies.

This got them dreaming. Denis, because he loved boats, and Ethel, because she was an island girl from way back. Denis commissioned a cruiser to be built, spending much of his off-duty time down at the docks. The builder was an odd chap who nodded a lot, seemed to understand, but never spoke. They assumed he was

Chinese. It turned out he was Japanese and would surface as a PoW camp commander in 1942 (Ethel insistent he was Gen Arimura Tsunemichi, whose military records bear out he was ambiguously 'in reserve' and 'retired' at that time before being recalled in late 1941).

The ever-resourceful Ethel set about enquiring about buying an island, which all belonged to the Crown Lands Office. So, naturally, she wrote off to King George V1 directly, beseeching him to let go of just one of his 'tiny, wee islands.' An answer in the affirmative was soon received: they could lease an island for $1 for 99 years 'provided that no Malay was interested in said island.'

Their cruiser was completed, named *Honora* for her birthplace in Manitoulin, Canada. And off to sea they went in search of an island to call their own paradise. They found it, just a 20-minute boat ride from their home, beyond Pulau Bukom. No wonder no Malay was interested in it – because it was called Pulau Hantu meaning Ghost Island. It was rumoured that the ghosts of old warfaring sailors rested – or more to the point, *didn't rest* – there. So they snapped it up for $1, and promptly renamed it Pulau Shorga (Heavenly Island).

They each had a little sailing skiff too, hers the blue *Api Shorga* (Fire of Heaven) and his, the *Api Neraka* (Fire of Hell). Friends often made up the crew, and Sunday morning races were a social highlight, followed by a lunch spread prepared by their staff (an extended Malay family who lived on the island).

Off the island, they were not big entertainers and socializers but a modicum had to be done. She was the more extroverted of the two, but as a teetotaller, would swan through the many cocktail functions bedecked in dazzling evening gowns and sparkling diamonds, rubies and pearls. But with never more than Orangeade in her champagne glass.

**

A newly minted captain, Cyril Wild, also arrived in Singapore after the War Office had discovered his Japanese linguistic skills. He was put on the staff of newly-wed Gen Sir Lewis Heath, 3rd Indian Corp, and posted to Fort Canning to work as an intelligence officer and interpreter. In typical fashion, he knuckled down to learning Malay before breakfast, and also tried to add Urdu to his lexicon. Tennis, squash and swimming occupied other down times.

In November 1940 General HQ Far East was formed with Air Vice-Marshal Brooke-Popham (or 'Brookham' as he was informally referred to) at the top of the totem pole. Lt Gen Arthur Percival, who'd attended Rugby School, was made GOC, a huge leap for a veteran who – despite his track record in WW1 and the inter-war years – had never actually commanded a corp before.

But this was typical of the Singapore bureaucracy of the day. And when people rose above their level of competency, rather than replacing them, they simply brought in another level beside or above that person, adding to convoluted dotted-line reporting structures. The resultant organization – civilian and military – was bloated, inefficient and ineffective. And full of paradoxical conflicts of interest: chiefly being to prepare fully for war, yet to maintain maximum production of the previous tin and rubber resources.
Everyone was in charge, but no one was in charge.

Still, the illusion of grandeur and invincibility meant that Percival moved into Command House, an 11.5 acre estate. It had six bedrooms, servants' quarters, tennis court, gazebo and a three-car garage. As Percival had left his family behind in England on this posting, he shared it with Air Officer Commanding, Air Vice-Marshal Pulford, who had also left his family behind. Not a bad bachelor pad! Around this butterfly-winged arched colossus – designed by Frank Brewer, the same architect behind the Cathay Building – was the Sime Road Camp, from where Percival's HQ team operated.

**

And still more Allies poured in to Singapore. The *Queen Mary* arrived in February 1941, full to the gunwales of the brawny, suntanned garrulous Aussies of 8th Division.

There was no room aboard for Father Brendan Rogers, a chaplain, so he had to wait for Good Friday to board the Holland America Line's *New Amsterdam*. 'It was a beautiful ship,' said Rogers, it hadn't even been properly converted so we had first-class accommodation and everything.' Ordained in 1937 the 25-year-old from Victoria initially put his name forward 'as a sense of adventure I suppose, a terrific amount of patriotism, but everyone was caught up in it.' He was accepted into the Army, and posted to an infantry training battalion, even though he was 'just acting as a priest in uniform, not doing any training, so I was dropping hints I'd like to get into the real show.'

Sometimes you have to be careful for what you wish for. 'We ended up in Singapore,' he said. 'It was like going on a picnic, a holiday. They were all keyed up,' he said of his fellow soldiers, who – even though he was not quite 26 – 'looked on me as an old man,' he laughed. 'Those fellows weren't really fighting soldiers but everyone had to be properly trained. They had to mix with others. Morale was really high.'

They landed at Keppel Harbour, straight onto a military train to Tampin, then put on a sideline track to Malacca where he was transferred to the 2/10th Australian Field Regt who occupied the St Francis Institution. His new digs were nine miles up the Port Dickson road in the servants' quarters of the Governor's Residence which sat atop the adjacent hill.

Several regiments were dispatched to coastal towns in Malaya, and Smiley's medical mate Humphrey was sent as a medical officer for the East Surrey Regiment to Kota Bharu in the far northeastern corner of Malaya's border with Siam. Smiley himself had a brief secondment as medical officer with the Argyll and Sutherland Regiment before returning to The Alex as surgical assistant under Col Julian Taylor.

'Taylor seemed to think highly of him and informed him he would be at the Alexandra hospital for good,' Fiona Smiley told me. 'Tom was naively disappointed thinking that he was missing out on the action.'

And yet more Allied arrivals flooded the island ...

'*Singapore*? I'd never bleedin' heard of the place in my younger days,' said motorbiking enthusiast Gunner Dick Lee, Royal Artillery. 'We boarded ship in Scotland – the ship was called *Empress of Japan*, funnily enough – and I thought we were going to the Middle East because that was the only place there was a war going on at that time. They don't tell you nothing. I never saw none of Singapore, straight off the ship on the train to a place called Sungei Patani, which was just near Ipoh, and that's where I joined the 11th Indian Division. They were building up the division. They must have known things in London that things could be a bit dodgy out there.'

Indeed, the tenor in Singapore towards Japan as a threat was changing. 'They used to come into Keppel Harbour in their boats with their Jap flags flying,' said Stan Sharpley, 'and we could see Keppel Harbour from Gillman Barracks and we'd say "Look at them so-and-so's coming in". And you'd see all the guns pointing out to sea.'

And as though 32-degrees wasn't hot and humid enough, temperatures and tempers would rise further when there were sporting fixtures involving the Japanese. 'Two Canadians come over and joined the battalion on a representative basis and they taught us baseball. The baseball league then consisted of Chinese, Japanese, Americans, Canadians, and the Loyals put a team in the league. And every time we came up against the Japs the baseball bats used to fly. Yes, we knew they were going to get at us some day or other.'

**

In February 1941, the Central Department in Tokyo called for a fortnight of War Exercises using Taiwan as the friendly HQ and Kyushu as the hostile territory. It was a bit of a shakedown of landings and testing of battlefield principles. Notably, the battledress and equipment was that which would be used in tropical theatres. Was the Southern push on? A few months later another 10 days of exercises were held in southern China.

**

30 April 1941. A secret cipher telegram from GOC Malaya to the War Office in London requested permission to expand The Alex – not even 10 months old – up to 600 beds. Was this realism at work, or pessimism in disguise?

This was to make up the predicted shortfall of beds needed in wartime. 2400 would be needed in Malaya for Europeans alone ('excluding Australians') and 5000 for non-Europeans. Currently all five military hospitals combined could muster just 1116 beds. Perhaps to soften the sell-in, a further telegram on 17 June indicated that the first phase expansion to 450 beds could be achieved by adding more beds to each ward and using existing verandah space. The only additional resources required would be 20 St John Ambulance nurses.

The next phase up to 600 beds, however, would require a total of 62 more staff, specifically 25 nurses, five surgical specialists, one anesthetist, and assorted cooks, ward boys, etc. That was a much bigger ask, especially to a War Office now heavily weighed down by a real war on its doorstep in Europe. Singapore? Far away. Even further from care. Denied.

**

26 August 1941. Another GOC Telegram to the War Office: 'Difficulty obtaining suitable accommodation expansion Alexandra Hosp above 450 beds. Propose drop expansion Alexandra and concentrate Civil Hosp Johor.' That ambitious plan was for another self-contained 700-bed hospital in Johor, on the southern tip of Malaya.

In line with this, a boatload of Australian nurses arrived to work at the 2/13th Australian General Hospital, under the ever-smiling and well-respected Matron Irene Drummond, based in the former lunatic asylum near the Sultan of Johor's Palace. Visits were arranged for them to visit The Alex to view malarial education films.

QA nurse, Kit Woodman, was posted to Singapore after escaping in 1940 from France. She was rather surprised at the stark contrast of conditions there versus in Europe. The main thing that struck her was the complacency. Day-to-day life went on as usual for most, people going off to their humdrum jobs in shipping companies or insurance firms. 'Singapore's preoccupation was with golf, cricket and the afternoon siesta,' she recalled.

She found the Sisters' Mess at The Alex comfortable, hardly believing the luxury of having one *amah* (maid) for every three sisters. The work kept her busy enough, mainly tending to those with tropical diseases and traffic accidents, and a lively social calendar kept the nursing team's mind off war. In the first few days of December she was posted up to the 1st Malayan General Hospital, Johor, where Margot Turner also worked.

**

On 5 September, Col Tsuji was appointed as staff officer to the growing number of forces now stationed in Indo-China.

To anyone believing that the Japanese attack on Malaya was meticulously thought out years in advance, Tsuji is unequivocal. 'I state beyond doubt and without fear of contradiction that not until September 1941 did we begin active preparations for military operations to the south,' he said. 'The Pacific hostilities were wholly and hastily prepared on the *doro nawa* model.' This is a Japanese expression meaning 'you catch a robber, then you make the rope to bind him'.

Long days and nights of planning, sitting on a mat, consulting maps and charts, ensued. His emerging signature style was one of rapid offensives based on taking initiative, yet with a 'win at all costs' mentality which showed scant regard for conserving the lives of his own soldiers.

Lt Gen Harukichi Hyakutake had been the commander of 18th Division. His two brothers were both admirals in the Japanese Navy, no less. He was promoted, and command of the 18th Division passed to Lt Gen Mutaguchi on 6 November 1941. Doubtless, some celebratory drinks would have been enjoyed because his 'considerable appetite for drink' was matched only by his voracious appetite for sex. His alcohol consumption accounted for the extra kilos he carried around his girth.

That day, the Order of Battle for the IJA 25th Army was gazetted. Mutaguchi was delighted, because the crack 18th Division and 5th Division had been selected for their meritorious performances in China. Another division was added: the Imperial Guards, also known as the 'Prince's Forces'. The difference was the Guards had seen no combat action since the Russo-Japanese campaign over 30 years before. Tsuji saw them as 'trained in traditional ceremonies, but they had no taste for field operations and were unsuitable for them.'

Yamashita got the nod to head up the Malayan campaign, while the less favoured Lt Gen Iida was given the 15th Army and Burma theatre, and the latter went off in a disappointed huff. Yamashita and Tsuji immediately had an ego clash, especially because Tsuji had build up intelligence and experience in tropical conditions which Yamashita did not yet have.

To this end, Tsuji made his own reconnaissance of northern Malaya, persuading Capt Ikeda, commander of a reconnaissance squadron, to fly him over the British colony. They took off from Saigon at dawn in a twin-engined Mitsubishi Ki-46 'Dinah', a reconnaissance plane capable of flying high, fast and far. The craft was unmarked and Tsuji wore an air force uniform in case they were forced down. They scouted its airfields, with rain clouds forcing them as low as 6500 ft. Tsuji reported his findings to Gen Terauchi Hisaichi, Southern Army commander, and fine-tuned their plans.

Tsuji sat on his mat and made a promise to the gods: 'Day and night I would abstain from wine and tobacco. I forgot instinctive desires and worldly passions, to say nothing of lust and appetite and even life and death. My whole mind was concentrated on gaining the victory. We will win. We *must* win.'

**

On the west coast, Denis and Ethel Mulvany's beloved beach was now wrapped in barbed wire, with military men and vehicles scurrying like ants at every turn. One day she found Denis talking to Bharose: 'I wish you'd go home for a holiday to India,' he said.

'I will return to India when *sahib* returns home,' replied their faithful servant. Denis handed him a military-issued ticket, implying this was his chance to escape Singapore now. Bharose chose to stay on.

Ethel, longsince involved in fund-raising, felt she could and *should* be doing more for the war effort. Given her previous ties to the Red Cross, that was her starting point. But there was no British Red Cross presence on the island. So of course she made an appointment to see the Governor of Singapore, Sir Shenton Thomas. Amazingly she secured a slot, further proof of her confident pulling power.

She was more amazed, though, by Thomas's insistence there would be no war, so why didn't she toddle along and join St John Ambulance which would be just fine? 'The meeting began poorly and went downhill from there.' She insisted that he contact the International Red Cross in Geneva to establish a British Red Cross in this British colony. Thomas rose to meet her fury, ushering her from his office, declaring that wasn't her place as a mere civilian to decide these matters. She discovered, however, there was an Australian Red Cross office, run by deputy assistant commissioner, Basil Burdett, himself a former art dealer, journalist and WW1 stretcher-bearer in the European theatre.

'Here I am!' she announced herself, offering up her skills and services. Again her confidence won out, and she walked away with an appointment as Superintendent, attached to the 1st Malayan General Hospital. Naturally, this was not quite the adrenaline-inducing immersion she was after: the strong and tall Canadian wanted to drive ambulances and lift heavy stretchers into the back of them. So that's what she would do.

**

At the northwestern tip of Malaya, Dick Lee, and his friend Tony were getting settled as HQ dispatch riders to commander Maj Gen David Murray-Lyon, who was nearing 50, and had earned an MC in the Battle of Flanders in WW1.

'The roads was quite good up there,' Dick remembered. 'Asphalt roads in Sungei Patani. That was quite a busy area and we were building up the division up there.' Four Indian Brigades (the 6th, 12th, 15th, 28th) were already mustered in Jitra on the Thai border. 'We was in Malaya, peace time, before it started, and then end up in a war that you didn't expect.'

**

30 November 1941. Orders from Tokyo reached Yamashita advising that the invasion of Malaya was to commence 8 December (local time).

Timing is everything. In December 1941, permission was finally granted by the War Office to increase Alexandra Hospital to a capacity of 550 beds.

One of those was given over to Sgt Norman Bryer, the RAF pilot. 'I entered Alexandra Hospital suffering from phlebitis [vein inflammation] in the calf, and was ordered strictly to "bed down".' This would have been torment enough for the usually active young flier, but fate had far, *far* crueller plans for he and Singapore.

The Mulvanys enjoyed their life in Singapore, shuttling between their grand home at 112 Pasir Panjang Road, and their own private island, Pulau Shorga, in their cruiser, *Honora*. Below: Ethel relaxes on Shorga.

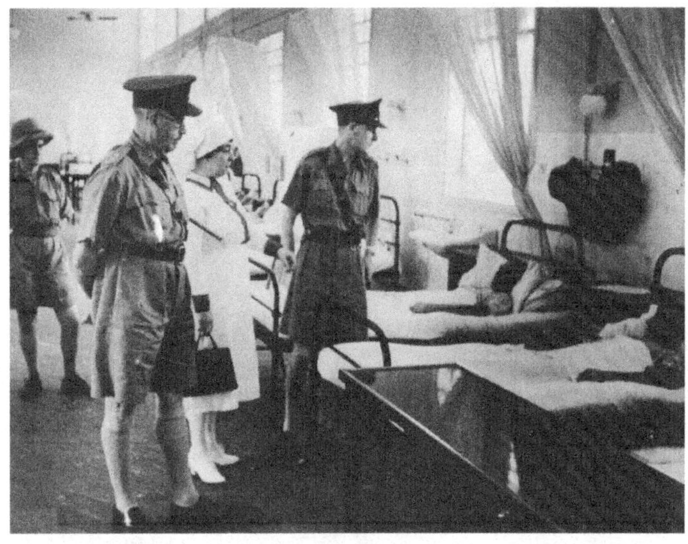

On the opening of the hospital, CO Col Craven and Matron Violet Jones conduct an inspection in the airy wards. Below: Maj James Bull (probably) operating his new radiography equipment, which would be destroyed.

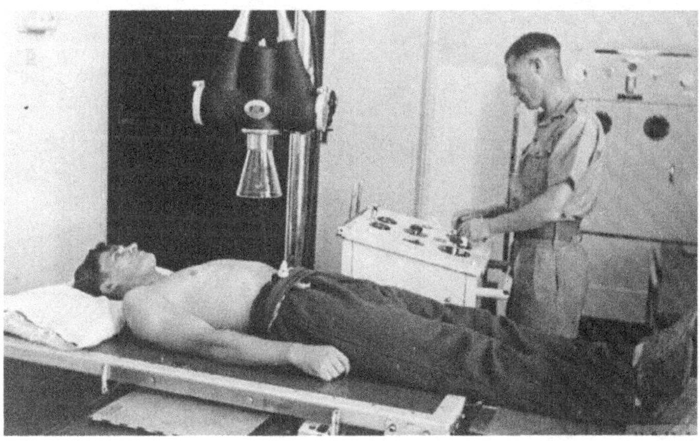

Clockwise from top left: Gunner Fergus Anckorn, Cpl George Poole, Sapper Danny Fraser, Sgt Norman Bryer.

Top: Pte Len Knott on duty at The Alex. Inset: Capt Tom Smiley enjoyed a 'happy year doing a great deal of surgery' at The Alex. Below: Bert Gurd relaxes with new girlfriend Rosa's family while training with the RAMC near Watford.

Gillman Barracks, home of Pte Stan Sharpley and the 2nd Loyals, and the site of their last stand. Below: Sapper Danny Fraser and his 36th Royal Engineers in training. They would be stationed directly behind the hospital.

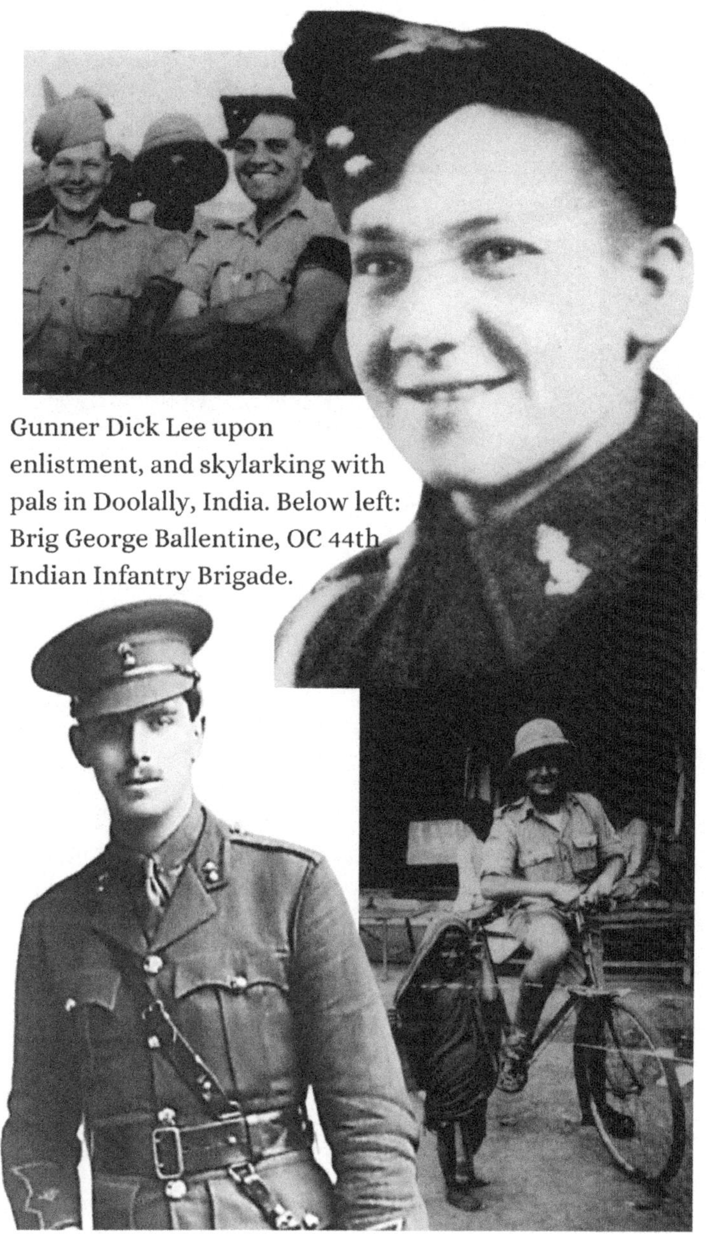

Gunner Dick Lee upon enlistment, and skylarking with pals in Doolally, India. Below left: Brig George Ballentine, OC 44th Indian Infantry Brigade.

Part 2

THE MAIN ACT

(Detail of memoir by Capt Petrovsky)

RISING SUN, SINKING EMPIRE

'We're right now, the Navy's here.'

2 December 1941. A crystalline afternoon highlighted the glittering blue-green of the water and the lush green of Singapore Island. The foreshores were crowded, all vantage points opportunistically snapped up for the word was being excitedly passed around: 'The Royal Navy's here!'

If the uncertain spirit of the local population, its expatriate residents, and even the Allied forces needed a lift, this would do it. The majestic grandeur and implied omnipotence of a fleet of battleships heaved to port into the Johor Straits towards the Sembawang Naval Base.

Today was the debut of the Far East Fleet in Singapore, although this was not the *Repulse*'s first trip to Singapore, but it was the first for *Prince of Wales.* The former looked menacing in its geometric camouflage patchwork paintjob, the latter painted up in amorphic blue-green-grey patterns.

Capt Tennant, commanding the *HMS Repulse,* had something else on his mind. Where were the fighter planes to escort them up this channel? Not one.

Anyone who was anyone in Malaya was there at the Naval Base, most notably Gov Gen Sir Shenton Thomas, Air Marshall Sir Robert Brooke-Popham, overall commander of the Far East, and General Percival, GOC, in his ubiquitous khaki Bombay bloomer shorts and long socks, peaked cap on, talking with Admiral Geoffrey Layton, dressed identically but in white. (Having handed over command, he and Lady Layton later boarded the *Dominion Monarch,* the same vessel which had brought most of the QA sisters to Singapore.)

And another naval figure was dockside too. Capt Tom Phillips, he of pale skin and close-set eyes, who was captain of the flagship *Prince of Wales* and Commander in Chief of the Far East Fleet. He'd taken a flying boat ahead to Singapore to meet with Air

Vice Marshal Pulford, and try and rustle up the rest of a decent flotilla, because now two destroyers from the Mediterranean were also no-shows.

Phillips to Pulford: 'If we need it, are you going to be able to provide us with air cover?'
'Yes, of course.'

This was the Empire's show of force. The media was there in force. Radio broadcasters. Film cameramen. Photographers. And the more global media exposure there was, the more it backfired on those senior-ranking officials who knew too well – or at least privately felt – this was a flimsy smoke-and-mirror show. Deep inside, even Percival felt that this was an imbalanced token fleet.

**

The Japanese were especially thankful for the media coverage of 'Force Z' as the flotilla was now named: it gave them definite names and ship class types to overlay on what their air recon had already spotted and reported from the air.

Intense training for their 22nd Air Flotilla had continued until late November when news came of the Colombo flotilla, which enticingly included what was believed to be Britain's most modern battleship. Matsunaga called forward three more squadrons, the 27 Bettys of Kanoya Corp. Now a total of 123 of the world's leading naval attack aircraft were poised to strike from Vietnam.

**

In that British flotilla of approximately 30 ships, was Francis Docketty, a 24-year-old bricklayer who'd signed up with the Territorials in 1937 then joined the 316th Royal Engineers who were rebadged as the 316th Royal Artillery overnight. 'We was a pretty boy Scottish affair in those days,' he said. 'Actually we felt like broomstick soldiers – just ploughing about in mud, one uniform, wellington boots. All the second-hand stuff would come to us.' Then one day, after clearing up a bombsite and debris in Bristol, they were taken to Southend and put on a ship. 'We didn't know where we were going – via Iceland, America, Cape Town, Bombay, Colombo.'

Through bomber and submarine scares, he sat on the forward machine gun, finger on trigger.

Watching them sail down the Straits of Malacca were Father Brendan Rogers and his fellow Aussies from the 2/10. 'We saw the *Repulse* and *Prince of Wales* come down the Straits. We thought, We're right now, the Navy's here.'

The fleet finally arrived at their secret destination: Singapore. 'I thought it was a filthy hole,' recalled Docketty. 'Very interesting, but they took us out to Nee Soon on the northern part of the island. We had a few days leave, and we'd walk about Singapore and have Chinese food.'

**

At dawn on 4 December Lt Gen Yamashita of the IJA 25th Army made an ominous observation through his heavy-lidded eyes – the sun and moon were both simultaneously visible as 27 troop ships slid out of Hainan, destination Malaya. This led to a rather poetic outpouring:

On the day the sun shines with the moon
The arrow leaves the bow
It carries my spirit towards the enemy
With me are a hundred million souls
My people of the East
On this day when the moon shines
And the sun both shines.

**

Fate continued to deal other hands randomly. Pte W Maynard, RAMC, was tasked as a medical orderly to accompany a party to India. 'I left on a temporary duty, escorting invalided patients. I was unable to rejoin my unit when this duty was completed owing to the fact that after hostilities had broken out no transports were then leaving India for Singapore.' As a result he luckily never returned to The Alex.

**

7 December 1941. An orgy of orange suffused sea and sky as the tropical sunset made its lazy curtain call on another idyllic Sunday. Only the streamlined hull of their 38-foot cruiser, *Honora*, disturbed the placid waters of the Malacca Straits, the Rolls-Royce motors purring them towards home.

'This is too beautiful,' said Denis, surveying the scene from behind the wheel. Ethel sat with long suntanned legs outstretched, a smile of radiant contentment a proxy for her reply.

Dead-ahead was Kent Ridge and the Bukit Panjang spine of green hills which framed the west coast of Singapore. She could also pick out Bukit Chandu (Opium Hill), and tracing a line down the hill she could spot their double-storey colonial bungalow along the coastal road. To the east a little was Labrador, newly bristling with six-inch 18-pound guns perched atop the low red-granite cliffs that fell away into the ocean. To their starboard Blakang Mati island loomed golden-green out of the water. Pillboxes poked from between palm trees. And 15-inch guns – the insurance policy of the Empire – added an ominous and incongruous tone to the otherwise languid landscape.

The couple were returning from their own little private island where they had built a small cottage sheltered by palms. Its main feature was an *atap*-roofed open-sided living area, replete with wicker chairs, where they could laze the days away as the warm waters lapped up against the 150-foot wharf they'd put in for *Honora*. At night the portable wind-up gramophone player would blare out tunes they, and often their guests, would dance to, relishing the sun-warmed sand on their bare feet under the Malayan moonlight.

This was a long way from care, especially with the nearest telephone being at Fort Siloso on Blakang Mati, about 10km as the seagull flies. As Denis – or Major Mulvany, RAMC, as he was by then – was on call at The Alex most of the time, he devised a rather ingenious work-around. When needed, the hospital would call the fort, which would send a soldier outside to beat a big old Malay gong *seven* times. Denis would then cruise back across to perform his surgery. Ethel would meanwhile go and feed the fish at the end of the pier, especially delighting in Minnie the stingray. In this agreeable way, they spent nearly three quarters of their time on the island. Magical times.

Soon after twilight their car turned up the driveway to their main residence on Pasir Panjang Road. Their exuberant dogs, Brutus and Bowby, bounded out to meet them.

From this grand portico-clad four-bedroom house they could enjoy the reverse angle view of the islands. In the past year they'd made it their home – colourfully furnished with Kashmir lamps, Persian rugs, silver tea sets, and other trappings of colonial life from several years with the British Indian Army. Bharose, one of their 22 Indian servants from those Cawnpore days, was here, plus Kuki, a Chinese cook who – when not incapacitated by generous inhalations from her opium pipe – served up delicious dinners.

Bellies full, and pleasantly sapped by the glorious weekend away, they retired for the night.

**

Elsewhere on the island that night, there was restless dissatisfaction, because army personnel had been confined to barracks. 'Many were irritated by these orders, grumblings were going on,' said bespectacled Capt Constantine Petrovsky, RAMC, of the No 4 Malaya Field Ambulance. '"What the hell? What's all this nonsense – why do we have to sacrifice our fun?" and "Those cross-eyed, short-sighted yellow bastards will never come".' He and his unit would far rather be whooping it up at New World, Happy World, or Great World, their nightspots of choice, than be stuck in their mosquito-ridden huts. 'They were swearing at this unnecessary infringement,' he recalled, as he retired to sleep around 11pm.

**

Soon after 11pm, Mihoro and Genzhan Corps of the Imperial Japanese Naval Air Service took off from an airfield in Saigon with a single-minded mission: Bomb Singapore. 'I and my crew got our Type 96 bomber and departed an airbase in Vietnam with 12 of 60kg bombs,' pilot Iwasaki Yoshiaki would tell me.

The proverbial dark and stormy night necessitated navigation lights to be switched on just to keep formation. Lightning zaps skittered over the South China Sea. The further they went, the worse the weather got. Matsunaga re-called all planes around 2am. But only Genzhan listened. Mihoro's 17 bombers ploughed on. Then the weather cleared. Singapore was clear. Sparkling even. Their targets were perfectly visible.

'Our target was Seletar Airfield,' said Iwasaki of his crew's specific briefing. 'We dropped all our bombs under strong searchlight and heavy anti-aircraft firing.' Some of that ack-ack came from the *HMS Prince of Wales*' high-angle gun crews, but no fighters were scrambled against them. One RAF torpedo bomber pilot, Sgt Norman Bryer, had been based at Seletar but had just been admitted to The Alex Hospital with inflammation in his leg, so luckily was not on the receiving end of Iwasaki's bombing that night.

**

'Wake up, Ethel,' shouted Denis from their upstairs verandah, 'the Japs are blitzing us!' They rushed down to the garden, dogs eagerly in tow, soon joined by their three servants, including Kebun, the Malay gardener. Bombs crumped and boomed from the Raffles Square area, and showers of sparks and flowery fireworks filled the air.

Leaflets drifted earthwards from planes. They featured a cartoon of a fat European rubber planter, and white men lounging, cool drinks in hand, while Tamil labourers slaved around them in the scorching sun. 'Burn all the white devils in the sacred flame of victory,' they exhorted.

But for now they all stood on the lawn at 4:15am, slack-jawed and mesmerized. Including the dogs. But the excitement proved too much for Bowby, who died frozen where he stood. Two hundred civilians were also casualties that night.

Denis and Ethel rushed upstairs. They threw on their uniforms, Ethel affixing her Red Cross armbands, scoffed down Bharose's hastily prepared breakfast, and sped off to The Alex, a mere five minutes away, to make themselves useful.

**

'In my sleep I heard sounds of gunfire, I thought I was dreaming,' recalled Petrovsky. 'I looked out the window of my hut and saw brilliant flashes of light criss-crossing the dark blue sky. I heard voices: "Why do they disturb our sleep?" The formation of twin-engined planes sailing along was brilliantly outlined by several searchlights. Puffs like woollen balls were bursting all around but the planes did not look worried, their triangle formation keeping perfect order. One must admit it was a beautiful sight.' But then the reality that this was not a drill snapped them into action. 'Suddenly air-raid sirens began their screeching wail, explosions of falling bombs. This was the real thing. What a scramble to get into slit trenches, the same trenches our troops grumbled so much about when they were ordered to dig them only a few days previously.' They watched the bombs fall on the city and the RAF base in Seletar.

'We stayed outside the huts and talked about this unexpected attack without declaration of war. None of us anticipated when we went to bed that Sunday night that this was the least peaceful evening we would have for many years to come.'

**

On landing at Saigon, Capt Iwasaki heard that the first transports had gone ashore on the north Malaya coast and Pearl Harbour had been successfully attacked, too. The day of infamy.

**

8 December. 'We are actually at war!' Capt Smiley wrote to Elizabeth. 'I've been in a genuine air raid and treated casualties. I got such a shock at 4am this morning when I wakened and heard planes overhead and saw flashes of the gunfire and the bombs. I don't believe anyone in Malaya expected such a thing last night. Last night I was feeling that war would never come to Malaya. Now that it has come I'm glad as it will be over sooner than later and I'll get home to you! We haven't started too well I'm afraid but that is always the way with us British, isn't it? I've been terribly busy today and I expect to be very much busier tomorrow. Today Col Taylor did all the

abdominal cases and I did all the fracture and lacerated work. I've been putting traction pins in femurs and all sorts of things today.'

**

Pulford received news that Khota Bahru airfield could no longer be held and the ground force was withdrawing, and first news had been received of the devastating fury of the Japanese torpedo bomber attacks on Pearl Harbor. The *Prince of Wales* and *Repulse* slipped anchors at 17:35, described as 'a pathetic sight' by Admiral Layton.

'We are off to look for trouble, and I expect we shall find it,' Capt Tennant told his action-hungry crew as the *Repulse* led the way down the rapidly darkening strait. He himself was more somber, better understanding the implications of Pearl Harbor and what it said about their woeful under-estimation of this foe.

'One night I was doing a late round of the hospital,' remembered Edith 'Woodie' Stevenson, at St Andrews at Siglap on the east coast of Singapore, 'when the First Aid men drew my attention to two ships far out to sea. They were the *Prince of Wales* and *Repulse* cruising north towards the China Coast.'

22:53 a signal was received by the *Wales*: 'Fighter protection on Wednesday 10th will not, repeat not, be possible.' And only a single Catalina would be flying recon for it in the morning. So, two mission critical factors that Phillips was relying on for this mission were duly blown out of the water. Oh, and one more thing: the estimated size of the Japanese bomber force in Indo-China was larger than anyone imagined.

**

10 December 1941. A beautiful clear mauve dawn broke around 5am, revealing an enemy reconnaissance plane directly overhead. By 6am the sleep-deprived Genzan Corps pilots in Saigon were clambering back into their cockpits and climbing slowly into the cool morning air, weighed down as they were with their lethal payloads and aiming for 10-12,000 feet, their optimal cruising altitude. Fuel consumption was crucial – they didn't know exactly how long this flight would be, and those massive torpedoes meant they could only

carry around two-thirds of their maximum fuel load to compensate for the weight. They expected Singapore would be their destination today.

By 09:30 95 Nells and Bettys were aloft in flights of nine planes, 34 of the 60 Nells with 600kg bombs, the rest with torpedoes. Captain Iwasaki and the other pilots sipped coffee from their thermos flasks hoping for added alertness when they'd need it most. They snacked on *ohagi* rice cakes over the endless and bare South China Sea. Nothing below. Still nothing. Some reached Singapore. Still nothing. Today wasn't their day so they turned around.

By 11:00 fuel gauges became a concern for some. Suddenly the radio crackled. It was Ensign Hoashi from one of the 'Babs' (Mitsubishi Ki-15) recon planes: 'Sighted two enemy battleships seventy nautical miles south-east Kuantan course south-east.'

11:30. Torpedo bombers off starboard. Low. About 3000 feet. Port side of the *Prince of Wales*. Groups of two or three. Diving in now. Full speed. Low. 500 feet. And ...

Torpedoes!

'Stand by for barrage! Stand by for barrage!' the Tannoys on both ships blared. Tennant on the *Repulse* called for a 45-degree turn to starboard, presenting only her slender stern, and a dozen torpedoes whooshed harmlessly past. Phillips tried the same: turning to port to present her bow. *Bang!* A geyser of water shot skyward and the ship immediately listed hard and dropped speed. Two torpedoes had simultaneously struck her Achilles heel – the rudders and propellers – jamming her in a portside turn, and ripping open her aft, her bowels rapidly swallowing the waters of the South China Sea.

Just as the rest of the 22nd Air Flotilla joined the feeding frenzy, goaded on under the conductor's baton of the excitable Hoashi. More planes. More bombs. More geysers. More desperate evasive dance maneuvers from the *Repulse*. They'd dodged 19 torpedoes in all. An unparalleled display of 'combing.'

Tennant turned to see where the *Wales* was. Far off to the south. Barely firing, barely moving, barely alive.

12:20. A flight of nine bombers appeared from the south, three peeling off to unleash on the *Repulse*, six darting for the *Wales*.

But as Tennant started to swing away from the incoming torpedoes, three planes switched away from the *Wales* to drop their torpedoes towards the *Repulse*. Having dodged the first lot, he was now presenting broadside to the second batch. 'Stand by for torpedo!'

You can only imagine that would be the longest 90 seconds of their lives ... watching ... waiting ... *WHAM!* The ship shuddered and listed to port.

More Nells rushed in. Soon eight tell-tale foam trails were headed her way. 'We successfully bombed the British ship *Repulse*,' Iwasaki told me. 'Our bomber gave the bulls-eye.' The *Repulse* swayed like a drunken uncle, taking three hits on the port and one on the starboard. 'Prepare to abandon ship,' was Tennant's call. The *Repulse* was leaning ever and ever to the port side. She was still underway. But her guns were now silent. The water calm.

'You've put up a good show. Now look after yourselves and God bless you,' Tennant broadcast with his megaphone to the throng.

Listing now at 60 degrees. Hundreds of her crew were walking up the deck then sliding wildly on their backsides down her oil-slicked side. *Slam!* Many hit the bilge keel, breaking ankles and spines.

Then the *Repulse* went down gracefully stern first. Tennant was still on her, wearing his tin helmet, but managed to float his way up out of the darkness, where some men dragged him on board a Carley float.

The *Wales* was hit on starboard by all three of the last torpedo runs.

'Abandon ship! Abandon ship!' called Phillips.

Fifteen hundred crew clambered – however they could – to get off. Ropes, nets, sliding down the *Wales* forecastle onto the rocking deck of the *Express*.

'The *Vampire* and *Extra* [Electra] quickly moved their positions and started rescuing survivors,' said Capt Iwasaki. 'Commander Thomas Phillip sent a message to the Japanese bombers – "Give us 30 minutes and we will rescue our men in the sea." One of our commanders then replied to the British ships saying "Our mission is completed. Please continue rescuing the survivors".' He ordered bombers to stop attacking them and kept flying over them.

'A large bouquet of flowers was dropped on the spot where British seamen who had fought so bravely were now sleeping quietly,' reported Col Tsuji, ever looking for poetic PR opportunities.

It was a victorious day for Iwasaki Yoshiaki and his fellow flyers of the 22nd Air Flotilla. Despite his own plane having its left wing on fire, they headed back to base in Saigon. 'The radio kept updating us on the situation. "Repulse completely underwater." We all shouted "Banzai" in the airplane when we heard the good news.' Iwasaki landed safely moments before his left wing burned down to nothing.

**

The *Express, Vampire* and *Electra* were full to the gunwales with 90 rescued officers and 1195 men from the *Prince of Wales*, and 42 officers and 754 men from the *Repulse*. Forty-seven Allied officers and 793 crew had been lost in those Kuantan waters that day.

Survivors were ferried back to the Naval Base, arriving around midnight in torrential tropical rain to welcome hot urns of steaming tea. A fleet of ambulances and trucks then ferried the serious cases to The Alex, and those with dental and other relatively minor problems were sent off to the Singapore General Hospital.

'When the war started in Malaya we were acting as a base hospital,' said Tom Smiley, 'though of course when *Prince of Wales* and *Repulse* went down, we accepted a lot of casualties.' Smiley saw this as the first real test of the island's military hospital readiness – and felt that they were not prepared for what was till then its busiest period.

'I'm getting all the surgery I wanted and able to be in charge of operations way beyond my four and twenty years!' he wrote to Elizabeth. 'Colonel Taylor is going to apply for me to become a graded surgeon which I can't quite believe.' This was a huge fillip given Taylor's pre-war eminence and experience.

'We had a large amount of cases from the *Prince of Wales* and *Repulse* – some of them were frightful burns – otherwise mostly foreign bodies in various parts including the abdomen. I've got all my wards in one special ward and I'm having great difficulty in giving them plasma because they are burnt all over their arm and legs and it is impossible to incise there. I've had to study *Gray's Anatomy* to find out where the superficial veins are and then find a suitable place. I've got one case who is absolutely terrible – nearly all of his epidermis well gone. Two or three of them are from Belfast and I've to tell them when I was last there and make up a story about Linfield beating Celtic or vice versa depending on their names!' he says, talking of the local football club rivals.

The next part of the letter is a 'canary in the coalmine' test of the Allied effort against the Japanese up-country. 'Casualties from Humphrey's unit are beginning to arrive and I'm beginning to worry about him as there is no word from him.' Humphrey Thomson was of course in Khota Bahru, one of the main Japanese landing sites in Malaya. He was killed in action there on 14 December. 'I'm so sorry that I didn't write yesterday but I only had a few hours sleep and fell asleep with my clothes on. We have had all sorts of cases – we had ghastly burns, fractured legs, particularly *os calies*, femur – quite a few tibias, perforating wound of the abdomen or chest. The chests are easy – we just leave them alone – perforating wounds of the abdomen are terrible and mortality rate is very high. Fractured skulls and ruptured membranes are very commonly assisted and large lacerated wounds involving any part.'

Indeed the doctors were perplexed. A *calcaneous* (heel bone) fracture is a rare thing, accounting for only about one percent of fractures, according to the American Academy of Orthopedic Surgeons. But here were hundreds of men presenting with this injury at once. Then it dawned on them – it was a 'deck slap' injury caused by the sailors jumping from one raised deck to another, or sliding down the ships' hull and hitting the keel, or even jumping across from one ship to another. Many required urgent surgery. For some it was weeks before they could put weight on their feet again, meanwhile resting immobilized. For others, it would take three months of immobilization to recover. Three months that would put them in the path of much graver danger.

Those that did recover were then assigned to *HMS Sultan*, the naval land base at Sembawang, ready to be reassigned to other naval craft as and when required. As it turned out, they soon would be.

The next morning Churchill was awoken by a call from Sir Dudley Pound who had vigorously opposed his half-baked Far East Fleet idea. 'I have to report to you that the *Prince of Wales* and the *Repulse* have both been sunk by aircraft. Tom Phillips is drowned.'

'As I turned over and twisted in bed, the full horror of the news sank in on me,' Churchill wrote.

'We then realized we were up against the 1st XI,' said David Wilson who was dug in with the Argyll and Sutherland Highlanders in northern Malaya.

A MAULING IN MALAYA

'They knew they caught us with our bleeding trousers down.'

8 December 1941. The first shot fired in the Malayan campaign was arguably by a Thai policeman in Singora (present day Songkla) who took a pot-shot at a moon-faced Japanese officer who was insisting on a right of passage near the Malayan border. The first shot grazed his arm, the second passed his hip. That officer was Col Tsuji. Within hours the anti-Western Siamese government flipped and flopped and Japan had the free run of the country for the next nearly four years without any further shots being fired.

Whilst one of the bloodiest phases of action for both sides, within a few days of landing in Malaya, the IJA 18th Division had firm control of the Kota Bahru, Gong Kedah, and Machang Airfields on the east coast of Malaya. Meanwhile, having landed in southern Siam and crossing quickly over to the narrow isthmus to the west coast, the battle-hardened 5th Division threw themselves hard against the 11th Indian Division at Jitra, which included dispatch rider, Dick Lee, soon to celebrate his 22nd birthday.

He ferried urgent messages, orders and instructions around for the likes of Maj Gen Murray-Lyon and his right hand man, Maj McIntosh. 'Our main job was reconnoitering with the brigadier, looking for new places for the guns to pull out and come back to new positions.'

However, the division – expected to hold out for three months – was mauled in around 15 hours in the Battle of Jitra, leading to Murray-Lyon being unceremoniously dumped and replaced by Brig Archibald Paris (who would later die hallucinating in a raft adrift off Sumatra). Tsuji meanwhile was leading from the front again, in a captured black car, occasionally using his revolver against defenders, and even stopping at bridges to slash, with his sword, at demolition charge wires left in place.

'The Japanese were very well prepared, you've gotta give 'em full marks,' Lee conceded. 'They were very well organized. They knew they caught us with our bleeding trousers down. "We've been there 90 years, who dare tread on our toes?" That was the British attitude. The Japanese lined it all up and they knew when to strike. Our trouble was being bombed all the way,' said Lee. 'Anything moving on the road they'd be swooping down, machine gunning, or these Zeros used to carry a couple of light bombs, mostly machine gunning, and they'd have a go.'

**

Another big problem was beginning to manifest itself: the morale of the Indian regiments. The 44th Indian Infantry Brigade was beginning to splinter and fracture. They were not directly engaged in the landings, but had borne the brunt of softening up by heavy shelling before and during the main landings by the IJA.

The Japanese played a masterful hand of propaganda. Leaflets dropped on the Indian lines targetted the Indians with messages along the lines that they were just the cannon fodder for white man's ambitions in Southeast Asia. It played to many Indians' feelings that they were second-class citizens even in their own country's army, and certainly their quality of life in Malaya was nothing to fight for. They were encouraged instead to defect, and they would be set free. They could hand in their arms and uniforms and in return get a pair of shorts, a bowl of rice, and – importantly – their freedom.

It transpired that 32-year-old Capt Mohan Singh Dib, of 1/14th Punjabs – who surrendered upon the fall of Jitra in the earliest days of the conflict – had switched sides and thus became the notional founder of the Indian Nationalist Army (INA), according to Maj Fujiwara Iwaichi, who had been active in Malaya and Burma pre-war with Indians in exile and Indian expatriates. These men were pressed immediately albeit informally into action, still wearing British-issued uniforms plus a Japanese armband, fighting against their former comrades down the Malayan peninsula and on to Singapore.

The British infantry and Allies mocked the Indians as weak and feint-hearted – with nicknames like 'the Galloping Garwalis' attributed – but by the end of World War 2, Indian soldiers had been awarded 30 VCs. So they cannot collectively be accused of cowardice or incompetence, although this was to prove a critical factor in the events around The Alex.

**

Penang fell on 17 December followed by a violent spree of looting and raping by men of the IJA 5th Division. Yamashita was incensed by such behaviour, summarily ordering the execution of three solders involved, and the close arrest of their battalion commander, Maj Kobayashi, for one month. Turns out that Kobayashi was a classmate of Tsuji's and Tsuji pleaded to defer the sentence because it would be bad for morale. Not only did Yamashita uphold it, but he made Tsuji personally announce the sentence.

'I want my troops to behave with dignity,' wrote Yamashita in his diary, 'but most of them do not seem to have the ability to do so. This is very important now that Japan is taking her place in the world. These men must be educated up to their new role in foreign countries.'

**

Yamashita was by now already confident of a Japanese victory in Malaya. So much so, he signalled Tokyo that the 56th Division, earmarked as a strike force for Operation Singapore, could be deployed elsewhere.

The IJA blitzed further southwards, regardless. Yamashita acquired a headache in the form of the arrival by train from Bangkok of Lt Gen Nishimura Takuma, commander of the Imperial Guards, whom he considered arrogant and aloof. Mutaguchi and Matsui, his other divisional commanders, he knew very well. Even though Tsuji was quirky and eccentric, his planning capabilities were well and widely acknowledged. But Nishimura, he was another matter altogether.

**

Capt Smiley, in a reflective mood, found the time to pen a rather heartfelt letter to his fiancee that evening: 'I wonder will our sense of values have changed after the war? I used to have such clear-cut ideas as to what I'd like to do and how exactly I should react. Somehow I just don't know the answers anymore. Oh Beth I feel so sad and lonely. The situation is getting worse. The Japanese are gaining day by day. The poor men in the ward – some of them with their faces all burnt trying to join in the Christmas carols. It really is pathetic and they look to us for moral support when I just want to break down and cry. It is a sad, sad life and war is a terrible thing.

'I wonder do these chaps suffer mental agony? I wouldn't feel it so much if I knew that they might recover but sadly many will be maimed for life and many won't make it. I feel so depressed although I try to be as cheerful as I can with them. I've got black rings around my eyes and look very tired which of course I am. I'm scared stiff of falling down on my job. I don't think I should have been given such a responsible job. I just don't feel that I have enough experience and all the time I'm thinking and wondering whether I'm doing the right thing or the correct procedure.

'The sort of operations I'm being asked to do usually take years of experience. If I let anyone down I'd feel really dreadful. I know if you were beside me you would give me encouragement and I'd feel your faith in me. Oh Beth isn't war so awful? The number of lies I have to tell when a patient asks me if they are going to be alright – I always say, "Of course, Laddie".' Well I must go to bed while the going is good. If we can find the courage and strength to get through this we'll both agree it was worth it in the end.'

**

A few days after Christmas the Army appealed for nurses. 'Bishop Wilson said one of us should volunteer, and I agreed to go.' Which is how Edith Stevenson found herself reporting for day-duty at The Alex on 28 December. 'Army work was a big change. I had to take orders instead of giving them,' she found. Then there was the sheer volume, laid out in four rows of beds and stretcher beds: 'In all one hundred and forty patients in my two wards, which normally were intended to accommodate forty.'

And her patients were of an altogether different nature: surviving sailors from the sunken ships in the British other ranks ward. 'Some had lost arms or legs, others had been severely burned,' she noted. As she was not part of the QA quorum she felt there was another subtext at play: 'The regular nurses were resentful of outsiders, trying to make them uncomfortable,' she said. Fortunately she found a sympathetic ear in Matron Jones. 'She was the kind of lady one instinctively liked and respected.'

Assisting her were a couple of orderlies, one older man and a younger one, 'a mere boy of sixteen.'

**

And so 1941 became 1942. The Allied lines were retreating ever southward under the onslaught of the Japanese. The Battle of Slim River was a decimation by the IJA. Simultaneously, more Japanese poured into the top of Malaya. 'They were dying to get out of Canton and go to the front to share with Takumi Detachment the glory of taking part in the fight of the century,' concluded Henry Frei, who would later intimately interview many Japanese troops of the crack 18th Division.

7 January saw its HQ Regiment, including Mutaguchi, 114th Regiment and 55th Regiment, sail from Canton to Singora, a journey that would take two full weeks. They were dissuaded from landing at Mersing in northeastern Malaya due to strength of the defences and mines laid there.

Meanwhile Allied reinforcements were pouring into Singapore. 'All the training of the division had been for Libya and for this purpose the treeless districts of Scotland and Wales had been chosen,' said Capt Hugh Pilkington, who had just arrived with 6th Royal Norfolks aboard the *Mount Vernon*. Their ominous arrival date was 13 January.

Aboard that same vessel were the 198th Field Ambulance, 5th Royal Norfolks, 135rd Regiment Royal Field Artillery, 2nd Cambridgeshires, 287th Field Company Royal Engineers, and various other regiments and corps which formed the 53rd Infantry Brigade, part of the British 18th Division.

Pilkington at least had the advantage of having lived and worked on a rubber plantation in Malaya for 11 years previously, and lectured the men on what he knew. 'It was therefore difficult to expect men trained in such surroundings to plunge successfully into some of the thickest jungles in the world.'

Many reinforcements and replacements came directly from India. But if their predecessors hadn't acquitted themselves too well, this batch was *very* raw material. Forty-five percent of the replacements for the 44th Indian Brigade were brand new recruits, mainly aged 17, possibly 18. They'd gone through hurried basic training with old rifles. But none had ever seen a tank before, not even a British one, let alone faced-off against one. And because they were freshly minted, their English literacy was probably not up to the levels required, a problem exacerbated by their British officers not being proficient in Urdu either.

If the new recruits were unsure of what they'd got themselves into, they were left in no doubt by those who'd already experienced Malaya. 'The impression they created on the new arrivals was one of despair and futility,' said the CO of the 4/19th Hyderabad Regiment, whose jungle-trained men had still copped a shellacking at the Slim River.

The reality of war was about to hit Stan Sharpley hard. 'One of me best pals, I was 50 yards off him when he got shot by the Japs. And there was another young Lancashire lad, Titch Crosston, and our CO had given us orders to withdraw because the Japs were coming over Yong Peng Heights. So I said to Titch, "Get on the back of this bike, we've got orders to withdraw". "Oh, I'll be alright". Never saw him again.' The rifle companies of the 2nd Loyals were decimated.

Percival directed the 53rd Brigade to Yong Peng because the Japanese had launched an all-out assault on the line at Muar on the west coast. Transferred under Malaya Command, the 44th Indians under Ballentine were in the firing line and not acquitting themselves too well against their experienced foe. All the new arrivals, including the 198th Field Ambulance crew, were to go. With the Australian Brigade sent to Muar to hold the line, it was expected that they might have at least a week or ten days to acclimatize, retrieve equipment, and prepare for the battle. Not a bit of it. They were on the move. On the double.

On 16 January, Tokyo Rose, the phantom voice of Japanese propaganda, was received loud and clear on radios, including that of the Australian General Hospital, in Johor. 'The voice told 13th AGH to be out of their buildings by 26 January as they were needed by the Japanese at that time.' How spooky to know that the enemy knew specifically where you were. What's more, within nine days the wards were dismantled and the whole hospital evacuated back to St Patrick's on the east coast of Singapore, amid the din of guns and bombs nearby.

'We crossed the Johor Causeway about 12 o'clock,' noted Pilkington heading north. They reached the road leading to Bukit Pelandok. Briefing over, Pilkington took his car down to the village of Medan, a Japanese mining town, some two miles away for a recce. 'On my return a Jap fifth columnist sharp-shooter had a crack at my car but a burst from a tommy gun stopped that nonsense. We were continuously bombed from the air and machine gunned. It was always a great relief when the Jap bomber formations, generally 27 at a time, passed us by and we heard them bombing someone else. Once while walking down the road a Jap fighter passed over my head, the pilot very kindly throwing a couple of hand grenades at me which burst harmlessly in the swamp.'

**

Someone who was far removed from all these developments was Robert Loveday, still languishing in Changi. He had appealed after his court martial sentencing, but the original sentence was upheld, and the *London Gazette* carried the official announcement of his cashiering on 16 January 1942.

Japanese internees in Changi, mainly civilians rounded up at commencement of hostilities, were shipped to India, where they'd remain inside the crumbling confines of Delhi's Purana Qila (Old Fort) until an arrangement was later made, after occupation, with the Japanese to return them to Singapore.

'In January, they started bombing during the day,' said Dr Constantine Petrovsky of the Japanese making the most of their air monopoly. 'You could predict their timing – 10 o'clock in the morning they used to come.'

Meanwhile life was fairly normal for most. 'We used to go to the movies,' recalled Dr Yeoh Sang Aun. 'Theatres still ran but didn't run the late show, so movies ran till nine or 10pm only. Sometimes there were air raids walking home in the dark. It used to be like seeing fireworks in front of your eyes, and it was an enjoyable sort of session.'

**

Ethel Mulvany took time to motor the *Honora* round the channel, but not before stocking it with food and filling its tanks, and heavy-heartedly handed it over to the Navy.

Another nurse reported for duty at The Alex. Brenda Macduff had trained in the UK before being posted to the Batu Gajah Hospital in Perak, northwestern Malaya. Her boyfriend back in Lancashire asked his friend out there, lawyer Ken Macduff, 'to keep an eye on her'. He did more than that – they quickly fell in love and married! He joined the FMS Volunteers as a private and, when the Japanese attacked, they both evacuated south to Singapore. Her experience was warmly welcomed here, and he would also go into action on the island.

**

On the morning of 22 January 42-year-old Lt Col Ian Lywood retired behind the lines, suffering from acute malaria. Pilkington gathered it was 'to rest with the transport column some ten miles back.' Both would be in for a surprise reunion shortly. Another of the Norfolks, Pte Arthur Haines, a 25-year-old former grocer from Wiltshire, also came down with malaria soon after landing in Singapore on 13 January, and was confined in The Alex, as was Bill Warbrick of 11th Indian Division, the 21-year-old additionally wounded in battle.

Malaria was a terrible scourge, also hobbling 2nd Lt Philip Paxton Harding, so off to The Alex he went. He had been in the 19th

Hyderabad Regiment before being attached as a captain to Dalforce (the recently-created Singapore Overseas Chinese Anti-Japanese Volunteer Army under Col John Dalley and other mostly retired British officers of the Straits Settlements Volunteers). 'Dalley's Desperadoes' they were nicknamed, being a last-ditch – though highly motivated – pastiche of local defenders.

19-year-old Pte George Britton of 2nd East Surrey Regiment was shot through both knees by a sniper after they ran into a Japanese patrol near Kampar. Cpl Bill Riley carried him to a truck, and he was sent on to The Alex.

**

The following day a broader withdrawal of all British forces to Ayer Hitam began. 'The Japanese Imperial Guards were fearless, skillful and magnificent fighters,' said Capt Pilkington.

They had certainly made their presence felt around Muar, Bakri, and Parit Sulong, the full extent of which would not be known by the Allies for some time, and feeds into the mystery of the events surrounding The Alexandra Massacre which would unfold within just three weeks.

Tsuji, who had recently survived his car running over a landmine, saw this battle around Bakri as a desperate 'war of extermination.' And the Imperial Guards *did* want to make a name for themselves, because prior to the Malaya campaign they were unblooded since fighting the Russian decades earlier, unlike the 5th and the 18th. However this 'very good division' – as Yamashita called them – wasted no time in spilling a lot of innocent Australian and Indian blood in sickening fashion in the aftermath of the battles around Parit Sulong. 110 wounded Australians and up to 40 Indians were tied together, locked in small rooms, teased, taunted and tortured, machine gunned, burned alive, then dumped in the river. Earlier a further two hundred Australian and Indian PoWs were beheaded and dumped in a mass roadside grave, just north of Parit Sulong.

In that horrific slaughter, it was Lt Kurabayashi's 2/7th Coy Imperial Guards who had captured the prisoners, and crammed them inside a Public Works Department building adjacent the bridge. All entreaties for water and medical assistance were ignored, indeed ridiculed. Curiously in one instance at Parit Sulong, a Japanese officer was dressed in full British officer uniform, minus the hat.

A short way south, Father Rogers and his 2/10th Ambulance were around Batu Pahat, while the violent and brutal Parit Sulong events raged. 'The Japs were push, push, push and our fellows had to draw back all the time because they were cut off.' The situation was getting critical.

'The colonel called me up one morning and said you are going to have to do a different job. Take all the unit papers and things, take one of the ambulances, and get out because we are going to get overrun if we're not careful. So I did.' He beat a hasty retreat to the 'ants nest'-like busy-ness of Singapore, ending up in the Cathay Building, where a convalescent ward was established.

Similary, Bert Gurd and his 198th colleagues were ordered south to Singapore from Singam Rengam, with new orders for the unit to be co-located at the Alexandra Hospital with the overwhelmed 32 Coy team running it.

**

And into the IJA mix now came the veterans of China, 18th Division under the hard-living, heavy-bodied, bull-necked Mutaguchi, who had landed in Singora.

Now, even at full strength of three divisions, the Japanese were at a numerical disadvantage of roughly 2:1 in Malaya.

Never mind bicycles, the 18th Div were to truck their way down the 1000km peninsula at high-speed to be in position for the decisive battle of Singapore. But one slight problem – there were no trucks available. Chief tactitioner, Tsuji, was soon on the phone to logistics teams of the other divisions in Johor, threatening them that they would have to go it alone if they did not give up their trucks for this collective cause. 300 trucks instantly materialized.

**

By midday of 23 January the withdrawal was in full swing. After waiting all night for a Singapore-bound train, the 198th Field Ambulance finally reached their new home base, The Alex, late that Friday afternoon. 'It is indeed impressive,' Bert Gurd felt. 'Here, we are in clover – *dhobies* to clean our boots, make our beds, Malayans to run the NAAFI, showers, radio, good food well served – what more could we want?' He felt optimistic, and that better things were just around the corner. Their arrival swelled the staff count in the hospital to about 180, according to QMS Lunt.

**

'By 3 o'clock all bridges had been demolished forward of the Causeway,' said Capt Pilkington. But cut and run as they did, the Japanese remained in hot and close pursuit. A mortar shell landed just 10 yards from a slit trench in which Pilkington sheltered. 'The concussion ruptured my right eardrum and seriously damaged my left.' But shortly, he'd have even bigger problems. 'About 5.30 the Japs were reported assembling in a hollow about 300 yards away and I went round making final dispositions to beat off this attack. While doing so I spotted a Jap sniper up a tree at whom I had a shot. I think I hit him as I saw him sag over a branch. But unfortunately standing up to take this shot over the grass exposed me to a Jap sniper in the rear who put a heavy bullet through my shoulder from the back. The shock spun me round and for a few minutes I thought I had been hit through the chest as all the pain was in the middle of my back where the muscles had been wrenched out with the force of the shot.'

His CSM Edward Kelf dragged him back. 'He helped me to the rear where Maj Cubitt ordered me back at once. I had no pain although I was, unknown to myself, bleeding dangerously down my back. I was joined by Capt John Stratford and another of my warrant officers, CSM Noel Twiddy, who had been detailed by Maj Cubitt to help me back.'

CSM Twiddy 'almost literally carried me this distance' as Pilkington was by now beginning to feel the effects of heavy blood loss. They still had to safely negotiate the next ¾ mile through the anti-tank mines. 'By now the pain was almost unendurable, but unfortunately the morphia I carried for myself and my men for such an emergency was in the breast pocket underneath my web equipment. Attempts to try and get at it, which meant moving the arm, had to be abandoned as I could not stand the pain.'

Stratford and the two sergeants made use of an abandoned bicycle and wheeled their captain a good half-mile. 'I was transferred from the pushbike to a stretcher under the care of the RSM and Cpl Cole of the RAMC tried to stop the bleeding. By now I was drenched with blood but he could do little to stop it. Capt Edward Griffiths, our transport officer, had collected a spare ambulance and was driving. This arrived almost immediately. The brigadier and John Stratford wished me good luck and I was loaded in.'

And so, drifting in and out of consciousness, he was triaged and passed through the full hierarchy of the Field Ambulance system. Large mugs of cocoa and brandy were then produced, and duly consumed, before he was loaded into yet another ambulance. 'Just before I left I was given more morphia and half a glass of neat brandy, with the result that the ensuing journey to the Alexander Base Hospital (sic) was like riding on a cloud. My orderly lit cigarettes for me, some more brandy and all was well with the world and when I was taken out of the ambulance I was merrily drunk. I shall always be grateful to the Australian Red Cross for what they did for me then.'

And so he was admitted to The Alex on 24 January.

'The officers' wards were at the top of the building on the fourth floor, open on both sides with broad balconies and very cool all day. I was whisked off in a lift and met at the top by a cheerful Scot sister who conducted my stretcher, feet foremost to her ward, which is no way to treat a living being! A big argument then took place as to the best method of getting me into bed, aggravated by my remark that I weighed 16½ stone without the masonry. However four orderlies and three sisters rallied round and I was lifted most gently into bed, but the movement was enough to start the pain again but more morphia quietened it down.'

**

The general situation was clearly beginning to play on medic Len Knott's mind, enough for him to dash off a quick telegram to his beloved Joan, saying: 'Please don't worry. My thoughts are with you. Fondest love, darling.' Which of course would have made her *immediately* worry.

**

Pilkington described the next ten days as living 'in a world of fever and pain with happy hours in between when I had morphia and sleeping draughts.' A barricade was erected around his bed to stop it being accidentally jolted. 'Anything I wanted or asked for was brought to me and the VADs were most charming and helpful in such little matters as lighting my pipe, cutting up my meals and, during the first few days, feeding me. I was thoroughly spoiled and enjoyed it. Clean sheets three times a day. Powdered and washed like a baby morning, evening and night and all the choicest tit-bits they could give me. For the most part I lived on M&B and Dr Clark's blood pills, liver, chicken and milk, with as much beer and whisky as I wanted. The latter always amused me as the sister would come round, carefully measure out the prescribed amount and then come back half an hour later and leave a bottle and some soda by my bed in order to get me through the night.'

Sister Currie took particular care of him, sitting on his bed administering liver to get his blood count up. But the fever did not abate, and a further operation was necessary. 'I had to be supported in a sitting position by two sisters, while the plaster was cut away, the wound cleaned and bandaged. On my return journey I found that a new bed had been prepared for me. A wooden fracture bed with an ordinary mattress, on top of which was a big Dunlopillo one with linen sheets and huge feather pillows. This mattress and pillow accompanied me on all my other travels, even to prison! I have never known anything so comfortable and veritably floated on air.'

To make things even better, he was soon put on the outside by the doors so that a continuous draught blew over him. 'Always afterwards I was given a large glass of brandy.'

Thick bath towels were placed under him, changed every

four hours because of the suppurating fluids. 'The surgeon, Maj Webster, was kindness itself, and I cannot say how much I owe to him. The sisters were one and all super-humanly kind, and particularly Sister Currie, Sister Bowers and the night sisters. The VADs, amongst whom was Betty Wiseman, loaded me with fruit and anything they could find.' Pilkington knew Wiseman from his pre-war life as a rubber planter in Seremban. 'There was one VAD who had been a children's nurse all her life and, not having any children to look after, took me over!'

**

Not only were patients flooding southwards, but surgeons too. Lt LE Vine was a health officer up-country with the Colonial Medical Service before being posted to the Malacca General Hospital (shared with 10th Australian General Hospital) before that was evacuated and he was moved to the Tan Tock Seng hospital then also immediately assigned to The Alex as a surgical specialist. He rated the surgical equipment here as 'good and with few deficiencies. But there was no neuro-surgical equipment in the command,' he lamented. The X-ray equipment under Maj Bull he rated as 'satisfactory' but noted there was no portable X-ray apparatus. Another thing that concerned him about the intense situation was that 'no specialist in any British or Indian hospital had a deputy really qualified to act for him when he might be off duty.' Or worse.

Elsewhere at the hospital, a group of eight Queen Victoria's Own Madras Sappers and Miners got to work behind the hospital, tasked with constructing an underground bomb-proof operating theatre, which would connect to the existing operating theatre block on the ground floor.

**

Still the Singapore media persisted in talking up the situation. 'The newspapers were frankly very optimistic,' said Benjamin Chew. 'But right to the last moment they still wanted to boost up our morale to say that we could beat them back.'

On 24 January Mutaguchi issued the order: 'We will depart

tomorrow for the front, in 50-truck convoys, each leaving at hourly intervals from 10am sharp.'

Little did Fergus Anckorn and fellow 55th Brigade troops aboard the *Westpoint* know, they were steaming towards a fateful date with Mutaguchi's men within a few short but intense weeks. Anckorn was hospitalized on board the ship with pharyngitis, but attended a rousing ship-board rally by Lt Col James MacKellar: 'Go in there and kill! Kill! Kill!' recalled Fergus of his address. 'There's no bloody cricket now ... just slash their throats and kill the little yellow bastards.'

On arrival in Singapore on 26 January, Fergus and company were billeted at an abandoned housing estate near the Tanglin Barracks.

**

Hugh De Wardener, of 4th Field Ambulance, RAMC, was sent northward against the flow of traffic, to a jungle aid station, located in a native hut in northern Johor. 'We had equipment, drugs, dressings. When the ambulances came in, you took a look, and unless you thought you could be useful, keep moving. I was mainly part of a retreat, which is no great fun. At an aid station you have to be alert because if people are retreating and you don't know about it, you suddenly find yourself on the front line,' he laughed nervously. His aid station copped the occasional mortar. 'Which is no joke. The decision not be be brave anymore saves your life,' he laughed again. 'We were being mortared, and I thought I'd better get into that slit trench – got in, and the next mortar landed right next to a tree I had been standing by. I remember that with great clarity: stop trying to be brave.'

The 36-year-old De Wardener was an interesting character born to French and American parents. His father fought for the US Army in WW1, meeting his mother – a singer studying her craft in Paris – after he stayed on in Europe after the war. De Wardener was born and raised in France, only learning to speak English when he was eight years old. Despite this he attended St Thomas' Hospital Medical School and became a British citizen. He met and married

Janet (who would be the first of four wives) in 1939, joined the RAMC, and now found himself in Malaya, subjected to some shelling and mortaring. 'I heard a terrible crack outside the walls, then I smelt cyanide. "Hey what are the Nips up to now?" and I thought I was going to die in the next few seconds. But then I was still alive, and I thought, that's funny, so I looked over the wall and it was an almond tree, which smell of cyanide.'

Sometimes he had no choice but to be brave. De Wardener had gone to collect the wounded one evening, near a bridge which was to be demolished. 'We went over the bridge, two or three miles ahead of the front line,' he said, when something rather surreal happened in the middle of the Malayan jungle. 'Someone recognized my voice in the dark: "That's the goalkeeper from Number 4",' referring to the Field Ambulance team he played for.

Soon after, he was in his ambulance traversing the main east-west road. 'We came across Nips trying to ambush us. I was armed with the driver's revolver and my own .45 revolver, a very big gun, so I leant out of the window rather like a Wild West,' he laughed, 'and I shot at these people with my two guns. I felt a bit silly.' The Japanese shot back at them. ' I was lucky and I was saved by the mattresses in the back.'

Perhaps one of those he triaged was determined dispatch rider, Dick Lee, who was in the firing line around Yong Peng on 26 January.

'That's where I got blown off the bleedin' bike,' he recalled, returning to HQ from visiting a gun site. 'I got dive-bombed. They was after an Australian convoy coming in the opposite direction, and these little Nip light bombers saw what they wanted to 'ave a go at. They dived down, and it all happened so quickly. The first bomb blew me across the road, and I hit the first bleedin' truck. The Aussies had come to a standstill and they were all jumping out, down ditches on the side of the road. I was doing about 40. Bleedin' lucky I was. I went up into the air, came down on my back. While I was lying there, the second one came down and dropped a bomb. And I looked at my leg and saw all the trousers fly open and the muscle was hanging out of my thigh, a lump of shrapnel had gone into it. I didn't feel no pain. But I'm lying in bleedin' oil and petrol, looking up at the bleedin' BSA bike smashed up like a concertina.'

The Aussies soon picked Lee up and had him on a stretcher, putting him in the back of one of their trucks. 'They took me back to Johor General Hospital, because it wasn't far from there. I had the right leg broken and the other leg had shrapnel in the thigh. I was black with all the oil and blood. I remember saying to the nurse on the stretcher, I'm apologizing for the bleedin' state I was in, so dirty. She said, "Don't you worry about that. When you wake up you'll be as bright as a new pin!"'

**

Around this time Denis and Ethel Mulvany's house at Pasir Panjang was bombed to rubble. They were fortunately not home, both working inhumanly long shifts. Bharose escaped harm, and came to present them whatever chattels he had salvaged, such as their wedding certificate, honeymoon photo album, and a few books. They moved, further north on the island, to reduce Ethel's commuting time.

'Our new house was on a hill where the view of the battle was a deadly looking business. We were standing watching it, awed by the horror of the deadly, gruesome beast, war.' She suggested Kuki take Brutus and try to make their escape across the Causeway back into the Malayan jungle.

Ethel (or 'Mul' as most knew her) now focused on her work at 1st Malaya General Hospital (MGH) in Johor, collecting the wounded brought down by train in her ambulance, a former pig lorry now emblazoned with Red Crosses: 'There's no train that pulls so heavy as one that's full of boys that are wounded.' She never got used to the shocking sight of bodies, blue-lit by the security night-lights, oozing vital fluids on the floor of the trains. One night, a badly wounded Japanese prisoner lay on a stretcher side-by-side with a wounded Ghurka. All prisoners were disarmed, but *kukri* knives were not taken from Ghurkas because of its symbolism to them. The Ghurka made to reach for his knife and stab the Japanese, but Ethel leapt into action and grabbed it. 'It's Red Cross. We're for mercy, you can't kill this boy.'

Apart from men 'torn to ribbons' other sights were simply abhorrent: Ethel saw dead bodies flattened on the road by tanks. 'Squashed flat, with old bits of khaki over some of them. The stench of all this is beyond man to lay words to.'

Ethel described these shifts as working 'like a mad person, like a hen with its head cut off and didn't know enough to fall down, robots going and going and going.' Their secret was Benzedrine, a new 'upper' wonder-drug, issued nine small yellow tablets at a time, to her and the medical teams. 'Who am I but a Benzedrine-loaded ambulance driver?' she once asked in a moment of existential angst.

As each train came in, she'd feel the pulses. 'You picked up the ones whose pulses told you "Take me, I'll live".'

Irish Sister Mary Cooper, QAIMNSR, and New Zealander Lilian Tompkins were on the staff here, the latter hoping to nurse in India one day. But she had visited her mother in Malaya several years earlier and stayed on to nurse there. When hostilities broke out she was directed to report to the Johor General Hospital. Margot Turner was putting in the hard yards too, especially as the Japanese noose drew tighter and the order to evacuate was made.

At one point she retired beneath a billiards table with another nurse and a bottle of brandy from the medical stores. 'After a number of swigs, the barrage became nothing like as terrifying,' Turner recalled.

**

'I woke up the next day, it was late in the afternoon, and there wasn't a soul,' remembered Dick Lee. The hospital had been evacuated, patients loaded onto vessels to carry them across the Straits to Singapore. 'I was the only one in there. I woke up in pain then because I had one leg in plaster and one was up in a cradle sort of thing. All the beds had been stripped of bedding, no mattresses or nothing. Just bare beds. And I could hear talking in the corridor. I shouted out for a nurse. She came in with a doctor and he looked at my bleedin' toes sticking out the end and they'd put the plaster on a bit tight and my toes were a bit blue. He says, "We'll have to cut the plaster down until we get you across the Causeway and they put a new one." By cutting down the plaster he released the tension on me leg and it was into the ambulance, across the Causeway to Robert Barracks. Because everything was such a bleedin' shambles you know. And Roberts Barracks was turned into a temporary hospital and the Red Cross flags were flying everywhere.'

Roberts Barracks was part of the impressive military infrastructure on the Changi side of Singapore.

En route, perhaps in that same convoy, Ethel Mulvany was in the lead ambulance ahead of a convoy of trucks. Ahead of her was a motorcycle dispatch rider. Suddenly the rider was headless, decapitated by a wire strung across the road. The bike rode itself another eighty feet, weaving drunkenly before toppling into a ditch. Pulling over, shrapnel started to fly. Two wounded soldiers were shoehorned into the front seat next to her, one a sergeant with a wounded arm, leaning over her. Under fire, he now caught a bullet in his jugular, warm and sticky blood spurting over Ethel's left side. She felt a sting in her calf. She clutched it, not realizing a sniper's bullet had narrowly missed its mark, just grazing her.

She gunned the ambulance as fast as she could. As it turned out, that would be her last ambulance trip, and she then joined the team at The Alex as a VAD.

An anonymous member using the pen-name 'Scipelai' of the 198th Field Ambulance penned a poem entitled *The Last Ambulance Over the Causeway* which is at once desultory yet speaks to the determined optimism of the RAMC corps to achieve their mission at all times, at all costs.

Lurching, reeling, spirit sinking,
Wounded, bleeding all the time,
Tattered clothes still smeared with slime
From the rivers dank and stinking,
Limbs already racked with cramp,
From the clinging, hungry swamp.
Escaping from the foe he's fearing
Through the jungle, fever blighted
For days his friends he'd never sighted
Until we found him in the clearing,

Fainting in the tropic heat
Half collapsing at our feet
Speed with the safety darkness lands,
Speed with him South, to meet his friends.

One advantage of a retreat was pointed out by De Wardener: 'As you are retreating it gets easier and easier to deal with the wounded – shorter distances and more people to deal with them.'

**

Mutaguchi had now arrived in Kuala Lumpur, and met with his commander, Gen Yamashita, whom he knew well and they enjoyed a cordial relationship. By 30 January, his 18th Division reached Johor, having endured six days of 180km per day bouncing around in the back of their borrowed trucks. The massive supplies of fresh ammunition they brought with them were most welcomed, too.

Mutaguchi had a pleasant reunion with his two detachment commanders, glad to see them alive, and braced for the final showdown. They had enjoyed an unopposed landing in the northeast, and saw no action along the east coast until Mersing and Kota Tingi, a mere 60km north of Singapore.

Constantine Petrovsky, now with his Field Ambulance No 4 in Singapore, could sense the noose tightening: 'In Malaya, you could already see the Japanese from this hill, when you climbed it, the Japanese going through the jungle. And there was a clearing and a Japanese flag suddenly comes out.'

A Japanese flag flew atop the Sultan of Johor's palace, used by the Japanese to survey across the Straits.

'An indescribable feeling seized their hearts when they laid eyes on Singapore, a short distance away,' said Frei based on his interviews with Onishi from the Imperial Guards, and others. 'The island for which they had come all the way from Manchuria.'

This *blitzkrieg* had defied everyone's expectations. Goering himself had advised the Japanese strategists that Malaya would take five divisions 18 months to conquer. Instead their three divisions had done it in just two months, covering averagely 20km per day, whilst fighting two battles and repairing four bridges each day. The lean and mean Japanese infantry had averagely lost 10kg from their frames in that short time, too.

Fortress Singapore was now besieged, with the Japanese waiting to pounce across the Johor Strait and finish off the job Mutaguchi and his men had arguably started way back in 1937. The sharks could smell blood.

THE BATTLE FOR SINGAPORE

'Sort of struck me then – what a waste of bloody time.'

1 February 1942. They issued all Japanese troops heading for the Southern front a substantial 18-chapter pamphlet that had been cobbled together by Col Tsuji and his team of researchers at the military research department in Formosa (Taiwan). They had tapped sea captains who'd sailed around Singapore, medicos familiar with tropical diseases, Japanese residents of Singapore and Malaya, aerial photographers, and military logisticians. Basically, anyone who could add some insight and dimension as to what lay ahead.

It was called: 'Read This Alone – And the War Can Be Won.' It trod a resolutely moral line, preaching for 'strong, correctly behaved and self-controlled' troops who 'demonstrate to the world the true worth of Japanese manhood.'

It started with the nationalistic purpose of the campaign, talking about how the 800,000 white colonizers had oppressed the 450,000,000 natives of the Far East. 'Once you set foot on the enemy's territories you will see for yourselves, only too clearly, just what this oppression means. Imposing, splendid buildings look down from the summits of mountains or hills onto the tiny thatched huts of natives. Money squeezed from the blood of Asians maintains these small white minorities in their luxurious mode of life.'

In a section called 'To reach the land is victory' it intimates that once they go ashore, victory is in the bag. 'Our opponents are even more feeble than the Chinese Army and their tanks and aircraft are a collection of rattling relics.' And on it went about how to feed horses, how to scale ladders from landing craft, and other essentials of kirimoni sakusen (blitzkrieg) style warfare.

Singapore was a prized scalp for the Japanese. And so it became a red-misted three-way race between 18th Division, 5th Division, and the Imperial Guards, as to who would enter Singapore town first and claim the prized Union Jack from the top of Fort Canning. Yamashita was the master puppeteer in this, playing his generals – Mutaguchi and Matsui – against each other to extract the most from them and their men.

**

Even at this last gasp stage the Allied reinforcements poured onto the island. Lt Col Sainter's 6/1 Punjab regiment arrived at the Seletar Naval Base, seeing tropical jungle for the first time. John Wilson, part of their number, recalled: 'From there we went by truck to Tuas on the west side of the island and took up posts at Tuas Village.'

Dr Yeoh, at the General Hospital, around 5km inland from The Alex, said, 'Being at a hospital we thought we really ... we were safe.' But on the first day of February a crater about 20-30 feet across was blasted into the area behind their tennis courts. The Kandang Kerbau Hospital and Tan Tock Seng Hospitals also each received a few shells, and the 13th AGH – operating out of St Patrick's at Katong – had part of its roof blown off.

Hugh de Wardener, assigned to Tan Tock Seng – an open-sided hospital for the elderly – noted: 'By this time, the RAMC had been concertinaed down – the regimental medical officers were on top of the hospital, so what's the point of us? In Singapore there was a huge amount of medical staff all compressed down.' A peptic ulcer was adding to his own woes.

A never-ending and ever-expanding influx of wounded warriors from Malaya, 10,000 by some estimates, was causing congestion and chaos in field stations and hospitals across Singapore. The 'No Vacancy' signs were up. Makeshift wards mushroomed in unlikely places such as the Raffles, Goodwood Park and Adelphi hotels. And schools such as St Joseph's Institute, Raffles College, Oldham Hall, Nan Wah and Chinese High School found themselves press-ganged into medical service. The Cathay Building and even Stan Sharpley's much-loved Union Jack Club shoehorned space for beds and stretchers.

The so-called Guns of February would build to a crescendo over a week to soften up the island before the Japanese crossed and landed. And the Japanese air force made the most of their monopoly of the skies.

'Each day the air raids intensified,' noted Edith Stevenson at The Alex. 'They were almost continuous during daylight.' She was moved to working night shift at this point. 'We had no idea how many patients to expect or what their condition would be. There were four rows of stretcher patients from one end of each ward to the other, 140 patients in my two wards, which normally were intended to accommodate 40.' She also made another interesting assertion: 'A large Red Cross was laid on the hospital for the bombing planes to see, but because we were near an ammunition depot, the planes had an excuse to bomb the hospital.' This large cross on the lawn was stitched together by one of the newly arrived nurses on the team.

Petrovsky was in the firing line out in the field. 'We were bombed for a period and they got our supplies hut. I was nearby and was lifted up in the air. It was a funny sensation, like you're flying, then bang on the floor. But no injury. And the order came in: "You can join Alexandra Hospital Military Hospital". That was 1 February. So we said, "Oh that's good, at least we'll have the protection of the Red Cross". Because in the Field Ambulance you're not supposed to mark yourself. Because we knew the end of Singapore was coming. Where else can you fight? In water? We can't.'

On arrival at The Alex, they were tasked to look after casualties. 'There were wounded lying in corridors, those big wards were full up, and beds near the other beds, and operations going on all the time. And suddenly late in the afternoon, an order comes: "Move away". They were pushing us somewhere else. And they sent us to the Cricket Club grounds, to open up immediately, to be active. And we opened up that building as a hospital and operated that day. Shelling was continuous, even you could hear machine guns going on. Only was the question: How long we're going to last?'

'Life began to be more rosy,' felt Capt Pilkington after 10 days recovery in the hospital. 'I was gradually able to use my free arm and legs and do a lot of little things like feeding myself and lighting my own pipe.' Also cheering him up was having the familiar – if 'undoubtably very sick' – face of Col Lywood in hospital with him, who was suffering from malaria. Lywood was his commander, a square-faced man with a determined gaze and a heavily receded hairline. From him, Pilk learned that his 6th Royal Norfolks had been cut-off on the Ayer Hitam-Batu Pahat Road, and had to hack their way through jungle and swamp to reach the coast, where naval destroyers ferried them back to Singapore.

Maj Cubitt of the Royal Norfolks was also admitted with a poisoned hand.

And an RAMC private, HP Futter, was transferred from Changi to The Alex in an ambulance, the orderly in which was Pte Arthur Collins. 'During my tour in Malaya, I was nearly always depressed,' said Futter, 'and rarely spoke to anyone for long, I had little interest in things.' Futter was admitted to a mental ward set aside for the seriously shell-shocked and delirious, where the shaven-headed Pte Josiah Thompson, who had transferred from a field hospital, was the orderly.

'In the hospital black out restrictions were rigidly enforced,' observed Pilkington, as 4 February showed no let-up in the bombings. 'No lights were allowed to be used after 7pm. All dressings etc had to be done with a pocket torch. Theoretically all doors of wards had to be kept closed, but the sisters refused to allow this owing to the heat. My door across which my bed stood was never closed except when I was having a dressing renewed. The night period in hospital – 6pm to 6am – was a nightmare for everyone, as it is impossible to keep cheerful for twelve hours night after night when you are lying in pitch blackness.'

Pte Frank Hill sent off a telegram to his wife Nancy in Kirkburton that day: 'All well and safe, please do not worry.' It would be his son's second birthday in just under a month. It would also be the last contact she ever had from him.

**

That night Japanese planes attacked the Empress of Asia – a large liner which held trans-Pacific crossing speed records – in the coastal straits due west of The Alex. The following morning the 2nd Loyals observed the large liner on fire, limping out to sea. What a helpless feeling to know their fellow 5th Loyals and others were on board that flaming vessel, plus much of the British 18th Division's materiel.

Fortunately, around 1000 were rescued by the HMAS Yarra and other smaller vessels and reached Singapore safely, although there were numerous burn victims. Among these was DF Carse, a steward, who was admitted to The Alex and put into Ward 17.

**

That night artillery bombardment opened up for three days on the western part of the island where the hospital and so many key military installations were co-located.

'The hospital was first bombed about 5 February, no one being hurt,' noted Pilkington. 'Next morning at dawn it was bombed again with a few minor casualties.'

The Allies were still posturing for a concerted defence of the island. Fergus Anckorn and his 118th Royal Artillery unit were ordered to fetch their guns and ammunition from the Polo Club, while the Allied defences were digging in on the northern and north-western shore lines.

The Allies had the numbers on their side. But perhaps they were mentally outplayed already, if the sentiments of Gunner Francis Docketty are representative: 'The high-ups seemed to be in such confusion. We wanted to have a go. We was all in Singapore. Here's me in me tiddly uniform, that is blue with red stripes and all the tiddly bits on it, walking into the Cathay Cinema, when the Japs were in Johor Bahru. And the disgusted looks on some of the Chinese faces who was fleeing the peninsula. Sort of struck me then – what a waste of bloody time.'

**

And the time was now. The balloon went up for the attack on Singapore on 8 February. The main assault took place west of the Causeway, with 5th and 18th Division IJA lying in wait opposite Kranji and Chao Chu Kang.

At the signal 300 boats of all types roared across the narrow straits to the mangrove swamps of Sarimbun on the other side. All hell broke loose. Some creeks at Kranji were filled with oil and set alight, burning the attackers' boats and their invading crews. It was

'Abikyokan' – the worst level of hell in Buddhist parlance – and the Imperial Guards suffered badly.

Mayhem and carnage ensued in the darkness. 'They kept riddling bullets over and we kept ducking,' said Docketty. 'You couldn't see the Japs ... they were in the trees around you, they were shooting off these pop guns, only tiny bullets ... Titch Holland, a tiny bloke, was going to toilet behind a rubber tree. A Jap grazed the top of his penis with a bullet, so he had to rush off and get it bandaged up. Only a little bloke about 5'1' so he's running around with this thing bandaged up, and pestering our commander Maj Alfred Glossop for a letter to take home to his wife to say it was a bullet and nothing else!'

Then the familiar pattern of falling back and reforming was adopted. 'They told us to go back, we stuck our defenses in one line across Singapore, and we made a stand there,' he says of the short-lived Jurong-Kranji line.

The IJA 18th Division had landed, opposing Australia's 22nd Brigade between the Sarimbun River and Berih River. 'The divisional boundary from the time of landing extended south and west of the Bukit Timah Road,' said Maj Gen Takeda, Chief of Staff of 18th Div.

There was stiff competition between divisions, causing ruptures among the commanders, and a competitive rivalry between the troops themselves. They hated to see the other divisions or regiments had arrived somewhere ahead of them. Yamashita and Nishimura were barely talking after a heated stand off in which the former regretfully told the Guards they 'could do whatever they liked.'

18th Division's aim was to get to the strategic Tengah Airfield, around 6.5 km south of the Causeway, by early morning. Thereafter to take the Jurong highlands, then Bukit Timah (Tin Hill), Singapore's highest point at just 164m. Then Singapore city lay dead ahead. Slightly held up, the 13,000 elite troops claimed Tengah Airbase around lunchtime.

Commander Ito and his men of 2/55th Regiment were immediately on the move: 'We advanced through the western sector of the island, towards Bukit Timah Road, and heading west again from there towards the Pasir Panjang Hills.'

As 3/114th Regiment attacked the west side of Tengah, a massive British counter-attack caused critical Japanese losses, including a company commander and five other officers.

'The 18th Div HQ unexpectedly encountered some British – possibly Australian? – soldiers who were fleeing from the defensive positions,' reported Staff Officer Hashimoto. 'I heard some explosions of hand grenades and screaming voices. Due to a fragment of the hand grenades, Gen Mutaguchi got wounded on his chest while staff officer Ino lost his legs. Another officer got killed and the other was seriously wounded on his jaw. Mutaguchi got a fragment in his left arm, but continued commanding the division. Gen Yamashita heard that Mutaguchi was wounded and soon sent him some wine at the Division HQ.'

Tsuji recalled 'I saw bloodstains on the left shoulder of his coat surrounding a small hole where evidently a bullet had penetrated.'

The forked road at Bukit Timah allowed the Japanese to affect a classic pincer movement, with 18th Div assigned to branch west, right to Reformatory Road, Kent Ridge, Pasir Panjang and Keppel Harbour.

**

Two sticks of nine bombs each were dropped across the buildings of The Alex that day. 'The Sister's Quarters were demolished while several slight casualties were caused in the mental wards,' noted Pilkington. 'It was terrible to hear the howls and shrieks of the shell-shocked patients every time a gun went off. Underneath my bed, with its two mattresses and my lovely plastered body, was a refuge for all during the air raids and it always surprised me the number of people who could get under it in an emergency!'

The orderlies of the 198th worked around the clock amid ever-increasing bombardment. 'I remarked: "I've got a birthday Sunday – if I live so long",' joked 35-year-old Bert Gurd.

And by the night of 8 February, it was feeling like an emergency. 'Miss Jones asked for eight nurses to stay at the hospital in the event of occupation by the Japanese,' said Edith Stevenson.

'She said there was a list on the dining room notice board. I went to supper, Miss Jones had put her name at the top of the list.' Edith added her name. The list was soon full, and she headed to her ward. 'A patient handed me a revolver. "Take this, sister, don't let the Japs get you". I refused his kind offer for I had no idea how to fire a gun and if the occasion had arisen I am sure I would have been a menace.'

Pilkington noted that, 'for the first time all the big guns of Singapore and Blakang Mati opened up at night on the enemy positions. The noise of the guns and the explosions of their shells, many of them 15", was almost unbearable, while the concussion on my eardrums drove me nearly frantic.'

Heavy artillery fire was was being exchanged in both directions, and on the first day of the attack, a large shell blasted a 20-30 foot crater behind the tennis courts of the General Hospital in Outram Road.

**

9 February. Fergus Anckorn's artillery unit was now based east of Kranji, protecting the northeast coast. 'The crescendo coming from the west increased and also spread around to our left. We were prepared for everything in battle except for one thing: the noise. The noise paralyzed you. In the middle of the night, the skyline to the northwest of us was glowing red and bright yellow, signifying some kind of tumult.'

He noted an absurdity amid all of this: 'Figures appeared, darting from trench to trench. Unbelievably it was local Chinese selling ice cream! They were taking no notice of the fighting and thinking only of the business they could do.'

Percival sent up two Indian infantry brigades to reinforce the Australian 8th Division, and ordered a counter-attack to retake the Jurong-Kranji line. But this was patchy at best. 'The whole position was a poor one,' Australian commander Gordon Bennett recalled as he walked the lines, 'poorly sited and platoons most extended. True the 44th Infantry Brigade was weak.'

Companies pulled back in incoherent hap-hazard fashion, many of them not informing neighbouring units nor their higher commanders. Bennett had no knowledge of condition of troops west of Bukit Timah, a large swathe of the battlefield.

Pilkington had a grandstand view of all of this from his top-floor ward: 'From my bed I had a splendid view of the battle of Singapore. I could watch the docks and town being bombed, the fighting on the hills, on the island, and in fact there was little that I missed.'

**

John Wyatt, of the East Surreys, was not alone in having a hell of a time. 'Around 14:00 the Japanese attacked us in force but we were able to hold them back for several hours with a series of bayonet attacks. It became even worse when I took a piece of shrapnel in my shoulder. I was in great pain, and also a seeping ulcer on my leg.' A volunteer was called to take him back. 'I managed to struggle out along a jungle path helped by Pte Nicholls.' Within a few minutes they arrived at a truck carrying 'Chinese Communist Guerillas', he was helped on board, Nicholls disappeared back into the jungle, and the truck set off for The Alex.

'I was appalled at the sight that greeted me,' he said of struggling down from the truck outside the main entrance of the hospital. 'Hundreds of injured civilians and soldiers were lying around on the ground, and I found it difficult to weave my way through the mass of moaning humanity.'

A doctor inside the main entrance soon triaged him and sent him upstairs. 'On the first floor a medical orderly, Cpl Sinclair, allocated me a bed, gave me some pain killers, and bandaged my throbbing ulcer, but he was unable to remove the shrapnel from my shoulder.' Sinclair was assisted by his Eurasian wife in this.

**

The IJA 18th Div had already battled their way to a point southeast of coveted Bukit Timah by late afternoon of 9 February. Mutaguchi was pleased enough with this, but typically Col Tsuji stirred him up by saying, 'You know, 5th Division just overran Bukit Panjang.'

'What? Then we shall overrun Bukit Timah tonight with me at the very front!' countered Mutaguchi. Tsuji then immediately went to Gen Matsui of 5th Division and played him off Mutaguchi. Matsui immediately ordered a breakthrough on Bukit Timah without waiting for nightfall.

Mutaguchi gave his troops a memorable pep talk this day. It was memorable because he rarely spoke to them en masse – in fact not in the five years they'd been in battle together. But he was fired up by the fact that tomorrow was Kigensetsu, the anniversary of the founding of the Japanese empire by Emperor Jammu 2602 years earlier. 'Tonight we carry out our final attack on Bukit Timah. Soldiers I pray for your battle success.' Pithy but powerful.

In their revved state, 18th Div's 55th Regiment advanced all the way to a southern three-way crossing, essentially the trunk road towards Singapore city itself. But they were scolded – that was 5th Division's territory. But where was 5th Division? Attacking Bukit Timah from all sides, per a last-minute change of battle order. 55th Regiment couldn't understand the rebuke.

'It was all very competitive,' explained Henry Frei, who interviewed these soldiers in their own language. 'Everyone wanted to be the first into Singapore. Why hand the finest morsel, the Grand Finale, to 5th Division? It made no sense from a military strategic point of view. If they dashed ahead, Singapore was theirs for Kigensetsu.'

Indeed, at this speed, it was highly possible they could cleave the Allies' defences and take the city for the Emperor Jammu's anniversary. But the dizzying speed and brazenness of battle tactics caused some officers to exhort Tsuji to move their headquarters further to the rear as it became more volatile and vulnerable. 'By heavens, no!' he responded. 'If we have to die, let us die together in the front line. We'll never get another such opportunity.' Maj Gen Okamura, the 18th Division ordnance chief, was killed in action on Bukit Timah.

**

Gen Percival responded by creating a close defensive perimeter, encircling Kallang, Paya Lebar, Thomson Village, Adam Road, Farrer Road, Tanglin Halt and Buona Vista to the west. The 2nd Loyals moved up to Ayer Rajah Road, and their armoured cars and carriers moved from Gillman to the junction of Ulu Pandan and Reformatory Roads, facing northwest.

The 44th Indians became quickly demoralized under incessant attack on the ground and from the air. 'The brigadier called the colonel and said we were more or less surrounded by the Japanese and we were to withdraw from Jurong to the West Coast Rd, and good luck to all of us,' Dr Robert Brown of 6/1 Punjabs recalled, in his light Scottish accent.

**

11 February 1942 was a 'Black Day' for the 44th Indians facing a full-frontal attack by the Japanese 18th Division. They were 'young, untrained, badly equipped, led by inexperienced British officers and VCOs' and the brigade simply 'melted away' according to witnesses.

The Indian regiment retired down the West Coast Road to Pasir Panjang, where they rallied briefly, before reaching Reformatory Road, and rendezvousing with the 2nd Loyals. But their retirement caused a gap in defences between the 1st and 2nd Malays, allowing considerable infiltration and progress by the Japanese. The 2nd Loyals found themselves surrounded and engaged in close-quarter bayonet contact.

As 18th Division waited for the 5th Division to catch up, the Australian 22nd and Indian 44th was able to regroup on the defensive line just south, and the big guns of Fort Siloso on Blakang Mati opened up onto Bukit Timah.

**

Petrovsky's field ambulance moved to a hill adjacent The Alex, the railway and the ordnance depot. 'That's where I saw my first casualty.' They were set up in a tent that was overrun by the Japanese, killing the Allied patients. 'He hid under the table and survived,' his son, Dr Nikolai Petrovsky, would tell me. 'He never spoke about that, he was probably embarrassed.' Embarassed, but alive, and assigned once again to The Alex.

John Wilson's company was ordered across the road to higher ground. 'There was an armoured car preparing to go up the road and we co-ordinated with that, and we made a hundred yards or so before we came under machine-gun fire.' Japanese machine gunners were on the hillside barely 100 yards away. 'Deployed the company in positions to cover this fire,' he recalled in cool measured tones. But Wilson and two others were hit. 'I hobbled with the help of a medical orderly to an ambulance not too far back.' And off to The Alex they went.

'A lot of people seemed to come in at the same time, ' Wilson noted of The Alex, who had to hand his pistol in at the entrance, where curiously their weapons were stockpiled. 'A doctor came to me while I was lying in the stretcher and decided the correct treatment was to put the leg in plaster, which meant I was immobile. I was then carried upstairs to the first floor.'

A lot were being sent off, too, in evacuation ships at this time. Bert Gurd worried whether his best friend (a medic only referred to as 'B') would return from each of these excursions to the dock. Pilkington was unlucky to not score a berth on one, although the team was trying on his behalf to get him away. Pte HP Futter, from the mental ward, was put on a ship – possibly the hospital ship Wu-Sueh – with 350 other patients, and evacuated to Java.

The riverboat Wu-Sueh had been procured by the Navy as a last-resort option, because it was actually a Chinese boat, with only a five-foot draught and not considered suitable as an ocean-going vessel. But it was hastily repurposed and pressed into service.

Those in The Alex considered not able to return to active service within two months were triaged and given priority for evacuation to Java, India, and ultimately to the UK. Lt LE Vine, only recently commissioned into the RAMC, was to escort this large shipment of seriously ill and wounded away from the island.

Sgt E Dronfield, RAMC, was also working on board the Wu-Sueh, and chatted to Cpl Jack Lewis. Dronfield was stationed at the hospital before being posted away but had still been back on duty to that unit often, as recently as early February. 'Lewis was among the party who brought them down.' He ascertained that 'the Military Hospital Alexandra was still functioning and had no casualties among its staff, but there was heavy fighting a few miles away at that time.' Dronfield left Singapore safely with the ship that day. Lewis would be dead within four days.

Sgt F Dartford remembered on this day also seeing Cpl James McEwen. 'He was employed on theatre duties in Alexandra Hospital. I personally spoke to him and wished him "Cheerio!" before I left for my own duties on Hospital Ship 44.' McEwen, too, would be dead within four days.

The Wu-Sueh made it through to Java safely, and then onward to Ceylon without interference from the Japanese. A couple of days later, Sgt Evans of RAMC 32 Coy was also lucky enough to be posted away from Singapore, thereby avoiding the terrible fate of his colleagues.

**

The Japanese were held up by stiff resistance and although they had captured their second key objective, Bukit Timah, their supply chains were getting run ragged – getting supplies and ammunition across the Straits was under-estimated in their planning.

But despite injuries, setbacks and supply issues, that night 18th Div were able to move west in the direction of Reformatory Road. 'The soldiers were dead-dog tired, some even dozing as they walked in pitch black, the darkness broken only by fireflies,' according to Frei.

Robert Brown's Punjabs received orders to push on to Reformatory Road 9th milestone, that road (now Clementi Rd) named for a boys' home that once occupied it. 'We started pulling out very late at night. I took the HQ Company out and it was very eerie because we knew the Japanese had infiltrated across and no shots were fired. Eventually we met up with others in the brigade and we went in a straight line down the West Coast Rd through lalang, rubber trees, and eventually reached West Coast Rd in the early morning, quite exhausted.'

This was just about 6km from The Alex, and 'as the fighting got closer, casualties poured in to the hospital,' according to Edith Stevenson. Even their own mess came under fire that morning. 'Planes flew over, strafing the Sisters' Mess. After the raid was over, there were holes through all the walls of every room on that floor, and most of the windows were shattered. There was a Bofors gun near the mess which may have led the enemy to think it was a legitimate target. They made the home uninhabitable. A phone message came from the hospital ordering all nurses to leave at once and take with them any valuables and immediate necessities. On our way to the hospital we saw Japanese snipers in the trees. They made no attempt to injure us, maybe showing respect for our uniform.'

Apart from the small suitcase Edith carried – in which she had her nursing certificate and some jewellery – she never saw any of her possessions again.

**

Matron Jones wrote in the middle of the battle for Hong Kong to the Matron-in-Chief, Far East: 'We are all very distressed about our people in Hong Kong ... I feel they will get fair treatment if only because of their training. Unless the Japanese have made great headway within the last eight years, they will appreciate anyone with medical or nursing skills, and they have so far spared anyone wearing the Red Cross.'

But she had since received via cable more details on the attack on St Stephen's Hospital. The news from Hong Kong was both grim and grisly, and certainly only contained a very brief summary of what actually transpired there:

For Hong Kong the balloon went up at 08:00 on 8 December (usually lucky numbers for Chinese feng shui followers), mere hours after Pearl Harbor and Malaya were surprised. With the rapid over-running of the island, a makeshift hospital had been set up in St Stephen's College at Stanley, at the back of the island.

In a murderous, rapacious move, leading up to Hong Kong's surrender on Christmas Day, the 229th Regiment had rampaged through the hospital, bayonetting and shooting patients, medicos and orderlies, and raping European and local nurses and VADs.

'Under orders from the Japanese a huge bonfire was built for the burning of the bodies,' according to Maj James Anderson, RAMC. Wood from nearby trees, doors and window frames were hurled onto the fire to keep it burning big and long enough to complete the gruesome task.

And little did anyone know, those 'grubby little men' – as Matron Kathleen Thomson described the Japanese victors – would feature further in this story because on 4 January 1942, with Hong Kong in the bag, the IJA 229th Regiment shipped out to take part in the Battle of Java and the Dutch East Indies campaign.

**

'Before we left Singapore we were told what had happened to nurses who had remained in Hong Kong in December 1941,' said Edith Stevenson, still at The Alex, 'and we had no reason to believe our fate would be any different.'

Just four nurses were now on duty on nightshift to cover the whole hospital and around 900 patients.

**

11 February. Lim Bo Seng, the brick-maker and biscuit impresario, slipped from Singapore and travelled to Sumatra with other Chinese community leaders, making their way to India. There he would later recruit and train hundreds of secret agents through intensive military intelligence missions in China and India.

Clearly the local Chinese knew the game was up for Singapore and they would be prize scalps for the Japanese. But the remaining territory would not be easily won over, proving to be some of the hardest-fought yards of the entire campaign.

'Fierce British counter offensive encountered with heavy shelling from the south side of the island, and the line was not advanced more than 1000 metres,' said Takeda, calling for postponement of their big advance.

Yet the Allies' artillery adopted a defeatist mindset. The Buona Vista battery, near the junction of Ulu Pandan and Reformatory Roads, boasted two 15-inch guns. But these were blown up in the early hours by the retreating Allies. (The Japanese managed to salvage and relocate one for their own use later.)

The Australian 22nd dug in stubbornly, but the 44th Indians were on the retreat again, retiring now to Buona Vista Road. Maj Rex Beale, a 41-year-old Aussie from Victoria, was injured around here and carted off to The Alex. The line was disintegrating once again. Capt Brown of the Punjabs had just arrived at the 9th milestone in the hilly Reformatory Rd area. 'We didn't really know who was on our right and who was on our left. All hell broke loose, some Japs had got down there in the rubber trees. We couldn't see anything, neither could they, but they were firing from the trees. We suffered quite a few casualties as dawn broke.'

The Japanese fighter planes buzzed in at tree-top level, machine guns chattering. 'They killed quite a number of soldiers. We were coming a little despondent, because it looked obviously like the Japanese were going to take the place. But how long no-one knew.'

Brig Williams shortened his front as Japanese troops now advanced with their tanks down the Jurong Road, Ulu Pandan Road, and Reformatory Road, rumbling unencumbered over barbed wire, trip wires, and even mines.

'The noise,' recalled Capt Brown. 'Everything happened so quickly. There was movement on the hill in front of us, and we couldn't see who it was. There was movement in the lalang, so I put a burst of machine gun into the ground above them to see what the response would be, and it was Australians. They let me know in no uncertain terms they were Australians and not Japanese,' he laughed.

'Just as we were moving off, there was a Japanese soldier up one of the trees and he started firing. The Japanese didn't worry too much about the soldiers – they went for the officer every single time to try and knock him out. This soldier got me and I rolled down the hill to the bottom. He got me through my right knee and all my ligaments were torn. I just fell down again, my knee had no support.'

An Indian Artillery captain assigned to Brown's regiment was nearby.

'What's wrong?' asked 24-year-old John Mortimer.

'I've been hit.'

'Can you come up the hill?'

'I can't walk!'

'Try crawling up and I'll give you covering support.' As the Punjabs gave him covering support, firing into the trees, he crawled up. 'Where the sniper was I don't know but he kept firing at me,' said Brown. 'I had to drag myself up the hill, and bullets were coming to the left and to the right, but none more hit me, I was so thankful.'

At the top of the hill, three Aussies came over and dragged him by the shirt over the crest. 'One of them put a field dressing on my knee, which was bleeding very profusely, and they carried me down to the battalion HQ at 9 Mile, where an ambulance was just about to go off with four wounded, and they put me on the floor.'

As he was being put in the ambulance, a few of his Indian officers and men stopped fighting to come and farewell him. '"Sahib! Sahib! We hope we see you again, that you are alright". That's the way they liked the British officers. They stopped the war! My colonel was even standing there waving his pistol telling them to get back to fighting, and then they did go back fighting.'

Mortimer himself was 'knocked off' (not fatally) around half an hour later. Many others were shot 'many of them lying wounded and carried down to ambulances,' according to Brown.

The frontline was moving so quickly, that by the time a dispatch had reached the strategic planners in Fort Canning, their response was out of sync with the new reality of the battlefront.

As Brown's ambulance hurtled towards The Alex nearby, bombs were falling around it. 'I remember one, two, three, four bombs. They weren't intended for the ambulance – no plane's going to waste four bombs for an ambulance – but we swung over to the left, and then to the right. There were some even more badly wounded than I were, screaming with pain.' With that, the ambulance screeched to a halt. 'Dr Young [possibly Pte Robert Young, 32 Coy RAMC] who'd been in the front of the ambulance, came back and gave us all a shot of morphia.'

Around 10:45 they reached the Alex. 'It was chaos in the casualty,' said Brown, 'with what seemed to be hundreds of people lying on the floor.'

He was not exaggerating. On this day 500 patients, including Dick Lee, were also transferred across from the Selarang Barracks Hospital on the coast at Changi, which had been bombed.

Signalman Lt Walter Salmon had been wounded by a mortar round, and was placed in a bed in the Officers' Ward on the top floor, along with others such as George Britton of the East Surrey Regiment.

Cpl Pease was one of many recovering from the Empress of Asia incident. The scene at the entrance to The Alex stunned him: 'What chaos!' said the corporal. 'Wounded men, blood, piles of discarded clothing and equipment, all stained with blood and soil, and the smell was terrible. As fast as each ambulance drove up and discharged its load, another was waiting to do the same thing. Nobody can imagine it unless they've seen it – what a ghastly, horrible, filthy thing it is ... men with legs torn off, heads split, and intestines ripped out. I cannot put into words the sights and sounds, the screams of agony.'

Despite all of this, Brown says the nurses and sisters were doing all they possibly could. 'They were excellent, and we all just lay on the floor and had to wait until eventually a nurse came and gave me another shot of morphia which made me rather dopy.'

It was a few hours before he was finally put on a trolley and taken to the X-ray department, where Maj Bull X-rayed him. 'He looked at the film, and said to me: "That's the luckiest shot I've ever seen, it's gone right through your knee but hasn't split any of the bone, but it's torn all the ligaments. And that's why you can't stand".'

He was wheeled back to casualty, knee heavily bandaged. 'Then I was taken up to the top floor of the hospital, the third floor, and I was on the balcony there for an hour or two waiting for a bed in one of the wards.'

Apart from horrific battlefield injuries, other patients died from more prosaic causes. One young soldier had tetanus following a pelvic injury. Sister Stevenson wanted to pass a catheter but he was 'too modest' to allow this initially, and died. Another died from smallpox. 'When the doctor asked if he had been vaccinated he replied, "No, my mother didn't believe in it".' Stevenson wished she could've spoken with both these mothers and let them know they died with bravery. 'Everything happened so quickly it was impossible to keep records of names and addresses.'

Recovering from an appendectomy was 27-year-old Gunner Edward Furness, from the 5th Field Regiment, RA. Welshman Harold 'Hal' Hart, a 31-year-old Signalman with the Malaya Corps Signals, was admitted to The Alex, suffering from, of all things, hemorrhoids.

Other cases showed altruism for those they considered worse off. 'An Australian soldier who had lost half his tongue refused injections for pain, he could not speak but nodded his head,' recalled Stevenson. 'He suffered in silence and was a real hero.'

**

Sister 'Tommy' Lucy was a former nursery school teacher – born in China because her mother was a missionary there before starting the Tanglin Nursery School in the Cameron Highlands, Malaya – had signed on as a VAD at The Alex. Bill Warbrick, wounded and suffering malaria, discovered that some of his belongings, including his money, had been pinched from his bedside locker. Sister Lucy took his cause to heart, apparently becoming distressed. 'I told her it was nothing to get upset about. She tried to get me on the last hospital ship out.'

Capt Smiley continued his tireless and inspiring rounds, as noticed by Sister Stevenson: 'He was working day and night continuously in order to save lives. One night I asked him what I was to do about pain-killing drugs. "Sister, do what you can to relieve pain. If the men ask for an injection, give them morphia. I do not have time to write on charts, so use your own discretion. The poor souls will have worse fate if the Japs come." His consent made it possible to give relief to the dying.'

Pilkington dished out kudos to the nurses such as Stevenson for their own heroics: 'The hospital was continuously under shell and mortar fire with the doctors and sisters working in steel helmets. A direct hit from a mortar bomb on the tiled roof above our ward caused one of the sisters to raise her helmet and say, "Come in. You needn't knock so loudly – I'm not deaf!"'

They eventually found Brown a bed in another ward nearby. 'There were eight other officers in the ward and I was in a bed in a corner. Later on, when I was able to walk, I went up to have a look at the ward where I'd been, and thank goodness I had moved because there was a hole in the roof where a three-inch mortar bomb had come in right above the bed.'

'It's quite an experience, the passage of their shells sounded like being in a tunnel when an express train hurtles through,' said Walter Salmon. 'The Japs' counter-fire was falling short and penetrating the roof of the hospital, showering us with debris.'

Salmon and Britton were among those moved to the dining room, the latter carried down by an orderly. Here they were laid into makeshift beds set up under the dining table, which was set with a long tablecloth that reached to the floor, and stacked with loaves of bread. Britton remembered himself and Salmon, plus L/Cpl Fred Shenstone and Pte Arthur Haines there.

'I estimate the total number of officers in this canteen to be about 40,' said Salmon. 'Both sides of the room had swing doors, like the entrance to saloons in Western films. So you could see under and over.'

**

High-level discussions were held. Brig Stringer, Commander of Medical Services for Malaya Force, recommended to Percival that Singapore should capitulate immediately for fear of an outbreak of malaria and other diseases related to lack of hygiene. As for the hospital itself, orders were received that the hospital was not to be evacuated.

Some precautionary measures were taken, and a group of NCOs were ordered by Command HQ to destroy all wine and spirits in the stewards' stores. The mixed emotion of hurling bottles of brandy and whisky down from the first floor verandah can only be imagined.

And, based on the Hong Kong experience and the general concerns that the Japanese were not observing the Geneva Convention, Matron Jones called a meeting for all nurses. 'We knew this was evacuation,' recalled Stevenson.

Newly-wed Brenda Macduff was in that meeting, too. 'The colonel in chief and matron interviewed all the nursing sisters personally and gave us the chance of leaving that day on a ship. They intended to only keep a skeleton staff. I decided to stay, as did many others.' The majority voted to stay on.

The wife of Geoffrey Rogers, the doctor who simply wanted to save some money and start a family GP practice in the English countryside, was among those who decided it was best to leave now.

'At 7pm that very night, the nurses who were anxious to leave embarked on the SS Empire Star,' said Stevenson. 1254 people, many of them troops, plus around 25 nurses from The Alex, crammed onto the refrigerated cargo ship with cabin space for just 16. Despite some bombing and some RAF casualties on-board, they made it via Batavia to Western Australia.

Among those on the Empire Star was Sister Olive Donaldson. Olive had been a nursing sister at the Malacca General Hospital and had married Dr William Donaldson from Aberdeen, who was the Medical Officer at the Malacca Agricultural Medical Board, in the middle of 1940. He'd also served on the Straits Settlement Volunteer Force Field Ambulance for the past four or so years, and now found himself stationed at The Alex.

Also, 'Tommy' Lucy had secured a berth, although one imagines rather reluctantly and with mixed feelings. The VAD had only a few days earlier married Peter Lucy at the Singapore Cathedral. He was now fighting in his armoured car with the Volunteers just a few miles northeast somewhere. Her true measure was how upset she had been by the casualties in the hospital. But also the personal interest she'd taken in Bill Warbrick's plight when his money was stolen. 'Before leaving she tried to get me out on the last hospital ship out, and when she couldn't, she left some money with a doctor to give to me to help me out,' Warbrick remembered. The nursing spirit exemplified.

'We had our last slap-up meal as by the next morning the hospital had been completely deserted by its Chinese and Eurasian staff, who had bolted to a man,' said Pilkington.

To a man, perhaps, but not to a woman. You see, whilst the QA nurses had been evacuated, what is lesser known is that a few VAD nursing volunteers had stayed on. One was Major – promoted to temporary lieutenant colonel the day the Pacific War started – Mulvany's wife, the ever-feisty ambulance-driving Ethel. 'She was a tough customer,' recalled Torbit. 'This is the same girl who'd broken her right arm playing softball sliding into home base, and went on to write and pass her exams with her left hand the following week.'

Another was Betty Fernandez, the locally born Eurasian wife of Cpl Jack Mace. Gallantly she had volunteered to stay and tend the wounded, no doubt also wanting to be in proximity to her RAMC husband.

The third was also a local lass, the daughter of a wealthy local jeweller married to 24-year-old Cpl Edward Sinclair, RAMC, who was ward master of the upper medical wards. His Eurasian wife, described as 'very attractive' by John Wyatt, had come into the hospital to support the flood of wounded from the west coast warpath raging around them.

In hindsight, not the smartest move positioning your hospital adjacent key military targets as they'd done in this western cantonment.

ALEXANDRA HOSPITAL MAIN BUILDINGS, 1942

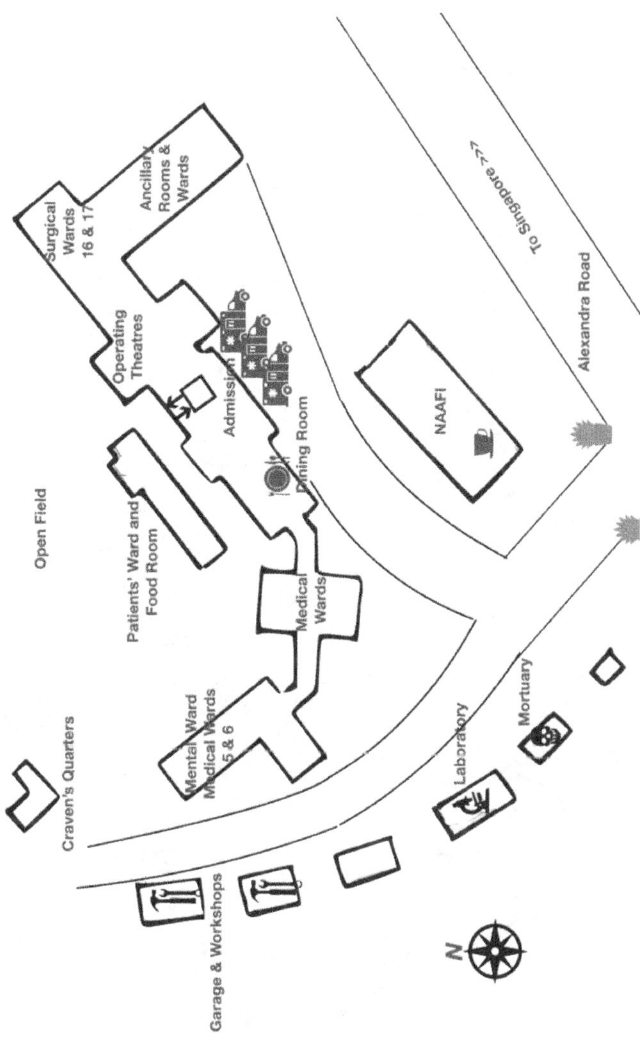

IJA DIVISION MOVEMENTS, FEB 1942

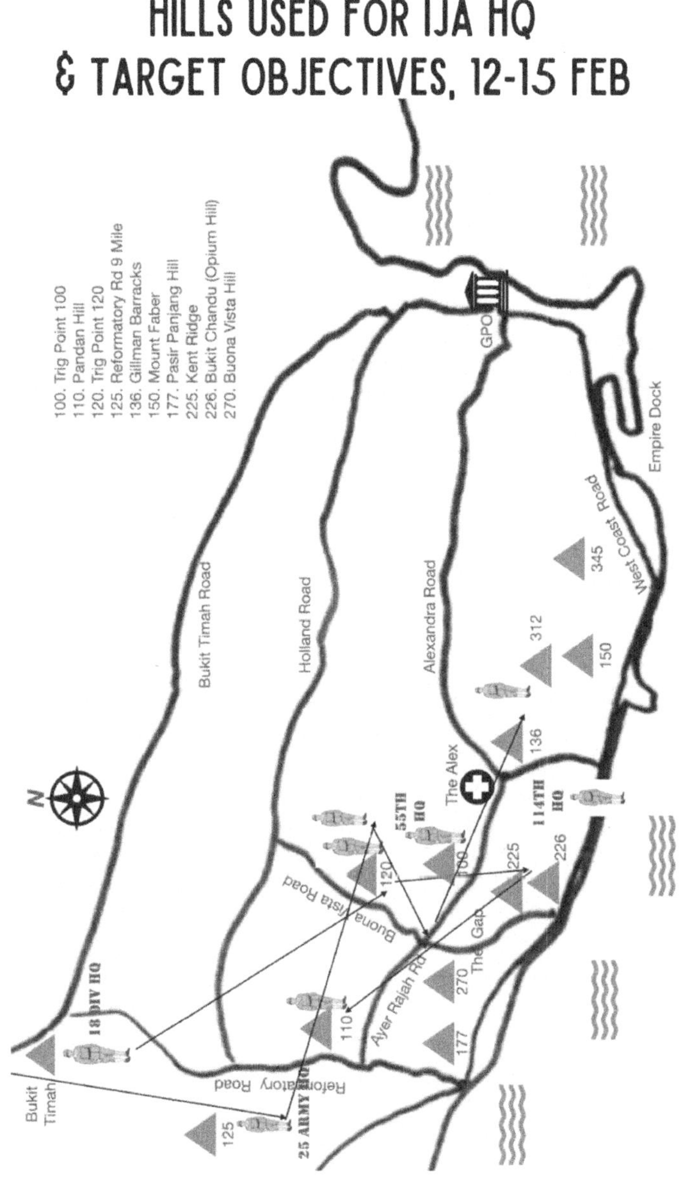
HILLS USED FOR IJA HQ
& TARGET OBJECTIVES, 12-15 FEB
100. Trig Point 100
110. Pandan Hill
120. Trig Point 120
125. Reformatory Rd 9 Mile
136. Gillman Barracks
150. Mount Faber
177. Pasir Panjang Hill
225. Kent Ridge
226. Bukit Chandu (Opium Hill)
270. Buona Vista Hill
N
GPO
Empire Dock
West Coast Road
Bukit Timah Road
Holland Road
Alexandra Road
345
312
150
136
The Alex
55TH HQ
114TH HQ
100
120
225
226
Buona Vista Road
The Gap
Ayer Rajah Rd
270
177
110
18 DIV HQ
Reformatory Road
25 ARMY HQ
125
Bukit Timah

WEST COAST WARPATH

'We felt like the meat in a very nasty explosive sandwich.'

11 February 1942. The southwest of Singapore was a key strategic area for the Allies, with a concentration of oil depots, ammunition dumps, and military camps in that corner of the island. The Allies had long since prepared to defend this area, and now created the 1st Malaya Infantry Brigade to shore it up.

This brigade – comprising the 2nd Loyals, 1st Malaya, and the 44th Indians – fell under the command of Brig George Williams, who'd been in Singapore since 1939 and was very familiar with this territory, because he himself was ex-Loyals who were based in the western Alexandra area.

The Malay Regiment had been impressive already, and they would soon tick all the 'proof of concept' boxes.

Williams had deployed the 1st Malays to hold a long ridge running parallel to the west coast known as Pasir Panjang Ridge. The 2nd Malays – formed just two months prior under ex-Lincolnshire's Lt Col Frederick Young, largely by scavenging men and officers from 1st Bn – held a line from there further north to the west of Reformatory Road and its junction with Ayer Rajah Road. The 2nd Loyals were in position around that junction to the north and southeast.

**

Mutaguchi gave his order to the division that it should make a tactical maneuver to the West Coast Road on the night of 12 February, driving a wedge to cleave the Allies and break through to reach Keppel Harbor.

From the outset 114th Regiment were in front on the right (west) wing and, by daybreak, entered a field following the edge of a rubber forest. Mortars started raining in, three 20-minute bursts, every 30 minutes. When the last attack finally died off, Mutaguchi moved his headquarters up, and called five tanks forward.

Maj James Andre was commanding the 1st Malay regiment and had some mortar platoon sections under him. He directed their fire on to the advancing tanks and infantry.

The Japanese had passed by three young girls 'around 20' working in the field earlier, and someone suspected they had betrayed them to the British. The girls, with short hair, were summonsed and brought forward, and each tied to a wooden pillar. As the heavy attack continued, the soldiers dived for their trenches, leaving the three girls tied standing in the open. 'When the shells began to fall, they went half crazy with fear,' said Master Sgt Arai. 'They cried out loudly. When the attack was over, they were still alive. Regimental Commander Okubo could not take it any longer and ordered a soldier: "Stab them!"'

Arai called out: 'Wait, don't stab them there, you'll only mess up the place.' The soldier looked at the officer, who said nothing, and returned to his trench. The soldier was somewhat relieved and walked away.

**

The 2nd Loyals saw a Japanese observation balloon going up, replete with spotters, who soon brought heavy shelling down on the 1st Malaya Infantry Brigade. Lt Col Mordaunt Elrington was in command of the 2nd Loyals. In October 1918 the 21-year-old had earned a Military Cross for 'exemplary gallantry' on the battlefield in France. Now 45, he had a huge responsibility, not just to his men, but to Singapore, and indeed the entire British Empire, to hold this once-languid corner of this tropical island.

The 2nd Loyals, with Pte Stan Sharpley in their ranks, were stubbornly holding, but the gaps with the retreat-happy 44th Indians were widening unacceptably now. So Brig Williams consolidated the 2nd Loyals and 2nd Malays back across Reformatory Road. Their line was deep here, from Ayer Rajah Road south to a feature known as Gap Ridge or just The Gap.

The 55th Brigade of the British 18th Division, would barely have time to recover from their 'sea legs' before being pressed into action.

The Malay Regiment dug themselves into slit trenches on Hill 125. Despite having plenty of spirit they had pathetically little in the way of weaponry other than rifles. 'They started fighting the Japanese with just rifles virtually,' observed Lt Penrod Dean, of the 2/4th Australian Machine Gun Battalion. 'And when the Japanese broke through them, the Malays took to them with bayonets, and with a bayonet charge they drove the Japanese back across Reformatory Road.'

There was no time for either side to dwell on little victories as the battle see-sawed its way down the coast. Soon, the joint HQ of 2nd Loyals and 2nd Malays was shelled, with heavy casualties in both HQ staff.

**

Bombs rained closer and closer to the hospital. 'An artillery officer, Lt Peter Rickett, was in a wheelchair and came and spoke to me,' said Brown, 'and we watched a plane coming down trying to bomb some oil tanks.' What a grandstand view given that those Normanton tanks were less than 500 yards away. 'He hit them eventually and one of them went up in a terrific explosion, and the heat ... you could even feel the heat coming across.'

Rickett, just a couple of months younger than Brown, pushed the Punjab officer behind a pillar. 'A lot of shrapnel was falling in the hospital grounds.' This shrapnel from aerial bombs caused the first fatality among The Alex's medical staff. Senior orderly Pte Hugh Lloyd, RAMC, was killed by shrapnel wounds in the abdomen, bleeding out from a severed abdominal aorta. The bomb was dropped near the railway line, a distance away, while he was sleeping on the verandah of the night duty quarters above the command lab.

'I went on duty and was told that Cpl Lloyd had been killed,' Stevenson said, as she reported for work that evening. 'The young orderly boy spent that night crying in the kitchen so I had to manage as best I could. When I returned to the wards, I was given a royal welcome. In response to the cheers I promised to do what I could do for the patients but said I only had one set of hands. "Don't worry, sister, just let us look at you. All we want is one of our girls. We thought you had deserted us".'

**

The 30-odd oil tanks of Pasir Panjang were billowing black smoke into the sky right in front of the IJA 114th. Sgt Arai was mesmerized by these despite all his previous action in southern China and Malaya. 'Why did our military bomb these tanks? What a waste,' he thought to himself as he ate tomatoes given to him by Sgt Katayama.

In the pre-embarkation pamphlet, the need to preserve and protect natural resources was a sub-head, which covered oil as essential to national survival. 'It is unlikely that the enemy will surrender it to us easily,' it read. 'We must expect them to try by every means in their power to destroy it first.'

So who damaged the oil tanks at Normanton? Was it a Japanese air or artillery strike? Or was it a scorched earth policy move by the Allies or an errant shell?

Bill Frankland later learnt that the Japanese commanders had indeed issued strict instructions to their pilots to avoid oil tanks as it was needed for their further war efforts. 'In fact, the pilot responsible for the attack was later disciplined for his actions,' Frankland maintained.

You can only begin to imagine the radiant heat from all those oil wells ablaze at once, in the already 32-degrees of tropical heat.

Commander Jim McMahon of NSW Fire & Rescue added his expert analysis of this situation: 'Thermal radiation is one of the great dangers of fire, the reason we wear fire gear, flash hood, helmets, etc.' He pointed out that radiant heat at 43-degrees Celsius causes pain to the skin, and skin burns from 45-degrees upward. 'Those oil wells alight are putting out temperatures from 850 to 1500 degrees or more. Let alone the toxic gases given off by them, causing oxygen effects, nervous system irritation, and the like. I couldn't imagine being within 50 metres of them without being clothed in proper Personal Protective Equipment.'

'At night Singapore Island was an awe-inspiring sight,' said Alex Drummond, cooped up at The Alex. 'Oil tanks at Pulau Bukom, Alexandra, Katong and elsewhere were beacons that lit up the sky.'

'We were attacking Singapore from Kota Bharu Airfield and my squadron moved to Kuantan airfield in the last few days,' recalled Capt Iwasaki. 'I saw a few black smoke coming out of oil facilities.'

The night was on fire, the air thick with acrid fumes. Oil was seen running down the railway line and Ayer Rajah Road storm-drain.

**

Signs that Singapore was a lost cause for the British included the sudden 5pm departure of all British guards and wardens at Changi prison – including the superintendent Capt Lily, who bolted for the city – leaving their prisoners to run amok. Heavy shelling continued from Japanese guns as distant as Johor Bahru, thudding into areas of western Singapore, 'causing an average 150 deaths a day' according to Miyozaki, who six months previously had been moved out of Loveday's cell into the Asian section of the prison. Loveday remained there.

**

Midnight ticked over to Friday. Had it struck any of the more superstitious British and Aussies that this day was Friday 13, an ominously black day? Possibly not – they'd had weeks and weeks of black days and things seemed only to be getting darker.

But the wins in this area were coming at a far greater cost for the attackers than any other part of the Malayan campaign. So far the Japanese 18th Division had lost 200 men on Singapore, and 300 were injured.

Arai could not sleep. His mind was busy thinking about those three girls back in the field they'd passed earlier. So he sneaked back surreptitiously and crept up to them in the blackness. Whispering, he got no response. He shook one girl from the side. Nothing. As he loosened the rope around her body he noticed the cold and wet blood. All three girls had been stabbed. 'Inside of me I felt a fiendish inhuman devil had come to attack them,' he said. 'One much worse than the enemy we were presently facing.' Arai went back to his trench with an unbearable feeling that, if his homeland were attacked, the same beastliness might be meted out to them. 'Violence begetting violence, a continuing sequence, one bad thing leading to something worse.'

Just then, the IJA 18th Division launched its main mighty offensive against Pasir Panjang Ridge. They pushed the defenders – largely 2nd Malays – back to Point 270 above The Gap. Buona Vista Hill, Hill 270, was the highest point of this coastal ridge.

**

HQ 25th Army could feel the shift of the battles swerve towards the west, moving its command post towards Trig post 120, beyond Tanglin.

But the optimism was not universal. General Takumi came to the command post and told Mutaguchi that it was difficult to continue attacking the enemy. Mutaguchi told him not to say such a ridiculous thing and forced him back to the frontline. Mutaguchi thought Gen Takumi's mental and physical tiredness was contributing to his pessimistic attitude.

The 1st Malays on Hill 125, after another punishing two hours of artillery and mortar attack, with heavy casualties, withdrew, the Japanese gladly taking over their vantage point.

Still dark, bar the raging oil tank fires, Mutaguchi shuffled the pieces around his human chessboard. 114th Regiment now switched to the left (easterly) flank, adjacent their rivals 5th Division, who they could see had an easy and straight run down Bukit Timah Road into Singapore. But ... why weren't they moving?

Breakfast for Arai and his men was always the other half of last night's leftover dinner – something dunked in red bean paste soup. 'No appetite during roaring shell attacks,' he found, and no time for lunch. 'Churchill supplies' such as British biscuits and powdered milk were often plentiful, and sustained them. 'On to Singapore was food enough,' he reflected.

At around 11am, a concerted push forward was made 'with 56th Regiment and 114th Regiment forming the front line, followed by 55th Regiment in the centre,' recalled Maj Gen Takeda. 'As far as I remember, no troops of 18th Division advanced (east) beyond the railway line. By the evening, the perimeter had been extended to a line north of the oil tanks between the railway line and the coast.'

Mutaguchi's recollection would be slightly different, recalling troops advancing *east* of the railway line. This is significant because the hospital is east of the track.

By midday, the Japanese had by now captured Pasir Panjang Hill from the 2nd Malays, who retreated south through the blazing Normanton Oil tanks down to the Alexandra Brickworks, and the Japanese managed to outflank the forward companies of the 2nd Loyals and the 1st Malays.

At 1pm Mutaguchi issued the order: 'Attack Hill 270. Advance along Buona Vista Road. Attack Pasir Panjang Heights. Then advance to Keppel Harbour.'

This changed everything and would set up one of the pivotal battles in this story. The Allies on this western flank were initially charged with defending the slopes and approaches to the Pasir Panjang Ridge. It was never expected that the full thrust of 18th Division would be thrown against the Malay Regiment directly. 13,000 seasoned Japanese versus 1400 untested Malays.

**

36th Field Company of the Royal Engineers came under Brig Williams' orders, and he'd positioned them at the intersection where Tanglin Road met with Alexandra Road, while the Bedfordshire Rifle Companies straddled the railway line, adjacent the Alexandra Road. Directly in front of them stood the Alexandra Hospital, sitting on the Ayer Rajah Rd borderline that delineated regimental responsibility.

Across the road, to the western side of Alexandra Road, two companies of the Loyals were stationed. On their right was the displaced 31st Battery RA – now only lightly armed having blown their coastal battery – who'd found an officers' mess to occupy. In this murky, confused bigger picture, a salient had been driven into the Allied lines, leaving The Alex unwittingly exposed in a no-man's land. It was around this time the nurses were given the order to evacuate not just from the hospital, but from the island, a wrenching saga we will explore a little later.

The combined might of the Japanese infantry and tank units jointly attacking Hill 270 was needed, along with the 1st Mountain Artillery Battalion and a company of the 14th Independent Mortar Battalion – 25th Army units both recently reassigned to 18th Div – firing in support. But even then it was a frantic struggle. 'The enemy position had concrete machine gun and artillery posts that were protected by barbed wire entanglements in front,' the IJA battle report said of the mini-fortress. 'Also the position was well supported by their artillery behind, that made attackers very difficult to attack.'

The Allied defenders had found a little hollow in the ground in an excellent position, and hammered the attackers from there. 'The rifles became so hot that they were difficult to hold with both hands,' said one lieutenant with D Company, Malay Regiment. They could have held out for a longer time but, with the continuous firing, were running dangerously low on ammunition.

Hill 270 (Buona Vista) was in Japanese hands by mid-afternoon, with Hill 177 (Pasir Panjang) soon to follow. The momentum had quickly swung to favour the Japanese, enjoying all the highest ground now. The commander of the Mountain Artillery regiment, Maj Col Takasu Katzutoshi assigned 1st Bn to the right wing unit and his 2nd Bn to provide artillery firing support. He himself followed 3rd Bn, and established his regimental observation post at Hill 200.

Mutaguchi would have been mightily pleased when 18th Div HQ advanced south down the road and reached their objective: Hill 110.

**

In addition to Normanton, the oil tanks on Pulau Bukom, about three miles offshore, were blazing away. And not just on land. The waters of Keppel Harbour in front of Blakang Mati were alive with dancing flames fueled by burning oil on the water's surface. The Loyals could scarcely believe their eyes, as it was a scenic view they'd often appreciated, and many had spent fun afternoons sailing those very waters in quite recent times. Just as the Mulvanys had.

1st Malay Rgt had retreated to Buona Vista Village without further incident, and were guarding the eastern edge of the coastal ridge and a couple of posts near where Alexandra Road met the coastal road. Familiar territory for them, because they'd been based within minutes of here on beach defences duty for over one year already, and many of their families actually lived around here.

The 5th Bedfords adjusted to a new position just southwest behind Alexandra Road astride the railway line, their left flank covering the end of Ayer Rajah Road immediately west of the hospital. The 2nd Loyals marched back down along Ayer Rajah Road, passing in single file through the burning tanks of Normanton in single file.

'The single file walking was to reduce the distance from radiant heat, but the intensity and exposure time would make it diabolical,' said Commander Jim McMahon. 'Tough buggers indeed!' They took up defensive positions in the Gillman Barracks area, their happy home for many years pre-war. What a peculiar feeling, one must imagine.

One of the Loyals, Capt James Johnson, rejoined his regiment after being in The Alex for a few weeks. Handy that they were just across the road by now. In Ayer Hitam, he'd been commanding a carrier platoon that ran into intense opposition. His fellow carriers were shelled, with a couple put out of action and their crew instantly killed or badly wounded. He managed to disarm one Japanese and killed another in the skirmish that followed, but was himself wounded in the leg.

**

By now the malaria-ridden Lt Paxton Harding was up and about and he and several other walking wounded left the hospital. He had an 'escape party' on his mind, and soon rendezvoused with others from Dalforce who were disbanded and tasked with forming an underground guerilla force. They felt Sumatra might be a suitable base from which to regroup.

**

Braddell Road, around the centre of the island, was the scene of sustained action, with a determined fightback by the British troops. Entrenchments and rifle ditches had been dug and, Somme style, the enemies were within grappling distance of each other. The Japanese, probably 5th Division, tried to rush them, or go around these trenches. Lance Sgt Oswald 'Ossie' Griffin – of 5th Royal Norfolks, like his father in WW1 before him – found himself in the thick of it, as the Japanese lobbed grenades over, many of which were duds or had slow fuses. Cpl Frost picked one up and tossed it back with devastating effect, winning a Military Medal. Branson, a medic, also won a Military Medal in this action.

'Then a Japanese NCO came over, with drawn sword,' military historian Neil Storey, great-nephew of Ossie Griffin, would tell me. 'Ossie was known as a good boxer. It took a bit but if he got the red mist, he'd go.' And go he did. 'Ossie goes for him with rifle and fists, and took him out.' Griffin sustained a sword cut to the left arm, but wanted to stay on and fight, until Maj Bob Hammond finally had to order him back for treatment. He was carted off to The Alex.

Wavy haired 24-year-old Pte William Armiger, also of 5th Royal Norfolks, went down with a gunshot wound to the chest, and was rushed to a field hospital, and the following morning ferried into The Alex.

**

Meanwhile, in nearby Thomson Road, artillery gunner Fergus Anckorn was in a battle for his life. 'Our gun had been hit, and I'd been sent down to get another gun from ordnance yard,' he told me, 'driving up the long straight road and a stretch of seven Jap bombers dropped the lot on me, like a diarrhea attack.' It caused an involuntary philosophical reflection. 'I thought someone's damn well trying to kill me. Well he's allowed to. He *supposed* to. He's like me, he doesn't even want to be in the war.'

He remembered it all in vivid frame-by-frame detail. 'In strange, mystical slow motion through my side window I was looking at a bomb coming down less than 10 feet away – so close I could have put my hand out and caught it. The rivets on it were plain to see and the Japanese lettering too. I saw the tailfins and a long spike on the front of the bomb as it went into the ground. I saw the bomb begin to explode as flames shot out the back of it. Unbelievably I saw all this and in that instant, thought, I'm dead. It's true what they say – parts of your life *do* flash before you. For me it was my fourth birthday party.'

With a deafening blast, the lorry lurched violently, 'and I was engulfed in metal hailstones. Blood was shooting out like a bathroom tap. The door of the truck was jammed, and I managed to kick it open with one foot, and ended up in a ditch unconscious. Someone found me and pronounced me dead. I was paralyzed from the waist down, and put on the wing of a truck face-down with a tourniquet around my arm. Under fire all the time as we drove, a bullet came in, creased my nose and went into the engine and stopped the lorry.'

His mind zoomed in and out of focus. 'Five of us were put in an ambulance, it was boiling, *boiling* hot. The driver of ambulance was a young Indian and he drove off the road, and just walked away. I was dehydrated and in a very poor state. Then he came back into the ambulance with a bottle of water.'

He was dragged across the road into the GPO, housed in the rather grand colonnaded Fullerton Building. 'It was a field hospital, full of people. I was told my hand would have to come off.' Fortunately an orderly recognized him as the conjuror who'd performed for their company back in the UK, and duly informed the surgeon who promised to do what he could to save those magical performing hands.

'13 Feb at 13:00. Two 13s in there!' he said, marvelling at the importune date and time. Later that afternoon, he'd be transferred to The Alex.

'There were apparently more deaths and wounding on that day than any other during the whole campaign,' observed Walter Salmon, he too a casualty of that ominous date. He was put into the Officers' Ward upstairs, late afternoon, near John Wyatt who said,

'We felt like the meat in a very nasty explosive sandwich,' as ordnance from both sides rained down near them. 'New casualties were arriving every hour – it was just total chaos.'

**

The Federated Malay States Volunteer Force (FMSVF) was also heavily engaged in the action around the area of upper Holland Road that day. A key part of their force was their Armoured Cars, manned mainly by mining and rubber men from the Malayan up-country.

Cpl Robert Veitch was nearing 29, 'tall, dark and heavy' according to Smiley. Veitch was a mining engineer who'd gone to George Heriot's School in Edinburgh, which had produced David McGregor, awarded the VC posthumously for his actions just prior to Armistice Day. Veitch came out to Malaya in 1937 to join his friends, the Littledyke brothers, for some adventure out east, and got a job with the Hong Kong Mining Company, and subsequently signed up with the Volunteers. He'd recently enjoyed leave in Australia, cutting it short and rushing back to join his unit just three weeks earlier.

Lance Cpl David Alexander was also Scottish, an assistant at the venerable Guthrie's trading firm, and had been in various volunteer outfits and companies between Singapore and Malaya since 1929. He was now 34, and married to a Queenslander, Margot, with a baby daughter, Christine. Margot and daughter had just got away on a ship to South Africa. He had no way of knowing if they'd made it safely yet.

Cpl Leslie 'Len' Best, an Englishman who'd been in Malaya for well over 10 years, was in the tobacco industry in Penang with Carreras Ltd. He was married to Cicely, who had just evacuated. Had she made it safely to India, he wondered?

Cpl Henry Francis De Camborne Lucy was simply known to his mates as Peter. He, Best and Alexander were all the same age, and the trio had all coincidentally been in this part of the world since 1929. Originally from Hertfordshire, just north of London, he loved the colonial life as a rubber planter and estate manager on the Amhurst Estate.

Aussie Sergeant John 'Jack' Slater was, like Veitch, a mining engineer. Originally from Bathurst, NSW, the 28-year-old had had stints in the Militia and the RAAF, before marrying Anne and picking up a job with Anglo-Oriental Mining in Perak. Almost immediately he signed on with the Volunteers. On New Year's Day – a rather intense six weeks earlier – he'd dashed to the post office in Kuala Lumpur to send Anne a telegram of well-wishes. What he didn't know was that she and their daughter Patricia had boarded the *Narkunda* two days earlier and had made it safely to Fremantle, Perth, by the end of January.

Slater picked up their story of 13 January. 'After being bombed and under rifle fire for days, two large shells landed among us and I collected a piece of shrapnel in the thigh.' Their armoured cars offered scant protection against heavy artillery. Bob Veitch, who was in a car with Peter Lucy, caught shrapnel in the lower leg, Lucy some in the arm, and Alexander in the leg. Worst affected was Best 'in the chest'.

The ambulance did its utmost to rush them to hospital but Best's wounds were too massive to save him and he died en route near Normanton. The rest were lucky enough to be able to be brought back through to The Alex nearby before it soon became inaccessible from that direction.

De Lucy was X-rayed, the last person to be done before Bull's precious machines were damaged and put out of action by bombs. This was his second stint in hospital, having been wounded by enemy fire in the defence of the Kuantan airfield on the coast due east of Kuala Lumpur on 4 January. He'd just rejoined his unit in Singapore, now *this*.

Adding to his woes were the fact that he'd just got married less than a week earlier to Dorothy aka 'Tommy' in the Singapore Cathedral. The VAD had only just shipped out on the *Empire Star* the night before he was admitted here. The vessel came under severe attack but made it through to Batavia then India. Of course poor Peter knew nothing of this at the time. So much for a honeymoon.

**

Two companies of the Loyals, including 31st Battery RA, were forward on the western side of Alexandra Road, occupying their Officers' Mess building and other officers' bungalows. Another company plus Battalion HQ used their Sergeants' Mess as a defensive position in which to set up. Another company dug in to defensive posts between Alexandra Road and the Tiger Brewery. The HQ company was spread around, with their trucks being concealed in the Heap Guan San *kampong*, west of the barracks towards the coast road. Here a makeshift Indian General Hospital was also set up, marked with Red Crosses, and this remained unshelled.

With the Gap Crossroads now unholdable, the 8th Div Aussies moved back from Holland Village to bolster the important Tanglin Barracks and Tyersall Park area. Brig Williams made the call at 6.30pm for a withdrawal after dark to the Alexandra Depots Area defence line.

And so, as the sun set on an ominously terrible Friday 13th, fine-tuning movements were being made by both sides on the real-life chessboard for the following day. But the superstitious jinxes were far from over.

The Alexandra telephone exchange was pre-emptively blown up, which caused vital communication problems between various units. Lt Col Elrington and Brigade HQ had moved around to Mount Faber by now and they had to find alternative ways to get messages out quickly and establish the situation.

The 44th Indian Brigade, temporarily defending the area west of the hospital moved back a little way to the line of Mount Echo, where Ayer Rajah Road met Depot Road.

C Company 1st Malays, the valiant defenders of Pasir Panjang Village, hopped aboard Bren carriers around midnight, and retreated through the lines of B Company who had set a road block at Buona Vista Village.

As for the rampaging Japanese, their 25th Army HQ was as far forward as Reformatory Road, where Maj Gen Takeda spent the night 'on the way to Trig Point 120.'

The badly battered and bruised 114th Regiment passed south of Hill 110 and arrived at 18 Div HQ at 20:00. They had suffered huge losses, 'reducing regimental strength by one third' according to their battle report.

It had been a truly Black Friday for all. Still the shells from both sides whistled and roared incessantly overhead and, around the Port, increasingly desperate and dramatic scenes were playing out as the expatriate population, vulnerable locals, and desperate deserters tried to flee the island.

SINGAPORE'S DUNKIRK DAY

'We all knew we were going to die. The sisters died bravely.'

Friday 13 February 1942. Previously, the Singapore Cricket Club had been a picture postcard of languid colonial charm and calm. Now, as an emergency transport hub, it was a dramatic and desperate scene of conflicted emotions. Confusion at what was going on and where the next steps would take them. Happy hugs of reunion with other sisters they may have trained with back in England or Australia, or served with further up-country in Malaya. And heartbreaking tears of farewell to close colleagues assigned to a different vessel.

A lottery in which none could necessarily win, but several would lose.

'I'm on the *Mata Hari*, how about you?'

'I'm on the *Vyner Brooke*.' Many of the Australian sisters from the 13th and 10th AGH were on this steamship.

For many of the sisters from The Alex they received their announcement:

'Oh, thank God, we're all on the *SS Kuala* together.'

Though it was mid-afternoon it felt like twilight already because of that thick pall of smoke which hovered menacingly above the city, providing cover for the Japanese planes which dashed and darted across the skies, looking for targets. Even the nurses by now could tell 'ours' from 'theirs' by the different roar of the engines.

Capt Bill Frankland – by now operating the 1st Malayan General Hospital out of the Victoria Theatre across the road since the Tanglin Military Hospital was evacuated a couple of days earlier – was assigned to ensure their safe transit to the harbour, and dished out Red Cross armbands which effectively served as passport proxies. Capt Petrovsky had also assisted to set up this new hospital and then moved on to the Chinese Girls High School to set up another. Little did he know the bullets – and bayonets – he dodged in doing so.

Their assigned buses soon started trundling their way through the city's smouldering streets, picking their way around car wrecks, tumbled shophouses, and bodies. Heading to the docks. With seemingly a million other people and vehicles, for that was now the estimated population of the island, having swelled to double its size of just weeks earlier.

The *SS Kuala* was a white two-masted cargo ship that had run aground on its maiden voyage exactly 31 years ago to the day, its single tall funnel adding more black smoke to the air as skipper Lt William Caithness prepared their escape. Knowing this vessel would likely not be returning soon to Singapore, the local crew were replaced by seamen from the *Prince of Wales*, and, coincidentally, wounded crewman from the same ship and the *Repulse* from the Alexandra were stretchered below decks too. The vessel seemed way too small to possibly fit the 600 clamouring bodies – including 100 matrons and nurses – waiting for her. Among the throng were teachers, shopkeepers, housewives, jewellers, milliners and planters.

The famed cake-baker Mrs Howe was lined up, as was Helen Monier, the lingerie lady. And Leonora King, the first female radio announcer in Malaya. She'd made tongues wag recently with a rather saucy talk at the Rotary Club in Penang called 'Plea for Pornography'. Perhaps not what one would expect from the wife of the Reverend Colin King, principal of the Bukit Mertajam High School, whom she'd married when she was just 18.

'It seemed madness to be trying to leave by ship at that late stage,' Brenda Macduff felt, especially as the docks were being bombed.

Edith Stevenson – dressed in her white nursing overall with a silver medal pinned to it – described as 'turmoil' the scene at the gate in front of the Ocean Building. 'I walked up the ladder to the deck in a daze,' she said. And still the Japanese planes swooped and buzzed, machine guns chattering away as the sisters disembarked from their transports at the dock, waiting for the launch to take them out to the *SS Kuala* out in the deeper sea roads. Sister Olive Macfarlane was killed immediately by shrapnel to the head, and Jean Duncan copped a splinter wound in the loin which was hastily patched up, but not after a bout of screaming and crying.

Husbands and even some grandfathers, staying behind because they wanted to fight for Singapore or because they'd not got permission to leave, did their utmost to remain stoic as they packed off their wives and children. Many of the big companies of Malaya were represented on the docks by someone seeing off their family – Bousteads, John Little, Evatt and Co, Borneo Motors, and many of the big plantation estates. John Dawson – the 54-year-old head of Guthrie's whose wife Ethel had evacuated ahead successfully on the *Empress of Japan* – jagged a berth on the *Kuala* and was ferried out to the vessel aboard the *Daisy*.

The robust figure of WW Duncan was at the dock, too. Normally with the Municipal Secretariat he'd just been appointed Director of Air Raid Precautions (ARP). He was still vacillating whether or not to send his Chinese wife and two Eurasian daughters off, but believed they'd be better off on a ship rather than caught up in Singapore once the Japanese came. He handed over a rattan basket of diapers and feeding bottles to his wife, Violet, for their baby. You can imagine the wrench.

Despite the high premium on boat passages, there were some no-shows. Two were Sion Abraham and his mum. 'Our bags were packed, the taxi arrived. It was a split-second decision – we decided not to go,' he told me.

**

As the last launch ferried the sisters out, a solitary suitcase was seen sitting forlornly on the dock. It was labelled: 'K Woodman, QAIMNS'. Back at the Cricket Club there was some serious urgency. A rather sleep-deprived Kit Woodman was blearily readying herself for night duty, because they had just decamped to using the Cricket Club and Victoria Theatre after the roof of their previous hospital at Roberts Barracks was blown off a few days before.

She was wondering why her colleagues had not roused her as she raced to the Club's hall. But a brigadier asked her angrily what she was still doing here. He hurried her towards his jeep and they drove to the docks as fast as the chaotic crowds and traffic would allow. She was rowed out to the *SS Kuala* by 'a huge man' in a rowing boat. 'When we came alongside he just lifted me up and threw me on board, and my case after me,' Kit recalled. 'My uniform was crumpled, my hair all over the place. Miss Jones (her former matron at The Alex) looked me over and said coldly: 'You girls will have to smarten yourselves up before we reach Java. She should have seen us when we *did* land.'

As the *Kuala* pulled away out of Singapore, Kit looked back. 'The once green paradise island now lay charred and smoking in a sump of foul oil. Flames and gun-flashes lit up the evening sky. My last thoughts were of my orderlies, left behind with the patients. Excellent men, all of them. What would happen to them now?'

'As we looked back we saw what seemed like a blazing inferno, as bright red flames shot into the air,' recalled Edith Stevenson. Had she looked to starboard, she might have seen Pulau Hantau, the Mulvany's paradise, now sporting an 18-pound gun, and perhaps their cruiser *Honora* flying the Navy's blue ensign and spiriting 17 escapees to safety.

Meanwhile WW Duncan, who'd just waved his family off, got involved in a scuffle in the dockside pandemonium and was stabbed by a desperate soldier, so off he had to go to hospital for a patch-up. It had been a momentous Friday 13th for their family.

**

It was 6pm and darkness couldn't come quickly enough for the anxious and nervous passengers and crew. The stream of ships pulling out from Singapore was redolent of Dunkirk with 80 vessels of assorted size and shape making their bid for freedom, but the flotilla was far too disorderly to be called a convoy. The *Vyner Brooke* – with 37-year-old matron Olive Paschke and 64 Australian Army Nursing Services sisters aboard – formerly being part of the Rajah of Sarawak's royal fleet, sounded more glamorous than she actually was.

'Singapore was ablaze – thick black smoke billowed high behind the city. There were 200 aboard – far too many for the size of this ship,' said 28-year-old Sister Flo Trotter from Sydney, who'd joined the 2/10 Australian General Hospital in Malacca almost exactly a year ago to the day.

The *Mata Hari* was also underway, and so was the *Tien Kwang*. QMS Edwin Buffton, who'd only joined 32 Coy RAMC a couple of months earlier to be in charge of statistics and casualty returns, managed to leave Singapore, saying farewell to colleagues Pte Robert Davidson, Cpl Frederick Dealtry, and Pte Stephen Minns. Also leaving at the same time were Capt John Kellett, Lt Edward Snoad, and S/Sgt C Crow. These RAMC men secured passage on one of the many ships, boats and assorted vessels, steaming across to Batavia.

'The *Kuala* was so suffocated with frightened talking flesh, one could barely move without having to step over someone,' recalled Wilhelmina Eames, travelling with her three-year-old daughter, Shirley. Part of a large and prominent expat family in Kuala Lumpur, they had evacuated down to Singapore, where her father had waved them off at the dock.

**

'Everyone was so excited to hear that Singapore would fall soon,' said pilot Iwasaki, 'but my squadron was ordered to prepare for enemy's counter-offensive and kept flying for search and destroy missions.' Which might have put them on a collision course with the heavy shipping leaving Singapore.

**

Saturday 14 February. Dawn revealed that the vessels had run straight into the gaping jaws of the Japanese destroyer fleet, with 'Operation L', a seaborne invasion of Sumatra, underway. The skies, too, were full of recon planes and scout spotters. There was no sign of the *Mata Hari*, and no radio contact overnight. Also, no sign of the *Vyner Brooke*, so the captains of the *Kuala* and *Tien Kwang* decided to hole up on the far side of Pompong Island in the Riau Islands chain and ride out the daylight hours.

The *Hosang* – which had carried 32 Coy RAMC from Shanghai to Singapore a few months earlier – was not so lucky, getting bombed near Palembang, before running aground and being abandoned in the Moesi River. (It was later rebadged as the *Gyozan Maru* before being torpedoed by the Americans and sunk on a reef near the Philippines.)

What nobody knew then was that the *Vyner Brooke* had hit a minefield and was somewhat disabled. Captain Borton decided it best to anchor overnight rather than risk hitting another mine.

Surreal scenes ensued on the *Kuala* as the nurses were requested to change out of their white uniforms to be less conspicuous, and foraging parties were sent onto the island to cut foliage to try and camouflage the ship. The six matrons on board, including Matron Jones, Matron Cicely West (from 1st Malayan General) and Matron Margaret Brebner (from Singapore General), plus Superintendant Ada Cherry (a keen competitive golfer of the Medical Auxiliary Service, whose husband Cecil was the managing director of Bousteads and Cold Storage), Matron Vera Spedding (from the 20th Combined General Hospital at Gillman) and Matron Winifred Russell (from the 17th Combined General Hospital), decided to meet in a cabin and discuss the status of the wounded who required attention.

Jones, West, and Spedding were all 51, Russell and Cherry both 54, and Brebner 57. The collective experience and cool heads in that cabin were a valuable asset. But that counted for nothing as next thing a Japanese bomb scored a direct hit on their cabin. Matron Jones and three others were obliterated. Two other QAs, Lorna Symondson and Helen Montgomerie, had gone to the Chinese and Eurasian nurses' area on the top deck, arriving just as a bomb struck that part of the boat, killing both – and many other nurses – instantly. 'The carnage was terrible.'

An older nurse, whom she knew from her nursing training school in North Staffordshire, tossed a cushion to Stevenson and called out: 'Put this over your bottom, buttock wounds take longest to heal.' As last words go, not especially propitious.

Fires broke out around the ship. 'A live version of Michaelangelo's *The Last Judgement*,' said the religious Stevenson, praying fervently, 'and blood made the decks slippery.' She slid into the sea to escape the flames, preferring to die by drowning than burning, and tied herself to a raft with nine others – including one 68-year-old gent – all non-swimmers who begged her to stay.

'I had never heard such mass wailing of hundreds of helpless fellow creatures as they were told to choose between the burning ship and the yawning depth of an unknown sea,' said Dr Chen Su Lan, a China-born doctor from Singapore. 'I shall never as long as I live forget those tormented screams. They broke my heart.' Sister Olga Neubronner, from the 1st MGH – who was due to celebrate her third wedding anniversary to her accountant husband, Guy, the following month – clambered into a raft, where she promptly miscarried. Even though the captain, Caithness, was badly wounded, indeed partially paralyzed, he soldiered on valiantly to ensure his charges were safe. (Post-war he was given the honour of leading the liberation parade by the Navy into Singapore for his efforts.)

If the coldness of the water was a surprise, the ferocity of the currents certainly was more so, quickly separating groups who'd vowed to swim, float, or cling together. Those who made it to the nearby island found the rocks slippery, and the jungled slope to the flat patch above, steep. But they were the lucky ones. Others were simply washed way to the side of the island, some washing ashore on Sumatra eight hours later. Edith Stevenson's group was rescued by a Chinese fishing boat miles away and taken to a stilted house where they gave her a sugar sack to wear.

The water was full of thrashing, splashing bodies. Some had lifejackets, others didn't. Those with lifejackets were about to find out that they were the unlucky ones because soon a Japanese plane returned, firstly machine-gunning those who had reached land, then focusing on the figures in the water with bombs and guns. Those with life-jackets couldn't duck under to try and dodge the raking bullets.

Matron Russell was killed in this way, the fourth matron to die that day. In all, 18 QAs (including Annie McGregor, Agnes Hervey-Murray, and Laura Coward who'd all worked at The Alex), five TANS (including Alice Ingham from The Alex), plus a number of Colonial Sisters and Indian Sisters were killed trying to escape the burning wreckage of *SS Kuala*.

'According to our Navy airmanship tradition, we never attacked civilian targets, and we never shot wounded enemy soldiers,' Capt Iwasaki, who was operating around Singapore at that time, would tell me. 'We all knew that Americans enjoyed shooting at our survivors. But we never did such a thing. It was the matter of our pride as a Navy airman.'

The surviving doctors, matrons and nurses set about getting the wounded settled on the clearing above the rocks. Among the wounded was Brigadier Walter Fawcett suffering a massive wound in the back (and some said he'd lost three fingers too). The 47-year-old – who'd earned a Military Cross for gallantry in WW1 – was en route to India to take up a posting as a Director of Military Operations because of his previous long experience there. Sister Macduff used a stretcher fashioned from sail and vine to make him comfortable.

Another who found himself stranded on Pompong was Lt Commander Terry, who'd survived from the *Prince of Wales* but was sunk again with a group of seamen on the *Kung Wo*. Almost all of the 80 boats that left Singapore that fateful day were intercepted, hit minefields, or shot up.

Including the *Vyner Brooke. Again*!

The morning of 14 February saw them spotted and bombed, the rather squarish and squat vessel sinking within 15 minutes off the tin mining island of Bangka, east of Sumatra.

'The planes grouped in two formations of three and flew towards us,' said Flo Trotter. 'We felt as if the last bomb had landed right beside us. There was the dreadful noise of smashing glass and timber.' They scrabbled about the decks gathering up dressings and drugs.

Capt Borton probably didn't need to make the call for the 300 passengers (mainly women and children) to abandon ship, but Matron Paschke – who had only two months earlier been promoted to principal matron aged just 36 – always led from the front, and ensured all her 63 sisters had jumped off before she abandoned ship. Being a farmer's daughter and not raised near the ocean, she jumped nonetheless: 'Keep an eye on me girls, I can't swim!' she shouted before leaping into the junkyard of debris that swirled around the boat, and clambered into a life-raft with seven others. Strong currents whisked them towards but past Bangka Island out to sea, and she was never seen again.

'But the Japanese hadn't finished with us yet,' continued Trotter. 'They machine gunned the deck and the lifeboats. They came back and machine gunned us in the water. Our tin hats came in handy! Five of us managed to grab a piece of railing, and one of the girls was quite a wag and started singing *We're off to see the Wizard* ...'

After 18 hours in the water, her group was swept around the lighthouse into a sandy cove. 'It was wonderful to feel sand under our feet.'

Others were luckier with the currents, and the first Australian sisters to make dry land lit fires to help guide others towards their beach, called Radji.

Sister Sylvia McGregor joined a raft with other Aussie nurses. They had aimed for the same beacon as Bullwinkel's crew. 'During the night I had given my uniform to make a sail, so arrived in my undies!' she said, of her unflattering long pale grey buttoned tunic.

Soon it was apparent there were a number of problems. Many had simply not made it to the beach. Among those that had were many badly wounded (those in the water when bombs were dropped suffered internal percussion injuries, although ladies with strong elastic girdles were less affected). Plus some initial foraging attempts turned up very little in the way of food on the swampy island.

So it was decided that they should surrender to the Japanese who, according to some local islanders, were at nearby Muntok. A party set off, with instructions that they were to alert the Japanese and return with stretchers to ferry the wounded. Rather than wait, all who were able to walk set off for Muntok, leaving just the nurses plus one civilian behind to tend to the injured party which included several British and New Zealander naval ratings and reservists.

**

That was quick! Here came the Japs. But no stretchers in sight. Stomachs would have tightened at that moment of realization that something didn't look or feel right about that. And what the sisters couldn't have known is they'd just summoned men from the IJA 229th Infantry Regiment, the self-same villains who rampaged their way through St Stephens College in Hong Kong just six weeks earlier. What were the chances?

With some brusquely barked orders from Capt Orita Masaru, all the men, including the badly wounded, were herded off behind a nearby dune under the guidance of Sgt Maj Taro Kato and Lt Masayuki Takeuchi. The soldiers soon returned, wiping blood from their bayonets. A stoker from the *Prince of Wales*, Ernest Lloyd, took the opportunity to escape and ran into the ocean. He survived to tell the tale, but was later recaptured.

The men disposed of, they set upon the women, ripping their uniforms open and raping them. Next, the 22 women were ordered to walk into the sea. My God, whatever next?

'Girls, take it, don't squeal,' said Sister Esther Stewart.

'Chin up, girls,' called the 36-year-old bespectacled South Australian, Matron Irene Drummond. 'I'm proud of you all and I love you all."

Rat-a-tat-a-tat-a-tat!!! Rat-a-tat-a-tat-a-tat!!! Once they reached about waist deep in the blue-grey waters, they were gunned down from behind. No one was spared. Or so the Japanese thought, because they collapsed their machine guns and trundled off. One nurse had been shot through her side above the hip. Vivian Bullwinkel momentarily blacked out, but the 26-year-old South Australian had her wits about her enough to realize that playing dead and floating among her colleagues' corpses was a smart strategy.

After she felt the coast was clear, Bullwinkel got back to the eerily deserted beach. There, a wounded British soldier with an arm missing, Kingsley, emerged from behind the dunes. They hid out for 12 days, and she cared for the man until he died. At which time she turned herself in to the Japanese again, carefully covering the bullet hole in her tunic with a water bottle so as to not make them realize she was a survivor – and therefore a witness.

'Vivien Bullwinkel came into our camp,' remembered Sister Trotter. 'She told us of the massacre of 21 of our nurses.'

'We all knew we were going to die,' Bullwinkel said. 'There were no protests. The sisters died bravely. Their marvelous courage prevented me from calling out when I was hit. I could not let them down.'

**

Meanwhile, back at Pompong Island a secret rescue mission was underway ...

During the night of 16-17 February, all women, children and wounded – about 120 in all, according to Edith Stevenson – were taken off the island in rowing boats and boarded the *Tanjong Pinang*, commanded by the rather dashing-looking Lt Basil Shaw, who in better times was a sheep farmer in New Zealand before signing on as a skipper in the RNZNVR. There were 17 officers and experienced crew on board, many of them New Zealanders or reassigned from *HMS Repulse* (in some cases both). This vessel was in the area after evacuating some specialist radar technology army teams from Singapore, so they could apply their talents in another theatre.

Priority was given to the stretcher-bound wounded. This was a very slow and delicate operation especially given the state of some of the evacuees. Among the worst was Brig Fawcett but he insisted on travelling 'because of important business in Sumatra' and his need to reach India. Brenda Macduff once again held his (good) hand and guided him carefully down the slope, over the red-pebbled beach, to the water's edge. She then remained behind to work a nightshift caring for the wounded who were not leaving on this boat.

Some recall Matron Brebner struggling down the hillside with her handbag under her arm, heartbroken about all her nurses who'd been killed. Another woman carried across the rocks and put into a rowboat was Mrs Nell Brewer. Her husband was the celebrated architect Frank Brewer who had contributed signature buildings such as the Cathay Building (Singapore's first 'skyscraper'), the art deco Capitol Theatre, and the imposing colonial Command House which firstly GOC Dobbie and now GOC Percival called home.

Doubling the difficulty of this trans-shipment was the fact that the *Tanjong Pinang* was less than 100' long, and she was already full with stragglers collected from other stops around the archipelago.

Cissy Mather, with three-year-old daughter Maureen, might have thought of her husband Jimmy because the cramped, crowded and airless conditions of the cargo hold were probably quite similar to where he had worked till recently: as a prison officer at KL's notorious Pudu Jail (and, unknown to her, would become an inmate at Changi within a few days).

With those from the *Kuala* sardined aboard, too, the best estimate would be 200 passengers on board here. These included Olga Stringer, a 50-year-old VAD nurse who was the wife of Brig Stringer and had added her feminine design flourishes to The Alex Sisters' Quarters. There is some thought that military rank was pulled to get wives and families of the officers away on a priority basis over other military families and civilians, but of course everybody was playing all the cards they could at that stage to get themselves or at least their families away from Singapore.

Lt Col FW Hennessey, RAMC, had managed to get permission for his 22-year-old wife and son, Tinker, to evacuate. Joan Wildey secured a berth, being the rather sociable wife of Brig Alec Wildey whom Maj Mulvany operated on and secured Ethel's berth from India to Singapore as a favour. Together they had initiated the Royal Artillery Changi Married Families Club in 1940.

One rather interesting case was to do with the wife of Brig Charles Seaver, honorary surgeon to the Viceroy of India. A 'Mrs Seaver' was listed on the *SS Kuala* and also the *Tanjong Pinang*. But intriguingly the real Mrs Francis Seaver had remained in Ireland for the entire duration of the war. So who was this mystery woman?

Ivy Evenett was the wife of 2nd Lt HJ Evenett of the Royal Engineers, and lived just opposite The Alex at 5 Royal Road, one of the oldest houses in the Alexandra area. How terrifying for her to see the frontline coming so close to her bungalow, and her husband was probably in combat action just around the corner somewhere. Did they even get a chance for a goodbye?

**

The irrepressible Sister Mary Cooper for one would have been tired of these shipboard evacuations – first with her hospital team from Johor to Singapore, then the *Kuala*, now this one. Most others had also got to this point in various stages, especially those from northernmost Malaya who made their way down dossing on friends' or relatives' couches and spare beds, finally calling on even strangers for a spare bed in Singapore as they got shoehorned south.

'As a nursing sister I remained on deck but all the passengers were below decks in the hold,' said Margot Turner. Probably a half of all passengers were below decks in what was actually a cargo hold. And there was limited cabin space above decks. Other Alex nurses on board included Daphne Clarke, Marjorie Fowler, Naomi Davies, Dorothy Tombs, Edith Pedlow (actually a music teacher who became a VAD at The Alex), and Charlotte Black, a 26-year-old Irish sister from The Alex who'd recently got engaged to a RAF officer, also boarded.

But the *Tanjong Pinang* didn't sail right away. Navigating these straits at night was too risky. Not that daytime seemed any safer based on their recent experience. The minutes ticked by one ... by ... one ... until they finally weighed anchor at dawn and steamed all day towards Batavia. Night fell and they kept on. Is that it? Somewhere on the horizon, a light. A lighthouse!

Then suddenly another light. This one closer. Shining right at the *Tanjong Pinang*. A loud shot rang out. A warning shot. But from where? It was hard to see beyond the bluish spotlight coming from nearby. The helmsman, Richardson, cut the engines and hove to. Was it a submarine? A torpedo boat? A destroyer? The skipper and signalman Daniel McHugh urgently flashed the message: 'We have women and children on board.' The searchlight seemed to check out the white ensign at the stern. By this time a boat of women and children was being lowered into the water. The Japanese opened fire, the first salvo blasting the boat to pieces and setting fire to the *Tanjong Pinang*. Six more shells thudded into her amidships.

Many of the nurses now rushed to the cabin for cover but were the first to be hit. Edith Stevenson reported there were only five survivors and, of all the nurses on board that vessel, only one survived: her.

Others, such as 20-year-old Malayan nurse, Choong Kwee Cheo, managed to get into another lifeboat, but that was soon shattered and they found themselves once again in the sea. 'It was terribly cold. We were floating around all night shouting for help.' They grabbed mattresses, lifebelts, splintered wood, whatever would float.

The speed with which the fire took surprised everyone and soon flames raged all over. The dog-loving Jean Shaw possibly prayed for her husband Jim to be there at that moment, because he was the #1 man in the Singapore Fire Brigade. There were a few couples on board, but Jim was too vital in Singapore to be allowed to evacuate.

'Mothers asked me to throw their children overboard into the sea so that they could get on rafts,' said Richardson. 'I threw many children overboard and women too. The fire was very intense.' The large strong frame of Kiwi Captain Basil Shaw was down in the water putting children into rafts. Two of those were Gwen and Colin Smith, the rest of their family was trapped below decks.

Mary Cooper was gingerly making her way towards a raft, both hands lacerated by the ship's rope as she slid down. Elizabeth Strachan, TANS, succumbed to a shrapnel wound in her abdomen.

'As I was making for the hold to see what help I could give,' said Sister Margot Turner, 'I met Mrs Stafford, a VAD, who told me it was useless to go down to the hold as all the people appeared to have been killed. The ship had heeled at an acute angle and I just stepped into the water, swam around, got hold of a raft.'

Then the *Tanjong Pinang* sank below the surface, not 15 minutes after being shelled.

Mrs Howe, the baker, Helen Monier, the lingerie shop lady, and Leonora King, the broadcaster, were all immediately lost in this melee, or sometime soon after. Of all the 60 who probably managed to get off the ship, only a quarter of those ever made it to land near the Tanjong Ular lighthouse on Bangka Island, or were picked up at sea. They were all adults, plus two teenagers.

**

But still unbelievably their problems weren't over yet. Seaman Robert Archer described their welcome: 'We got ashore on a beach on the southeast end of Bangka Island at about 18:00 on 22 February. We were robbed that night of all our money and possessions, except clothes, by a party of about 20 Malays armed with poles and knives.'

This group included two sailors from the *Repulse*, Seaman James Baird and Alfred Hissey, the latter nursing an injured left wrist. Alex sister, Charlotte Black, was with his group – as were six other sisters who all died en route from over- exposure – but was suffering from a nasty septic wound. 'We could get no medical help for the nurse. Her leg was badly poisoned. She died on the night 23/24 February. We buried her body on the beach about five miles to the north east of the village of Rambut.'

'During that first night we picked up 16 people,' said Turner. 'I was on the raft for four days during which time all the sixteen people either died or fell off the raft through exhaustion.' One of them was QA sister Beatrice Le Blanc Smith, 'who had concealed a terrible wound.' Delirious 'madness' combined with dehydration befell many, the sun literally frying their brains and bodies.

'On the night of 21 February I was picked up by a Japanese cruiser and taken to Muntok Camp on Bangka Island and interned,' said Turner. She was so sun-blackened as to be unidentifiable as British. Sister Mary Cooper was brought into that camp at the same time. The Kiwi captain, Basil Shaw, was summarily executed by the Japanese near the Tanjong Ular lighthouse after reaching Bangka Island looking for help.

Choong Kwee Cheo ended up floating on her raft with six others for six days, until they too all passed away, and she linked up with another raft with another Chinese or Eurasian nurse and they reached a small island near Bangka where they were rescued by the Japanese.

**

With all their survival instincts and resilience infinitely tested in the previous few days, one wonders how much thought they were able to give to the rapidly unfolding situation they had left back in Singapore. Especially the nurses, since leaving the Alexandra Hospital just after lunchtime on Friday 13. The frontline had moved quickly around the strategic Alexandra Cantonment epicentre, and just 24 hours later some of the fiercest last-stand pitched battles were taking place literally on the doorstep of the hospital.

HEADING FOR THE HARBOUR

'Then the enemy's guns and artillery firepower became stronger.'

14 February 1942. Nutmeg trees and secondary jungle smothered Hill 226, also known as Bukit Chandu by Malays, or Opium Mountain by the Chinese in reference to the State-owned opium factory operating at the southern base of its ridge. Three kilometres east lay the Alexandra Hospital, and the Alexandra Barracks and Depots – seen among the distant treeline – would only be about a 15- to 20-minute march if unimpeded.

After midnight on 13 February, the rather battered but unquestionably resilient Malay C Company evacuated to a low rise west of the Opium Factory, some 50 metres inland off Pasir Panjang Road. This was directly adjacent the Mulvany's bungalow, from where the major and his wife had watched the initial bombardment of Singapore from their front lawn. It was also west of a storm drain, estimated at around six metres wide, which ran down from Normanton Oil depot, and now was full of burning oil. Occasionally this flared up into an impassable wall of flame.

The Japanese had set the *beluka* (grassy undergrowth) on Chandu on fire which, combined with the smoke from Normanton, meant that visibility was severely hampered and fighting done at extremely close quarters. Pepys Road, named just a few years earlier for Johor General Advisor Walter Evelyn Pepys, ran across the hill and hosted a few bungalows dating back to 1910, built by the Colonial government for senior officers. Some now seemed to house military and food supplies.

On Opium Hill, 2nd Lt Adnan Saidi – with 42 men in his platoon – was observing ragtag groups of Punjabi soldiers making their way slowly in ranks of fours up the slope. He was immediately suspicious. British units didn't typically march in fours, rather threes. You mean ...? Damn, Japanese disguised as Punjabis! As they reached the firing lines of the Malay Regiment, they felt the full brunt of C Company's Lewis machine guns. Other rifles opened up too –

finding their deadly mark. After all, four of the top marksmen in the 1941 military competition in Singapore were drawn from C Company. Most of the charading Japanese died in the first fusillade. Others rolled or crawled down the steep hill to safety.

Two hours later, the Japanese regrouped and launched an all-out assault, outnumbering the defenders on the hill by at least 10:1. The Malays were by now already short on ammunition and supplies, but fought with their all in keeping with their motto *'Ta-at Setia'* meaning 'loyal and true.'

Harry Rix was made of stern stuff and a natural leader who'd been head of house at Sherborne School, a school prefect, in the 2nd XV rugby team, and a useful all-rounder in the school's 1st XI cricket team. He'd gone on to study law at Cambridge and, because he'd gone out to be a solicitor and advocate in the Supreme Court in Malaya, signed on locally. 'The company officer Capt Rix maintained close personal touch with his men, and showed disregard for danger which inspired his men to equal efforts,' said Dol Ramli, the regiment's biographer. 'He gave orders that the position should be defended to the last man and the last round, and the majority of the C Company followed his example and died fighting.'
He was tragically cut down at the age of 41, just a day before hostilities would end.

Finally after a desperate battle with the Malays standing and holding their ground, the Japanese broke through. All Malay officers, with the exception of Lt Adnan and 2nd Lt Abbas bin Abdul Manan, had been killed in the vicious onslaught with close-quarter exchanges of grenades and automatic rifle fire. Adnan was laying down withering fire with his Lewis gun to devastating effect. He copped a serious injury but kept shouting encouragement. '*Tuan*, if I should die today, I am quite willing as long as someone can look after my family,' he shouted to a fellow soldier.

**

Lt Jack 'Hugo' Hughes was a tough kind of guy. South African by birth, he'd moved to New Zealand to farm before moving to Malaya in 1930 as a 23-year-old. As an assistant planter, he was doing his bit when he signed up for the FMS Volunteers. His wife, Frances, evacuated with her mother, grandmother, and their baby boy, Gerald, not yet two. They made it safely to Fremantle. A great relief to him, but just two days later, he was fatefully attached to the Malay Regiment. In the cascade of mortar fire that rained down on these hills, he took a blast to the leg, and was rushed to The Alex, where his leg was amputated.

Soon, the Japanese were savagely mopping up. Some captured survivors were massacred, and Cpl Yaakob, in the chaos of the carnage, fell on top of a pile of dead soldiers, taking the chance to lie motionless and play dead. He unwittingly witnessed a gruesome spectacle. This involved the hero Adnan who, according to differing reports, was either hung upside down from a tree and bayonetted, or had his throat slashed many times and was stuffed into a gunny sack. Or both. *'Yell! Stick! Turn! Retract!'*

The only officer who survived that brutal bout on Bukit Chandu was Lt Abbas bin Abdul Manan who, with four of his men, fought their way backwards through a raging oil blaze, eventually leaping the flaming trench. Many fell short in their desperate attempt to ford it.

Lt Gen Percival later heaped praise on the actions of the regiment in that action: 'The Malay Regiment showed what esprit de corps and discipline can achieve. Garrisons of posts held their ground and many of them were wiped out to a man.' Six British officers, seven Malay officers, and 146 other ranks had perished, largely in those preceding two days of battle on Opium Hill.

But the Malay Regiment – who'd done founding officer Maj George Bruce so proud on Bukit Chandu with their fighting spirit – was to pay even more heavily for its gallantry in frustrating Mutaguchi's 18th Division advance to be the first to reach Singapore town.

**

The 'fog of war' was thickening into opacity, even as nighttime lifted only to reveal a smoke-filled tropical dawn. Did anyone know, or care, that it was Valentine's Day? Certainly many of the men were married, some engaged, many with sweethearts left fretting at home.

Frustration was seeping into the IJA 18th Division too. 'The right wing of my division could move to Hill 130, northeast of Keppel,' observed Mutaguchi, 'but there they were pinned down. The left wing unit could secure a hill northeast of the oil tank but they were pinned down by the British again. After this, both of them couldn't move forward much at all.' _Suddenly the surging sprint into Singapore was not the sure thing it might have been assumed by the Japanese. And pushing rapidly towards the town from the east were the Imperial Guards.

**

During the day the smoke from burning oil in the harbour and the oil dumps settled to create 'a gloomy pall' as Drummond saw it from his hospital bed. The ward doors were kept closed but bullets and shrapnel came through the windows and ventilators and ricocheted around the walls. More shells flew over them, intended for the IJA 55th Regiment (in reserve on Pasir Panjang Heights) or possibly even the 5th Division further east.

'Had the British not noticed how close the 114th had got?' wondered Arai. They were just 1.5 km from Blakang Mati now. Keppel Harbour could be taken tomorrow. They avoided the reportedly mined road, using its edge, along to Pasir Panjang Heights.

Meanwhile, Takeda had set up his command post at Trig Station 120, and battle orders for the day issued resulting in a shuffling of the troops. '114th Inf Regt was ordered to take Hill 225 and Hill 226.' Arai recalled the Tiger Brewery was also a military objective on that day. Perhaps it was just wishful thinking on his part?

The *Soshi Shenso* battle plan for that day also includes some crucial directives which impacted what happened next: 'Koba Regt (55th Inf Regt) was ordered to move north side of the beach fortress but then ordered to be the left wing unit together with 1st Mountain Artillery battalion and a mortar company, deployed at the west area of the Hill 150 and was newly ordered to attack the British force in front and reach Keppel Harbour on 15 February. 55th Regiment moved along the railway to the south and the regimental commander ordered 2nd Bn (Ito) to attack Hill 312 and the Keppel Barracks and reach the south of the Hill 345, while 1st Bn (Kagawa) was to be ready to move to the left side of 2nd Bn if necessary.' Maj Kagawa had stepped into Maj Koda's boots as OC 1/55th, after Koda was wounded at Bukit Timah and was not with his men for the remainder of the Singapore campaign.

Typical IJA battlefield tactics involved deploying mortars and machine gun crews as far forward as possible to fix the enemy and tie them down, while other infantry units would then attempt a flanking movement.

Mortar battalions typically set up around 600-1000 metres behind the front lines and targeted positions 1000-1500 metres beyond the front lines.
The 14th Independent Mortar Battalion, commanded by Maj Tanaka, used Type 98 32cm spigot mortars. Tsuji reported that they had eight 40-cm (16-inch) mortars. These mortars were noticeably bigger than the standard three-inch models, and were carried around by means of a handcart. Devastatingly effective weapons.

Fellow Japanese talked about the awe of this company's 'ghost rockets' and the overwhelming sound they produced, which were as fearsome to them as to the enemy.

**

At 8am 14 February, an observation balloon went aloft, and by 08:30 shells peppered the Gillman Barracks and Alexandra Depot areas, wreaking havoc with transport and causing massive Allied casualties. Brig Williams was trying to make his way forward to where the Loyals were, but the Depot area was under artillery attack, and many of the hutments – the cause of such controversy during construction – were ablaze. Mortars (many captured from the British) were thudding in among the Loyals, and dive-bombers screeched down from the sky. Worse still, it looked like the island's main magazine was at risk of a direct hit.

All the while, Maj Andre was a positive encouraging force to his Malay troops, aided and abetted by RSM Ismail bin Baba who 'showed great courage and coolness while under fire ... and carried out his duties with great devotion' to Andre, valuably bridging the gap with the other ranks. Andre would win the DSO for his efforts here. 'He maintained a high standard of efficiency and morale ... and he was invariably cheerful and cool in emergency,' the citation would read.

The 1st Malays operating from the ridge ejected enemy patrols trying to overrun the bungalow area where the Loyals' B company was.

With The Alex hospital now effectively isolated between lines, there was little traffic on the roads around, and only about six men, mostly dazed stragglers, found their way into the hospital that morning.

Around 11am, the Machine Gun Company descended with 1st Bn to the main road that runs northeast of the hills. 'We advanced in the late morning ahead of the main strength of the regiment,' recalled Capt Soejima. The main regiment seemed to be somewhat in disarray. 'The advance was delayed until about 11:00 on account of British shelling and the reshuffling of troops necessitated in order to place 56th Regt in the second line reserve in the rear,' recalled Maj Gen Takeda. '114th Regt was brought round to the right of the line (ie the hill sector of Pasir Panjang), and 55th Regt on the left, to advance through the oil tank sector towards the railway line. One battalion of 56th Regt, through some misunderstanding, advanced with 55th Regt, though it was meant to have stayed in the rear with the rest of 56th Regt.'

By now the noon-day sun was overhead, although it was struggling to be seen through the swirling palls of smoke.

'At about noon there were indications that the British were retreating from the Keppel area,' said Nasu of the 56th, 'but this subsequently proved to be false. It was decided that we should give pursuit to the retreating troops. The regiment hastily assembled on the road north below Pasir Panjang Hills. 1st Bn was assembled first and, as the rest of the regiment was still not completely formed up, this battalion was sent on ahead along the road north below the

Pasir Panjang Hills. When the rest of the regiment had formed up, they advanced at the head of the column about an hour or so behind 1st Bn.'

Ito from 2/55th Regiment, born in the cherry-blossom laden prefecture of Aichi, south towards Osaka, shared his perspective: 'About noon the regiment proceeded down from the heights towards the main road that runs northeast of the Pasir Panjang Heights in Singapore town. My battalion, 2nd Bn, was the first to begin the advance along the main road. This was after we had eaten our midday meal. I think 1st and 3rd Bn followed behind us and 56th Regt followed behind them. I advanced at the head of my battalion without sending any patrols ahead of me, the regimental commander having ordered a rapid advance into Singapore City, believing that the fighting was almost over.'

As for 3/55th Regiment, their OC, Tsugawa, said: 'My 3 Bn was in reserve behind 1st and 2nd Battalions and behind regimental HQ. Our position was east of the main road and slightly north of the oil tanks between trig points 100 and 150. Shortly after we reached the oil tanks, they received a direct hit and burst into flames.' It's an important detail that there were a couple of battalions and companies ahead of them, including regimental HQ.

Capt Umemoto, adjutant of 55th Regiment, confirmed this order. 'The 55th Regiment was ordered into the front line. The column of march was formed in the following order: 2nd Bn, Regimental HQ, 1st Bn, and 3rd Bn. 55th Regiment advanced towards Singapore city along the road running northeast of the Pasir Panjang Heights. Our regiment, with 2nd Bn at the head, were the first troops to enter the area south of Pasir Panjang. As far as I know there were no divisional or army troops ahead of us. When 2nd Bn reached the oil tanks, these were already on fire.'

The attacking force started moving south along the railway line, appreciating its flatness and firmness under foot. 'In the afternoon,' Capt Soejima said, 'we had reached the oil tanks. By this time the oil tanks were ablaze and we skirted around them to the north. I don't think we regained the main road again that day.'

But Mutaguchi and his Divisional HQ were having a rough time of it while calling the shots from Hill 110. After 114th took over

Bukit Chandu, he decided to move forward his HQ, 'but he had to return the HQ to the original position at Hill 110 due to British heavy artillery firing.'

**

Meanwhile, the 1st Malays manning the Buona Vista roadblock could finally hold out no more, and Japanese tanks broke through. Hand-to-hand fighting with the infantry following behind them ensued. But a little further down the road, the D Company Malays were exacting some sort of revenge of their own. Overlooking the Alexandra Brickworks area, D Company and their battalion HQ – well armed with 3-inch mortars – plus an assorted battalion fused from 5th Bedfordshires and Hertsfordshires and the badly mauled Leicestershires and others, saw two companies of Japanese openly marching down Pasir Panjang Rd.

2nd Lt Alistair McKenzie, a 26-year-old seconded to the Malays, said: 'Imagine our surprise and delight when the Nips appeared marching straight down the Pasir Panjang Road – in fours! We let them go to within 100-150 yards of D Company HQ and then let them have it with machine guns first and then with mortars.' Pte Sulong Ahmed reckoned it was with a lot more than that: rifles, Lewis guns, rifle grenades, anti-tank rifles, and even revolvers. 'Almost every man of the first company was slaughtered and a lot further back too. A Loyals officer up on the right counted 94 bodies on that part of the road that he could see alone,' McKenzie reckoned. A further 300 were wounded. Most likely these were 114th Regiment personnel.

This further aggravated the would-be conquerors this close to their goal. And what they did next was to take local villagers as human shields to mask their advance.

B Company of the 2nd Loyals, and the 5th Bedfords (under 30-year-old Capt James Robinson) were dug-in in front of the British other ranks' married quarters, facing Ayer Rajah Road. While the defenders' job was made trickier by the wall of local civilians, including women and children, the Japanese pushed along ahead of them. Having to fire over their heads, they took them on solidly for an hour, trading blows as the Japanese advanced.

**

Things were moving fast, though, as the Japanese prepared to attack Hill 150, Mount Faber, 500m to the *southeast* of the hospital. The Singapore-city side. 'The 55th Infantry Regiment's axis of advance was through trig points 156 and 150,' confirmed Mutaguchi. The Alex lies roughly but undeniably between these two points.

Adding further kindling to the impending fire was the not inconsiderable matter that the 55th Regiment were seriously aggrieved. The last few days had been expensive for them, losing none other than their commanding officer and a platoon commander. Why *now*? After all the hard yards of the Malayan campaign and the easy landing on Singapore? Why, with Singapore city and harbour – the glittering prize – finally, unbelievably, in sight, were the mighty 55th Regiment now accruing such heavy casualties?

At 1pm with all of the 55th Regiment units ready to attack at the west side of Hill 150, the enemy's guns and artillery firepower became stronger.

Ito's 2nd Bn was still on the move ahead of the pack._'We reached the oil tanks that extend right and left of the main road at about 1300 hours. As the oil tanks were ablaze we had to make a detour to the northeast of the tanks, a Malay guiding us back onto the main road south of the tanks. I regained the main road about 10 minutes later, still ahead of the battalion which was forced to follow windingly behind me in single file along the narrow path.' They wouldn't be able to fan out due to the heat emanating from those tanks anyway. And the roar and thunder emanating from them must have been something. The oil tanks were no more than 300 yards from the nearest northwestern wing of the hospital.

'When I regained the main road, everything was very quiet and hushed and I thought that all the fighting was over and that the enemy had completely withdrawn from that area. A few minutes after regaining the main road I think I noticed to the upper left of the main road, well off the road, two large buildings. From an upper story window of one of these buildings I saw hanging a large Red Cross flag.'

His next statement would be as thick and murky as the air around him: 'I think I was later told that the buildings were definitely a hospital.' 'I think' and 'definitely' seem contradictory terms – but let's give him benefit of the doubt given his statement was made nearly four years after the event – but one would be very surprised if the largest military hospital outside of Britain was not clearly marked on maps, or was at least known about and mentioned in battle briefings.

But it is significant because it places the 2/55th Regiment virtually at the boundaries of the hospital (but with no impediment to accessing it anyhow).

'Advancing south of this hospital I was approaching a fork road that branches off from the main road when I saw two or three British soldiers dart across the main road from ~~left~~ right (southeast) to ~~right~~ left.' These directions were scribbled out and transposed in his post-war statement but not countersigned. 'Immediately after this we were fired upon from the front and from the ~~right~~ left.' The left would be the direction of the hospital. East.

Where Ito and battalion were at that stage is south of the oil tanks, and the fork describes the intersection of Ayer Rajah Road and Alexandra Road, with Alexandra Barracks, Gillman Barracks and Depot Road rising up directly on their right.

'Realizing that there were enemy positions facing us from positions left of the road and from the barracks on a hill right of the road, I disposed my battalion as follows: 5th Company (if I remember correctly) stretched across both sides of the main road north of the fork and 6th Company (I think) to advance to take the positions on the hill. 7th Company (I think) was to follow in the rear of this company in reserve. I had thus committed my whole battalion to battle.'

'Then the enemy's guns and artillery fire power became stronger,' said the *Senshi Sosho*. 'The enemy machine guns shot from concrete positions were so accurate, and the artillery firing stopped us from moving forward over the road. The regiment that was deployed on the ground had no appropriate support and casualties started increasing. Commander Koba ordered men at the frontline to cover themselves and this stopped their attack during the daytime.'

Meanwhile, behind, all the other battalions, companies, and regiments were slowly reaching the oil tanks, in line of sight with the hospital. 'We were out of touch with the main strength of the regiment behind us and the battalion HQ ahead of us,' recalled Capt Soejima, OC of the Machine Gun Company. So a battalion HQ was ahead of them, presumably 1/56th Battalion under Matoba. While unconventional in British military behaviour, we've already established that this was standard Japanese modus operandi, to get their HQs and officers as far forward as practically possible.

**

Switching perspectives, this is what the Loyals faced: 'Some Japanese started advancing along Ayer Rajah Road, coming into contact with B Company 2nd Loyals and the 5th Bedfords who managed to repel them solidly for an hour until they broke through into the bungalow area.' Ironically it was where some of their officers' families lived in some of the beautiful big tropical 'black-and-white' homes.

Heavy shelling continued to exact casualties, with even 14 of the Loyals' stretcher-bearers themselves becoming casualties. The rest, notably Cpl Charles Wanless, scurried around devotedly doing their duty, earning himself a Military Medal for his bravery on that day.

Of the Malays, Pte Ahmed was seriously injured in the neck. He and all wounded were taken to makeshift hospitals in Singapore town itself, in six of the Loyals' own trucks – in the absence of any ambulances – arranged by the quick-thinking Capt John Jesson.

This was telling. Because, adjacent, the British Military Hospital Alexandra now sat totally isolated and vulnerable in some kind of no-man's land.

ADVANCE OF 18TH DIV IJA TROOPS MID-DAY, 14 FEB 1942

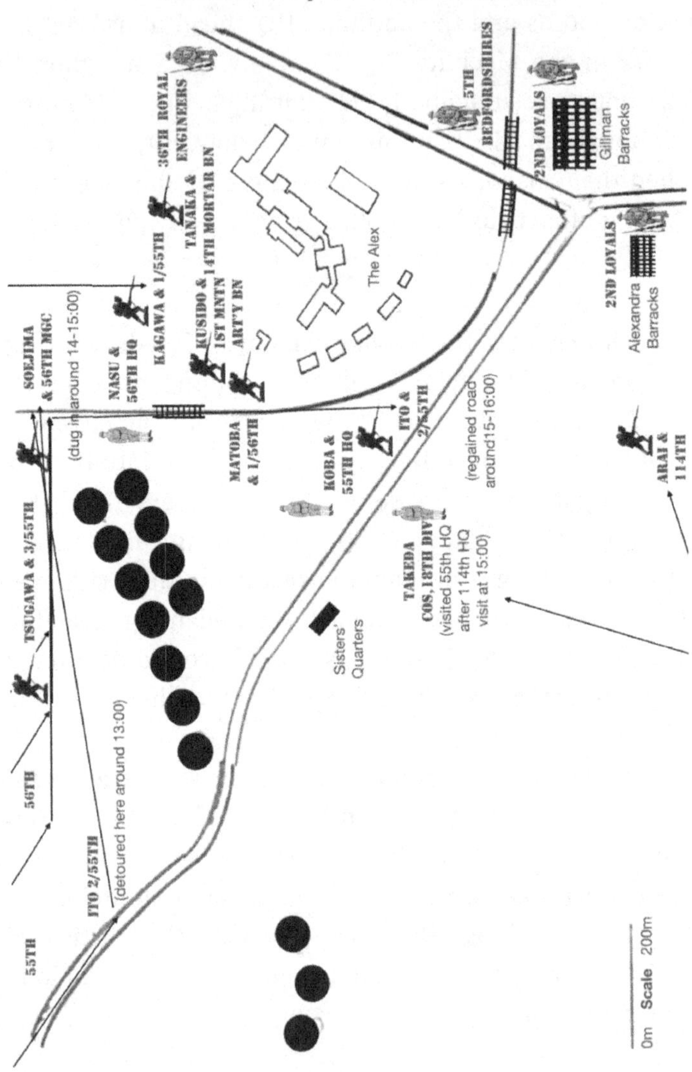

THE PERFECT STORM

'The soles of my shoes were thick with blood.'

14 February 1942. They could hardly believe it. Keppel Harbour. The heart of Singapore. They would be there. *Tomorrow*! An exciting yet daunting thought. Taking on Fort Siloso, one of the world's most heavily fortified sites, would be extremely dangerous. Arai's mind wandered: 'Loved ones at home, family and friends.' Schooldays images shot in and out of focus. Then the rugged battles came to mind. 'My dead and heavily wounded comrades. There had been little laughter, no frills, lots of loss.' But now they were here – tantalizingly near the finish line. A mere 1.5km away.

In the hospital, patients and staff noted the rising intensity. 'The water supply was cut off, shelling and air activity became intense, and some shells were bursting in and around the hospital,' said the injured ship's purser, Carse. 'The enemy were then drawing near the rear of the hospital from Ayer Rajah Road.'

'I was awoken just after 08:00 by the noise of heavy bombs landing all around the hospital,' said John Wyatt, nursing an injured shoulder.

But roads around the area seemed suddenly devoid of traffic because the hospital was effectively in a no-man's land between lines. About half a dozen stragglers from nearby battlefields found their own way to the hospital. 'I think they may have been lost,' said Smiley. 'Plus several Chinese from the neighbourhood.'

Part of the endless parade who'd arrived at The Alex was injured gunner and budding magician, Fergus Anckorn. 'When you're unconscious, you don't know if you've been under for 30 seconds or a week. You just wake up,' he said. 'The next time I woke up I was in The Alex in a bed. It was full of people, some lying on stretchers between beds. My arm was strapped up and hung from a hook above my bed. On the end of my arm was a large dressing like a huge boxing glove. I was desperate to know if I still had my hand or not.' There seemed to be a total lack of staff around, until he sighted an orderly coming down the ward. 'He was hurriedly putting up blackout boards on the windows, even though it was daylight.'

Gunner FT Moore from 9th Coastal Regiment even noticed there was little or no traffic in the wards. Some sort of ominous pre-storm calmness amid the chaos. Now the hospital was being hit by both sides, reported Australian Pte Alex Drummond, a Victorian who'd joined the 2/29th just seven months prior, and was in Ward 17 at the far eastern end of the corridor.

Upstairs in the officers' ward, Capt Pilkington, had a clearer vantage point. 'The battle was raging in the hospital grounds, with our own artillery now searching for the Japs amongst the oil wells.' He was reading *Gone With the Wind*, which had launched to great fanfare three years previously. 'Naturally I'd got to the part where the hospital was under fire,' he said. In the movie version, the doctor character, played by Mickey Kuhn, said: 'They're dying ... hundreds of 'em,' as stretchers and bodies were borne past him in an endless parade.

Smiley was doing his rounds as usual. 'Then someone called out: "Doctor, doctor ... do something here ... he's bleeding like hell." Indeed, my blood was dripping down on the man below,' said Anckorn who was attended to by Smiley. 'He looked younger than I was, pleasant but serious,' is how Anckorn saw him. 'I got the idea he was blonde headed, about 5'8' or 5'9', a good thin figure.'

The sounds of gunfire and shelling increased, as though building to a symbolic crescendo.

'The shells were dropping short around the bleedin' hospital, and you could hear the bleedin' shells going over the bleedin' top, near the hospital, outside,' said Gunner Dick Lee, RA, who was receiving a blood transfusion, with one foot in plaster, the other up on a cradle. 'Hours before, the medical officer came around and says, "The Japanese are advancing – you can expect they'll be in the hospital soon". And the medical orderlies were attending to the wounded and this officer says: "If the Japanese come in, you won't understand them, they won't understand you. But everybody must stay where they are, you'll be a walking wounded, don't walk about, don't make yourself busy, busy, busy. Stay where you are, in your beds, lie down, and if they come in, put your hands up, let them see that there's no resistance." Got the set up have ya?' Dick said, his voice rising, and cracking.

**

Orderly Bert Gurd realized it was St Valentine's Day, and probably cast a fond thought in the direction of Rosa at home with her family in Watford as he drew breath and took a quick 'tiffin' break. He glanced out from the verandah towards the railway line. 'I saw some troops in single file, they wear foliage as camouflage, and one carries a Japanese flag. In spite of this, one of our officers declares they are British.' He went back to work, while the volume of rifle and machine gun fire escalated all around for the next hour.

Maj James Bull, the radiologist who'd scanned the worst of the worst cases in the hospital, was also on one of the verandahs of the hospital. 'At about 1pm Japanese front line troops approached the hospital grounds and infiltrated around the building. They were firing with small arms and machine guns.'

'I hobbled across to the window,' said John Wyatt, in the upstairs ward. 'I was stunned by the sight that met my eyes across the grounds. Japanese soldiers were advancing across the hospital grounds. They were dressed in full combat kit consisting of green tropical uniforms, steel helmets, rifles, bayonets, and machine guns. They were heavily camouflaged with small branches. Seconds later all hell broke out downstairs.'

Pop! Pop! Pop!

Small arms crackled to life, too close for comfort. 'I was with six others,' recalled Cpl James Torbit in the dispensary. 'There was a burst of small arms fire and a number of our soldiers – about platoon strength – were retreating across the open space behind the hospital, followed by a force of Japanese soldiers. By this time the stray bullets were hitting the walls of the corridor.' He wisely closed the door of the dispensary.

Cpl Johnson was toiling away in the over-crowded Admissions area of the hospital. 'We observed our troops withdrawing on either side of the hospital,' he said. 'And could hear the Japanese only a few hundred yards away. I do not know the

Japanese unit involved. I did however see a number of Sikhs who were dressed in British pattern khaki drill, but were wearing white armbands, and fighting with the Japanese.' This was the origins of the Indian National Army at work, comprising traitorous turncoats.

'The advance of the Japanese troops was witnessed by me personally,' said Bull, sitting upstairs. They came from the direction of the railway line, which curves around the western front of the hospital, veering north away from the oil tanks. They poured around ancillary hospital buildings such as the garage, laboratory and the mortuary. A small RAMC group was working in this area. Those in the command area saw this first wave pouring in and made a mad dash for the main block but as they ran across the lush lawns, they were caught in the open by machine gun fire. Maj Clarence Calder and Sgt George Williams died where they dropped. Cpl Robert Saint was hit in the arm, badly wounded, but straggled his way to safety.

**

The first Japanese wave was a platoon who infiltrated the hospital front and barracks block around 3pm. There would be two more main waves – a second platoon hitting the rear entrance of the Admission room, medical wards 5 and 6, and the patients' dining room ward. Then a third platoon would wash in through the windows to the operating theatre block and surgical wards 16 and 17.

Although we narratively treat these waves individually there was not a great time difference between them, and amid the chaos and confusion they would've felt like simultaneous events.

It was to be a two-day tsunami of terror.

'I was lying where the corridor leads out down a couple of steps to the grass outside, at the end of the line,' said Gunner Dick Lee, probably referring to the western end of Block 4. 'You come up these steps onto the corridor. In other words, anyone coming from the outside in, I was the first one.'

This would be his first up-close encounter with the Japanese, despite being bombed and harassed from the air so many times.

'All of a sudden I could hear screams,' recalled Lee. 'And shooting outside the door. Whether they caught up with people and bayonetting outside I don't know, but I could hear screams. And a few shots here and there now and again. And then it just went silent. For, it could be a minute, maybe less than a minute, it went silent. A little sense told me somebody was near me. And I looked up and two of the biggest bastards you've seen – we'd been told they were little blokes, they were little people, wore glasses, can't shoot straight all that shit they were giving you beforehand. They were part of the Imperial Guard, could've been. And the one nearest me, he had his rifle in his left hand and his bayonet – about 18 inches long – and he lifted up the sheet with his bayonet to have a look under. Because I had me leg up in a cradle. I don't know if he thought I had a fuckin' machine gun or something underneath, I mean you don't know what they're thinking. And as he looked at me he grinned down and I could see this bleedin' gold tooth he had in his mouth, and he let the sheet down, and he's rabbiting, talking away to his pal.'

Bull was upstairs, about 20 of them sitting in a room. 'I was called out of the room by a British medical orderly who asked me to see a Japanese soldier outside. When I got outside, there was no evidence of the Japanese soldier, and the orderly had gone.' He then headed for the CO's office, just nearby to the left, 'to see if he knew what was happening.'

The CO's office was on the second floor above the nurses' rest room, which in turn was directly above the main Admissions portico at the entrance. Craven, Maj Hugh Henderson (the registrar), and the chaplain were in his office considering the option of surrender at this point.

'From his office window I saw two Japanese soldiers about 150-200 yards away, one with a rifle and one with field glasses,' said Bull. 'Thinking there might be some doubt in their minds as to whether we were still a hospital, although Red Crosses were still displayed on it, I fetched a Red Cross flag from nearby and held it up to them at the window.'

BANG! A sniper took his shot.

'They had a shot at me through the window and missed, so I thought I'd better get out of the way.' There was the clamour and crumping of more mortars at this point, which probably disguised and covered any sounds coming from downstairs. 'I had absolutely no idea at this point what was going on.'

Downstairs near the entrance, a Japanese soldier, watched by Capt James Bartlett, RAMC, entered the gap of an overlapping blast wall. Bartlett strode out to meet him, presenting no threat with arms raised, then indicating the Red Cross brassards. He was shot at point-blank range, falling into the adjacent ward duty room.

BANG! A hand grenade exploded. He survived.

George Johnson, working in the Admissions room, picked up the story: 'The Japanese were nearly all the Ainu type and appeared to be frontline troops.' Ainu are an almost European-looking race, very early settlers in Japan, although typically from Hokkaido in the far north. They have rounder eyes, fairer skin, and more body hair than the typical Japanese of Yamato descent. Which doesn't really tally given that the 18th Division was sourced from the Kyushu region of the far south. Thus opening the doors to further possibilities of who the perpetrators might have been.

'About 30 men were employed under the command of Lt Weston in the Admissions Room,' said Johnson. Many of those were seconded from the Dental Corps, and pressed into assisting the orderlies. 'Weston ordered us all to sit down on the floor and then took a white sheet from the examination couch and held it out the back door of the room as a signal of surrender. A Japanese Ainu soldier came along and plunged his bayonet through the sheet and into Weston's body.' William Weston, aged just 27, bled out and subsequently died.

'As soon as Weston was bayonetted the rest of us in the room made a break through the front door,' said Johnson. 'Some of the men ran out of the main door of the hospital and were promptly fired on with rifles and machine guns by Japanese troops who had infiltrated round either side of the building.'

Probably cut down in this moment were Padre Henry Smith, 29, of the Royal Army Chaplains who was attached to 2nd Gordon Highlanders, and one of those seconded Dental Corps personnel, Staff Sgt Sydney Walker, 33. Jack Mace, a 26-year-old RAMC corporal, made a desperate dash for the Admissions Room front door, only to be cut down by rifles and machine guns which were now sited at the side of the hospital.

This was witnessed by his Eurasian wife, Betty Fernandez, a VAD in the hospital, who saw him then taken away by the Japanese, and she was unsure if he was alive or dead. The well-built Arthur Collins, a 5'10" 29-year-old RAMC corporal, was usually stationed at the Selarang Reception Station, and often acted as an ambulance orderly. He was unlucky to be at The Alex on this day, possibly having just delivered patients to the hospital, and was standing in a doorway when he was suddenly attacked. 'He received a bayonet thrust in his back, coming out through his abdomen,' according to Stringer. 'He was left for dead. The lucky corporal got up when all had gone, and managed to get to the surgical ward where I saw the wounds myself.'

'Japanese fighting troops now ran into the hospital and ran amok on the ground floor,' said Lance Cpl Bob Mutton of the 4th Royal Norfolks. 'They were very excitable and very jumpy and neither pointing to the Red Cross brassards nor shouting the word 'hospital' had any effect.'

Ossie Griffin, with his sword-slashed arm, resolved to stall the invaders while enabling others to make a getaway. 'All you men who can get to the lines, get out if you can get out,' he shouted. 'Don't let them see you're wounded, cover up if necessary. Get out!' This was told to Neil Storey by Sgt Allison and Pte Jack Riseborough, both fellow Royal Norfolksman present. 'What else could you do? The Japs are in, around, blood on their bayonets, blood on them. Ossie got the red mist.' His defiant delaying action enabled some, like Allison, to make it back to their lines. Alas, the small band of brave resistors were never seen alive again.

Other defiant but deadly actions took place. 29-year-old Lance Sgt Gordon MacDougal from the 2/20 Battalion AIF was laid up with a wounded arm. He bravely tried to disarm a Japanese soldier with his good arm, but was killed. His unit mate, Lt Harry Woods from Mudgee – who'd recently showed bravery on the battlefield patching up a Dalforce member under heavy fire – survived the massacre and the war.

'As the Japanese came in the front of the building, those who were mobile ran out the other side of the building to escape,' remembered Bill Warbrick, lying immobilized. Others ran into the corridor which ran along the back of the hospital and encountered Japanese soldiers who were just breaking into the building, and who promptly bayonetted them. Sgt Thomas Sheriff, RAMC – a 28-year-old of medium build who liked to wear his dark hair brushed back – was bayonetted three times, then carried into a ward by orderly Pte John Lynas, but took two full days to die what must have been a most slow, lingering, painful death.

'The Japanese must have seen that our men were unarmed and I have no doubt they bayonetted them out of sheer brutality,' said Johnson.

**

In the hospital kitchen, a desperate scene was playing itself out. RA Gunner Richard Gwillim lay badly wounded on the floor. Two RAMC orderlies wearing their Red Cross brassards, Pte Harry Saye and Pte Arthur Bruce, 23, were attending to him. Bruce gave Gwillim a drink of water and redressed his wounds, and Saye went to the wards to fetch something.

Ping! A shot ricocheted off the floor, and two Japanese stormed into the kitchen. As Bruce stood up, he was shot three times in the stomach 'probably by a tommy gun'. The two Japs stood over Gwillim, who was splattered with Bruce's blood and playing doggo, pretending to be dead.

The Japanese soon lost interest and left. Gwillim, understandably hysterical, managed to pull himself up and find his way back to the main wards. Then a grenade was tossed through the window of the Ward Office, adjacent the kitchen in the northeast corner. RSM William Ridout tried to shoo the Japanese from the wards, but his hand and arm were shredded, and later amputated.

**

Enter the third platoon from the northeast end of the hospital, racing along the corridor and tossing grenades, shooting and bayonetting all whom they passed. But in their hurry, they missed a few. Such as Torbit, with his dispensary door pulled shut, who had sheltered seven others even as they could hear the footsteps running past their door and the shots fired.

George Poole was another. The 33-year-old regular RAMC orderly from Sheffield had seen Japanese brutality in northern China when he was posted there in 1938 and didn't want any part of this here. 'They sent the Imperial Guard in – their crack troops. They came through the hospital with fixed bayonets and did-in everybody they could find. We had no guns, there was nothing we could do. A friend and I hid in a linen cupboard and buried ourselves in the blankets.'

Orderly Cpl Joe Nutter didn't care about medals for bravery, either. He and three other RAMC orderlies bolted for the space above the hospital's central elevator. And there they hid undetected for three days before emerging unscathed.

Despite his very recent appendectomy, Gunner Edward Furness was quick-thinking and quick-acting. He managed to grab some of his clothes, climb through a window and make a mad dash for it. He made it back to Allied lines, and even found his artillery company, although he might have ruptured his wound in the process, because he never made a full physical nor mental recovery.

On the left of the corridor another larger group comprising two medical officers and FC Stuart – the senior representative of the Australian Red Cross Society – plus 16 patients had sheltered in Operating Theatre #2 and remained miraculously undiscovered.

Irshad Ali Khan was a civilian employed by DCRE Alexandra after it had opened, and was part of that group. 'I myself, my brother, his family and other friends were in the ground floor operating theatre. The Japanese soldier opened fire on us – in the firing my brother-in-law, cousin and some friends were killed. Then they moved to the other wing of the building. Some of us hid in a room for our life. Then the Japanese soldiers came back looking for us, but they saw some dead and injured by their gunfire so they did not bother about us. God almighty saved our lives.'

Other Indian civilians weren't so lucky. 'Three Indians employed in the boiler room were killed and badly mutilated,' said

Brig Stringer. 'Their skulls were smashed, their abdomens ripped up with their intestines hanging out.'

Saye had made his way to the wards. 'Some were two in a bed and under the bed. With groans and shouts for water, it was like bedlam. The soles of my shoes were thick with blood.' The sickly smell of human blood rose with the suffocating heat of the day. 'The *Banzai* charge had arrived. They jumped over the verandah, raced up the corridor, killing whoever they saw. The Japs threw a hand grenade in the Surgical Ward Toilet-OR Office, raced over the verandah as far as ORI Billets, where they shot one of our men. I can still hear him now shouting "Water! Water! Water!"'

Saye later managed to make his way back to the kitchen. 'When I left to go to the ward, that was the most important move in my life. When I went back later, poor Bruce was lying on the floor of the kitchen, dead. He was riddled with bullets.'

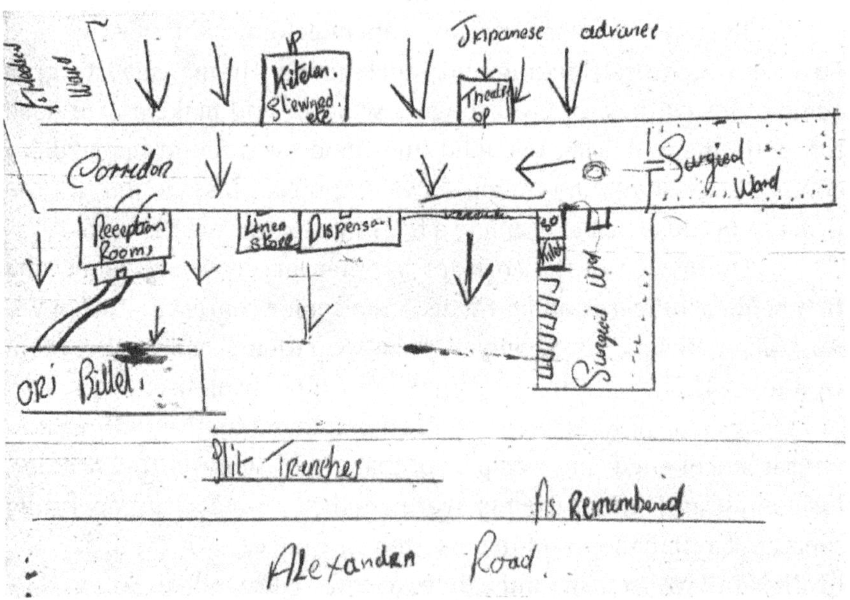

The verandah invasion drawn by Pte Saye, RAMC.

The Japanese now focused on Ward 17 downstairs. This is probably where Fergus Anckorn was. 'Isn't that a Jap soldier?" he asked.

'Yes, it's a Jap.'

'I'd never seen a Jap before at closer than three or four miles,' he said. 'Suddenly I could hear many feet coming into the ward and a kind of thumping noise. *Thud! Thud! Thud!* "They're bayonetting everybody," said the man next to me, calmly. There were no cries, no screams, nothing. I pulled up my pillow with my one good hand and covered my face. I muttered "Poor mum". I must have looked dead so they left me,' he thought.

'Funny thing when you realize you are going to be dead in 10 seconds, there is no fear at all. There is nothing you can do about it, there is nothing to fear because you will be off the planet. I did not hear one person cry out. It's amazing isn't it? Once you realize it's all over, there's nothing to worry about.'

Duke University behavioural scientist, Dan Ariely offers a possible explanation: 'In the case of pain, expectation can release hormones and neurotransmitters, such as endorphins and opiates, that not only block agony but also produce exuberant highs (endorphins trigger the same neurotransmitters as morphine).'

'I looked around and thought: My God, we're all dead,' said Anckorn. 'I was the only survivor of 71 in the ward. I never thought, that was a close one. I just thought, God, I'm alive! In action you see so many getting killed, it just becomes a way of life. I didn't even think I'm lucky *I'm* not – then I passed out.'

At 57, CQMS John Hartery was nearly double the age of most of those around him. But that afforded the long-serving RAMC regular no special immunity from the thrusting bayonets. At 51, Australian Cpl William Warren was a WW1 veteran and had been the managing director of Anglo-Oriental Mining up in Perak before attaching to the Singapore Observer Corps the previous month. Wounded, he was holed up here, but would die in April of his injuries.

Medical orderly Pte Len Knott was so traumatized by the brutality to his innocent bed-ridden patients, he and other medics stepped outside to vomit. A system in shock.

**

Immediately behind the hospital, perhaps just a couple of hundred yards, were the 36th Royal Engineers who had hastily repositioned themselves here from in front of the hospital amid the fluctuating fortunes of the frontline the day before. One imagines they should have seen Ito's battalion moving up on the road to their immediate left.

'We thought of moving to the left or to the right to get a better view through this gap,' said Daniel Fraser, just 25. The officer in charge was Maj John Montresor from Kent, who was slightly inexperienced to be dealing with such a complex situation, having joined the RE Corps in 1935 but having only served as a lieutenant in Palestine from 1939-40 before shipping to Malaya.

'Just as we were thinking of moving, the Japanese had entered the hospital on the north side,' said Fraser in his even Scottish brogue. 'There was nothing we could do about stopping the Japanese because they were into the hospital at the time. And next we heard screams and noises, we knew what was happening, we couldn't do a thing about it. Because with international law you are not allowed to touch a hospital, you should go round about it. So our officer said we can't do anything, we must wait till they come out, which I think is quite the right thing to do.'

But was the hospital clearly and obviously marked as such?

'There was a Red Cross flying from the mast,' recalled Fraser, 'also an international flag, international Red Cross. No way they could mistake, even when they went into the place, that it was a hospital.'

**

Meanwhile, upstairs in the Officers' Ward, there was also a sense of helplessness. They could hear the cries for mercy but could do nothing to help. And wondered whether they were in for it next.

'It was horrible to be on the second level and to hear all the ...,' John Wilson trailed off, '... but I didn't witness the massacre because I was immobile. But I could hear the noise. One of the surgeons came up and told us to stay where we were and not move with what was going on.' So Wilson lay there in bed, in the same dirty clothes he'd come off the battlefield in, with his binoculars. 'That's all I had.'

John Wyatt panicked. 'I suddenly remembered that I still had the dead Japanese officer's watch that I had taken from him back at Kampar. God, if they find that on me I'm definitely dead. I got out of bed, limped as quickly as I could to the toilet, and with great difficulty placed the watch on top of the cistern, then quickly got back into bed.'

Frederick Bales was a driver with the 6th Royal Norfolks, and was recovering from an operation for synovitis on the knee. 'I could just walk, but I was in bed,' he said. 'The building was first rushed by shock troops, and I heard the sound of shooting and men screaming from the ground floor. As far as I know these shock troops just passed through the hospital, shooting it up on the way.'

'The doors and windows of my room were closed,' remembered Peter Lucy. 'And the fact that nothing could be seen added to the terror of listening to the terrible screaming from below. Everybody lay quietly, without panic, listening to the firing and screaming while rifle bullets were flying through the room and plaster from the ceiling was falling on the beds. The roar of planes flying low over the hospital, and the serial machine-gunning together with the intense shelling added to the tremendous roar of battle.'

It is hard to underestimate the cacophony bouncing around those walls.

'At this stage, a soldier stood up from his bed, said that in civilian life he was a parson in Norfolk, and he thought we would like him to say a few words,' recalled Lucy. 'He said we all know what to expect in the next few minutes, and asked everyone to have faith, knowing that God is present in this room watching every man, and now was the time to show faith and courage.'

Capt Brown was another who heard the screams and yells. 'And I knew then they were in the hospital,' he said in a flat tone of voice, very matter of factly. 'We had no idea what exactly was happening. But then ... there was confusion downstairs. And we kept waiting for them to come upstairs, but they never came up. We didn't know what was happening. People were too terrified to go downstairs to find out what was happening.'

With the exception of one unidentified Aussie. 'And this Australian came walking down the stairs with his arm in a sling, whether he had an arm wound or a shoulder wound,' said Dick Lee, who was in a bed at the bottom of the staircase. 'He had his pyjama trousers on, so the top half of his body was bare. He's come down with all this screaming and shooting outside. And as he's come to the foot of the stairs more or less opposite where I was, he stopped and leaned against the pillar. And a Jap walked straight over and shoved the bayonet straight into his gut. As he stepped back, I saw the Aussie put his other hand up to his stomach and all the blood was running out of his fingers and he just slumped down to the floor.'

Medical orderlies sprang into action. 'They came and took the Aussie away and later I found out he survived the bayonet wound,' said Lee. 'But it was after that there was groups of them started to come in. You could hear screams, shooting outside. And of course the first lot that come in are pointing to their wrist, their watch, their rings. And they're wanting all the stuff. The first bunches that came in were getting all the plunder. The watches, the rings, the pens, and everything, whatever there was. Then the shooting started further down the corridor. I could hear shooting, I could hear screams, they were going into the wards and shooting. Then they go out and another lot comes in.'

The demands to turn over their valuables started up all over again. 'And you're trying to tell them and they can't understand you that their pals have got the gear,' said Lee. 'And they're tipping them off stretchers, they're going into wards, tipping over beds, looking under the bleedin' mattresses, thinking we're hiding the stuff. And bayonetting and killing. And a chap who was lying three stretchers away from me, a Jap bayonetted him a few times on the bleedin' stretcher, near me and of course medical orderlies – there were nine or ten of 'em – well we got together. Where I was lying, they got nine or ten orderlies that was trying to help the wounded, got 'em outside, took 'em outside the door where I was, along with a British officer, I don't know if he was a medical officer or what, and I could hear a lot of talking and shouting outside. And all of a sudden I heard some shooting and some screams, then they sent the officer back in, as white as a sheet. They bayonetted and shot 'em outside.'

**

Many patients from downstairs found their way to the upper floor wards, urgently seeking shelter and a hiding place wherever they could find one. 'Some ran upstairs and told us the Japanese were in and were bayonetting the patients,' according to Capt Brown.

'Why don't you get under your bed?' someone said to him.

'Because there are already three people trying to hide under my bed,' he replied. A screen was erected around Betty Fernandez's bed for her protection.

'By now this hospital was in Jap hands,' said Capt Pilkington. 'And, except for an occasional bullet from one of our snipers, the battle had died down. The Japs now took matters into their own hands.' A sudden round-up of walking wounded – anyone who was alive and able to be harried out of bed – started.

'One of the chaplains in a medical unit was there, and said some of the Japs peered around the corner but didn't take any notice of him,' said Father Brendan Rogers, chaplain of the Australian 2/10th. 'The chaplains were not armed, you see.' Does this somehow imply that others there were?

'They collected the staff of Reception,' recalled Torbit from his nearby dispensary, 'less three men – one shot in the thigh, one bayonetted through the chest, and the RSM [Ridout] who'd had his arm blown off with a grenade.' This was confirmed by Saye: 'The Reception was reached by the charging Japs, being full of staff and refugees, and these were herded out of the hospital. All those patients who could walk were kicked out of bed, went out, and were never seen again.'

Much shouting. 'Two or three soldiers peep into the ward gingerly, bayonets to the fore,' is how Gurd saw it in Ward 5 & 6. 'Lance Cpl Jones came in and announced: "Everyone except bed patients to come outside with their hands raised".' Jones – at 43 and married – was a little older than most around, and also served with the 198th Field Ambulance. 'Patients – some in pyjamas, some half-naked, some barefoot – crowded along,' recalled Gurd.

'The patients were collected in the lobbies and were taken outside the hospital,' said Bryer, who'd been relieved of his ring and his watch.

'Some with limbs recently amputated,' added Peter Lucy, adding to a ghoulish spectre. 'One man whose arm was in plaster had it forced behind his back and re-broken,' John Wyatt heard.

**

In the upper wards was Lt Charles Mounsey, 35, originally from London but a Rubber Estate Agency Malaya man of some 14 years' standing, and an agent for the Societe Internationale de Plantations et de Finance in Kuala Lumpur. He had been in action with the FMSVF 2nd Bn but was laid up here with a wounded leg which would've hampered his very good game of tennis and cricket. He even boasted his own Charles Mounsey's X1 cricket team in Selangor. His wife Audrey was also a keen and competitive tennis player, and she had returned to the UK in the middle of 1940 with Serena, nearly six, and Simon a year younger, and both surely fretting for their father.

Another who was wounded in the leg was Capt Richard de Warrene Waller, who'd shipped down from a halcyon stint in Hong Kong. A 20-year-old Artillery gunner, Dick was posted to Hong Kong in 1936. His background was military through and through, with his father being a Royal Artillery colonel who served his career in India after winning a contest to get an army commission, no less. (His grandfather was head brewer at Guinness, and married Eliza Guinness, a grand-daughter of the founding brewer.) His great-great uncle, Col Robert Waller, was in the Bengal Horse Artillery, and had seen action in two Sikh Wars and the North West Frontier. In 1842 he was taken hostage, with his wife Annie and their daughter Selina, when Akbar Khan incredibly persuaded Gen Elphinstone to hand over several women, children and wounded officers in return for supplies and a safe escort for his army. The family was released nine months later.

'The Wallers are Southern Irish Protestants. The Wallers are soldiers,' his son Robert Waller would tell me. Dick was born in India and, aged six, went on to boarding school at Wellington College, established in 1853 as a memorial to the Duke of Wellington who was a famed military tactician, perhaps most remembered for his role in the Battle of Waterloo. Many sons of soldiers were Dick's classmates, and rugby and plenty of physical activity was high on the agenda in the vast acres of forested school grounds. The tall young man moved on to the Royal Artillery – a proud moniker since 1720 – being commissioned as a RA captain after time at Woolwich Arsenal, the artillery equivalent of Sandhurst. He was soon after sent on his own Asia adventure.

'He would have been 21 and probably his first overseas posting,' daughter Louise Kidd told me. 'So lots of excitement and adventure. The voyage out was a highlight for him. He said it was the best three weeks of his life.' En route to Hong Kong, they docked in Bombay where he was excited to see the Taj Mahal. 'He meant the Taj Mahal *Hotel*!'

Life as an officer in Hong Kong involved a lot of leisure time. 'We did half a day's work for half a day's pay,' Waller would say. In the afternoon, uniforms were swapped for sporting gear, and time was spent variously golfing or sailing in the rugged bays of Hong Kong and the South China Sea. The general experience was akin to some kind of 'heaven' for a young military man.

With the Royal Artillery 118th Field Regiment, who had just arrived in Singapore weeks earlier, it's probable that his battery was assigned to airfield defence around Seletar on the east of the island. 'He was injured when strafed or bombed while in a vehicle,' said Robert. 'He had one or two visible bullet wounds.' Now Dick lay on the floor of a boardroom with a mattress, surrounded by about 30 others. 'A RAMC orderly came up and said that all doctors and orderlies were to go downstairs.'

Was it just medical staff or was it patients too? No one was quite sure, and certainly no one was going to volunteer. Should we, shouldn't we?

The picture was clarified with the sudden arrival of two Japanese soldiers upstairs. 'I did not see the Japanese fighting troops until they arrived on the first floor and entered the wards,' Mounsey said, reflecting the experience of many similarly and unfortunately indisposed here.

'From their appearance these were frontline fighting troops,' said Waller. 'They came into the room and ordered all of us to go downstairs. The unit was equipped with what looked like a four-inch mortar. They were excited but from their appearance I do not think they were drunk. An officer who was on crutches just behind me was motioned back, and the other officers who were behind him also fell back. The Japanese soldiers were in a great hurry and did not stop to bring them with us.'

Estimates of how many patients were in the hospital range from about 800 to upwards of 900. 'The hospital staff numbered about 15 officers and 300 orderlies, all of whom were British,' according to Smiley. It is generally agreed that around 50 were killed and 200 rounded up in that first shock wave.

**

The second wave was triggered by one of the most contentious events of this story.

A witness reported to George Peet, editor of the *Straits Times* for 17 years, they saw Indian soldiers firing a machine gun from behind the gateposts of the hospital grounds before the Japanese came in.

Some RAMC reports have it that 'a British regiment (Indian I believe), entered and set up machine gun pits in the actual hospital grounds. When this unethical move was discovered by the Japanese they literally "saw red" and charged into the hospital grounds.'

Surgeon Smiley took a quick break around 2pm, retiring to the balcony on the front of the hospital. 'I saw Japanese troops on the railway line,' he said. 'We could also see Japs outside on the hill. They were creeping slowly towards the Officers' Quarters at Alexandra Park, then occupied by the Loyal Regiment. At the same time the Japanese were sending explosive missiles over the hospital and an occasional one hit it. Then I went down to the operating theatre.'

'The Japs put on a full-scale attack in this area,' said Pilkington, perched up in the Officers' Ward, 'driving back the British and Indian troops, who actually withdrew through the hospital wards.'

These Indians were seen and corroborated by many from their hospital beds: 'Some IORs (Indian other ranks soldiers) retreating from the Japs ran into the hospital compound, fired from the ground floor of the hospital, then withdrew,' according to Lt Charles Jackman of Royal Signals.

Fellow signaler Cpl Bill Cowan, 32, saw the lot: 'Some of our Indian troops, like idiots, retreated through the hospital and some of them opened fire on the Japs from the roof,' he said.

In hot pursuit, another platoon of Japanese troops poured in through the rear entrance of the Admission Room, this time, focusing on the Medical Wards 5 & 6, plus the Patients' Dining Room, where 100 forlorn patients lay mostly on the floor.

'We heard both rifle fire and machine gun fire which seemed to come from close by,' said Salmon. 'Later we heard shouts and screams and saw (under the swing doors) the legs of Jap troops running along the corridor. These terrible cries were coming from all parts of the hospital. An orderly, I think it must have been Cpl Sinclair, came into us and said, "Keep quiet and you may be lucky and escape notice in this small room".' Easier said than done, because one of their number – a burns victim from the *Empress of Asia* – was delirious. 'No Japs entered our room but the poor fellow kept screaming and shouting. Mercifully he died later that evening and all was quiet in the room.'

Peter Bruton's well-researched meta-account reads as follows: 'A number of patients lying on the floor of the temporary reception ward in the patients' dining room heard the sound of a light machine gun being fired very near to them. The hollowness of the sound suggested that the gun was being used in a confined space. As they listened and watched through the open double-doors, they saw a group of six Indian soldiers carrying rifles. They were retreating along the corridor from the Medical Wards and went past the Dining Room ward. These soldiers then ran out of the main entrance to be closely followed by a party of Japanese fighting troops.' Seeing the boots of the Japanese running up and down the corridor would have been a heart-stopping moment.

'For an hour the Indians were firing from the balconies and windows,' according to Pilkington, 'but were eventually driven out, but a great many patients had been killed.' The fact that they used balconies implies they were not just beating a hasty retreat at ground level but actively using the cover of the hospital, and benefitting from its raised and protected vantage points. Saye is another one completely convinced of this action taken by the Indians. 'There is no doubt in my mind that the Indian troops did get across the corridor and out the other side. They had no alternative other than to stand and fight.'

'Turbanned Indians ran along the corridor and jumped the low fence into Alexandra Road,' said Aussie 2/29th member, Drummond, who was holed up in Ward 17. 'The Indians were unarmed. Japanese troops appeared as the Indians disappeared.'

But who were these retreating Indians? Were they Punjabis from the hapless Indian 44th who Drummond described as 'a disorganized unarmed rabble of very scared men'?

Others point to them being specifically from Queen Victoria's Own Sappers and Miners Group, Indian Engineers (or Madras Sappers and Miners as they were historically and more colloquially known). Two companies of these 'small, tough and wiry men' were active in Singapore, the 15th Field Coy under Maj Robert Muir and 13th Field Coy under the aptly named Maj Whiteman.

'Rumour has it that the Indian Sappers and Miners digging a tunnel at the rear of the hospital had made a run for it when the Japs advanced and passed through the hospital building,' said Gunner Moore. There might be some veracity in this, given that eight Sappers of Queen Victoria's Own Madras were engaged in making an underground bomb-proof operating theatre behind the hospital, connected to ground floor operating block, according to Drummond. The question is why this theatre wasn't conceived of, nor executed, earlier? There exists a small maze of tunnels, which the author has visited, that do run under that area of the hospital. But the sappers probably never completed their task.

The reality may well have been a combination of both, with the Indian 44th in total and utter disarray by this stage, and the entire beleaguered 2/10 Baluch regiment having deserted that very day (two of their commissioned officers became senior INA officers). The Sappers may well have been among those seen scarpering across the corridor and out through the other side of the hospital, whereas those from the 44th might well have been part of a larger force generally withdrawing through the hospital area because by mid-afternoon the frontline had advanced to Alexandra Road, south of the hospital.

It was everyman for himself with the 44th Indians. So how much blame can we apportion to commanding officer Ballentine, or his three senior officers: Ingle, Southern and Sainter?

**

But everyone saw differing fragments of the whole. 'No combatant troops were seen in the grounds,' according to Bull.

'At no time did I see any Allied fighting troops inside the hospital,' said orderly Gurd, whose life was about to be violently turned on its head. Yet more Japanese were inside, and heading for Gurd's ward, beating and bayonetting as they went. 'One choice specimen dashed up to me and smacked me on the tin hat with his bayonet, which I promptly abandoned.' Others threw their helmets down in a pile. Out into the sunshine they went. 'In the corridor our hands were tied behind our backs with rope and we were also roped to each other in groups of about eight.'

Many who could barely move under their own steam were included in these human chains. 'A few patients who could only walk with difficulty were allowed to put their arms over our shoulders so we could help them along. We were hustled out of the hospital by the north wing.'

Amid all this madness, Fergus Anckorn came to again, and something altogether different was taking place. 'Suddenly all the walking wounded were being walked out of the ward,' he said. 'Hands tied together with barbed wire, and behind them a soldier with a bayonet.'

'What are they doing?' I asked.

'They're using them for bayonet practice.'

Back in Ward 17 the ward door burst violently open. 'They opened it with a hand grenade,' said Drummond. 'Then an orgy of sadism began. They first fired indiscriminate volleys from rifles, then knocked down and bayonetted all orderlies in the vicinity of the door. They then set out by any means possible to terrorize the patients. They began to loot for valuables, and destroy what they considered to be of little value. This was done with inhuman brutality, those not fortunate enough to have valuables were jabbed with bayonets, tipped off their beds, and clubbed with rifle butts.'

Poor old William Armiger. Already suffering from a serious chest wound, the Norfolk private had at some indeterminate time been finished off in cold blood, leaving behind a three-year-old son at home, also called William.

One of many curious incidents then occurred in Ward 17. 'The Japs asked one walking patient if he was a Gurkha, whereupon the two Japs began to whack him – with all the strength they could muster – across the chest and head with their rifle butts. His face was soon a mass of pulp, but he remained on his feet till the Japs collapsed exhausted on the beds. The Gurkha turned to the other patients and attempted to twist his smashed face into a smile. Then, drawing himself up to full height, he spat on the floor in front of the Japs in a gesture of complete contempt.'

Pte Harry Saye noted what happened next as obviously word of the Japanese advance had reached back to Artillery. 'All was still in our ward when – with a whistle and an explosion – the first shell dropped in the grounds. *Ours*! For the next two hours we were bombarded by our own artillery who must have been firing from the docks of Singapore. Shells were bursting all over the hospital area – in the grounds, the roof, etc. We all held our breath as each whistle grew nearer, breathing a sigh of relief as the shell burst away from us. The Japs just got behind the rear high walls of the hospital.'

**

Medical orderly, Pte Sydney Hoskins, was beavering away in the Reception Room, then headed upstairs. 'I had gone upstairs on the first floor and from the verandah I could see Japanese troops infiltrating into the hospital grounds.

His colleague, Johnson from the Admission Room, went up the main staircase of the hospital. As he reached the top, he found himself facing a group of about 60 officers and men on the landing, craning their necks to work out what was going on below, and about to come down. Torbit interpreted it that the British officer with a white flag had collected a number of clerks and patients around him and was looking for an opportunity to formally surrender.

'I told them what was going on,' said Johnson, 'and shepherded them back upstairs, and then remained on the half-landing to watch events.'

Local VAD lass, Mrs Sinclair, was married to 24-year-old Cpl Edward Sinclair, RAMC, the fair-haired medium-built and much-admired ward master of the upper medical wards. When they realized the Japanese were incoming, Sinclair hatched a plan. 'He decided to dress her up as a man,' said John Wyatt. 'As the corporal tried to dress her she clung to him in terror, this made the task difficult but he managed to push her out of the door hoping she might get away.'

From the second wave, at least two Japanese ventured up the stairs to the Officers' Ward.

'Two soldiers came running up the stairs and burst in through the swing doors,' recalled John Wyatt in a small ward of just five patients. 'One was over six feet tall, the other short, and for a moment they just stood there motionless looking down the ward. Although I was petrified it was quite amusing to see that one of them held a squawking and wriggling duck under his right arm. After a few seconds the taller Jap moved to two heavily bandaged soldiers nearest the door and, after searching their wrists for watches, proceeded to bayonet both of them to death. My whole body started to go numb and I began to come to terms with the fact that I had only a few minutes of my life left. I was certain that they would work their way down the ward killing all of us.'

Cpl Sinclair stepped forward, offering them a tray of bread he was holding. 'Bread? Bread?' *Clang! Bash!* 'With cries of "*Kurrah! Kurrah!*" they knocked him unconscious with heavy blows from their rifle butts. They then dragged him out of the ward and that was the last I saw of that brave corporal.'

Soon, they were back and now intent on ransacking whatever valuables they could. Then a Japanese officer appeared. 'Seeing what happened he screamed and shouted at the two soldiers and shoved them out of the ward,' said Wyatt, who had his eyes firmly shut by now. 'As he turned to leave he apologized to the three of us left alive and said in English: "I am sorry but my men are tired and hungry – they have been fighting without rest or food for many days".'

Tired, hungry, and revengeful for the hold-up and high cost of the last few days of fighting.

Wyatt was relieved that his life had been spared. For now. 'When I opened my eyes the other two soldiers who had not been bayonetted had disappeared. I have no idea what happened to them but hopefully they escaped from the hospital.' Perhaps the closed-eyed Wyatt had been passed over as dead already, a convincing act. Because the bodies of the bayonetted two still lay in their beds near the door, but his buddies had probably been rounded up.

'An order was passed to us that everybody was to go downstairs to the ground floor,' said Hoskins.

'Cpl Thomas Gordon of the hospital staff then shouted from downstairs that we should take our tin hats off and come down with our hands above our heads,' said Johnson. He relayed the message. Gordon was 'short and very sturdy, with a dark complexion,' according to Pte Futter, and had recently moved across from the Auxiliary Medical Depot at Tanglin.

Just then, according to Gunner Moore, two Japs went upstairs and gave the instructions. 'These two seemed more humane than the others for they motioned patients on stretchers to remain behind.' One of those remaining was Capt Hugh Pilkington in his full body cast.

But the upstairs party was still made up of 'patients who could only just hobble, some had only one arm, some were in plaster, and others were obviously very ill,' according to Torbit. 'Many of the seriously ill showed great signs of distress.' It is likely that in this upstairs Officers' Ward was injured Australian, Maj Rex Beale, who'd arrived off the battlefield just three days earlier.

Betty Fernandez's ruse behind the makeshift protective screen was soon detected. 'She was last seen marching out with this party with her hands tied behind her back,' according to Brig Stringer.

'She was taken away during the looting and her fate can only be a matter of conjecture,' according to Alex Drummond.

And so another conga line of crippled and those on crutches was hastily formed. One officer seemed to take pity on the worst of the cases bringing up the rear, and motioned them back to their room with a grunt. It was probably not out of sheer humanity, more that they would slow down what was next in store for the group.

A medical NCO tried to hide behind a door. The Japanese officer spotted him, strode across, pulled the door open wide, slapped him about the face vigorously, then walked away. Doubtless shaken, did he realize how lightly he got off? For the unfolding operation was gaining sinister momentum, as they left the sanctuary of their officers' loft.

'At the foot of the stairs were two Japanese soldiers who directed us into the rear corridor, where there was a double line of Japanese troops, stationed about a yard apart,' explained Johnson of the 100-yard corridor. 'We were compelled to run the gauntlet between these troops, who struck us with the butts of their rifles as we passed them.'

By simple mathematical deduction, this gives a clear indication of the number of Japanese troops involved: approximately 200. There are 180 in an IJA company, adding weight to the theory that this was an organized company-strength maneuver.

'We passed through a door leading outside,' said Johnson, 'and were there rounded up by more Japanese troops. We were then tied up either individually or into parties of varying numbers: I was one of a party of about 50, all tied by the wrists with the same length of rope.'

**

Wyatt's painful ulcer was playing up. 'It was the size of a half crown and was a mass of heaving, squirming maggots. With no one to dress it I had to do it myself with a bandage and some scissors I found on a medical tray. I lay on my bed with my eyes firmly closed for what seemed like hours, playing dead, giving thanks for my salvation. I remained firmly under my sheets on the first floor.'

**

All the while 'bullets were striking the back of the hospital where the operating theatre was situated,' according to Smiley. With no electricity, one can only imagine how dark, difficult and dangerous conditions for surgery were. It seemed that the corridor between the sisters' bunkroom and the main theatre would have been a better lit and better protected place.

'We decided to operate in the corridor,' said Smiley. The table was brought in and we had just finished a case and were waiting for another to arrive when we became doubtful of the advantage of our selected site owing to the now more advanced position of the Japanese who could be seen clearly outside 50 yards away.'

Suddenly, the third attack wave was bursting in through windows around the operating theatre and surgical wards 16 & 17.

RAMC QMS Sgt Edward Lunt, who would be turning 43 in less than a month, was in the corridor between the staircase and Wards 15 & 16. 'There was a large number of wounded congregated underneath the staircase in the main entrance hall for safety from the shelling. I saw about 12 Japanese enter the corridor near wards 16 & 17.' They were armed with a machine gun and rifles. 'They first fired into the duty room of wards 16 & 17, and then sprayed the corridor in my direction. I was in the line of fire and saw the crowd near the staircase move down the corridor towards Wards 5 & 6. I crawled to safety round the corner near the staircase with the idea of contacting my CO, Col Craven.'

His description of the troops is very detailed. 'They appeared to me to be forward guerilla troops. They had full kit, camouflaged headdress, cloven shoes (worn out). They were filthy, smelled, and appeared to me to be drug-drunk from the glassy appearance of their eyes. I don't know what regiment they were.'

**

That is the big question. Who were these foul-smelling men? Many patients identified them specifically as 'Imperial Guards'. Others described the green tropical uniforms, which were the distinct signature uniform of the Imperial Guards. But, especially as the war dragged on, variance in quality and colour of fabrics was wildly inconsistent. Photos of some Japanese regiments show men standing shoulder to shoulder in every shade from near-white bleached khaki to grey to green.

But the Imperial Guards were not supposed to be anywhere near this operation zone. This was 18th Division territory. And to their east was 5th Division, and then even further east came the Imperial Guards Division. But they were underemployed in the Singapore campaign, and had also been told to 'do whatever they liked' by Yamashita in a heated spat after landing. Perhaps they were just following his orders to the letter? Because what would soon unfold did carry hallmarks of their treacherous work around Bakri and Parit Sulong in Malaya.

Interestingly, the 13th AGH in Katong had found itself in no-man's land from 11 February. 'The Singapore Volunteer Force retired from the Changi area leaving no fighting troops between the hospital and the enemy,' Cpl Lex Arthurson wrote. But then, just two days later, with a grim situation looming, he noted: 'The crack Imperial Guards had by-passed us, leaving observers and troops to keep a discreet eye on the hospital. Our sagacious CO made sure that all arms were collected and dumped outside the hospital's boundary – a sure sign of a non-military establishment.' This was not the case at The Alex, where it seems weapons were stockpiled in the Admissions area at reception. 'The first Japanese soldiers to visit the hospital appeared more curious than hostile,' he noted of 13th AGH's situation.

Whoever these attackers were in the Alexandra, in the wards they found prone patients, in splints, plaster casings, and complicated weighted pulley traction systems. Some Japanese couldn't resist pulling on these, eliciting yells of excruciating pain from the patients, and encouraging laughter from their sadistic colleagues.

'Some of us went into the theatre again, looking for a protected spot,' said Smiley. Others rushed in from the corridor now. 'Bullets had just passed through the corridor where they and the patient were. The Japanese were outside the operating theatre!'

But dedicated to the core, Smiley insisted the Saturday surgical show must go on. 'One patient was bleeding from a severe shrapnel wound in his ankles.' This was Veitch, the armoured car Volunteer. Allardyce – the Irishman who'd previously worked in Japan – anaesthetized Veitch.

Apart from Allardyce, the operating theatre team that fateful day was devoted dad Capt Rogers, pacifist and idealist Capt Parkinson, Pte Alfred Sutton (just one month short of his 23rd birthday), Pte Kenneth Lewis, the fair-haired, mediumly tall orderly who gave generously of his time to the Salvation Army, and Cpl James McEwen, a tall Scot with darkish hair.

'Some of us attempted to get out and bring the patient into the Operating Room but Japanese bullets splattered the walls around us and we retired,' said Smiley. 'I went to the door of the operating room and – showing the Red Cross on my arm – waved the Japanese to come in.

WHIZZ! 'A bullet passed me and hit Pte Lewis, who was some yards behind me, on the left shoulder. I then instructed the staff to stand in the middle of the room with their hands in the air. A moment later, a Japanese jumped into the room. He signalled us to come out of the room and this we did with our hands up.'

They found themselves in the corridor facing 10 Japanese. 'They signalled us to walk on, which we did. A Japanese then lunged at me with his bayonet, hitting my cigarette case in the left breast pocket of my shirt, and knocked me against the wall.'

Capt Parkinson, 30, walked on and got out of sight. 'But Rogers was bayonetted on the right chest and fell,' said Smiley. Other accounts have it that he was 'bayonetted twice through the throat and died at once' and another 'at the back of the thorax' and twice more even as he fell. The Japanese then set on the remaining foursome of Sutton, Lewis, McEwen and Smiley.

'I received three bayonet wounds and decided to fall down,' said Smiley. 'In doing so I pushed Sutton down and shouted to the others to fall down and pretend to be dead.' Compliant and quick-thinking Sutton was the only one of the team not inflicted by bayonet wounds as he followed Smiley's lead. Lewis – already nursing a shot shoulder – was felled and killed by bayonet blows. He was just 24. Multiple bayonet wounds also finished off McEwen, 28, whose young wife was waiting anxiously for him back home in Perth, Scotland. (She wrote several times to his friend Sgt Dartford post-war wanting to know the fate of her husband: 'I informed her that he was alive and in good health on 10 February 1942.' Finally he had to come out with the gruesome truth that he hadn't made it.)

The tall, slight, ginger-haired Parkinson didn't make it much further from the group. As he turned into the main corridor he was struck down by a bayonet. The idealistic medic, who wanted no part in this war, was brutally slain and dead at 30.

'Sutton and myself lay on the ground while the Japanese stood talking and for some time after they'd gone,' said Smiley. 'While laying there I saw many orderlies and patients running up the main corridor with their hands in the air.'

His chest must have been heaving with the exertion and adrenaline coursing violently through his veins. To play dead convincingly must have required unthinkable self-control.

**

'The Japs hardly came up to the first floor, and I was on the first floor,' explained Bull. He and CO Craven's team had been upstairs all this time discussing the next steps. 'The noise of the battle was considerable, and we did not know exactly what was happening inside the hospital, but decided that we would all go downstairs to the ground floor and see if anything was happening around the front entrance.'

Plenty, apparently. Because all three waves had gone through before they ventured downstairs, based on who and what they saw next. Such response could be criticized for its tardiness, although who can blame them for not venturing down? Craven especially had demonstrated medal-winning bravery in the line of fire in WW1 when he summoned stretcher-bearers to attend to his wounded men.

'On reaching the foot of the stairs we found the recently dead body of one of the medical officers who had obviously been bayonetted,' said Bull. 'Along the passage was another, similar treated, lying in a pool of blood, and nearby in the operating theatre the RAMC anesthetist who had recently anesthetized the patient in the theatre was also lying dead, shot through the heart. The patient on the operating theatre had been stabbed to death by bayonet.'

Indeed, unbelievably, the anaesthetized Veitch was killed on the operating theatre where he lay. But perhaps his death was the 'best' one of all – if such a thing can be said –because he was unconscious and completely oblivious to the manic madness unfolding around him.

Smiley identified the patient as Veitch. He didn't see the killing, but he did see the body.

Some of Bull's recollections about Allardyce are way off the mark here because the anesthetist was still elsewhere in the hospital and worse was yet to befall him. 'The surgeon, Capt Smiley, was lying on the ground outside the theatre feigning death, having been bayonetted three times, but without serious injury,' Bull noted.

Smiley added his perspective: 'After what seemed like 15 minutes I saw the commanding officer, Lt Col Craven passing along the corridor. Sutton and I called to him and soon we were among those who remained.'

The grateful Sutton dressed Smiley's wounds, which were – in the surgeon's medical parlance – to his '*iliac fossa*' (groin) and '*thenar eminence*' (thumb). They then put Smiley on a stretcher and carried him to a ward. Oddly Smiley observed that, 'They did not molest patients in bed or orderlies in the wards' and furthermore in another account that 'the main wards were undisturbed.' Perhaps in that section where he was taken, which is possibly why he was taken there. Because by now, presumably, all the 'up patients' – those able to walk – had been rounded up and herded outside.

CO Craven, along with his cohort of senior officers, plus the uninjured Sutton, were taken prisoner and made to sit on the floor outside the Stewards' Rooms, and some out on the cookhouse verandah. It's odd that no senior medical officers were manacled and marched outside.

Initially armed sentries guarded them but, perhaps bored, soon left for some lucrative looting instead. This gave Sutton the opportunity to investigate when he heard desperate cries from outside. He found Cpl Robert 'Ginger' Saint, wounded member of the RAMC party working outside, brought him back inside, and splinted his arm with an old handbrush before dressing it.

**

'Patients and personnel numbering about 200 were taken outside the hospital,' according to Lance Cpl Bob Mutton, 4th Royal Norfolks, 'and had their hands tied behind their backs with slip knots, one length of cord being used uncut for groups of four or five.'

An estimated 140 were from the ground floor wards, admission areas, and those walking wounded who'd been huddling beneath the entrance hall stairway. About 60 were officers, doctors and administrative staff from the upstairs and officers' wards area. Among these, Stringer estimated, there were 10 officers (including one Army chaplain) and 73 Medical other ranks.

'As the crowds moved towards Wards 5 & 6 they were met by a further contingent of Japanese who apparently gathered all together,' said Lunt.

'Most of them were patients who could manage to walk or members of the medical staff of the hospital,' noted Bryer, dressed only in his pyjamas and shoes. 'Many of them were in no fit state to walk.'

Pte Lloyd Hayes was caught up in this melee, as his friend Pte John Willard from Brighton watched on helplessly. Willard was waiting to be tied up in the next group when the Japanese suddenly changed their minds. The lieutenant colonel and padre of Hayes' dental unit also were 'saved', and all taken prisoner.

Why some were selectively separated and spared is not known. Perhaps impatience and time ticking: this was a time-wasting nuisance distraction from that prime objective for the competitive and impatient infantrymen – being first into Singapore.

Medic Pte Hoskins was among the procession herded down from upstairs. 'Japanese troops were stationed at all the main points along the route,' he said. 'On the way down I saw three British dead bodies and one Japanese corpse in the hospital. The Japanese troops appeared to be excited, but as far as I could judge, they were not drunk.'

One can only speculate about that Japanese corpse. Perhaps it was the injured Japanese who was hospitalized here earlier, and given a mercy killing as a 'useless mouth' by his own unsympathetic team. Or he had possibly been mistaken for a Gurkha? Certainly no one has reported a Japanese invader being killed by the patients or staff.

Downstairs and out the door they went, to an open space of ground 'about 100 yards south of the hospital, where about 200 prisoners had already collected, all walking wounded cases, one with his arm and chest in plaster,' according to Waller. 'Our hands were tied behind our backs with small pieces of rope and we were then tied together in parties of six each.'

'Our hands were tied behind our backs and we were tied together with a long rope in groups of about twenty," recalled Bryer.

**

The two groups – the first the 'downstairs' group, the second the 'upstairs' group – were then ordered to move off, and taken in different directions. This action was shielded from the view of the 36th Engineers by the main hospital buildings. 'Our steel helmets were taken from us and we were taken to a small Chinese village between five and six hundreds yards from the hospital,' said Bryer in the first group which came to a halt there. 'All this time we were coming under rifle fire and many of us were hit. 'We then were marched about another four or five hundred yards and halted again for about 15 minutes. A dozen or more were untied and given shovels to dig a big hole. I and many others presumed it was for a mass grave.'

Then, more adjustments were made. 'We were tied more securely than before. The Japanese used rope and also strips of clothing which they took from a Chinese hut nearby. We were then taken close to the main road and to a European style house which appeared to be half a mile from the hospital.'

Gurd recalled the dense undergrowth they had to forge through, and the heavily-armed Japs lining the route. 'Our captors beat our legs as we failed to go fast enough.' Twice, bursting shells caused them to stumble to the ground. On reaching the railway, they were allowed a rest, before being counted again by a 'Nippon officer who, from his behaviour and clothing, we guessed to be of fairly high rank. The Japanese troops were in full battle kit and unshaven. We go through a culvert, under the line passing a dead Malay, then up the slope beyond and into a paddock.' A short wait. 'Here we are finally herded into a row of outhouses, the *ayahs*' (maids) quarters.

That main European bungalow was the Sisters' Quarters, the same one given the 'feminine touches' by Stringer's evacuated wife, Olga, who was at that very moment floundering in the waters of the Dutch East Indies. But that was not to be their final destination. It was the rather ramshackle buildings behind. 'We were then marched to the servants' quarters of the hospital Sister's Mess, about 200 yards away from the main hospital building,' said Hoskins.

Stringer's estimate of 'about 300 yards' is more accurate in terms of the Sister's Mess. Johnson, who put it as 'a quarter mile' away, remembered that 'fighting was still going on in the immediate vicinity and we had to take cover from fire more than once.'

'We did not go direct to the Sisters Quarters, but fetched a circuit and halted about a quarter of an hour on the way,' said Johnson. 'At this halt our valuables were taken from us.' This second group went around the rear of the hospital's outbuildings, chiefly a large garage workshop with several bays.

'We did not go direct but fetched a large circle, calling at what appeared to be a Japanese company or battalion headquarters,' said Hoskins, many also noting a considerable number of corpses of Allied Indian troops – and one Malay corpse – along the route. 'A Japanese soldier who was wearing a sword said to me: "In Japan we give you the sword!"'

Remember, the IJA modus operandi was to have HQs operating much further forward than Allied units would. There is a lot more contentious and juicy speculation about who that high-ranking officer might have been.

Waller remembered the torturous walk as being 'encouraged by prods with bayonetted rifle butts.' He also had clear recollection of this stop. 'We were taken away to what appeared to be either a company or battalion headquarters. We waited there about 20 minutes while a Japanese soldier harangued us for a few minutes on the criminality of fighting Japan. A Japanese officer was also present but I do not know his rank.'

If it was a battalion HQ, it would be commanded by a lieutenant colonel. If it was a company HQ a captain would be in charge. In a reinforced regiment such as the 55th, a body of around 147 men would typically be present in a fully-manned battalion HQ post, or around 30-40 in a company HQ post. The compacted nature of the battlefield at that time doesn't preclude a forward regimental HQ post either.

The identity of this officer is a key part of the mystery because he was clearly complicit, if not directly instrumental, in proceedings. So let's see if we can pinpoint which Japanese brass were in the area at that time more precisely ...

**

Takeda Hisashi, Chief of Staff of 18th Division 'visited HQ of 114th and 55th Regiments, reaching HQ 114th around 1500 hours. HQ by that time had been established south of the Pasir Panjang Hills, near the West Coast Road. I later visited HQ 55th Regiment about half a mile away,' he said.

So the 114th HQ personnel were probably a little too far west at that time, and in any case a regimental HQ seems to be too large a body to fit the above descriptions. What about the whereabouts of the 55th Regiment HQ personnel?

Capt Umemoto Togoro of HQ 55th Regiment: 'Making a detour round to the northeast of the oil tanks, the battalion regained the main road between 1500 and 1600 hours, and almost immediately ran into British opposition. The whole regiment's advance was halted and Regimental HQ, 1st Bn and 2nd Bn dug into defensive positions in the vicinity of the oil tanks and remained there until about 2000 hours on Feb 15.' So this puts them extremely proximate to the orderlies and soldier-patients' march across the rail line at the time. But it does rather put HQ 55th Regiment personnel squarely in the spotlight of that HQ position and ranking officer.

Who else might have been around?

Col Nasu Yoshio, OC 56th Regiment, shed some further light: 'When we reached the oil tanks about 1500 hours between Trig point 100 and Trig point 150, these tanks were ablaze. On account of the intense heat and the heavy British artillery, we decided to skirt northwards around these oil tanks. Skirting around we came out on the railway line. Just as we reached the railway line (1400/1500 hours) a message came from the front saying that our 1st Battalion had crashed into the rear of 55th Regiment, which had halted and that they were withdrawing slightly and digging in.' This also placed them on a collision course with the captive groups walk to the Sisters' Quarters at about the right time, in about the right place.

Nasu's account tallies with Umemoto so far. 'I therefore ordered the halt,' continued Nasu, 'and the rest of the regiment took shelter and began digging in for the night.'

**

With an apparent eerie lull inside the hospital, the orderly George Poole and friend stuck their noses out of the linen cupboard. 'It seemed like hours that we were there before things went quiet and we got out of the hospital.' The keen footballer – who'd played for the RAMC team in Hong Kong in the mid-1930s – ran as fast as his legs could carry him, diving into a drain and hiding there for two days, without a morsel of food, until they were captured and sent to Roberts Hospital.

'On the 14th we heard what's happened in Alexandra Hospital,' recalled Capt Petrovsky. 'And then at that time we said: "How lucky we were to be ordered out and didn't stay in Alexandra Hospital." The Japanese soldiers when they fight, they don't think. They were looking for alcohol of course.'

**

From that battalion or company headquarters stop, the second smaller group of chain-ganged Allied prisoners then passed through a drain tunnel under the railway embankment, across Ayer Rajah Road, then to some 'flimsy' brick buildings set back about 50 yards from the road. John Wyatt, though not part of this party, described it as 'part of the old hospital's Sisters' Quarters. It was a red brick two-storey house raised above the ground on piles with a block of outbuildings surrounded by a small courtyard.' They arrived around 4pm.

This row was divided into three rooms of approximately the same size, each between 10 and 15 feet square. Facing Ayer Rajah Road, with our backs to the Sisters' Quarters, we'll call the leftmost (northern) area Room 1, the centre space, Room 2, and the rightmost (southern) one Room 3.

Each room had double doors opening onto a courtyard, where several reported seeing a 'European-looking officer' sitting when they arrived. Each room also had a window looking onto the Ayer Rajah Road and railway line just in front. They faced the European bungalow 'which was built on piles and which had a staircase leading up to it from the door of the room in which I was imprisoned,' said Bryer in Room 3. 'We were so tightly packed into these rooms that there was insufficient room to put two feet on the floor. All the time, the sounds of firing, shelling and bombing were all around us.' He calculated around 70 others in the room with him, and assumed around the same amount had gone into each of the three rooms.

Bert Gurd was shoehorned into Room 1, probably used as a toolshed before, with 57 patients, soldiers and orderlies. Waller went into the same room, recalling about 36 imprisoned there. He noted an Indian Commissioned Officer, some Indian soldiers, and Pte John Bunney, 29, of the RAMC in Room 1. Bunney, who came from a food chemistry background, was tall, dark, but not necessarily handsome because of his irregular teeth, and wore glasses.

Curiously few other names of the many jammed in there were recalled.

'It appeared to have been a toolshed,' said Capt Waller, who was – with Capt John Brown, the 22-year-old Dental Corp officer –

the senior officer present in that room. 'The windows were nailed up by the Japanese.' Through a gap in the barricaded door, Waller spotted some movement. 'I saw some Japanese soldiers taking away about one dozen bottles of whisky from out of the Sisters' Mess.' More Churchill supplies. And very welcome ones for battle-weary troops at that.

Little is known of Room 2 in the middle of the block, with Lt William Logan, RAMC – the soft-voiced, bespectacled 35-year-old doctor, sub-in-charge of the Mental Ward – being the only confirmed occupant. 'Logan was in the room next to mine, but I saw him go in,' said Hoskins, in Room 3 adjacent. As a medical officer Logan had been with the medical branch of the Straits Settlements Volunteers for four years prior, having lived in Singapore since 1936.

Others potentially in Room 2 included RAMC men Pte Thomas McDougall, L/Cpl Donald McKenzie, Pte Joseph Mattimore, Pte Robert Rodger, and Cpl Andrew Stoker, all of whom were seen being marched away by orderly John Lynas, and not listed as being in either Room 1 or 3.

Pte James Walker and Pte Ivor Griffiths, both of 32 Coy RAMC, were possibly in this room as they were not noted by others in rooms on either side. Or they might've been killed back in the hospital already. Dr Donald Irvine, who graduated from the University of Glasgow in 1933 before moving out to Taiping as a Health Officer with the Malayan Medical Service, subsequently signed on with the FMS Volunteers and perished on this day, either here, or elsewhere in the hospital.

And so to Room 3 on the right hand side, with our back to the Sisters' Quarters and facing east towards the road and railway.

Estimates range from a low of 40 from Hoskins to a high of 70 from Bryer as to how many were shoehorned and sardined into that steamy space. For now it was late afternoon in this turbulent tropical hell. Singapore's average 80% humidity can rise as high as 96%, and February is the driest month of the year, so less chance of a relieving evening rain to quell the heat. Because of this, a 30-degree day can often feel in reality more like 36-degrees. Then add to that the radiant heat from flames leaping from the oil tanks nearby.

'These conditions were torture to sick and wounded,' said Bryer, 'and to aggravate the situation we had had no water for twelve hours before we were made to leave the hospital, the water main having been broken. We all were suffering the torments of ever-increasing thirst.'

Some of those he was jammed face-to-face with included Capt William Walker, 26, of the Dental Corps, Squadron Leader Eustasius Griffiths, 38, a New Zealand doctor assigned to the RAF Medical Service, Cpl Thomas Gordon, 27, and Cpl Hugh Mitchell, 22, both of the RAMC.

Bryer also remembered a fellow RAF aircraftsman being present (probably Griffiths), plus 'some members of the Cambridgeshire Regt, and some Indian ranks of the Madras Sappers and Miners. There were also some other Indians who were wounded. Standing next to me were two Indian soldiers – one turbanned North Indian and a Madras Sapper and Miner, a sergeant.'

One speculates whether these sappers were the same ones who were seen bolting through the hospital having abandoned the work they were doing?

'We were still bound when we got inside,' said Hoskins, who felt the shelved room might have been a pantry, 'but managed to untie ourselves. The Japanese closed the shutters over the windows.'

The British other ranks he remembered sharing the claustrophobic space included Cpl Idris Isaacs, Pte Charles Williams, Pte Ivor Griffiths, L/Cpl Glenalvon Ritchie, Cpl Carl Deltry, Pte George Oliver, Pte Harry Rose, Pte Wilfred Watts, Pte Herbert Harris, Pte Adolphus Andrews, Pte John Bunney, and Cpl George Johnson, all of the RAMC.

It seems Bunney, 29, is erroneously recalled as being in both Rooms 1 and 3, as was Brown, RADC.

Also from the RAMC was young Cpl Sinclair with his Eurasian wife – who had been disguised as a man and pointed out of the ward – but obviously was not able to affect a complete escape. Luckily they were together here. One wonders if they were able to actually be face-to-face in this scrum, or somehow painfully separated by other poor bodies in between them?

There was also Pte Lloyd Hayes of the Dental Corps, and a 'Gunner Dean' of the Royal Artillery, probably George Dean of the 3rd Ack Ack regiment.

Bob Mutton was not there but had heard later from a fellow PoW that 'they were literally jammed in so tightly it took minutes to raise one's hand from the side to above the head, sitting down was out of the question, and people were forced to urinate against each other.'

Johnson confirmed it: 'We were packed so tight that we could not move, and found it impossible even to sit down.'

Hugh Mitchell may have been the youngest of the RAMC Company – Andrews and Ritchie were a shade older at 23 – but he was ever the team player no matter the extremeness of the adversity, just as he'd been pre-war. 'Where individuals were stacked so tightly that they could not move,' Mitchell's father later heard from Bull, 'Hugh managed to remove his stockings, which he then held above his head and waved them around and around thus creating a draught. He remained cheerful and encouraged the others, setting a magnificent example. That was Hugh Mitchell all over.' As Bull was not present, the source of this anecdote is most likely from Bryer, Johnson or Hoskins.

**

By this time of the sweltering afternoon, the 1st Malays had retreated from Buona Vista village, and they – together with some Loyals – fiercely defended the ridge just south before being overrun. Singapore was finally fighting back in a stubborn and stoic stance.

Meanwhile the fighting frontline was seemingly stalled nearby. Around 16:00, the Japanese brought up an infantry gun and fired it over open sights into the Loyals' B Company position and the Company's HQ bungalow. Allied brens and mortars retorted, taking out the Japanese gun crew, who were soon replaced and continued to fire off single rounds at point blank range as and when they could. The main fight then moved forward to the Tiger Brewery area.

But there were still Japanese in the hospital. '40 or 50 men were herded into the corridor and a guard placed over them,' said Gunner

Moore. 'Later the guards went away and Capt Bartlett, the RAMC regular, went out to investigate but found no sign of the Japs. The party remained there till dawn.'
A couple of Japanese at least now found their way to the second floor wards. 'About 5pm, two came up and stole everything they could lay their hands on – watches, rings, etc,' said young Norfolks' driver, Frederick Bales. 'There were some Japanese Imperial Guards with them and they took complete charge and stopped the shooting, and I saw no atrocities committed. The Guards behaved correctly and tried to get things organized again.'

Once again, odd that the Imperial Guards were *two* divisional boundaries away from where they were supposed to be. And even odder that they were *stopping* irregular behaviour given their appallingly brutal behaviour around Parit Sulong, Johor, which was the sort of behaviour unfolding at the Sisters' Quarters outhouse. Identical modus operandi.

Pilkington agreed with Bales though: 'By now the hospital was denuded of everyone except those absolutely bed-ridden. We were not molested in any way but were warned that there must be no smoking or talking.'

Sunset was about an hour away yet, a smoke-filled twilight lending an ominous atmosphere to this macabre setting.

The 55th and 114th Regiments 'halted on a line north and west of Keppel Barracks,' according to Maj Gen Takeda. Ito's 2/55th Battalion fought until nightfall, with darkness usually eclipsing daylight around 19:15 each day in Singapore. 'The troops fighting on the hill had suffered severe casualties, inflicted to a great extent by machine gun fire from within a building above us,' explained Ito. That would be the Alexandra and Gillman Barracks up to their right. 'The fighting on the road was static, with periodical exchanges of fire.' So for possibly the first time in the Malayan campaign, but definitely within the Singapore campaign, the Japanese were not forging their way ahead at lightning pace. And their losses were beginning to have operational implications.

'As the Machine Gun Company had suffered heavy losses since landing at Kota Bahru,' explained Soejima, 'our company strength was below 40 men. I gave the order that two of the machine guns be buried as we would not be able to carry all four on the following day. We buried the two guns and dug in for the night northeast of the oil tanks.' He was adamant that the company had not split up at all during this day. But it still had them within a few hundred yards of the hospital. 'We were out of touch with battalion HQ and regimental HQ. I believe the rest of the battalion was ahead of the Machine Gun Company and the main strength of the regiment behind us.'

**

Given the distances involved, a mere 100 yards from the railway line in front of the oil tanks to the northerly wing of the hospital's main buildings, most fingers must circumstantially point to the 55th Regiment.

More specifically to the advance guard, which was Col Ito Kojiro's 2/55th, followed by the Regimental Machine Gun Company. These machine gunners were especially aggrieved because they'd just lost their platoon commander in the furious fighting on the road just behind.

'I saw the corpse of the machine gun platoon commander,' said Ito of Commander Sako, 'and judging from what I saw I think that the firing there on the main road was so close that no part of that company would have been able to stray as far left of the company as the hospital.' But if the machine gunners were *behind* his battalion how did Ito see that corpse unless he – and presumably others – was able to move relatively freely to-and-fro the front line?

Remember, it's only 100 or so yards, and there were no British troops active immediately *north* of the hospital at this time, because all others had withdrawn through, around, or behind it.

**

CO Craven and his coterie, including Bull, remained seated outside the kitchen where they had been instructed all evening (and would do so throughout the night). The Japanese returned periodically to check on them. Each time, they'd take away prisoners. Now was the time for L/Cpl William Steel and Pte Harry Copperwheat to be hustled away. Just 24 and 25 respectively, both these 198th Field Ambulance personnel were already married, thus adding more poignancy to their demises.

Just as the final glowing red rays of the setting sun cast an extra ominous gloom on the fire-lit twilight, the Japanese summoned a medical officer and two stretcher-bearers. Capt Allardyce, the cleft-chinned side-parting wearing Cpl Patrick MacDonough, 27, and Cpl Fernley Wilkins, 38, stepped forward. 'They either wanted me to treat their wounded or to treat me as a hostage,' the Japanese-speaking Allardyce imagined.

**

By 20:00 the main body of the 114th Regiment, punching across from the west coast, finally reached Alexandra Road. That was enough fighting for them for one day. 'The regimental commander decided to stay the night,' according to their battle report, 'and prepared for an attack on 15 February.'

But Ito had other ideas. 'I was determined to make a night attack on the enemy hill positions, but unfortunately it never got dark that night, flames from the blazing oil tanks kept the sky aglow all night. I sent word to the regimental commander to send some of the regimental artillery to dislodge the enemy machine guns. During the night one piece of divisional mountain artillery arrived.'

Koba, the bald-headed commander of the 55th Regiment, had ordered 1st Bn to conduct a night attack on the Allies who were deployed 300 yards northeast of Hill 312 (the hill along Depot Road). This was probably the Bedfordshires, or possibly the 36th Royal Engineers. 'Many flares and signal shells were shot at the British base. Men on the ground were extraordinarily tired but could not sleep due to tension, and spent the night eating the small amount of rations left.'

**

'That night we saw nothing of the Japs,' said Smiley, now patched up and recovering from his earlier ordeal, 'but could hear the guns around Singapore.'

'There was no thought in anyone's mind to leave when the shells got nearer,' according to Pte Harry Saye, who earlier witnessed the dreadful death of his kitchen colleague, Bruce. 'With the raging fires from the oil tanks, no lights, no water, no food, but still the RAMC were doing their job,' he said with no small amount of pride. 'The dead were still unburied but no-one was allowed to move.' And some were still dying. Lt Mounsey observed one hospital orderly, who'd been shot in the leg and bayonetted in the stomach earlier, being rescued but succumbing to his wounds during the night. He praised Bull, Webster and the hospital padre for their 'extreme calm and coolness' during this period. The dead were laid out in the Medical Ward on the ground floor, which was by now full.

And other atrocities were still being waged in the hospital, albeit by a different foe this time. Furry, four-legged ones. 'All the stray dogs appeared to be in the hospital,' said Capt Pilkington, 'and rushed barking and growling up and down the wards. One officer had had an abdominal operation for which a tube was used to drain the wound. The dogs got hold of one end of this and a tug of war ensued. The dogs eventually won.'

So it's probably almost an understatement for him to call that night 'a ghastly nightmare.' Could there have been a longer night in all of history?

'The ward was lit by brilliant flashes from the burning oil wells, with people trying to quieten delirious patients. No one in our ward could do more than move slightly in bed, and there was no one to carry out the normal sanitary procedure, with the result that to the stench of suppurating wounds was added every type of smell. For twenty four hours we had no food nor water.'

Many of those delirious might have been in the area assigned to mental patients, including HP Futter.

Sleep was proving hard to come by for both sides, each with a different form of anxiety gnawing at them. For his part, Bull said: 'I can remember lying all night in a corridor just wondering what was going to happen next.'

**

'From time to time during the night, Japs passed down the corridor,' said Salmon, still prone underneath the dining ward table. 'It was pitch black, we had no electricity.'

**

Stretcher-bearer MacDonough was killed by shrapnel outside the hospital, according to Gunner FT Moore. Of Wilkins there was no trace but he died too that night. Leaving only Allardyce – who had anesthetized the patient Veitch on the operating table – from that recently seconded medical party to turn up elsewhere. At the Sisters' Quarters outhouse across the road, he was shoved into the already-bursting Room 3 where Hoskins, Johnson, Mitchell, Bryer, and company stood suffocating.

'We were left in the hut all through the night without food, water or adequate ventilation,' said Johnson.

'There was only room for a few of us to sit down. Conditions were very bad for the patients,' Hoskins understated. The bindings on his wrist dug deep cuts into the skin of the short medic, who stood just over 5'6" and weighed 60kg, and sported a tattoo of a deer on his upper-left forearm.

According to Bryer 'everybody was clamouring for water.' He'd not had a drink since the Friday at the hospital.

'Many of the men suffered severely as a consequence,' said Waller. 'There was a lot of noise among the prisoners owing to their extremely nervous condition.' After all, Japanese and British artillery fire was flying all about as the night attacks wore on.

Some false placatory promises were made. 'Two or three times during the night we heard the voice of a man who spoke perfect English and who appeared to be standing outside of our room,' said Waller in Room 1. 'He appeared to be trying to pacify us and at one time said: "If you will keep quiet I will try to get you back to the hospital tomorrow." This man was definitely not a prisoner himself, and was described to me by someone who saw him as being tall, fair, and with European colouring. The general conjecture in the hut is that he may have been German.'

Which brings us to another interesting parallel. Was he one of the fair-skinned Japanese Ainu soldiers? Or if we backtracked to the horrific massacre of Parit Sulong in southern Johor, there were sightings of suspected 'German' advisors there too. The echoes with this scenario, just a few short weeks earlier, are systematically sinister at best.

Could it be that some of the underemployed Imperial Guards – supposedly on the eastern side of the island – had gone rogue and insinuated themselves into this action, or that Tsuji, who sung their praises, had encouraged or even ordered them to reprise their dastardly role here?

**

15 February 1942. And so Chinese New Year 1942 dawned. This was usually a joyous occasion of firecrackers and feasts. There were fireworks aplenty of the artillery kind, but of food and water there was precious little. It was the Chinese Year of the Horse, which ironically is characterized by the element of fire, symbolizing energy and enthusiasm. It was certainly the year Mutaguchi hoped to be riding that great white stallion victoriously into Delhi. It was his frequently vivid daydream, and now that they were here nearly at the gates of Singapore, everything seemed to be falling whimsically into place.

Plus the weather gods were smiling, with another 'splendid' day promised. They'd had no rain since landing on Singapore.

'You're pitch black!' the unwashed Japanese of 114th teased each other, mainly from the accumulated soot from the oil tank fires. The cooler night air allowed the soot to settle nearer ground level.

'Sergeant, we found a wash place. There's no water but we've been able to wash ourselves with beer.' So much for the destruction of all alcohol. Row upon row of beer had been found in a nearby house, or possibly purloined from the brewery. Someone handed Sgt Arai two bottles. In this place, Arai was able to look at his face in a mirror for the first time since landing in Songkhla, southern Siam, three weeks earlier. A 'strange bearded face' stared back at him. It was burnt, grimy, dirty. Even in the biggest battles around Nanking he'd carried soap and razor, but not here. He'd not brushed his teeth since Johor, one week ago. He set about brushing his teeth with the beer, gargled with the rest of the bottle, and spat it out.

His ambitious orders for that day were to take Hill 130, 136 and the Empire Docks. Ito was happy because his one piece of mountain artillery had arrived, so he was all set to throw his men forward into another concerted push.

The 1st Malays had evacuated their coast road post during the night. Down to just four platoons now, they took up a position on Bukit Chermin, one and a half miles due south of the hospital. The Allies' left flank was now dangerously exposed because Lt Col Erlington of the Loyals had not been informed of this move.

There was also wild speculation that the Japanese had landed overnight on Blakang Mati. Brig Williams had called for a reserve defence line on the forward slopes of Mt Faber and Mt Washington as a result, and moved his HQ to the area of Singapore's civil prison, four miles south of the hospital.

**

And with daybreak, the rumble of artillery re-commenced.

'Wires were down, constant shelling and bombing,' is how Father Rogers remembered that morning as he moved from the Cathay Building to St Andrews Cathedral at first light. 'Explosions and stuff. A lot of ammo depots near the harbour caught on fire and they were going *bang, bang*!'

Shelling of the 'Keppel Barracks' (as Tsuji called it) was happening at the rate of once every 10 minutes. The troops on Mt Washington and the coast road were also receiving heavy attention from these guns and mortars. This was noted in the hospital by Gunner Moore: 'By this time, enemy shelling was at its maximum and shells were bursting all around.'

'We felt like the meat in a very explosive sandwich,' is how John Wyatt felt in the hospital.

'During the heavy bombardment from Johor Bahru, nearly 2000 were killed in one day in the Alexandra area near the hospital, according to British records,' noted Miyozaki Mamoru.

The gallant Loyals were still very much in the fight nearby, lobbing mortars onto one corner of the Tiger Beer factory, and the quarry adjoining the Chalet Spur. This held the Japanese in check. But then – *disaster*! – they ran out of mortars. The Japanese charged forward from the high ground, visiting massive damage on the Loyals' consolidated CD Company. Lt J Simpson led a small group on a valiant, daring, but ultimately short-lived hand-grenade attack run. The Japanese surged forward again.

**

In the hospital, the officers decided to get things back to normal as much as they could. 'It was decided we should return to the wards,' said Bull, who, along with the CO and other ranking officers, had sat obediently outside the kitchen all night. They found a few tins of food to sustain themselves.

QMS Lunt – who had been fired on the previous day – tried to hold a roll call 'as far as possible' and estimated that 'about 80 staff and 80 patients had been marched off. Investigation of the hospital and wards found 'about 38 patients and staff shot or bayonetted in the hospital.' Among the dead were Lywood – the commanding officer of the 6th Royal Norfolks who had been recovering from malaria – a Hurricane pilot, and that sole Japanese patient.

Allied orderlies were prevented from treating patients, many of them now delirious with thirst and infected dressings, but the gallant doctors carried on undeterred.

'How's the wrist today?' Fergus Anckorn remembered Capt Smiley asking, 'in a very doctorly way. He just had a plaster on the side of his neck and his jaw, as if nothing had happened. Doing his rounds like any normal doctor, on any normal day.' Incredible, given what he'd been through.

'Capt Smiley was my surgeon afterwards,' said Dick Lee, 'and of course in doing his rounds, attending to the wounded, he was telling us the story of what went on in the theatre.'

**

Back at the Sisters' Mess outhouse, the morning revealed the devastating toll that the unimaginably long night of captivity had exacted.

'One patient in the room with me died in the night,' said Bryer in Room 3 on the right.

Artillery man Waller reported machine gun fire 'and what may have been the sounds of fighting. It seemed an Allied counter attack may have been under way. Shelling from our own artillery started in the morning and continued intermittently every half hour. A Japanese, who from his appearance and dress I judged to be an officer, looked through the window and swore at us. They were angry about the noise in the huts during the night, and were inflamed by the whisky which had been carried away from the Sisters' Mess.'

'Allied shells began to fall in our area,' said Hoskins in Room 3. His room-mates, started thinking of escape.

'I could not understand the language of the turbanned fellow,' said Norman Bryer of the Indian pressed up against him, 'but, by his gesticulations, I guessed he was suggesting the possibility of escape. The Sapper and Miner spoke Tamil, a language I learnt as a manager on the estate because the labourers were Tamils. He told me that he had a pen-knife in the breast-pocket of his shirt and that if he knelt down behind me I could feel into his pocket, take out the pen-knife and cut the cord tying our hands, and then we would be in a much better position to attempt escape if any opportunity occurred.' Bryer managed to get the pen-knife and cut the cords of that Indian and himself.

'Escape seemed a chance at long odds if all of us made a concerted, organized break, and then it was a possibility to overwhelm the half a dozen Japanese guarding us. Although we were almost all disabled by wounds and sickness, some of us would escape but most would be killed. I was not optimistic about my own chances of being among the few to escape but I thought I ought to propose an attempt, being a sergeant.'

Even in such a dire predicament, such thoughts and plans had to be channelled through the ranking officer. In this room it was Capt William Walker, RADC. 'I suggested to him that he should take the lead in a mass attempt to escape,' said Bryer. 'He excused himself because being a dental officer he was a non-combatant. Next in rank was a quartermaster sergeant.' Clearly there was mass confusion in the heat, literally, of the moment. Because Squadron Leader Griffiths was in this crowd, a rank which is equivalent of major in the army. But he was probably in his pyjamas without insignia, and also a non-combatant being with the RAF Medical Service in any case. Or possibly too weak to speak out. A quartermaster sergeant cannot be positively identified among the list of internees in Room 3, but Bryer turned to him next. 'I invited him to assume leadership. This man so rudely and so contemptuously rejected my appeal that I tried to get at him and hit him with the only thing available – a tin hat. But we were still so closely packed together I could not reach him.'

Bryer was dejected by the emphatic rejection, and resigned himself, as shells kept exploding all around. So deflated was he, that he remarked to the man next to him: 'It would be better if a shell burst on us and killed us all.'

**

The Japanese *Senshi Soshi* battle report for that morning read: 'At 10:00 the artillery focussed on the enemy's artillery units while the frontline mountain artillery was moved to the frontline where infantrymen were deployed. The right wing attacked the Hills 130, 136 and 345, while the left wing unit attacked the hills of 312 and 345, and took over.' This makes a mockery of subsequent claims that they were 'dug in' near the oiltanks until after the ceasefire. These hills (apart from 130) are all beyond the hospital heading towards the city.

The Japanese moved forward on Gillman Heights, a few hundred yards southwest of the hospital, and on to Keppel Harbour front, 2.5 miles south of the hospital. But the Aussie defenders on Hill 130 were giving it their all against 1/55th. And 3/55th were pinned in position for nearly three hours, suffering many dead and wounded.

'The distance between the enemies was only 200 metres and the battle became more like urban combat,' said the *Senshi Soshi*.

'The enemy used strongly built houses in front of them and gave barrage fire to stop us. Because of this the regiments couldn't carry out effective attack and their speed of moving forward got weaker.'

'The Japs avoided the Australians, and attacked the British,' said Sgt Stanley Bryant-Smith of the 2/29th Australians. 'The British fought hard around the Alexandra area. We were watching this battle, and believe you me, it was a real battle. The British, like us, only had small arms, rifles and bayonets, and artillery was only light artillery. The Japanese had big heavy guns, heavy mortars, and dive bombers.' At least their tanks had been neutralized.

'We had such fierce battles from the morning of February 15,' said Mutaguchi. 'Towards the end of the battle of Singapore I came to have a strong respect towards the British soldiers' great resistance.'

**

One report had it that as the starving prisoners called for sustenance from inside the brick outhouse across the road from The Alex, Japanese soldiers outside devoured tinned fruit. Thank you again, Mr Churchill.

Around 11am, Johnson felt the shellfire was now zeroing in, concentrated in the immediate vicinity of their huts. Closer and closer until Room 1 received a direct hit. Doors and shutters were 'blown open.' From a spot near the window in Room 3, Johnson could see sentries posted all around the hutment building.

'A Japanese officer opened the door of our room and said in very halting English: "We are taking you behind the lines, you will get water on the way",' said Bryer. A couple of Japanese with bayonets fixed grabbed two prisoners and led them away. The door was slammed shut again.

'The Japanese began to take prisoners from the building in twos,' said Johnson. 'Twos and threes,' according to Waller. They would've been grateful for the extra breathing room, and space to stretch finally, or even sit down, while waiting their turn to get the precious water they'd been promised all night. The prisoners were taken out and disappeared off to the right, as seen by others facing towards the Sisters' Mess.

From his spot just inside the door, Bryer could spy through the cracked wood. 'I was able to see that they were tying them back-to-back. The soldier took them out very roughly and hit them several times with the butt of his rifle.' He also spotted a machine gun mounted at the top of the stairs that led up to the bungalow opposite. 'The machine gun was trained on our door, and there were two Japanese soldiers lying beside it, apparently in readiness to fire.'

'There were four Japanese 'Ainu' type soldiers engaged in this, working in relays of two,' said Johnson. 'Two of them would go past with two British prisoners and disappear round the corner, and as they disappeared the other Japanese would be coming back for more prisoners.' They'd hold up two fingers and wave the next two out of the room.

But ...

'Suddenly we heard blood-curdling screams,' said Bryer. 'Cries of "Oh my God!", "Mother!", and "Don't! Don't!" There was so much sound of battle fire that it was impossible to tell if the screams coincided with shots or not. The Japanese were bayonetting the prisoners, wiping their weapons, and returning to open the door and grab another couple. The screams of the victims left me in no doubt about our imminent fate.'

'We thought they were being taken away for a drink, but I saw a Japanese soldier wiping blood off his bayonet and heard groans and screams,' said Waller.

'Almost immediately after they disappeared round the corner, I could hear cries of anguish,' said Johnson, 'and as the Japanese passed the window on the way back I could see blood on their bayonets.'

The heat and screams and shots and shouts carried on for twenty minutes till around noon. 'Owing to the lack of water, most of us were very strained,' said Bryer. 'One man with me tried to hang himself, and another cut his wrist.' Many had had no water now for 24 hours, dehydration clouding their senses and shutting down their minds.

'One of the Japanese had a large piece of cloth, and I saw him wiping blood off his bayonet as he went back for the next batch,' said Johnson. 'So far as I could see, only four Japanese were engaged in this task of bayonetting our troops, but there may well have been other Japanese troops waiting round the corner.'

In a period of twenty minutes or so, he estimated at least 100 British prisoners passed his window, including about 20 or 30 from Room 3. 'During the whole time, a Japanese officer was sitting at a desk in the doorway of another wing of the same building, within my vision, and he could see what was going on.'

As a manacled group passed out of sight, another shell thudded in dangerously close to Room 1. 'One of the windows was blown open by a shell,' is how Waller saw it. 'Some of us got through the window.' This is when Gurd and company also decided to hot-foot it.

A Japanese machine gun crew opened up at point blank range, their standard-issue Type 99-1 gun spitting out 550 angry rounds per minute. 'The two men in front of me were shot,' said Waller, noting the Japanese were 'frontline fighting troops, equipped with what appeared to be a four-inch mortar.' He scooted away to a position slightly north of the outhouse block near to the oil tanks, and found a hiding place, where he remained secreted for over 24 hours.

Gurd ploughed on amid rifle fire, darting and jinking, amazed that he was spared that long. 'Several figures are in front of me. At least two. They reach the road and turn right, I do likewise. By now a Jap with a Tommy gun is racing across to cut me off.' Bert's pyjama-clad companions veer sharply to the left off the road. He followed them through waist-high grass. 'We are now running parallel and some trees have screened us from the Jap.' Rifles crackled. 'Still by the hand of providence I go on.' A gully. 'Down in this gully there must be water. Yes, a tiny stream. I throw up my hands and drop forward, and crawl towards the stream, conscious that I have lost a shoe. I push my face into the water and drink deeply. Then I rest to get my breath back.'

'*HELP! HELP*!' a voice shouted out.

'Someone behind me is shouting,' said Gurd. 'I turn back and, after crawling for some time, discover Capt Brown.' Brown was the young dental officer from his toolshed prison room. 'I found him with a bullet wound near the base of his spine. He had been bleeding freely. He smiles pathetically. I plugged his wound to the best of my ability with my own field dressing, but it is hopeless.'

Oh, no. The Japanese have spotted them.

'A ring of grenades came round us. One pitches about three yards away – it happens to be a dud.' Brown handed over the valuables collected earlier for bribing the guard. Snipers were now onto their scent. Brown urged Gurd to take better cover, but Gurd – ever the caring medic – wanted to fetch him some water and there was no container handy. 'I take off one of his shoes and, after making him as comfortable as possible, crawl away, telling him that I may be some time. His last words to me were, "Do what you can but for God's sake look after yourself".'

Rifle fire crackled and popped all around. Gurd became disoriented, unable to find that stream. More rifle fire cracking and kicking around him. 10 minutes, 20 minutes, 30 minutes. 'I am forced to take cover in some very thick jungle undergrowth. Here, I believe I lost consciousness, to wake up being bitten by ants, *thousands* of them.' A rustling noise. 'Two Nipponese are apparently hunting for me. They pass about 10 yards away.'

**

'A shell either hit our building or was a near miss,' recalled Bryer at the other end in Room 3. 'The blast blew down the door and blew open the window shutters and brought down many roof tiles. The air was full of dust, creating a fog, and I realized our few guards would be unable to see, especially the machine gunner facing the door.

'The rest of us made a break through what remained of the windows,' said Johnson, 'and nearly everyone was shot down. When those of us in the room made our break for the open, we left behind a few who were unable to move. They probably numbered ten at the most.'

The young, sporty, medic Mitchell bolted from the same room but was 'mown down by machine gun fire.' On the other side of the hutment, Bryer made his dash through the choking dust and debris. 'The door had been loosened by shellfire, and we made a bolt for it. I don't think that the machine gun which covered our door opened fire, because if it had done so, most of us in the room would have been killed.'

As it turned out they were, as many escapees ran directly into the line-of-fire of other chattering machine guns. But the options were few, so escaping at least gave them a slim shot of survival, versus a certain brutal death by bayonet. *'Yell! Stick! Turn! Retract!'*

'I made a dash for the door, turned left, and ran around the building towards the railway line,' said Bryer who had cleverly managed to put the building between himself and the machine gunner as he ran in the general direction of Singapore city. 'The machine gun covering the door did not open fire. I ran over the railway and across the road which runs parallel to it.' He ran across the 'open country' for around 100 metres, and noticed he had company. 'I saw, on my right, the Indian soldier with the turban being intercepted by a Japanese with fixed bayonet. I altered course slightly,' he said with typical English understatement, 'and continued running as fast as I could. There was a lot of barbed wire, which I hurdled over, how, I don't know.' The young tennis-loving Air Force man did extremely well given that he had been hospitalized with leg inflammation issues for nearly three months. A few hundred yards more, legs pumping. 'I was near the Alexandra Hospital.'

Presently, Hoskins joined him, and they joined forces on the fly, down the Alexandra Road zig-zagging to avoid enemy fire. 'All the time we were running, bullets were whistling past us.'

Then Hoskins pointed to a car, shining in the sunlight beyond, suggesting they could drive it to Singapore. 'A British officer was lying on the ground dead, and all the car tyres were flat, so we resumed running,' said Bryer. A large amount of money was found on the officer. Rather unusual, unless he was preparing to make an escape from the island and needed to pay a boatman or somehow buy his way to freedom out of Singapore. Bryer and Hoskins immediately resumed their zig-zagging run.

'We got on the road leading to Singapore and I was mentally congratulating myself for avoiding the bullets when I felt an enormous punch in the back. I was bowled over like a shot rabbit and all the breath was knocked out of me, and I could hardly breathe,' said Bryer. 'I looked down and saw a lot of blood and a large hole in my right breast.' The 7.7mm shell is the same as that from a .303 rifle, and that bullet would remain lodged in his body for the rest of his life.

'What's the matter?' shouted Hoskins.

'I'm done for. Go on!' Bryer told him.

'Come on!' egged Hoskins.

Hoskins recalled it in wildly different detail: Bryer was shot in the ankle. 'But he told me not to wait. He said something to the effect of, "Don't wait, I'm just doing up my shoelace!"' Hoskins ran past the hospital and reached a hut on the other side of Alexandra Road, where an Indian and his family gave him water. 'When I saw two Japanese soldiers approaching the hut, I went away and was picked up by a patrol of the Beds and Herts Regiment. I was taken to company headquarters, and thence given a lift in a staff car to Singapore.'

That made it one survivor.

It also proved how close together the opposing sides were, and underlines counter-intuitively too how surprisingly easy it was to move around within the area surrounding the hospital.

'I was left lying in the road, not able to breathe except in small gasps, thinking I was dying, and hoping it would not take too long,' said Bryer. 'Thinking of my mother and God, and regretting I'd only lived half my life.'

The tropical sun beat down, roasting Bryer on the bitumen where he lay crumpled. 'It occurred to me that I could die more comfortably in the shade of nearby bushes, so I crawled there. Immediately I moved, bullets began kicking up dust all around me.' Luckily his breathing came more easily now. 'I realized I might not die as soon as I had thought.' He steeled his resolve to make his escape complete. Easier said than done ... he could only move along with his 5'10" frame bent over.

Soon, a patrol of three Japanese soldiers overtook him. 'I must've presented a strange sight, dressed in the pyjamas I was wearing when removed from the hospital, and covered with a lot of blood. One of the Japanese thrust at me with his bayonet. I instinctively turned sideways. After three more thrusts the Japanese took the bayonet off the rifle and hit me on the left side of my head.'

Bryer feigned being knocked out. 'I fell to the ground and after a few minutes the Japanese patrol left. I stayed motionless where I fell.'

Next, a machine gun detachment arrived. 'They set up their machine gun near where I was lying and kept firing for some time, ignoring me, then they moved on. They must've thought I was dead.'

**

Chaos had a firm grip on the surrounding battlefield.

Lt Col Elrington was still without any brigade HQ communication – and didn't even know where they were. So he called the commanding officers of the 1st Malays and 5th Bedfords together. They consulted on a withdrawal plan. The 2nd Loyals would move backwards to Mt Washington, a coastal-facing southern slope further towards the city, dotted with grand colonial mansions and covered in coconut and rubber trees, and the Bedfords to Henderson Road, just over a mile southeast of the hospital.

But the Allies were still inflicting big damage, and frustrating the IJA 18th Division's aggressive intention. 'We did not advance at all,' according to Soejima of the 56th Regiment Machine Gun Company, who were last heard of dug in northeast of the oil tanks, more than suspiciously close to where the machine guns had guarded and mown-down the servant's quarters outhouse inmates. 'About noon I was hit by flying shrapnel, and taken to a place of safety in a rubber plantation,' he said.

The Allied machine guns around the Depot Road and Gillman Barracks to the west of the hospital were still doing a good job of pinning down the enemy. 'The divisional artillery could not succeed in silencing the machine guns,' said Ito, who was in the thick of that action, 'as its exact location could not be determined. 'The fighting continued until after noon, when the company fighting below on the road reported that the enemy facing them had withdrawn. It was then realized that the enemy had also vacated its positions on the hill.'

Elrington's withdrawal plan had been enacted.

**

English signaller, Lt Walter Salmon, while conceding 'exact times are vague' seems to think it was on that Sunday morning (rather than the day before) that the first Japanese actually came into his dining room ward. Certainly possible, given that generally that morning the ground floor areas and corridors of the hospital were jostling with Japanese troops, setting up for a final infantry push towards Singapore. It also tallies with the fact they were undetected and unmolested the previous day. But that was about to change:

'He was filthy dirty from head to toe, he had no firearms, only a knife with a blade about 18 inches long hanging from a string around his head,' said Salmon of a Japanese officer who suddenly entered. 'He went to the first patient lying on a mattress on the floor and tried to snatch the watch off his wrist. The officer tried to push him off. The Jap then picked up a boot lying nearby and smashed him over the head and took the watch. He then walked around the room taking watches, cigarette cases and anything that took his fancy.' Others were urinated on.

The signaller was busy reading a book, *Clive of India*, trying his best to ignore the thieving officer. 'He came and sat on my bed, staring at me, swinging his knife to and fro. I kept looking at the book. It seems an eternity before he saw my silver identity disc round my neck, snatched it off, and went away.'

Pte Britton described Japanese soldiers rushing in, grabbing piles of bread off the dining table, while he and four other soldier patients watched in disbelief from their makeshift beds, hidden by the long tablecloth, as the invaders gorged on the loaves inches away from them. They went luckily unnoticed. 'The Japanese soldiers paid no attention to them,' he told sister Elsie, 'their only interest: the bread.' But their orderly was marched out and bayonetted. Britton and company remained in hiding there 'for days' until it was safe to emerge. Perhaps at that point he was wondering why he'd ever lied about his age to get into this situation. Too late now.

**

'Tsukkakare!' Charge!

'We caught them running out the back,' said Daniel Fraser, whose 36th Royal Engineers were now engaged head-on with the rampaging enemy behind the hospital. 'They came out of the back of the hospital within our firing range, and as they came charging over this dump of soil ... we got them full with the machine guns. So much so that they dropped the flag, and I think one or two of them got away. They were fired on continually and we run down quite a few of them, and they were through.'

What became of that flag? It could tell us so much about who those invaders really were because often they were signed by the men of the unit, scrawled with slogans and inspirational mantra.

'Wc were waiting on another charge, but they came from a different direction, from a hillock,' said Fraser. 'We machine gunned them as much as we could till they disappeared altogether too far back. But then we had to move because they were getting round us. They put field guns on us and we had to make a run for it, and we got to the biscuit factory which was vacant by that time. We picked up some biscuits, because we were hungry. Filled our pockets with biscuits, and marched 100 metres down the road.'

**

Maj Lyndsey Webster and 28-year-old Capt William Young were notably active around the wards despite Japanese orders that no patients were to be treated. Young had been with the Malayan Medical Service in KL since the previous year, having married Peggie, a New Zealander, only the year prior to that. She had successfully evacuated to Sydney. Having joined the FMS Volunteers, he found himself attached to the Malay Regiment, was wounded just a week or so before, then assigned to the staff at The Alex.

'Around noon, the orderlies and doctors still surviving were allowed to return,' said Pilkington. 'In a few hours they worked wonders.'

'For those of us who were walking wounded, there was nothing much they could do,' said Capt Brown. 'They couldn't operate on my leg anyway. It was just left with the dressing from two days before.' Doctors scurried around doing what they could. Any remaining corpses from the hospital and immediate grounds discovered were placed in Ward 6, with the padre and Pte Charles Ellerington taking charge of this grim task.

**

And still the climax of the Battle for Singapore was reaching a crescendo and thundered around them. 'Our own guns were ordered to fire on the hospital,' said Pilkington, still bed-ridden in the Officers' Wards upstairs, 'and they proved to be far more accurate than the Japs. With a few salvoes they completely demolished the top floor of one wing and removed most of the roof elsewhere. Two shells burst by the stairwell by our ward and for two hours bits of shrapnel and ceiling were raining down on us like snow. This was, I think, the worst period of the lot as, added to the inferno, was the choking thick fumes of cordite.'

A state of tension dominated this day, according to Brown. 'We assumed the group were still in the little house,' he said of his colleagues and orderlies who'd been marched off and nothing heard since. Water was still almost non-existent. 'There was food but people weren't hungry anyway,' said Brown. Hungry or not, patients were fed progressively throughout the afternoon.

**

A Japanese infantry gun – possibly the recent arrival Ito had pressed into action – was still wreaking havoc around the area on the defending Loyals B Company, who were using a rapidly-deteriorating colonial bungalow as their HQ. But with each shell they became more vulnerable. Maj Patrick Leighton emptied three magazines of his Bren gun at the infantry gun. The order to retire was given, and not a minute later a shell scored a direct hit on the trench they'd hurriedly left. His exploits that day earned him a Military Cross for gallantry.

B Company stumbled across Alexandra Road, to a huge storm drain, carrying their wounded with them. They pulled back through A Coy's position and the highly important Depot Road area, to Henderson Road. This was still just over a mile south of the hospital and the Sisters' Quarters, showing how dense and compressed the battlefield around the hospital had become, and how many Japanese companies and battalions had possible access to the hospital in the 24 hours since the hospital was first over-run.

On regrouping, the B Company Loyals were shocked that only 25 men and three officers were able to keep fighting. CD Company, already a composite company due to casualties, was even more devastated, with just 17 men and three officers – including Capt Thomas Brook – fit to fight. This band of just 48 was again renamed BCD Coy, put in reserve, and ordered back to Marlborough Camp, just to the west of the Depot, for a much-needed rest.

**

Allied HQ was now feeling the heat directly. In Fort Canning, much discussion and debate was afoot regarding the possibility of Singapore surrendering. If there was any doubt where Percival stood on this issue, he had ordered all cars and vehicles to be driven off the harbour wharves to impede the Japanese fleet from easy berthing, and to deny Japanese forces access to left-behind transport.

Percival's official car was in the line-up to be pushed, when a quick-thinking Singapore Harbour Board employee, Australian Jack Stein, whisked the small flags off Percival's car before shoving it over the edge. That group then made their escape to Java, carrying the flags as a souvenir.

At the Ford factory in Bukit Timah, just after 16:00 hours, Percival was being doormatted by Yamashita.

The Allied party had arrived with lowest-ranking officer, Capt Cyril Wild, holding a huge white flag aloft, and Brig Kenneth Torrance carrying the much-prized and symbolic Union Jack, which the Japanese divisional commanders had all dreamed of ripping down first from Fort Canning. Brig Thomas Newbigging made up the rest of the home team.

Arthur Lane, a musician with 1st Bn Manchester Regiment, added some colourful insight to this scene, based on his later friendship with Wild. 'What you did not see was Wild throwing the white flag down and shouting to Percival: "This is stupid and I want no part of it, let's go back". Nor did they show Percival shouting back and ordering Wild to pick the damned flag up. Wild refused and the flag was picked up and carried by a Japanese officer,' according to Lane.

On the other side of the table, apart from Yamashita, were Lt Col Sugita Ichiji, Intelligence Officer with the 25th Army, and 2nd Lt Hishikari, a general's son and Yamashita's official interpreter.

The Japanese propaganda machine made sure this historic moment was captured in all its grainy glory by their film crew. Yamashita could be seen rampantly thumping the table, while Percival was cowered and the surrender signature was soon forthcoming.

The truth was far more prosaic according to Japanese-speaking Wild: 'At these surrender negotiations, Hishikari's translations were very hesitant. Yamashita finally lost patience with him, banged his fist on the table, and told Sugita to take over. Yamashita said it was Hishikari's time-wasting hesitancy which infuriated him and he had no intention of bullying Percival.'

**

But Mutaguchi knew none of these goings-on, and was himself growing wildly impatient with his division's stalled progress. He wanted to visit the front-most lines to rev up his men, but Staff Officer Tsuji pleaded him not to. 'Your men at the frontline are doing so good,' said Tsuji, 'but please do not go there because the commanders of the frontline would feel that you came because you were not happy about their slow progress, and many of them might carry out unreasonable charges that could eventually cause more mens' death.'

Mutaguchi insisted he was going there to encourage them because he cared about them so much. 'Tsuji understood and cried, and Mutaguchi understood how hard his men were and cried.' Viewed another way, could it be that Tsuji had something at or near the frontlines to hide? Like an outraged hospital, for example.

The British were lobbing 6- and 9.2-inch shells into these strongholds around the hospital. The 114th – desperate to reach its target of Hill 136, Gillman Barracks – crawled forward through the rubber trees on their stomachs. Just then some shells burst on Hill 130 only 1000 yards away, killing a couple of their HQ staffers. Anger welled up in Arai as he cursed the British Artillery.

The Loyals HQ Coy, under Maj Francis Barnes, used these fusillades to retreat to Mount Washington around 16:30 while the enemy was pinned.

Maj Gen Takeda also felt the lack of progress as he visited the HQ of 114th and 55th Regiments 'which were still in the same positions as on the previous day. The line remained practically static on account of heavy firing from the direction of Keppel Barracks which lasted until around 17:00 hours.'

Nasu's 56th was also pinned in the same position as yesterday, dug in near the railway line.

'The British Infantry appear to be on the verge of surrendering,' thought Arai, 'yet their artillery keeps pounding us. They should all be shot,' he said. But Arai wouldn't get that chance in Singapore ...

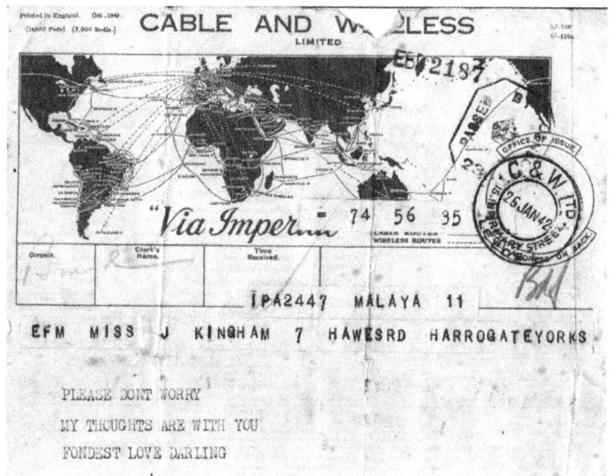

CABLE AND W[illegible]LESS
LIMITED

"Via Imper[illegible]" 74 56 35

IPA2447 MALAYA 11

EFM MISS J KINGHAM 7 HAWESRD HARROGATEYORKS

PLEASE DONT WORRY
MY THOUGHTS ARE WITH YOU
FONDEST LOVE DARLING

CANADIAN CORVETTE IS SUNK; 23 LOST

FINAL EDITION **The Lethbridge Herald**

BIG BATTLE SHIP PRINCE OF WALES AND BATTLE CRUISER REPULSE ARE SUNK

Windflower Reported Lost In Collision

TWO BRITISH WARSHIPS SENT TO BOTTOM

Japanese Report States Both Ships Attacked From Air

Top: Telegram from Pte Len Knott to his sweetheart, Joan. Centre: The sinking of the *Wales* and *Repulse* sent shock waves around the world. Below: PoWs were simply listed initially as 'missing' or 'PoW' without any details.

REPORTED MISSING

COLONEL J. W. CRAVEN

(P.A.) AUCKLAND, March 22.
Colonel J. W. Craven, medical superintendent of Auckland Hospital, who was officer commanding the Alexandra military hospital in Singapore, is posted missing. He also held the position of senior officer for the Malayan medical services.

Singapore burns in February 1942. View from The GPO Building (top) and the Normanton Oil Tanks (below).

The Alex, with Red Crosses clearly marked on the roof and Alexandra Rd in foreground. Below: Looking less than pristine during the war after the artillery bombing.

THREE ATTACK WAVES, 14 FEB 1942

PATHS TAKEN TO SISTERS' QUARTERS OUTHOUSES: 2 GROUPS

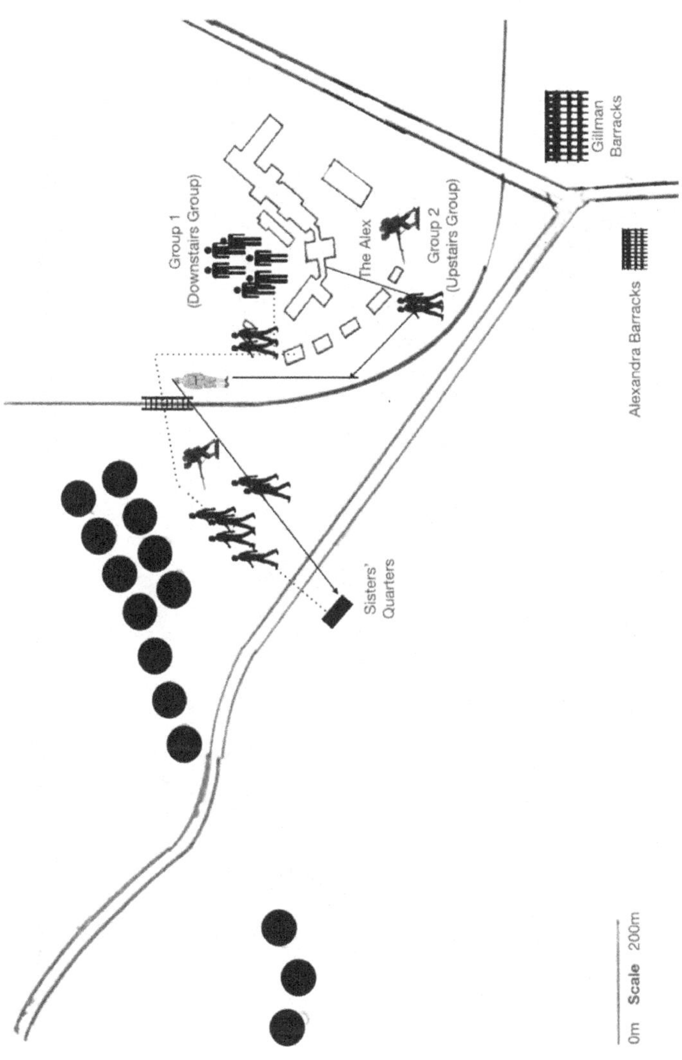

SISTERS' QUARTERS OUTHOUSES 14-15 FEB 1942.

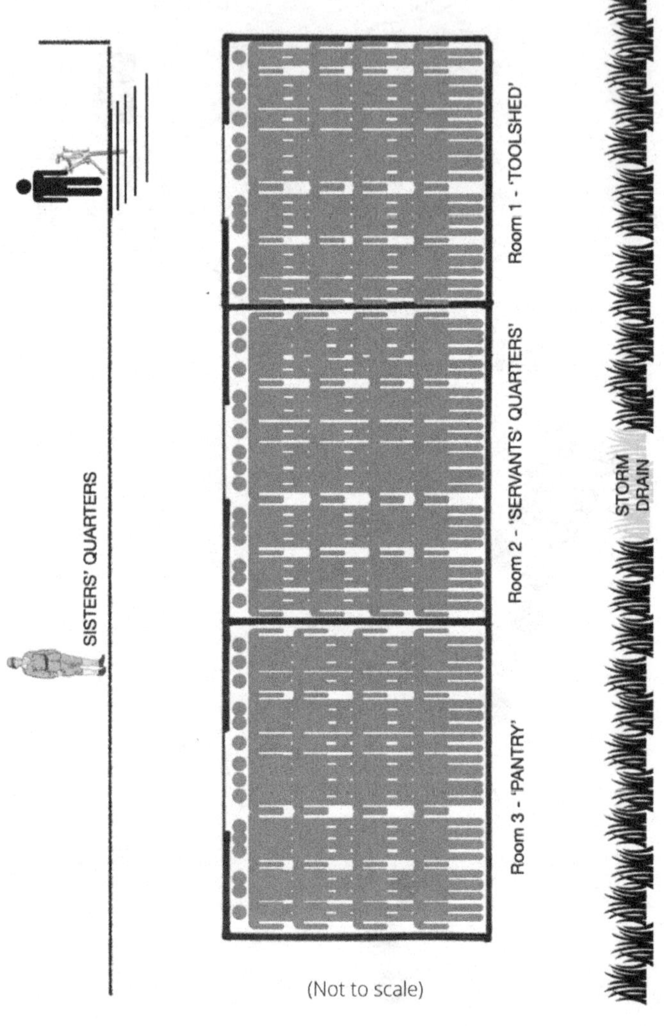

(Not to scale)

SISTERS' QUARTERS INMATES -- ROOM 1 'TOOLSHED'

Capt John Brown, RADC
Pte John Bunney, RAMC
Pte Kenneth Butler, RAMC
Pte Bert Gurd, RAMC*
L/Cpl Jack Jones, RAMC
Pte Frank Onslow, RAMC
Pte Stanley Pearce, RAMC
Capt Richard Waller, Royal Artillery*
Plus others including Indian Army Commissioned Officer,
and some Indian Army soldiers.

*= Survived

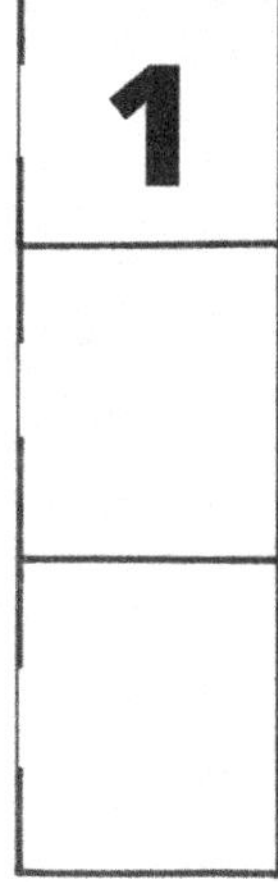

SISTERS' QUARTERS INMATES -- ROOM 2 'SERVANTS QUARTERS'

Lt William Logan, RAMC
Pte Joseph Mattimore, RAMC
Pte Thomas McDougall, RAMC
L/Cpl Donald MacKenzie, RAMC
Pte Robert Rodger, RAMC
Cpl Andrew Stoker, RAMC
Plus others unnamed, possibly
Cpl William Doherty, 2nd Argyll & Sutherland Highlanders.

(No known survivors)

SISTERS' QUARTERS INMATES -- ROOM 3 'PANTRY'

Capt Ransome Allardyce, RAMC
Pte Ronald Allgood, 2nd Cambridgeshires
Pte Adolphus Andrews, RAMC
Sgt Norman Bryer, RAF*
Cpl Carl Deltry, RAMC
Cpl Thomas Gordon, RAMC
Squadron Leader Eustatius Griffiths, RAF Medical
Pte Ivor Griffiths, RAMC
Pte Herbert Harris, RAMC
Pte Lloyd Hayes, RADC
Pte Sidney Hoskins, RAMC*
Cpl Idris Isaacs, RAMC
Cpl George Johnson, RAMC*
Cpl Hugh Mitchell, RAMC
Pte George Oliver, RAMC
L/Cpl Glenalvon Ritchie, RAMC
Pte Harry Rose, RAMC
Cpl Edward Sinclair, RAMC
Mrs Sinclair, VAD
Capt William Walker, RADC
Pte Wilfred Watts, RAMC
Pte Charles Williams, RAMC
Plus Indians, Madras Sappers & Miners. Gunner George Dean, RA?

3

ESCAPE ROUTE: SYDNEY HOSKINS 15 FEB 1942

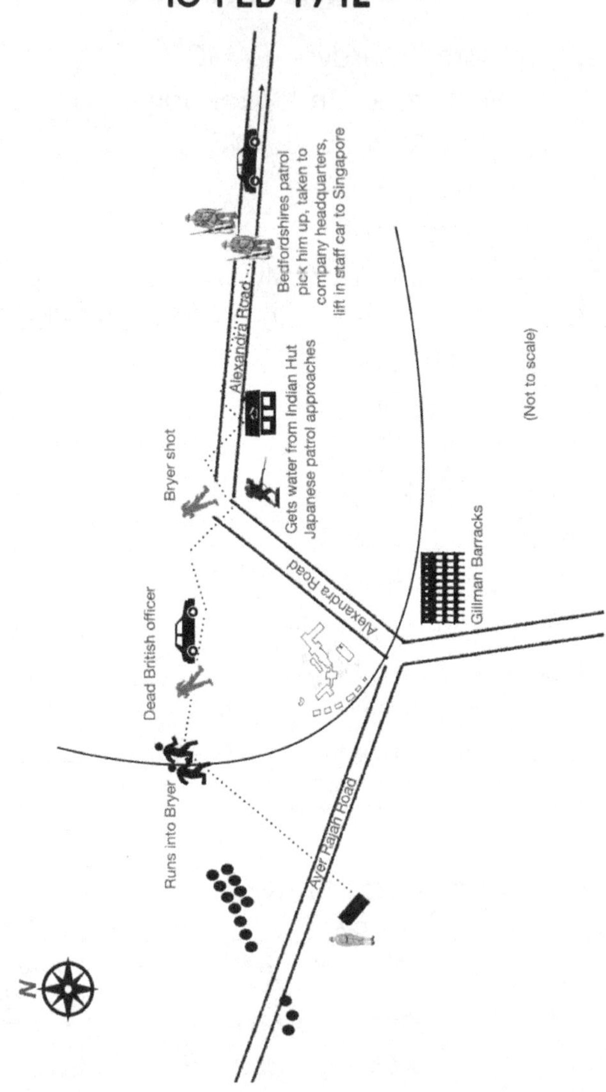

ESCAPE ROUTE: NORMAN BRYER
15 FEB 1942

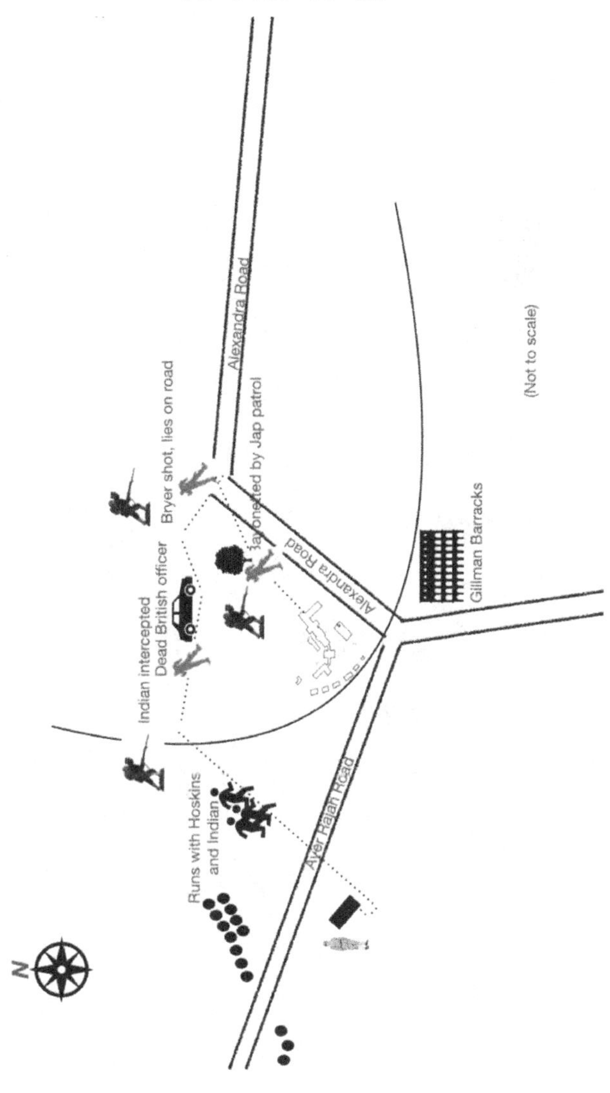

ESCAPE ROUTE: BERT GURD
15 FEB 1942

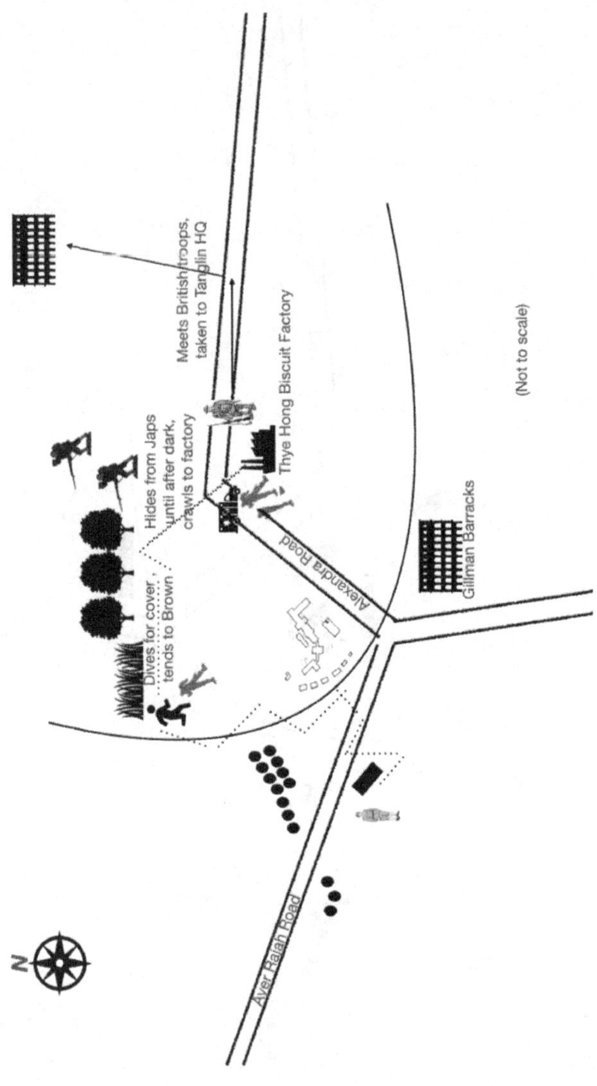

ESCAPE ROUTE: GEORGE JOHNSON
15 FEB 1942

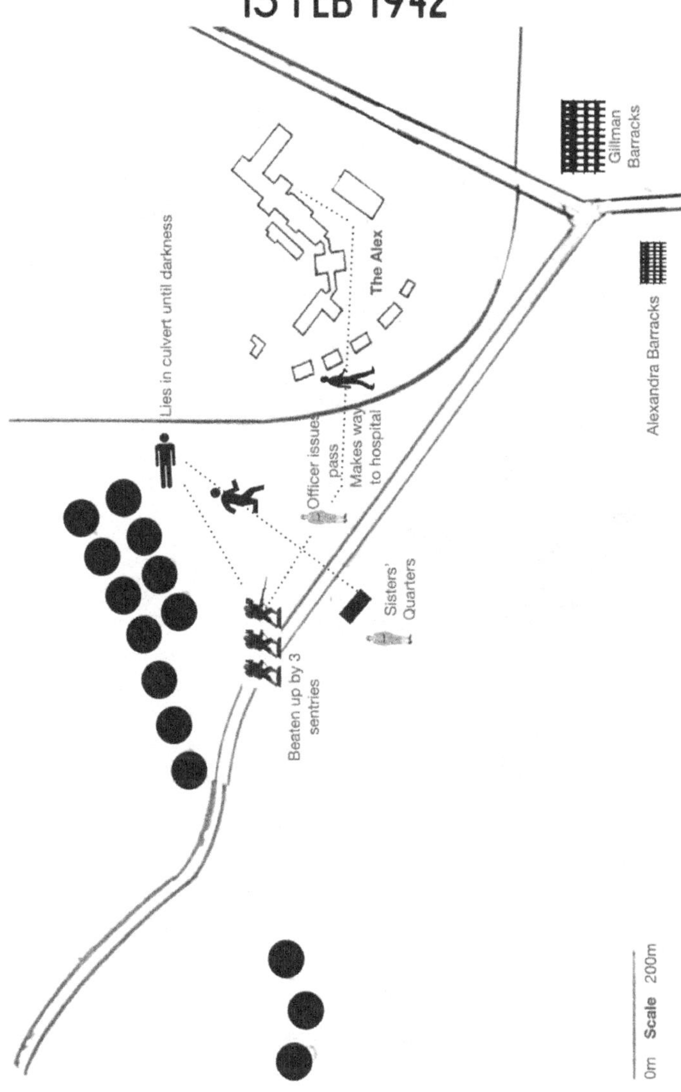

ESCAPE ROUTE: RICHARD WALLER 15-16 FEB 1942

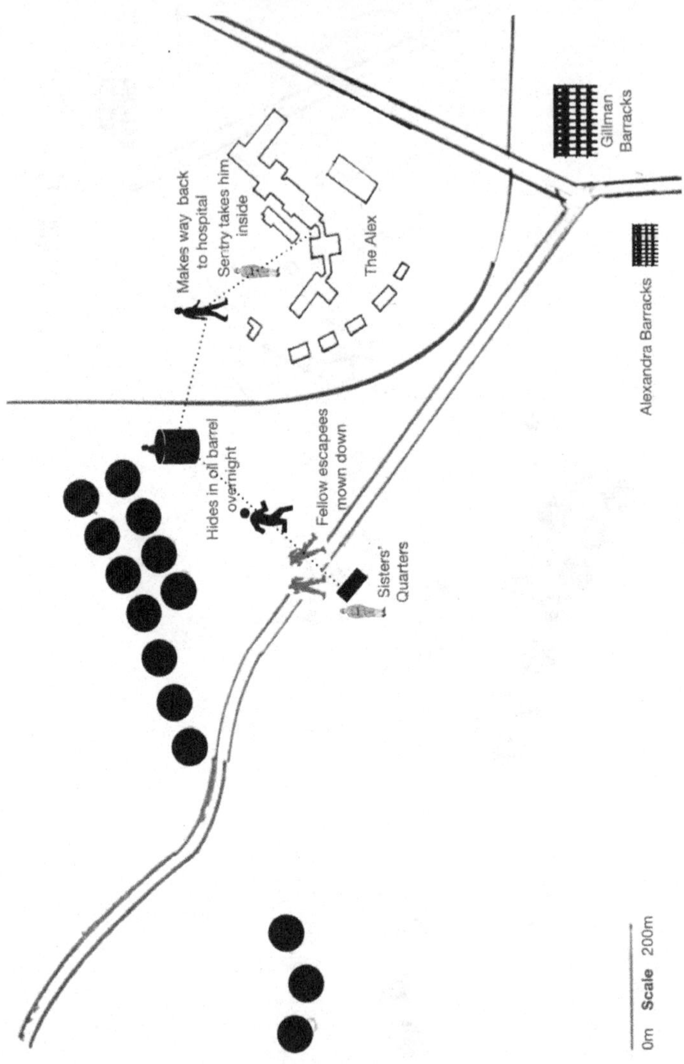

POSITION OF 18TH DIV IJA TROOPS EVENING, 15 FEB 1942

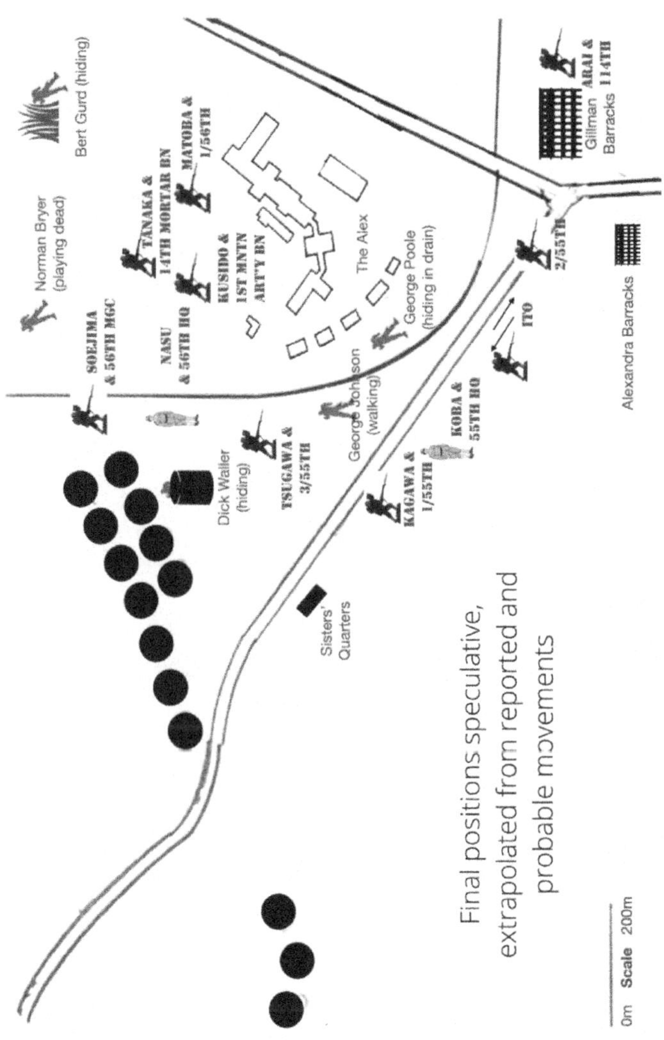

CEASEFIRE AND SILENCE

'An eerie calm had fallen over the island.'

15 February 1942. That evening at the hospital, the Japanese were still bundling people away. 'Col Craven kept enquiring for the patients and orderlies who had disappeared,' noted Smiley.

Around 18:00 another group of 20 orderlies and soldiers, including Sgt Anderson and Pte Sutton, were rounded up. Was the good fortune of Sutton, the only one uninjured among the operating theatre group, about to run out? 'Their hands were tied,' according to Gunner Moore, 'and they were led to a monsoon drain near the Sergeant Major's quarters, but were given cigarettes and raisins.'

Was this to be a firing squad 'last request' type of situation?

**

'About 18:30 everything seemed to be very quiet. I got up and looked for water,' said the Air Force man Bryer, who was still playing dead, which was now less and less of a stretch for him. 'I was tormented and desperate with thirst. I felt that I must quench my thirst before I died. I would be happy to die if I could drink before I died.'

Behind him in that sinister twilight he could make out the silhouette of The Alex. 'I could see the outline of the large building. Not a glimmer of light to be seen and, having been removed from there, I presumed the hospital empty. I thought if I could get inside I might find some water, *any* water.' He staggered towards it.

'While trying to get in, a door opened and someone with a hurricane lamp enquired in a quavering voice: "Who's there?" It was a medical orderly, someone who knew me, and knew I'd been taken out of the hospital the day before. A surgeon, Maj Nadell (sic), joined the orderly and they asked me about the others. I replied: "All dead!" Maj Nadell thought my story would alarm other patients so I was put in a small room by myself and examined by the major. The high velocity bullet had entered my back and been deflected by a rib and come out under the arm.' A field dressing was applied. 'I pleaded for water and was offered champagne, beer or any any other drink except water. Water was what I wanted above all. Finally they asked me if I would have some hot sweet tea instead, and I accepted that. After the tea I was allowed a long glass of crystal clear sparkling water for which I had visions during my long period of thirst torment.'

That made it two survivors.

Bert Gurd was still hiding in the undergrowth, not sure if he'd been there half an hour or four hours. Probably the latter because next he heard a lot of cheering. 'Can it be that our boys are driving the Japs back?' he thought. 'Foolishly I emerge from my hideout, and get to my feet. Immediately I hear "*crack-crack*" so I drop down and wait for darkness.' Twilight soon gave way to darkness. 'As soon as it is dark I make my way towards the road that runs along in front of Alexandra.' He'd made it about 1.5 miles beyond The Alex, when suddenly fires erupted behind him. 'Tremendous fires, making scenes of my former hideout as clear as daylight.' The Japanese clearly wanted to track down and extinguish all survivors, that is, witnesses.

'Near the exit to Alexandra I find an ambulance with its two occupants – a driver and orderly – killed. Other cars I come across, their radiators either polluted or dry.' He crawled and staggered along the open road, expecting to be hailed or challenged or worse. 'But there is absolutely nobody about – it is uncanny.' He spotted the Thye Hong Biscuit Factory and several figures lurking around it. 'They appear to be unarmed. When I am near enough I see their turbans. Friends. They examine the buckles on my shorts, apparently deciding that I am not Nipponese. One speaks a little English, or rather whispers – everyone is whispering. They take me to the rear of their quarters and feed me on biscuits and water. The English-speaking one later fetches his officer who tells me of the capitulation – hence the cheering that puzzled me. The officer hears my story then, as he is on his way to Brigade HQ, lets me accompany him.'

So off to Tanglin they went. 'I am interviewed by several officers of different ranks, all of whom are in no condition to understand me – none of whom believe me.' Clearly they believed that being inebriated was the only state to enter captivity.

'Nevertheless I contact one who is more rational, shall I say, than the rest. He sees that I get a splendid supper and a shakedown.' As he prepared for bed, Bert remembered the valuables in his pockets, passed to him by Capt Brown. 'I discover I have lost the watches not the rings. Then I remember those Indians had gone through my pockets deciding whether I was British or Nipponese.' The time, he was told in the absence of a watch, was 01:30am. 'I had been imagining it was about 10pm. So Sunday 15 February was over, that day on which, so many times, the hand of God was my protection – and I have been spared to thank Him for His mercies.' All in all, a hell of way for Bert to spend his 36th birthday.

That made it three survivors.

**

From his drain hide-out near the hospital, medic George Poole made an astonishing observation: 'Behind the building were petrol storage tanks that the Japs had set alight and any survivors they found were made to walk into the blazing oil.' This was not corroborated by anyone else – there again he was the only one in such a position outside of the hospital to see it, so it cannot be discounted as a very convenient and effective means of disposal.

And what of Capt Allardyce, who had anesthetized Veitch on the operating theatre, and was roped into this incident at the last minute? He was found among the massacre victims, thus becoming the third Allardyce child of their father, a humble tailor, to be killed at war.

Stringer reported that 'the rest of the party were butchered and are believed to be buried in a long trench at the back of the hospital, where excavation should reveal their remains. An Army chaplain saw a long trench filled in with fresh earth.'

**

Ito now realized that the British enemy had vacated its position on the hill in front of him at Gillman Barracks. 'I gave the order to advance,' he said. 'The company on the road and some of the Machine Gun Company were the first to start, but before the two companies on the hill were ready to move off, the order for the 'cease fire' came through.'

And slightly behind him was Umemoto, adjutant of the 55th Regiment HQ: 'I was in the vicinity of the burning oil tanks at the time of the fall of Singapore.' As was Tsugawa, OC 3/55th Regiment.

Just a little east of the hospital the 36th Royal Engineers were dug in. 'Our last bivouac was right opposite the Chinese cemetery on the left hand side of the road facing Singapore,' said Daniel Fraser, who'd had an especially torrid few days, mentally and physically. 'There was vacant land on the right. We came to a patch of ground with a tree sheltering it, so we bivouacked there right under some trees. And the Japs were still firing so we entered the cemetery to get better vision. There was continuous rumble of gunfire, shells, etc. We were fired on then all of a sudden there was dead silence. I thought it was a spell ... five minutes, then ten minutes, then it will start again. Nothing happened so we wonder what had happened.'

The guns that had boomed in, on, and around Singapore all February, fell silent.

'Now is the time to run,' thought the ever-ambitious and determined Arai, quickly covering the 100 yards between his position and his coveted target Hill 136. This was right in the thick of the British Empire's major depots and military materiel. They scaled the 50-yard incline to find 'a large two-storey concrete barracks stood on top of the hill, with the walls painted black and, above the entrance, a big Red Cross sign.' This would have been the 20th Combined General Hospital, or the 27th Indian General Hospital, both at Gillman Barracks.

'To our surprise 60 pale faces stared at us out of pyjamas,' Arai said. 'Those who sat upright and those standing next to their beds all held their hands up high, indicating surrender. Only a moment before I had entertained the idea of killing them all, even in surrender. But now looking into the ashen faces of these wounded soldiers, the thought quickly faded.'

Through an interpreter, the major in charge was asked what he knew of British dispositions. 'He respects international law and from that stance takes a neutral view. He knows nothing about military matters,' Arai was told.

Arai hit the major with full force on the left cheek, sending him sprawling. 'I myself was astonished by my sudden action, unable to control my rush of adrenaline,' Arai said. 'Was it a reaction to all the shelling I'd endured over the past 10 hours and the great loss of dead and wounded suffered in the past final hours?'

The slapping increased the major's desire to be compliant. 'According to the major this was Gillman Barracks and housed around 1000 patients.'

'Where on earth is the British infantry?' Arai thought. 'It was unbelievable to simply leave behind 1000 wounded soldiers to their fate,' he thought to himself. 'Abandoned by their own soldiers, the frightened eyes stirred neither pity nor sympathy in me.'

**

Fractionally south, the Loyals were digging into their positions on the high ground above the barracks around Henderson Road and Mount Washington when some Japanese suddenly appeared.

A Coy fired on them, possibly the last shots fired in the battle for this smoking southern island. 'They'd already bombed the hell out of Singapore,' said Pte Stan Sharpley. 'There was nothing to stop them, nothing at all.'

Nothing, that was, except an unconditional surrender. 'At 20:00 suddenly the Army HQ made a call to the Division HQ saying 'The enemy surrendered,' said the *Senshi Soshi* battle report. 'The 18th Div shall soon terminate your combat action, stay where you are tonight, and maintain the highest alert toward the enemy.'

Arai sensed a sudden commotion from the back moving up to their front. 'It seemed to be coming from the coast, through the valley, rising up the hills, like a growing tidal wave to engulf us,' he said. 'The roar grew closer and louder. One could not see their silhouettes but the force of their voices was shattering: "*Banzai! Banzai! Banzaaai*!"'

A shout mixed in: '114th Regiment! The enemy has surrendered! Hold your attack! Stop your advance!'

**

'They blew a whistle, a very powerful whistle,' said Bull, 'which we heard even though we were about five miles out of Singapore.'

'All of a sudden all firing stopped,' observed Pilkington. 'We heard the sirens sounding the All Clear, immediately followed by the *Banzai*s of the Jap soldiers. An eerie calm had fallen over the island. Singapore had fallen.'

'The noise suddenly stopped,' said the patched-up Smiley, 'and we knew it was over.' Or was it? Medic Harry Saye, who had witnessed the brutal slaying of his colleague Arthur Bruce in the kitchen, was apparently about to suffer the same fate.

'At about 8pm I had been rounded up with a few orderlies and lined up by the hospital kitchen,' he said. 'We thought 'This must be it.' When the air raid sirens went all over Singapore, we knew the end was here, we had capitulated. We were released by the Japanese and went back to the ward. Suddenly a great roar and *Banzai* cheers came from the Japanese lines.'

Anderson, Sutton and others rounded up earlier were also, incredulously, released.

Capt Robert Brown of the Punjabs was upstairs near Pilkington in the Officers' Ward. 'Then we heard '*Banzai! Banzai! Banzai*!' all around the place, and we knew that the island had obviously fallen. The doctors came in said the war was over, and we were informed officially that we were prisoners of war. The tension relaxed completely. We didn't want to be prisoners of war, but we knew the fighting was over, we had to become resigned to that fact now.'

**

Around Mount Washington, a car with its headlights on approached from behind the Loyals' position, and the brigade intelligence officer reported that Percival had capitulated. All firing was to cease by 20:30.

All 289 other ranks remaining in the decimated battalion retired immediately to their home base, Marlborough Camp, directly adjacent. A couple of hours later, Lt Col Erlington – now the veteran of fighting in *two* world wars – addressed his company commanders:

'I congratulate you on fighting so well,' he said. 'Through no fault of yours you have been ordered to surrender. Remember the lads who have fought and died, and show the same spirit of duty and discipline in defeat. Do nothing to bring discredit on the Loyals as prisoners of war. God bless you.' Erlington was immediately awarded the DSO for his gallant leadership of his men down the west coast.

**

But it seemed that whatever IJA elements were working inside the hospital were not directly connected in to HQ's communications. So their horrific war was to drag on that agonizing bit longer still. Because Bryer – who had just returned to the hospital merely hours earlier after his outhouse ordeal – was in the firing line again. 'More Japanese came into the hospital and tried to make me go out of this hospital again. They took some orderlies and patients and bound them, but returned them the next morning.'

Pilkington supported this story of the late night removal of personnel *after* the surrender. 'All doctors and orderlies were removed but this time we were prepared and things were much better,' he said. 'Before they left, the doctors gave the delirious a heavy shot of morphia. Those who had died had been wheeled, beds and all, on to the verandahs. There was peace and calm again with only the lurid glow of the oil wells to disturb us.'

Suddenly alone with their thoughts, it must have been a conflicting mass of emotions for the Allies. The war was over, but another less-defined battle was about to encapsulate them as PoWs.

How did they *really* feel at that moment?

**

'We had our last battle at Mt Faber, on our own football field, then up into Mt Marlborough Camp,' said Pte Stan Sharpley of the 2nd Loyals, who were among the last defending troops at the Admiralty oil tanks. 'That's where we surrendered, where we had to lay down our arms. We were given orders by our own people. We didn't want to surrender. It was heart-rending for us younger soldiers. We couldn't believe it.'

But they were completely surrounded. 'There was only 123 of us there, facing three or four thousand Japanese troops.'

'When we heard we were going to be Prisoners of War a few of us got together and said, "Let's bugger off, like". We were immediately collared and told, "Don't try it because you won't get 10 yards". Some lads were so desperate they threw themselves into the Tiger Breweries vats rather than being taken prisoners of war.' What a way to go!

**

Some *had* buggered off, like. Including the chisel-featured Paxton Harding. He and his Dalley's Desperadoes band had found their way down to Clifford Pier, the waterfront abuzz with manic movement of craft and people seeking a way out. He bumped into Lt Col Patrick McKerron, a WW1 veteran and old Malaya hand of two decades' standing. McKerron had been in charge of recruiting and preparing adequate volunteer forces, now – resigned to fate – was well into a bottle of bubbly with his brother-in-law, Charles Vlieland, who happened to be Secretary for Defence, Malaya, and Commander CP Robinson, Deputy Harbour Master in Singapore.

Paxton Harding and co mentioned their desire to get to Sumatra by whatever means, and Robinson recalled there was a derelict boat anchored off the island. The *MV Kembong* was a fisheries research vessel nicknamed 'The Ice Box' for the refrigeration units and tanks that took up all of its lower deck space, and most of its upper deck. At a push, it could sardine 30 aboard. But they needed a captain. Lt Commander Geoffrey Whitaker was soon located, while John Wyatt-Smith – who'd worked in forestry in Kuala Lumpur – commandeered a badly holed motorboat to ferry small groups to the *Kembong*, passengers bailing furiously to keep her afloat.

Finally, all were aboard, the engines coughed into life, and the anchor raised by 8pm. They were underway for Batavia, which they would reach relatively uneventfully.

**

Allied dispatch riders buzzed in every direction around the Alexandra area. 'Then a dispatch rider come up on a motorbike and handed a document to Maj Montresor telling us to lay down our arms, and that Gen Percival had capitulated,' said Daniel Fraser. 'So we weren't very happy about that. Although you didn't say too much to each other, individually you felt lost. Everything had gone, everything you tried to do in this war. It's a terrible feeling when you're told that.'

'A terrifying time,' Francis Docketty of the Engineers remembered it as. 'Then the bloke came around on his motorbike and said we have to pack it in, the war's over. And Maj Glossop took us to the top of the hill and said, "Well, fellas, the war is over". Everybody was cursing. "Why can't we go ahead, we've got the men here?" And after a while we said, "Well, what do we do about it now?"'

'Then these minute little Japs came around the corner. Comical, really. You laugh when you first see 'em ... the British Army is running away from this lot? Hats perched on their heads, their trousers – Bombay Bloomers you could almost call them, longer, with tight puttees around, not done up properly, and they looked a ragged mess.

'Maj Glossop and Lt Doojars asked for a volunteer. Well, Muggins was the volunteer and I went to the bottom with the white flag. The Japs were after me wristwatch and I wouldn't let them have it. I thought they were going to stick a knife in me but they didn't, and the officer shouted at them and they stood back.'

'How did the other ranks feel about the surrender?' asked Aussie Alex Drummond. 'One man expressed the feelings of most when he put his in verse:

Singapore.
A mighty Island Fortress, the guardian of the East.
An up-to-date Gibraltar, a thousand planes at least.
It simply can't be taken, we'll stand a siege of years.
We'll hold this place for ever, and reduce the foe to tears.
Our men are there in thousands, the defences are unique.
But the Japs would not believe it, and took it in a week.

It is not clear how and when Fergus Anckorn was transported from The Alex – having witnessed the bayonet attacks in his ward on the Saturday – to waking up in a makeshift hospital in a school.

'I woke up on the floor of a girls' high school,' he said. 'I've got no idea how I got there or how long I was out for. I said 'Why is it so quiet?''

'We're in the bag?'

'In the bag? What bag?'

'We're prisoners!'

'I was never taken prisoner, I just woke up and was *told* I was a prisoner. I thought someone was supposed to come and grab us and make us prisoners but we were lying on the floor. So I was out for two days. I was still paralyzed, like a tree.'

Curiously, Maj Denis Mulvany does not seem to have been in The Alex on the weekend of the massacres. There is no mention of him by anyone. Perhaps he had worked overnight and taken a rest after a protracted shift and was then unable to reach the hospital again? Or possibly sent off to open or man another makeshift hospital. Wife Ethel of the Red Cross remembered exactly where she was at the point of surrender. 'I was coming through a ward in the Post Office Building [now the Fullerton] where we had extended our hospital. I stopped at the foot of a badly wounded soldier. I seemed to be rooted there until he said, "Is this what we fought for?" The horrors of capitulation were just too stark in their hollow monotone. What was there to hope for?'

After nightfall a young Japanese sergeant entered her makeshift hospital. 'He was neither angry nor drunk, just staring impassively ahead as he strode through. All he wanted was to be seen.' But outside, a different story was brewing.

Ethel had just taken a body out to the temporary morgue on the verandah, when she spotted a mob downstairs. 'Violent, gross, more animal than animals.' Keeping this angry mob at bay was a line of Japanese soldiers, backs to the hospital building, blocking their entry.

**

And what of the Japanese reaction to the surrender? 'The announcement stirred some jealousy: 5th Division must have gotten into Singapore much before us,' said Arai of the 114th. It was a 'mixed set of emotions' that assailed the members of the 18th Division. The surrender had not come from their part of the city. They had wanted so badly to be first. After all they'd reached the furthest point of the campaign target, Keppel Harbour.

But the jealousy was misdirected. 5th Division hadn't made it to the city either. They'd been bogged down on Bukit Timah Road all this while, pressing only as far as the key MacRitchie Reservoir, and low on ammunition. The Imperial Guards had effectively severed the east coast, and taken Kallang Airfield.

The Japanese – presumably the Imperial Guards – came in to St Patrick's on the East Coast Road. Cpl Croft was there, feeling rightly nervous as that makeshift hospital, too, was in no-man's land until the Allies capitulated. Many of their nurses had got away on the *Vyner Brooke*, for all the good it did them, and eight Australians, three Straits Settlements volunteers, and a number of European and Indian civilians – all of whom were by then prisoners – were shot. Cpl Croft was the sole survivor of that incident, so his report could not be corroborated.

**

Tsuji was walking down the hill from his Buona Vista Road HQ and was called back to take an urgent call. 'I subconsciously dropped the receiver and thought: Ah! Seventy days of fighting ... Keppel Barracks and the death struggle ... Jitra's bloody battle. It seemed a dream. Only a few moments ago we were engaged in a life and death struggle. Perhaps I am dreaming, I thought. I pinched the flesh of my thigh hard through my trousers. From several places in the firing line cheering voices rose. The Japanese national anthem *Kimi Ga Yo* spread in a wave over the battlefields.'

Of the surrendered Allies he scathingly described them as looking 'like men who'd finished their contract work on a suitable salary, and were now taking a rest from the battlefield.'

Possibly having moved forward to Gillman Barracks now, Tsuji worked late into that night drafting the transition plans of Singapore from the British to the Japanese, based on the China format of an auxiliary 'police' force drawn from within the divisional ranks to prevent a repeat of Nanking.

As for Mutaguchi, the moment of surrender – as much as he had anticipated it – probably also surprised him when it finally came because his men were in the fight of their lives. 'The battle of Singapore was such a fierce battle for the 18th Division as more than 4000 men were either killed or wounded,' he said. 'The battle finished while we were fighting so hard. Right after we heard of our victory, I gathered all units under my command and ordered them that they shall bow toward the direction of the Emperor's palace in Tokyo to send their faithful mind and gratitude and that they shall pay their unlimited appreciation towards those great spirits who got killed during the campaign.'

**

At 10:30pm on the night of 15 February 1942, Commander Okubo issued Order #70 – the final order of the Malaya campaign – from Gillman Barracks, adjacent The Alex:

1. The enemy has surrendered. We extend condolences to the fallen British Commonwealth soldiers.
2. The regiment will retain its present position throughout the night.
3. Each unit will gather its forces and disarm the enemy according to orders. One detachment will inspect the wounded enemy assembled in Gillman Hospital.
4. I remain on Hill 136.

It is significant that he singled out the 'Gillman Hospital' for inspection. Was there some confusion regarding the identity of the Alexandra Hospital, and the makeshift barracks hospitals across the road that Arai had encountered? Because they both apparently held around or upto 1000 patients. Or did he mean to imply *all* hospitals in the Gillman area?

In all, the hospitals and other makeshift facilities and units in Singapore housed 9000 sick and wounded upon capitulation.

Arai did not try to hold back his tears. 'Slowly the soldiers settled down, each with his own memories, letting one scene pass after the other, with a heavy heart,' he said.

25th Army Commander Yamashita wasted no time in issuing glowing citations that very night. For Mutaguchi's 18th Division the citation read:

'During the final attack on Singapore island, this division, on the right wing of the Army, forced a landing against strong enemy resistance, pressed on to the rear of the Tengah Aerodrome, and in a night attack broke through a strongly fortified position, seizing the high ground to the south of Bukit Timah, thus sealing the fate of the enemy. Then attacking along the southwest coast of the island, in the face of heavy artillery fire, it broke through the enemy line and captured the high land in the vicinity of Keppel Barracks, the key position of Singapore.'

The ambitious and rather egotistical Mutaguchi must have been mightily chuffed to be singled out in such effusive terms:

'Under the leadership of its distinguished and resolute group commander, the division demonstrated the traditional intrepid spirit of the Japanese Army, and in recognition of its great achievements I hereby bestow this citation.'

Tsuji, the architect of much of 25th Army's movements down the peninsula and through Singapore, also heaped praise on the 18th Division: 'There were strong bonds of affection throughout the 18th Division,' he said. 'Not only were the rough Kyushu coal miners physically strong, but they showed an extraordinary sense of loyalty to their comrades and officers, irrespective of rank. Ah! Indeed in Malaya one saw and shared the true spirit of the Army.'

Mutaguchi must have felt himself well vindicated, five years on since launching the Marco Polo Bridge incident: now Japan had Singapore in its loot bag, largely thanks to his *bushido* spirit, and those of his hardy men.

The spirit which had thus far seen Guam, Wake Island, Hong Kong, Manila, Borneo, Malaya, and now Singapore fall. Within three weeks, the Japanese would also occupy the Dutch East Indies, and within a few months, the American garrison on Corregidor, Philippines, would capitulate.

While Burma and possibly India were the ultimate crown jewels in the Japanese battle plans, Singapore gleamed as a highly symbolic and strategic victory.

MOPPING UP THE MESS

'You could smell death. That made me sick.'

16 February 1942. Early Monday morning, medics Anderson and Sutton – who'd been removed the previous evening – were returned to the hospital, but their hands were not untied till nearly noon.

'Early in the morning the victorious Japanese troops entered the hospital and looted it,' said Bull. 'Watches were removed from patients and staff alike and any valuables which appealed to the looters.' They also looted patient lockers. 'There were many unpleasant scenes and one patient was bayonetted through the shoulder but survived.' That victim was Australian Pte Brain.

'Seemingly thousands of Japanese troops came into the hospital and started to loot it,' according to Bryer, who had seen more than his fair share of atrocity by now. 'One of them hit me on the head with a bayonet. I also saw Sgt Wood, RAMC, hit on the head because he told one of the Japanese soldiers that it would be poison to drink a bottle of whisky which he had found. They took stocks of food, cigarettes, medical spirits, and anything else which appeared to them to be of any value. I also saw Japanese officers looting and carrying away things.'

Fruit tins were bayonetted open, the juice drank and the fruit thrown away. Food store rooms were used as latrines.

'Our peace was rudely shattered by hoards of Jap soldiers starting to loot the hospital,' said bed-ridden Capt Pilkington upstairs in the Officers' Ward. 'What they didn't want, they smashed. Whatever they wanted they took at the point of the bayonet, even tipping people out of bed and leaving them to lie on the floor.

'The place was a shambles, with shouting drunken Japs. I myself was not molested, being treated more as a curious animal in the zoo, as I don't suppose they'd ever seen anyone encased in plaster before. One Jap came to me, leant his rifle and bayonet against my wounded arm, seized my tin of tobacco, emptied the tobacco out, pulled a canary out of his pocket, stuffed it into the tin, stuffed a lighted cigarette into my mouth and left grinning.'

Could a more surreal situation be conjured, even with a mind shot full of morphia?

'Fortunately I had dropped my gold ring down my neck into my plaster from where it was eventually retrieved by an orderly with a buttonhook,' he said.

**

The 2nd Loyals had laid down their arms and remained in Marlborough Camp. Fortunately, they were able to draw fresh clothing, food and medical supplies because this camp had been under the Royal Army Ordnance Corps. During that day, a Japanese patrol came to the camp, and their commander passed on congratulations on the splendid fight they showed.

The Royal Engineers 36th Coy held in the same position as the previous night. 'In the cemetery. We came down onto the road, we took the bolts out of the rifles and stacked all our arms so they couldn't be used,' according to Danny Fraser. 'Then we threw down all our arms in the one heap.'

**

'I thought I had to visit my wounded men before anything, and then to visit the wounded British soldiers,' said Mutaguchi. 'All units were led to new locations that were designated by the Army and I told them to have some rest,' he said of his victorious 18th Division units.

Tsuji meantime led the first group of IJA officers on a 'first triumphal entry' into Singapore city, Japanese flags fluttering from his car as it wound its way from the Ford Factory past 'shell craters, burnt-out cars and trucks, and other traces of the recent severe fighting.' He summed up the state of Singapore as 'a whirlpool of chaos.'

He drove on to the former Malaya Headquarters at Fort Canning, where the likes of Percival, Wild, Webster, Croft, and Loveday had all done their bit over the years. One can only imagine the swell of his chest to look southward from there to spy the Dutch

East Indies waiting to be invaded next, and northward to see the Rising Sun fluttering from the top of the shell-scarred Bukit Timah.

But Tsuji declared Fort Canning unsuitable as the operational base for 25th Army HQ, and drove on to the Raffles Institution instead. Here, despite it's shell-pocked exterior and blood-splattered walls, he set up shop. Journalist-turned-spy Miyozaki was released from Changi and drove down to Beach Road. 'Much black smoke gathering all over the island,' he noted, 'and in the streets I did not see even one single person. All the roads were quite dead. Every house was closed up. I did not see even a single cat or dog. It was a ghost town. It was still burning everywhere and everywhere was black smoke. I felt it was something like hell.'

Miyozaki was appointed an advisor to Defence Headquarters, a military rank, although he was not a military person, and taken to meet Col Oishi of the Kempetei at Fort Canning. Meetings over, he headed across to Raffles College. Here Gen Kawamura, Defence Commander, briefed him: 'The soldiers are never aware of international laws and also they are strangers in this place. Keep your eyes open to protect the good citizens and see that no mistakes are done by our soldiers.'

Of particular concern to Miyozaki was a battalion of 1000 soldiers from Matsui's 5th Division who had been seconded as Auxiliary Kempetei to garrison and keep the peace on the island. 'They were very young soldiers ... 21 or 22 ... mostly from Hiroshima district. Not well-educated because they were countryside people, very strong for fighting, very brave, but not much commonsense,' he said. 'They can die well when ordered, they were not afraid to die.' So this was the hardline mentality the Allies had been up against all along.

'I didn't see Col Tsuji, I think he was outside. So I never met him. He was the one who made the plan for the Chinese massacre,' said Miyozaki of the *Sook Ching* ethnic cleansing massacres – accounting for tens of thousands of Chinese – which would shortly follow in Singapore.

**

It was after an hour and a half's wait that the Royal Engineers 36th Coy came face to face with a Japanese for the first time. 'They were unlike descriptions of Japanese,' said Fraser. 'They were not small. There was not one under six-feet tall. That was the Imperial Guards, number one troops. And we sat on the side of the road but they passed by, didn't speak, just went right past us, and couldn't get in quick enough to Singapore. All they were interested in then was loot.'

The Imperial Guards? Again, what were they doing so far over to the west, across the divisional boundary of the 18th? By my estimation, the nearest they should have been was five miles east of the hospital. Several witnesses have claimed they encountered the Guards in and around the hospital. So perhaps they *were* the culprits in both the hospital as well as the Sisters' Quarters atrocities. Certainly it followed the form they'd displayed down the peninsula. And they had the motivation to make a name for themselves as bad and hard men on the battlefield, because they'd started Malaya without the miles on the clock that the 5th and 18th Divisions had.

They also had the aggrievement of being sidelined by Yamashita after his spat with Nishimura on the eve of crossing into Singapore for the final assault. The modus operandi at the Sisters' Quarters certainly echoed their shocking form at Bakri and Parit Sulong in terms of how the prisoners were bound, corralled into small rooms, then machine gunned. But only positive identification by the Royal Engineers of those they machine gunned down coming out of the back of the hospital could nail them for sure as the somewhat surprising prime suspects in this massacre. Unless, of course, the British had simply believed their own bulldust about the Japanese race, and horribly underestimated the size and physicality of their foe, remembering the 18th Div were big, rough Kyushu men.

'The first stare was the best – and that was their attitude,' said Fraser. 'But we had no ammunition, we had taken the bolts out of the rifles to make them useless. I believe that we could have shot quite a lot of them after they had passed us, but we would've been overcome and then the rifles put to their use. So we just sat there.

As Fraser and company sat there devouring a tin of beans, Maj Montresor approached.

'I want six volunteers,' the major said.

'So I stepped out,' said Fraser. 'I was chosen to go back up towards Alexandra Hospital, because we had lost some chaps along the line, to get their IDs, marking the spot.'

The Engineers were allowed to send six men back to the hospital to collect discs off the dead solders, to confirm their serial number and name. 'And they went to the back of The Alex hospital. So we tried to tell them we were picking up discs and then they let us do this. They showed this respect for the dead. They never interfered with us, just walked past us. So we carried on, nearly at the hospital, and we were looking for our lads, or anybody.' They collected discs from Indian, Australian, and British soldiers who didn't make it. 'Then I decided to chat to my mate, Ned,' Fraser said in a particularly slow voice, referring to Pte Edward Marshall, 23. 'He said, "C'mon, there might be somebody living at the hospital".'

They found the hospital in 'a terrible state,' as they entered the ground floor level from the back.

'The corridors had blood splattered all over the place. It was just a shambles. There wasn't a living soul. That made me sick. You could smell death. Well I've never seen ... it's the first time I've seen such blood. Slaughter. In the corridors. We gave a shout, "Anybody there?" but no answer ... I don't think any of us wanted to go any further. We had had enough.'

They looked into two wards: 'The two of us ran out ... I was violently sick. Terrible! Just ... well, no sane soldier would've done what they did.'

What they saw next – possibly outside the dining room ward – could never possibly be unseen ...

Two doctors were pinned up against the wall, big swing double doors, with a bayonet. They were either coming in or trying to get out, and the two of them had bayonets right through them, and right into the door, and the soldier couldn't pull it out. They were just hanging there like that. They just went berserk, it was a slaughterhouse. Others had sword cuts, Japanese swords. One chap wasn't dead – he was sliced with two cuts around the waist and he was still living. So a Japanese soldier came along ... We didn't know the language very well at that time. He looked at him and he just took his revolver and *POP*! He killed him, right in front of us.'

Fraser and colleagues were wearing steel helmets. 'The sun is strong as you know, and he knocked my helmet off. So I didn't bother putting it on again. We held up the discs so they knew what we were doing there, so we picked up the discs.'

They also saw bodies of 'nurses', or at least VADs. Fraser never stipulated how many they saw but possibly one of these was Betty Fernandez, whose husband Jack Mace had been machine gunned. 'Some of them had been raped then bayonetted. Gutted by a knife. Every bed had a patient on it, just blood-soaked, shot and bayonetted. I saw the corridor, I saw two wards, and that was enough for me. They must have been raving mad.'

They reported back to Maj Montresor who in turn got in touch with High Command. 'I believe that a party with some Japanese officers and our officers went back up to that hospital to make sure it was cleaned up,' said Fraser. 'We weren't supposed to be in there, I can tell you, because it had been pretty well cleaned up by the time their officers came. By us going in there, set off the alarm before they had a chance to do a bit of cleaning up. I don't know who cleared it out ...'

The Royal Engineers then moved down to Normanton Camp with specific jobs to do: 'Get the water back on, go down to the docks, unload ships. Every day brought its own story.'

**

Around 10am, some Japanese medical staff turned up at the hospital and looting ceased. 'As Chief of Medical Branch HQ 18th Division it was my duty to go round visiting the divisional field hospitals and inspect the casualties,' Col Suzuki Susumu said. 'I was in no way responsible for the administration of the welfare of Allied hospital patients. These matters were dealt with by HQ 25 Army.' In a conciliatory touch, wounded Aussie Pte Brain's shoulder was stitched up by one of the Japanese.

'The hospital was not being used by Japanese,' Suzuki maintained. 'There was no intention of using it for 18th Division. I went there because, hearing there was a British hospital in our sector, I thought I should like to see it, to find out what conditions were like there, and to see whether the hospital was in need of any assistance.'

And so his party set forth for The Alex, *on foot*, which gives an indication of the proximity of even the HQ personnel let alone the frontliners.

'I and about two or three others including my batman walked to the hospital and met the commanding officer, a lieutenant colonel, a big broad man,' he said, presumably referring to Craven. 'He told me that Japanese soldiers were coming into the hospital looting. I myself saw some Japanese soldiers come in and immediately ordered them away. The OC also told me the hospital had been bombed from the air. He did not tell me that any of his patients or his staff had been killed or brutally treated. I think he felt some restraint about complaining to me.'

'I hardly speak any English at all,' said Suzuki. 'As it was difficult for the OC and myself to make ourselves understood, I sent for an interpreter from 18th Div. When he arrived we started inspecting the hospital. I was struck by the number of patients. I did not notice any signs of their having been ill-treated. I think I went up to the first floor, too. I remember telling the OC that he could have the windows open (they were kept boarded up during the daytime). I left the hospital after about an hour, telling the OC that if he had any further troubles he could contact me.'

'On my return to 18th Div HQ I asked a staff officer that steps be taken to prevent unauthorized Japanese soldiers from entering the hospital. I do not know to what unit or formation the Japanese soldiers who looted the hospital belonged. I believe a sentry was posted there as a result of my request. I never heard from the hospital again and imagine that everything went well after that.'

'A Jap doctor arrived with a party of men and cleared the hospital of looters and to clear up the carnage,' is how Alex Drummond saw it.

Guards were duly called and stationed. Bull assessed the situation: 'After this a high-ranking Japanese officer appeared and went round the hospital with the British commanding officer. He could not have avoided seeing the corpses of the British medical officers which were still lying in the corridors wearing the Red Cross armlets but he made no comment and he made no apology of any kind to the commanding officer.'

Upstairs, Brown and other officers lay, awaiting whatever unimaginable horror might unfold next, when the boot steps of the inspection party drew nearer: 'Some soldiers started going around the wards, one British doctor, Col Craven, OC of the hospital I think, and there were two Japanese officers with him. They were very dishevelled, didn't have caps, and they had rifles taller than they were, great big muskets, and he said: "Gentlemen, this is what has defeated you".'

'They probably only had one uniform,' reckoned Brown, correctly, 'and some of the shorts and trousers torn, and no caps. They looked terrible!'

'Squadron Leader Barnes, who was on a bed in the centre of the ward, called to me and said, Bob, two soldiers have just come in the window at the side of your bed.' Indeed, there were long French windows beside him. 'They were standing behind me and said: "Watch!"'

Brown had on a Rolex, and slid his hand gently under the sheet. 'But they had spotted it and – as they weren't carrying guns – they pulled my hand from under and said to give it to them. I shook my head and pulled my hand away. One of them twisted my hand up behind my back and started pulling off my watch. And the other took his bayonet and pushed it just into my throat, pushing me back into the pillow. Probably just a few seconds but it felt like a few hours, and I lost my Rolex watch.'

Even more soldiers came in. 'They walked around our beds taking watches, pens, any valuables they could see, and we all had packets of cigarettes, and they took all our cigarettes except one packet per man was left. But there was no more bayonetting or shooting that day.'

Pilkington was in a nearby bed: 'Japanese staff officers arrived and started to beat up their own looters. Pandemonium had raged before but it was nothing to what went on for the next half an hour. Eventually a grinning staff officer appeared and told us not to worry. He had settled everything and there would be no more looting. He was as good as his word and in order to enforce his orders stationed a machine gun company round the hospital with orders to shoot anyone attempting to loot. These orders were carried out and several looters were shot. This officer very kindly brought back all my tobacco, which had been removed, in my haversack. Four pounds of it plus quite a lot of someone else's!'

**

A kind of normality rapidly returned. A meal was served, along with half a cup of water. 'Wounds were dressed for the first time in days and I, much to everyone else's annoyance, was given clean sheets!' said Pilkington.

'We were in a state of tension, absolutely,' recalled Brown. 'And some doctors who had survived came around and spoke to us, did what they could. Some were very ill. They still had some medicines left. I don't know if the Japanese took any away, I never heard.'

One of those doctors was Smiley. 'I came under his care,' said Brown. 'His right hand was all bandaged up, presumably where he'd tried to ward off a bayonet, and it was all cut. I didn't ask him – I didn't think he'd want to talk about it.'

The depleted ranks of the RAMC orderlies were noticed. 'Sad and empty gaps in the ranks' as Pilkington called them. 'The two orderlies that had looked after me so kindly were dead, as was Col Lywood, my CO, who was one of the walking wounded killed on Saturday.'

The numbers were made up by the arrival of that double-pistol-pumping medic, de Wardener, who was sent off from the Tan Tock Seng hospital to The Alex by his colonel. En route he had his first contact with a Japanese soldier. 'Here was a *real* Nip. Singapore, being Empire, was filled with roundabouts, a disease we put on every country. Now the Nips are not used to roundabouts, probably never seen them before. This roundabout was quite big, but there was a little low wall and then lawn on the top. And I saw this Nip came out of a road full pelt on a motorcycle and he went straight into the wall, and he flew through the air, did a somersault as he landed, and stood up. And I thought, My God, these blokes are well trained. I was very impressed by that. His motorbike was no good but he was alright.'

From there he went to The Alex. 'When I arrived the hospital was working well. There was a lot of to-ing and fro-ing. It was not panic or anything. No Japanese guards. The Japanese didn't come in, they were kept outside, this was part of the surrender terms. I didn't know anything about the Nips having gone in and murdered a few people at that time.'

**

Then mid-morning, another curious sight presented itself. 'After hiding for two days I walked back to the hospital and was there picked up by a Japanese sentry and taken inside,' said Richard Waller.

That now made it four survivors from the Sisters' Quarters incident.

How nervous he must have been, re-appearing at the scene of his departure 48 hours earlier, especially in the face of Japanese sentries, not knowing what their reaction might be.

'The Japanese had put a regular guard on the hospital and permitted the staff to carry on their duties,' said surgeon Smiley. 'We heard nothing of the people who had been marched off until Captain Waller, RA, arrived into the hospital covered in oil. He played against me as a centre three-quarter for an infantry unit. He ran down the hill and hid in the oil until everything was quiet and then crept into the hospital covered in oil.' While he was tall, with the build of a runner, let's not forget he was in hospital being treated for shrapnel and bullet wounds in the thigh and ankle. So presumably adrenaline has enabled him to run for his life.

Smiley was under the impression that *all* had died except Waller, which is slightly odd given that Bryer and Johnson had already made it back to the hospital the previous evening. But we must remember the size of the place, and the amount of extra-ordinary goings on. It is totally conceivable that such news did not make the full rounds, especially as Bryer had been secreted away in a small room for this very reason of containing the news.

**

'Later that day, I was shifted into one of the wards,' recalled Bryer. 'On the same evening an elderly Japanese officer who wore a beard and appeared to be a general came in and said to us: "I am very sorry for you." Japanese guards were put on the hospital and thereafter we had no trouble. I have no idea who the Japanese troops were who came into the hospital. Neither on the 14th when they took us away, nor on the 16th when they started to loot the hospital, did they appear at all drunk. On the contrary they appeared very cool.'

A Japanese officer who appeared to be a general. Who might *that* be?

'One of the army surgeons told me that there was a British hospital and I decided to visit the place after I visited my men,' said Lt Gen Mutaguchi Renya. Col Noda was in charge of 18th Division medical services. It was decided that he would also visit the hospital with Mutaguchi.

'I didn't know there were hospitals there but some of the military doctors of the division told me so,' said the general. Hard to believe the divisional commander had no prior knowledge of this massive piece of military infrastructure, or that it wasn't marked on a map of the west coast. 'And that was why I visited there after I visited my men who got wounded. I always believe that professional military personnel would fight so hard to complete their mission during combat, but once it is over, then both sides start shaking hands for each other and cry for each other's hardship with deep emotion.'

'When the Japan-Russo war occurred, such moments came up often,' Mutaguchi wrote. So I was determined that I would have to act the same way based on *bushido* when I encounter enemy in the future.' Such an encounter was right before him now.

'The Japanese GOC called at the hospital at 3pm,' Craven said. 'Through an interpreter he expressed regret for the hard time the hospital had had, and assured me that the Japanese were hard fighters but kindly captors and that we had nothing to fear. The Japanese proverb about nursing the wounded bird to the hunter's breast was quoted to us as assurance. Before leaving he visited parts of the hospital and finally I was told that I was to regard his visit as being that of a direct representative of the Japanese Emperor, and that no higher honour could be paid us.'

Mutaguchi was on a charm offensive, as he had been in eerily similar circumstances back in Peiping, China, five long years earlier.

When I visited the hospital, I saw nothing strange or suspicious either,' Mutaguchi recalled. 'I visited the wounded British soldiers at the hospital in order to pay my respect to their services for their country as a representative of the Emperor of Japan. The Emperor of Japan said we must treat local civilians and wounded enemy soldiers with sympathy. As a representative of His Majesty, I told the wounded British soldiers that I would like to pay respect to all of them and acknowledged their entire service for their mother country.'

It was this 'representative of the Emperor of Japan' statement that resounded around the walls, and stuck in the craw of those assembled for his conciliatory words. Apart from sounding arrogant, it drew a straight line for many between the throne and this type of terror.

Especially as this representative did not seem all that aristocratic.

'I would describe this Japanese officer as: age probably 50, height 5'2', broad face, squat, not an aristocratic type,' said Waller. 'He was accompanied by 15 or 16 other Japanese officers. By this time the corpses had been cleared away.'

Lunt saw this figure as significantly taller than Waller did: 'When the divisional commander arrived he apologized for what happened. I do not know his name but he was tall for a Japanese and spoke fluent English. He was about 50 years old, 13-14 stone in weight, five feet seven or eight inches in height.' Perhaps Lunt had mistaken Mutaguchi for Suzuki, for how would they know who was who? Plus the Japanese insignia would be unfamiliar to British soldiers, too.

Actually Mutaguchi was a shade over 53 at that time, and three months older than Craven who was accompanying him. This age advantage, slim as it was, is an important pointer in Japanese culture, given their obeisance to those more senior in years.

'The Japanese divisional commander came to the hospital in white gloves to show he apologized for the crimes committed,' said Pilkington. 'He saluted every dead body where it lay still in its bed and gave permission for them to be buried. He told us that we were now prisoners of the Japanese Emperor and that we should be well looked after, that water should be brought to us and electric light and food. Needless to say, none of these things ever happened!'

Near Pilkington lay Brown: 'A Japanese officer with his interpreter came into the ward and just stood, looked around at us.'

'Who's he?' Brown said to the officer in the next bed.

'That's Yamashita, I'm sure of it.' According to Brown, he was 'very fierce looking, the first officer we had seen. Not very tall, very stocky, with his jackboots. He was striding around the ward, his sword flapping at his side, and it was rather frightening.'

Then the officer spoke through his interpreter. 'I think it was Gen Yamashita. Because the order had been given for the people to be bayonetted in the hospital and rounded up, he said he would do something about it. He also said there would be no more looting as there was a guard put around the hospital, and he said water would be brought immediately to the hospital.'

Lorries rolled into the hospital with 60-gallon drums of water, which continued for some time, according to Brown.

Perhaps the most surprising recollection of Mutaguchi's visit comes from Walter Salmon in the dining room ward. 'Mutaguchi came into our small room. He sent one of his men down to the Ration Stores and he came back with a box of either apricots or pineapples. They were opened with a bayonet (where it has been I shudder to think) and he came round feeding us with a dessert spoon.' Apart from that, they'd enjoy only one cup of water per man per day, and a few dry biscuits.

More Japanese appeared at the hospital, just to have a look around apparently, and then most disappeared.

Suzuki, having visited earlier and credibly established some sort of order, reappeared for a second visit at the same time as his divisional commander. 'I again visited Alexandra Hospital with Lt Gen Mutaguchi, who had a staff officer and other persons, including an interpreter, with him. On this occasion I was following behind the divisional commanders' party and I don't know whether he spoke to the officer commanding the hospital or not, or whether any mention was made of any brutalities committed by the Japanese.'

Indeed there was.

Bryer had managed a quick debrief chat with Craven after the visit was concluded: 'Col Craven told me afterwards that the Japanese had informed him that the prisoners had been shot because they had tried to escape and that they had been buried in a mass grave.'

'The Emperor of Japan told us to make sure we must treat not only local residents but also wounded or surrendered enemy personnel with thoughtful care,' Mutaguchi continued. 'And as a division commander of the Japanese Army I would like to pay my deep respect to all of those British soldiers who were wounded or got sick for their sacrifice and loyal attitude for the nation by fighting so great.'

The recumbent Dick Lee: 'I remember this Japanese coming in, further down the corridor from where I was lying, and he started speaking. I thought it was Yamashita, but it wasn't. It was some other big shot, who came in with an interpreter. I remember some of the words that were said. His interpreter says: "This officer is apologizing for the over excitement of his troops coming into the hospital". My troops are overexcited, that's the sum of what he was saying. And he was saying there'd be no more Japanese coming into the hospital, there'll be a guard put round the hospital. And it'll all get back to normality. And he said, "When you go home your king should salute every one of you. You're all brave men".'

But there was still a lot ahead of them before they'd reach home. If, indeed, they would ever make it home. For they were now officially PoWs of the Japanese.

**

Spare a though for poor John Wyatt still in his small upstairs ward. 'For two or three days I stayed in that ward on my own, with the bodies of the two soldiers who had been bayonetted for company. I was terrified as the Japanese were patrolling up and down the corridor outside, and, once when I hobbled outside the doors of the ward, they pushed me back in at bayonet point. I never got a wink of sleep and I existed on some biscuits and some stale bread that Corporal Sinclair had left behind. Eventually a couple of Japanese soldiers came in and took the bodies of my two dead comrades away, much to my relief as I was worried that they would begin to smell.'

The hospital dead were buried in the evening after the visit of Mutaguchi. 'A start was made later that day to bury those killed within the hospital,' said Bull. 'It was not until the evening of the 16th that any permission was granted by the Japanese to bury the dead. The state of these corpses by this time, remembering that it is a tropical country, can easily be imagined.'

Really, Dr Bull? Perhaps not easily by us ordinary civilians.

'I was very relieved when the wonderful padre, Rev Henry Babb, came in to see me,' said John Wyatt. 'He was most reassuring and made me feel as though I might just pull through this terrible ordeal. He told me that I should not try to escape as he had just seen two brave men shot whilst trying to do so.' A service given that day by Padre Roberts would have offered some consolation to the survivors.

'All was gloom in the ward, but we could now get about the hospital a bit more, which we did,' said Pte Saye, of the main medical ward. 'The corridor was littered with dead, which we buried, with the padre officiating, at the slit trenches by the Alex Road in a mass grave.'

Pte Edward Varney, RAMC, was one of those tasked. 'They were buried in slit trenches in front of the Alexandra Hospital,' he said. Frederick Bales, 23-year-old Norfolks' driver witnessed this operation: 'I saw the bodies of a lot of patients, about a hundred, carried out and buried in slit trenches, Pte Lewis being one of them.' Mounsey witnessed a hospital orderly who was initially rescued but died during the Saturday night. 'His grave and the graves of about 15 other persons who died as a result of Japanese action in and around the hospital can be found in front of the building.' A rather low estimate, but realize he was upstairs in the officers' wards, and his mobility and visibility would have been hampered.

Pte John Willard buried his friend Lloyd Hayes in the hospital grounds, and placed an oak board bearing Hayes's name and number 7538777 on the grave, and at the foot of the grave planted a flamboyant tree. His touching tribute would sadly not survive the war.

Saye recalled how the hospital slowly eased back to normal operation: 'During these crucial days there were no women in the hospital. Some of the more experienced NCOs of the corps were doing medical officers' work, passing catheters, taking out shrapnel, etc. Some Japanese even came for treatment.'

Back to stretcher-bearing 13 hours a day already, Bert Gurd was ferrying patients up the stairs from the theatre. He took a moment to survey the surrounding scene from upstairs: 'The city lay like a stricken animal. Festooned over all were miles of broken cable, while craters in the streets have been hastily and roughly filled in. The only pulsation of life was an occasional staff car of the occupation forces – speeding along the lifeless streets, and of course the ubiquitous ambulances bringing their loads. While several shrouded forms await their journey in the other direction.

He also noticed 'army lorries, gleaming limousines, trade vans, ancient tourers, sports cars, in every possible state, parked – if parked can describe their position' on either side of the Alexandra Road.

The busy work schedule helped take his mind off things: 'My own ordeal of the previous weekend gradually became a memory, although an extreme lassitude was felt, much as though one was the loser in a boxing bout of many rounds.' Up and down the stairs he trundled. 'This gave one little chance to think of that nightmare such a short time ago, one is so weary of work that even the stench of unattended wounds goes unnoticed. One night he passed out, helped to bed by his fellow orderlies, with no recollection of it. Although possibly an 'improvised aneasthetic' – alcohol me thinks – had played a part,

He pointed out that the surgeons worked day and night for a week until a 'forced halt' was called despite the escalating caseload. They had literally worked themselves to a standstill.

Meanwhile the occupation forces had to invent activities to keep themselves busy. Gurd awoke one morning to find a parade of guards outside the hospital chanting their prayers to the morning sun, and going through the motions of PT in full uniform half-heartedly and 'so grotesquely' it almost made him laugh.

Then came a trundling parade of captured Bren carriers and the like. But what did bring a cheer to the face of his patients was the steady tramp of hundreds of feet along the road outside. 'This time the tunes of *Tipperary, The Long Long Trail* and other songs tell us they are not invaders.' PoWs marching their way to various camps.

'Looking back on those three days,' Hugh Pilkington said, 'I am still surprised how cheerful we all kept. There were more jokes and laughs then than at any other period.'

**

A handwritten letter from survivor Lt Walter Salmon, who was in the dining room on the ground floor of the main building, claimed that the Japanese soldiers responsible for the massacre were executed right outside the hospital.

'After the apologies Mutaguchi saluted us and left. Some 10 minutes later there was a heavy burst of rifles fire outside our room. We thought, Oh my God, now he's gone they have started the killing again. However, an RAMC orderly came into the room and said breathlessly that Mutaguchi had rounded up some of the Japs he found in the hospital and had them stood against the hospital wall and had them shot.'

Sapper Daniel Fraser concurred: 'And Gen Yamashita (sic) was assumed to have executed 10 officers for what they'd done and what they'd allowed to be done. They must've been raving mad.'

Brown of the Indian Army was upstairs at the time: 'How true this is, I don't know, but he did have a number of his soldiers shot for the incident. It's hearsay, I heard it several times ... probably a bit of truth in it.'

Lt Thomas Bond of the East Surrey Regiment was more specific: 'It was generally understood and accepted by many of us in the PoW camp at Changi that the day following the incident the Japanese commander had visited the hospital to apologize and ordered the execution of three Japanese – a platoon officer and two others (ranks not known) – for their part in the incident.'

Irwin, in his post-war meta study, concluded that: 'This mass killing was apparently ordered by a very junior Japanese officer who, when more senior officers appeared on the scene some half an hour later, was shot with some others for his part in the outrage.'

Perhaps this was 18th Division officers dealing with their own within the hospital, unaware that 25th Army HQ had other plans, or even that there was the Sisters' Quarters massacre?

**

'I saw from a distance what I imagined was a hospital,' said Capt Umemoto, of the 55th Regiment. 'This was one or more big buildings painted black.' How amazing that he would see them as 'painted black' given that they were white but caked with layers of soot from the raging oil fires across the road. 'There were Red Cross markings. The buildings were over to the east of the railway. I also saw a two-storey white building on the west side of the main road, which I believe was used as Nurses' Quarters. I never went into the hospital myself, nor did I receive any report that any of the men of our regiment had entered it either. Furthermore, I did not hear any rumours to the effect that any Japanese soldiers had ever entered the hospital.'

**

And if anyone had enough energy to notice, amid all the pandemonium, they would have seen a bedraggled figure part-crawling, part-limping back towards the hospital. 'I lay up in a culvert until after dark,' said George Johnson, the young medic who'd bolted from Room 3, 'and then went back to see what the position was. I was picked up by three Japanese sentries, who beat me up very thoroughly with rifle butts and boot heels. I was seen by an

English-speaking Japanese officer, who gave me a pass and left me to make my own way to the hospital.'

That made it five survivors from the Sisters' Quarters outhouse ordeal. That was all. There would be no more known survivors.

**

So what was the full and final extent of the carnage of the Alexandra Hospital Massacres? There were many estimates made by those within the hospital, those associated with the hospital, PoW campmates, war crimes investigators, and so on.

If we take the lowest estimated figures for patients and orderlies in the Sisters' Quarters outhouse and average them for the three rooms we end up with a casualty number of 114. If we take the highest estimates and average them we end up with 190. These, averaged, give us 152 killed at and around the outhouse.

'Altogether 11 out of 21 officers on the staff of the hospital were murdered and about 70 of the 140 other ranks,' according to Bull, talking only of the RAMC men.

'Nearly 300,' Cyril Wild, the lead war crimes investigator put it at. But in an 8 May 1946 memo he talked about 'the killing of 20 medical officers, 60 medical orderlies, and 150 wounded men (figures from memory).'

'350 Deaths' is written on an undated evidence sheet from within the War Crimes Liaison Office.

Smiley weighed in with: 'I am informed and believe that between 250 and 300 personnel, including officers, orderlies and patients were killed.'

Averaging more than a dozen reliable viewpoints, the average is 260. Given a number of 152 in the outhouse, this means about 108 were killed in the hospital massacre itself. The average age of those killed was 28, with the medical staff – with several older long-serving regulars, officers and NCOs among them – being typically older, while their patients skewed younger. One third of those men murdered were married.

The youngest victims were patients Cpl William Doherty of 2nd Argyll and Sutherland Highlanders, and Pte Douglas Gibbs of 2nd

Cambridgeshires, both just 20. Both were murdered at or near the outhouse massacre site.

The youngest murdered in the hospital itself was Pte Ronald Allgood, also 2nd Cambridgeshires, just 20. Pte Arthur Bruce of 198th Field Ambulance was the youngest staff member killed in the hospital, being only 23.

**

A lorry had meantime driven Bert Gurd to 1st Malayan General Hospital in the Fullerton Building. With the angry Japanese mob dispersed from outside these Post Office hospital wards, Ethel Mulvany noted the human-heartedness of two Japanese soldiers. They brought in a wounded English soldier on a stretcher. (This was probably Cpl Victor Burns, 28, of the 5th Suffolks.) 'They placed the stretcher on the floor at my feet, bowed to the soldier they had brought in, then turned and walked out of the ward.'

'It was a sniper,' said Burns. 'One night one of those lads got me. And do you know they came and dressed my wounds and brought me rations and water each night after that.'

'I was just held by the spell of the horror of war as I listened to this dying boy,' recalled Ethel. She stayed on at the temporary hospital for a few weeks before they were packed up and transported to prison camp hospitals, with Bert Gurd being part of the 28-man RAMC party who evacuated them for their foot-sore journey to Changi.

**

The survivors of the Malay Regiment reassembled on 16 February in the Keppel Golf Links area, and on the following morning, eight Malay officers and 600 men were separated from British officers and marched off to join the Indian prisoners-of-war at Farrer Park. A massive majority of Indians had by now defected to or claimed allegiance to the newly formed Indian National Army, meaning they were turncoats, now sided with the Japanese. The nearly 45,000 Indian soldiers captured on Singapore were encouraged to join the Indian National Army. Many would soon be camp guards of their former British masters at Changi. Those who didn't willfully join were 'strictly punished'. Blindfolded and bayonetted into trenches.

Many Indians had defected but would the Malays follow suit?

'My husband Ibrahim Sidek and his friends were told by the Japanese to take off their Malay regiment uniforms and accept release,' said Sharifar Khadijah binte Hamid. 'They refused. They didn't even want to remove their badges of rank. A week later the Japanese executed them.' His body was never found, and her only keepsake from her devoted husband was his army-issued tin mug.

**

On Tuesday 17 February, the clocks changed to Tokyo time and 25th Army HQ ordered Nishimura and his Imperial Guards to be ready to ship on to Sumatra within three weeks. Kempetai guards – made up with individuals seconded from the 5th, 18th and Imperial Guards divisions – already stood watch on corner streets of the city, where the shophouses were festooned with little fluttering Rising Sun flags.

**

'For several days we were kept in the hospital,' said Capt Smiley. 'All efforts by Col Craven to get the Japs to tell what had happened to those people were of no avail, though of course we could not say that we knew. During the intervening days, the Jap officer in charge of the hospital treated us with great courtesy, though little food, and we were not allowed to leave the hospital.'

'We were pretty much left on our own,' remembered Bull, 'although on occasions the odd ordinary Jap soldier would appear and walk around in a rather aimless fashion. I can remember being in a room where there was a suitcase belonging to one of the sisters who'd been evacuated. A Jap came in, slit the case with his bayonet and started going through her clothes and found a powderbox. He opened the box and all the powder came out, and he obviously thought it contained explosive or something, as he backed away in fright!'

No more medical supplies came in, and the food stocks were depleted. So the Japanese started sending in rice. 'We had rice two to three times a day,' said Capt Brown. 'Some tinned meat now and again, from before they came in. We seemed to have enough because no one had an appetite anyway.'

'An Army chaplain attached to Alexandra Hospital was strolling in the rear of the hospital when he saw a long trench filled in with fresh earth,' said Stringer. 'This had not been there a few days before. He was seen by a Japanese officer and was driven back to the hospital by threats.' So if the previous victims had been buried in the slit trenches at the *front* of the hospital, what then was this trench at the rear, and what did it conceal?

As the Deputy Director of Medical Sevices, Malayan Command, the Japanese ordered Stringer to 'break up all military hospitals' and transfer the patients to PoW camps. 'For several weeks after surrender conditions were very chaotic and my task of administering the medical services was made very difficult if not impossible. In my capacity as senior medical officer in charge of the British prisoners of war it was my duty to take statements from as many of the eyewitnesses of the Alexandra Hospital massacre incident as I could. I took these statements from actual eyewitnesses as soon after the event as was possible in the circumstances.'

Most people in the hospital – including the escapees from the outhouse themselves – were only aware of one survivor, or perhaps two at most. No one realized five had made it. There again it wouldn't be something you'd want to trumpet too loudly for fear of incriminating yourself to the Japanese. A possible sixth existed: Gunner George Dean, 28, of 3/6 Heavy Ack Ack regiment, RA. He was seen to be in Room 3 but yet he is not listed on the Commonwealth War Graves Commission roll (and was later working on the Thai-Burma Railway). So perhaps he understandably chose never to talk about it nor come forward as a survivor and make a deposition.

Stringer said a 'L/Cpl Simpson, RAMC, got away and got back through our lines,' too. This was Daniel Simpson, who was never mentioned by others in the outhouse (although we must concede the lists are very incomplete) nor did he step forward to make a deposition later.

**

And so the job of discharging and transporting the patients began, triaging and slowly sending them off to various points in Changi, primarily Roberts Barracks. You can imagine there might've been some keenness to get out of The Alex post-haste.

'We were confined to one wing of the hospital and remained there till we were sent to Changi some days later,' said the dispenser, Torbit.

But the deaths hadn't stopped, as patients continued to succumb to their wounds. Among those to die on 18 February was Sgt Ian Chalmers, a Scottish mining engineer of the FMSVF. At least his 24-year-old bride had got away safely to Sydney.

'The Japs ordered the evacuation of the hospital to Changi Barracks,' said Pilkington. 'The exodus started with all the fit people that had by now congregated under the protection of the hospital. Over the next two days everyone who could walk was sent off to trudge the 16 miles to Changi. Some of them had only just had arms amputated but the Japs were adamant: No transport for anyone who could walk. Many of these were two or three days on the journey,' says Pilkington.

'When Col Craven protested and said, "These men will die if they have to walk", the Jap said, "Our soldiers are dying for their country, your soldiers can do likewise",' according to Salmon. 'A very painful ride over the very rough bomb-pitted roads,' he remembered it as.

'The Japanese wanted the Alexandra for their own injured,' said Capt Bob Brown. 'I was moved to Robert Barracks in Changi. It had been made into a convalescent hospital to take the strain off the Alexandra. But they kept the very sick in Alexandra. Our doctors and (male) nurses who were left took charge, and they had to work very hard because there weren't many doctors left, and there weren't many male nurses.'

Smiley stayed behind at the hospital to help bury the dead and clear up the mayhem, eventually joining the other PoWs in Changi. He was awarded the Military Cross and mentioned in dispatches twice for his acts of bravery in the hospital.

**

Capt Bill Frankland, who just five days earlier had assigned the finger of fate by designating nurses to certain ships, saw his first Japanese on this day. 'I was in Victoria Theatre with about 150 patients, and I went past the Cricket Club to the Padang and I saw a Japanese – because you still didn't see Japanese, it was amazing – early in the morning and in the centre, right on the cricket pitch, he was defacating. You couldn't get a more public place, but as far as I was concerned, that was a cricket pitch he was doing it on, and I was a cricketer. That annoyed me!'

**

Meanwhile Cyril Wild in Fort Canning continued his invaluable work as interpreter and liaison officer between the Japanese and British, but then once the Japanese were more organized and firmly in control he was sent off to a PoW camp (initially River Valley).

Sapper Danny Fraser 'celebrated' his 26th birthday, his first of several as a PoW, far from the close-knit Fraser clan of Brandon Street, Motherwell.

**

By 19 February conditions inside The Alex had relatively improved, and Pilkington was operated on again. 'By now we were getting reasonable meals of biscuits and tinned food with two pints of strong sweet tea and two pints of water. I was operated on for the last time.' In his ¾" thick plaster cast made by six doctors, he was taken back to the top floor, where he was nursed by other officers who were now able to walk about. He himself would be staying put here quite a while longer.

Just three weeks after the massacre 'the lucky corporal' Collins, who Stringer had seen bayonetted through the back and out the chest, 'was walking about fit and well.'

'During this period quite a few patients died because they couldn't get proper attention,' said Maj Bull, 'and some of them had been badly wounded. We felt dreadfully depressed as we thought that the Japs were winning everywhere and that they were unbeatable. Of course they were terribly cock-a-hoop.'

That very day, Japanese bombers and Zero fighters targeted Darwin, in northern Australia, scuttling 11 ships, damaging the business district and destroying 30 planes at the RAAF air base. 243 Australians were killed. This incident – dubbed 'Australia's Pearl Harbor' – signalled their intent on Australia and widening the war front beyond just their purported 'Asian Co-prosperity Sphere'.

SCATTERED IN ALL DIRECTIONS

'We left the hospital at Singapore cleaned up.'

20 February 1942. One of the Royal Artillery, the 'Broomstick Soldier' Francis Docketty, upon capture, had been sent to nearby River Valley Camp on the Singapore River. 'Just *atap* huts, long low huts, 40-feet in length about 16-feet wide. It was a degrading place.' One of his fellow PoWs there was Cyril Wild.

PoWs from there were sent on a working party in the neighbourhood. 'They sent us to Alexandra hospital, clearing up there,' Docketty said. 'They decided we'd be labourers, clearing up all the blood and stuff. A mess there. They slaughtered everybody there. We were dragging them out of cupboards. And rooms. They murdered patients, nurses, doctors, soldiers. They were all buried in the grounds of Queen Alexandra (sic) Hospital, and we had to clean the place up.'

Luckily he had a sense of humour, or chose to exercise it in these situations, to keep himself going. One such example happened at the River Valley Camp. 'This Aussie had eggs smuggled in his *fundoshi* (nappy-like garment) and came to attention really slowly,' laughed Docketty. 'The Jap officer gave him a slap and told him to do it again, to come to attention smartly. So now he's got yolk running down his leg, and when the Jap saw this he reckoned he had dysentery. The Jap said, "You are sick", so he got off his working party. Those sort of things stick in your head.'

The Engineer, Daniel Fraser, had already seen the horrific sights of the hospital and his experiences immediately post-capitulation did not improve. 'Singapore was a right shambles, I felt sorry just to look at it. During the time we were travelling from Normanton to the docks there were some ghastly sights, horrible for any human to have committed. There was one chap stone dead, bullet right through the head, and he was a dispatch rider, he'd been shot right off the motorbike.'

And there were some atrocities on the locals that foreshadowed the Japanese behaviours as the new masters of this land. 'Civilians, you didn't see very much of them in the streets, but you had a sight of what the Japanese were capable of. Upto 12 bodies a day pulled put of storm drains, teenage girls, elderly. The girls had been mishandled by the Japanese. There was a fence and they had tied these girls, mainly Eurasian girls, and they had tied them spread-eagled to this fence. They stayed there for over a fortnight and that was for the pleasure of the Japanese troops.'

And still, the wounded from the Alexandra and other outstations were arriving at Roberts Barracks. Among them, Fergus Anckorn: 'The Japs decided I was fit enough to be taken to Changi, threw me like a sack of potatoes in the back of the lorry, with both my forearm bones sticking out,' he said. 'Hellish journey, and then threw me out at Roberts Barracks. I was on all threes. And I thought I must find someone to take care of me. While I was crawling I came across our divisional commander, Maj Beckworth-Smith – the man who'd so heartily approved of my magic show at the divisional concert party that he called me 'his conjuror' and often playfully saluted me in jest before I saluted him. Now here he was sitting by himself, very dishevelled and disconsolate. When I reached him I said, "Hello, sir". But he didn't even look at me. He seemed lonely ... and lost.'

Anckorn was admitted to the gangrene ward. 'The smell was disgusting, like a cheese factory. It looked like I might lose my whole arm – the back of my hand was completely open with the all the tendons exposed. So they put eight maggots in there and plastered over it.'

Anckorn was lucky to get a lorry. Slater, the armoured car Volunteer who'd been hospitalized for shrapnel in the thigh, had to march the 16 miles to Changi. 'I just staggered into Changi about 5pm,' he said. 'I had lost all my kit, the only thing being possessed being the shirt, shorts and boots I stood up in, and had to find myself a place on the concrete floor for the night.'

**

Smiley was still toiling away selflessly and diligently at The Alex. 'We received no violent treatment causing any serious injuries, but from time to time we were prodded with the butts of rifles and slapped on the face by the Japanese who appropriated our personal belongings, including watches, cigarette cases, etc.'

By now, all but the worst cases had evacuated the hospital, and on 27 February a final order came through from the Japanese. 'The medical staff, orderlies, and patients were ordered to leave the hospital and to go to Changi. We removed some of the patients by ambulance and some had to walk.' Others, like Pte Britton with his shot-up knees, seemed luckless, being moved to Changi by wheelbarrow, cart or any other conveyance with wheels that could be found and utilized.

Pilkington was one of the last to leave the hospital. 'I was evacuated by ambulance, and with me I took my rubber mattress, pillows, sheets, books, etc.' His prized luxury Dunlopillo mattress would remain with him throughout his time in Changi.

Bull described this period in The Alex as quiet. 'By this time we had water, but I don't think there was any electricity on as I remember there was no possibility of doing any X-ray work.'
Perhaps 'quiet' was a good thing in the vein of 'no news is good news'.

'When we moved to Roberts, no news from the Alexandra came filtering down to us,' noted Brown. Lex Arthurson saw it differently: 'From Glyn White, we learnt about the incident at Alexandra Hospital,' he said.

Although the general conditions in Roberts weren't very good, there were plenty of doctors and orderlies from the recently arrived British 18th Division to help out. The tireless Capt Bill Frankland headed up the dysentery wing. In a reunion moment with his 'great friend' Capt Smiley, the latter recounted the harrowing saga of the operating theatre attack and that lucky deflection of the potentially fatal bayonet blow by the cigarette case. 'He said, "You see, if wasn't a smoker I wouldn't be alive!' Franklin chortled as he told me.

The Japanese somewhat surprisingly allowed RAMC staff to take whatever medical supplies and equipment they needed from

The Alex. For those medics, patients and soldiers transferred to barracks at Changi, the productivity of the RAMC continued apace. 'The hospital was re-established immediately in part of the RE Barracks at Changi and surgery continued on a round-the-clock basis until the vast backlog was cleared,' said Torbit.

Craven was at this point promoted to full colonel status (backdated to 30 April 1941) in order that he could pull rank where necessary over his Australian counterparts, Col Pigdon, CO of the Australian 13th AGH, and Col Glyn White.

Col Glyn White of the Royal Australian Army Medical Corps took over command of the staff and 2500 patients at the combined Allied PoW hospital there. He arm-wrestled with his counterpart Col Sekiguchi who had provided just five ambulances to move 9000 patients within seven days. White ended up with three weeks to move them, with twenty three-ton trucks, fifty-five ambulances, and one car. Plus they managed to surreptitiously sneak 4500 hospital beds and 7000 mattresses out.

Pte Harry Saye was on one of the last ambulances out of The Alex, no doubt pleased to forget the scene of so many ghastly experiences for he and his colleagues. 'We left the hospital cleaned up – all beds with blankets, pillows, bedding, etc, equipped. So ended the attack on Singapore and BMH.'

**

On 2 March medical staff from various institutions were assembled. Ethel Mulvany had her sticker-laden trunk packed with books, her precious bible, and a lipstick Denis (who would turn 38 in just three days' time) had found in the glovebox of their car before they abandoned it. Trucks were lined up, passengers assigned. Before boarding she slipped him a quick note:

'My Own Dear Boy, this is a dark cloudy day but behind the clouds this morning there was the brightest star. My darling, I am so proud of you and your work.' He tucked the note away, and would keep it for the rest of his life. Then the trucks started up and rumbled down the road on that humid Monday afternoon. 'His truck left about the same time as my truck. We were sitting in the back and he went on one angle of the road, and we went on another. He never looked back.' Ethel ended up in E Block at Changi Gaol (where Loveday had been held), opposite the generously named 'Rose Garden'. Denis was sent off to a PoW camp on Singapore (possibly Kranji) where he worked relentlessly as a doctor until being assigned to Changi in September 1943.

**

April 1942. The 'Changi Telegraph' grapevine was working overtime from Day One of their captivity, as all were eager to learn the fate of their former colleagues, friends, officers, men, family members.
Who'd made it? Who'd not? Did you hear about poor old so-and-so?

There were probably some uncomfortable meetings. Loveday, the cashiered Engineer who ran the construction Corruption Ring, might have bumped into Inspector Bunnens, the man who'd come and searched his house one night, because they found themselves caught up there together. Francis Vaux, the chess-playing counsel for the prosecution in his case, also ended up in Changi. Awkward!

'About a week or so in to our time at Changi rumours started to circulate of a Japanese massacre at Alexandra Hospital,' said Australian Dr Rowley Richards. 'We had long suspected what our enemy was capable of, so acts of violence were not surprising but to hear of such brutality so close to our new home, and to women and the sick, made us realize that any threats made by our keepers were likely to be fair dinkum. This news made all of us angry – as well as frustrated: it further highlighted how helpless we now were to retaliate. We thought we had experienced hell during the last week of the Malayan campaign, but we were still to realize that there were many depths of hell under the control of the Japanese, and each would be worse than the last.'

'We in Changi heard the number [in the massacre] to have been 'more than fifty',' said Lt Charles Jackman of Royal Signals.

Col Craven ended up as SMO in Changi, working alongside Lt Col Edward Holmes who was camp commander. Craven's health would deteriorate significantly during captivity. 'During May 1942, at the request of British Malaya Command, I compiled a full and detailed report of the incidents surrounding the overrunning of the Alexandra Military Hospital by the Japanese,' said Craven. 'I handed this report to Brig Stringer. I retained a copy of this report.'

And so, bit by bit, sense was being made of that senseless thing.

**

One of the PoWs in Changi was Cpl Dennis Redman, RASC, who was attached to the Fort Canning HQ. He was tasked with secreting documents regarding the massacre, which included a report entitled *The Affair at the Alexandria (sic) Hospital.* 'He told us a story of him carrying documents, throughout his imprisonment, in his water bottle,' his daughter Vickie Quinn would tell me. 'These were given to him by a chaplain, I believe, for safekeeping.' Post-war, he received a letter of thanks from the Imperial War Museum singling out 'the manner in which you brought the report home.' It seems these were buried for security at various points of his internment. The padre might have been Padre Noel Duckworth, who helped Wild secrete documents in his two attaché cases (the other used for clerical vestments).

George Peet, who had been the *Straits Times* editor, was a civilian interned in Changi: 'I recall a working party from our camp being sent to the Alexandra Hospital, possibly in late 1942, and reporting on their return having seen slit trenches filled with human bones.'

Indeed all were officially listed simply as 'missing', others as 'prisoner of war' but detailed information was scanty and hard to come by.

And news filtered in from further afield, too, such as Australia, India, Dutch East Indies.

'We heard that fifty of our sisters who had landed from a bombed boat off Sumatra had been machine gunned because they refused to accede to the Japs' demands,' said Capt Pilkington. 'But there was also our pride when we heard that two of our sisters had continued helping the wounded when their boat was sinking in shallow water and the Jap planes machine gunned the survivors mercilessly. And of their heroic journey through the jungle with the survivors. The matron, Miss Jones, was killed, some we know got safely through, others were bombed at sea and drowned or were machine gunned on the beaches. May God preserve them, they were a grand crowd.'

Pte Stephen McLean, who had been RAMC in Singapore until around February 1941, ended up in India. It was here in March 1942 that he chanced upon two RAMC corporals who'd escaped Singapore. 'They were Cpl Green and Cpl Chandler. They told me that only eight other orderlies got away.'

The injured Indian Army Capt Brown was now up and about: 'Once I could walk okay with bandages on my knee, I asked if I could join my unit. I found them down in Changi Village.'

44th Infantry Brigade HQ was given the police station and shop areas, according to Brown. 'We stayed for two to three months, the Japanese didn't bother us. We were eventually moved up to Y Block and Z Block, the former RAF quarters on the hill. Not too bad at all!' All the Indian rank and file troops were notably absent. A large percentage of them were now INA, and en route to Burma to fight alongside the Japanese to take India.

And not all Allies were happy to be stuck on Singapore island either. Escape had been ruled out by most now because the Japanese clearly owned the surrounding land and sea.

But this didn't stop the opportunistic Engineer Daniel Fraser from contemplating it when he was based at Changi and tasked with loading and unloading the docks. 'We stayed behind one night, during change round at the docks, three of us tried to escape. We'd seen a boat lying tied up at the Keppel harbor and we said if that boat is still there we would go for it. We managed to get onto the boat, it had a motor but no petrol. We thought of rowing out to an island, rigged a mast ... but never got out of sight of land. Crossed straits and went to find food and water, walked straight into a Japanese camp. So we were brought straight back. We got a slap or two and what have you.'

Had they reached Sumatra, ironically he might've been up against the Imperial Guards again – if indeed that was who they'd gunned down coming out of the back of the hospital – because they were now firmly in control of that part of the Dutch East Indies.

**

Meanwhile back home in Canada, there was great community concern for Ethel Mulvany's welfare, with the newspaper talking about 'anxiety as to the fate of the former Manitoulin girl' as she and her husband were attached to a military hospital in Singapore. 'We have had no word from them,' said her brother Harvey Rogers. All were simply and unhelpfully listed as 'missing' or 'prisoner of war' for several months.

**

In Changi, almost no time was wasted in rebonding with colleagues from their units. The 'One Nine Eight' Club was set up for members of the decimated 198th Field Ambulance now tasked with running an infectious diseases hospital out of the Changi Post Office. A journal was soon published, called the *Oner* (short for Singapore Changi PoW No.1 Camp journal) and in it a clear desire to bond around their dreadful Singapore experiences:

'Although we shall all wish to forget the Army, the war, and prison camps as soon as possible, we shall not, I am sure, wish to forget the friends we have made whilst in the 198th.

'With this end in view, the idea of a Club has been mooted, the chief objects of which will be an annual re-union – probably in the form of a stag party – and the publication of a quarterly newssheet. Correspondence between members will also be encouraged, and, it is hoped these measures will help to strengthen the links of friendship forged in such trying times.

The southern section of Britain would be initially co-ordinated by Pte Alfred Emary, 38, holed up in Hut 3, and the northern section by Pte Luther Taylor, 25, holed up in V Block. Their optimism was to be admired, for there would be many greater difficulties ahead in the short term than that.

One article in the hand-made publication (only one copy was possible for there was no means of reproduction) was entitled 'The Battle You Have Won:'

'Yes, won! Things, I know, went badly for you from the start. Harrassed without respite by a relentless enemy, in a country strange to you, retreating, bombed, cornered, you carried on. Failures there were, but cannot the lives saved by the RAMC be counted a victory, a victory over disease and death?' And so it went, exorting the men to face any future troubles – 'and there may be plenty still to come' – face them with the 'cheerfulness and determination with which you faced those others.' This inspiring author was sadly uncredited.

Bert Gurd was quoted, dreaming of returning to a simple life on the farm and raising a family with Rosa, once this was all over. He was assigned to the Southern Area Hospital where the new foe was 'the demon dysentery'. In his spare time he enjoyed dips in the sea nearby, and popped across to see his 198th pals 'to the utter surprise of one or two who had given me up for dead or at least missing. How good it is to hear their dialects again, the broad Yorkshire brogue, and the quaint sing-song of your Norfolk native, and how glad we are to see one another.'

His time at Southern Area was among his most pleasant memories as a PoW because of the reduced workload. 'I am rested in mind and body,' he said.

**

All the various hospitals on the island were now run by different divisions of the Japanese. 'Kendang Kerbau by the Navy, Woodbridge by the Military,' according to Matthew Jubang who worked at the latter for a time.

The Japanese were formally moving into The Alex: Medical Corps 6091 to be precise, using the facility as a military hospital. In a weird twist, Irshad Ali Khan, the civilian who had survived the shooting and witnessed such horrors among his co-workers, ended up working for the Japanese at Woodbridge.

'Then I was asked to stop work. So my friend said, "Let's go work at the military hospital in Alexandra".'

He and a few others volunteered to work in the lab at The Alex. 'No other job, if not. My wife and child came back at this time, everything was peaceful. I stayed in the hospital quarters. But we only worked half-day, no shift. Start at 9am, finish at 3pm. Follow Tokyo time,' he laughed. 'Work very easy also. We sometimes come late. The Japanese say, "Why you come late?" I say my bicycle punctured and what not, they excuse us, so we take our sweet time to go to work. The Japanese were very kind to us because they want our service. Lucky I only had two kids during the war, otherwise difficult to look after them. Lucky I was working for the Japanese – they give rations so we have enough to eat.'

Also working for the Japanese at The Alex was Capt Man Singh of the Indian Army Medical Corps. But a few months later he was interned for the rest of the war for declining to join the INA.

**

Some of those assigned to stay and garrison Singapore might have been beneficent, especially among the medical corps. But what became of the victorious and blood-thirsty Japanese front-line troops?

'After they had occupied Singapore, the Japanese Army must go on to Sumatra and Burma, leaving only one brigade here,' said Advisor to Defence HQ, Miyozaki. On 19 February, a few short days after claiming Singapore's scalp, Southern Army Supreme Command ordered the 25th Army to invade northern and central Sumatra, and the Andaman and Nicobar archipelagos.

Most of the IJA 5th Division was sent north to garrison Malaya and also to quell some Chinese Communist uprisings. The division was subsequently posted to actions on Rabaul and Guadalcanal, before island-hopping on the Dutch East Indies group, where they would surrender in 1945. (Their HQ building, in the grounds of Hiroshima Castle itself, would be obliterated by the atom bomb.)

As for the Imperial Guards (Konoye) Division under Lt Gen Nishimura, they had received their next orders, too. But they were not headed northwest, they were heading south from Singapore.

Tanaka's 14th Independent Mortar Battalion shipped to the Philippines and participated in the mighty artillery attacks on Bataan and Corregidor which overwhelmed the Americans in April and May 1942.

**

29 February 1942 Mutaguchi's 18th Division was withdrawn to Kluang, in central Johor, Malaya, to prepare to embark for Burma.

'After about 10 days on Singapore Island after the surrender, I returned with the regiment to Johor Bahru to prepare for forthcoming operations in Burma,' said Ito Kojiro, whose 2/55th battalion had put in solid but frustrated work around The Alex.

And by 25 February all of HQ 18th Div had returned to Kluang, with medical staff such as Suzuki Susumu among them. There was a little time to lick wounds, write letters home, and generally take stock of their unimaginably fast victory. Why, it'd only been about four weeks since they'd been through here fighting their way south to Singapore, and now that trophy was in their cabinet.
Some of their wounded comrades were ready to re-enter the fray, too. The 33-year-old Noguchi of 2/55th Machine Gun Company had been injured, like Mutaguchi, soon after landing Singapore, then hospitalized in Johor ever since. 'There was not much time to discuss anything about the events which took place during which time I was absent,' he said. 'I have heard that our unit were subjected to heavy British artillery fire, suffered heavy losses. I have never heard of Alexandra Hospital or any British hospital on Singapore island,' shedding light on the tone of such reunions, and the content of what the regiment had been through. They'd finally won, but with heavy losses which seem to have taken the sweetness out of their victory.

**

Their focus was now firmly on Burma. 'At the end of March I landed in Rangoon,' said Ito of 2/55th. The rest of his regiment had landed about a week earlier, and Ito and battalion were ordered to proceed independently to Kengtung under direct command of HQ 15th Army. 'On the way to Kengtung we were ordered to halt and withdraw towards Taungyi. I remained on garrison duties in Southern Shan States till the end of July.

**

Col Tsuji was at once hero and villain. He had grandstanded his strategic role in the victory a little too much, and the generals sought to drag him down a notch or two. He was summoned back to Imperial Headquarters in Tokyo. But not before he had painstakingly masterminded the cold-blooded *Sook Ching* massacres around Singapore. As soon as he arrived back, he started agitating for a role in the Philippines, where Homma's troops were bogged down.

He accused Homma of being too soft on the enemy, and even went to the stage of issuing fake orders under Homma's name ordering assassinations on high profile Filipino politicians. He saw a similar solution there – simply to kill all the captured PoWs, both Americans and Filipinos – the former for being colonialists, the latter for being accomplices. 'They surrender after sacrificing all the lives they can, except their own,' wrote the *Japan Times and Advertiser* on 28 April. 'To show them mercy is to prolong the war ... the wrongdoers must be wiped out.'

And so it happened that between 7000 and 10,000 died on Death Marches and from other privations. But the Japanese got their victory, Tsuji was hailed back in Tokyo again as the 'god of strategy', and Homma was forced into retirement as ineffectual, only to be hung for War Crimes in 1946.

Tsuji, ever the self-promoting political animal, also lobbied against Yamashita, the 'Tiger of Malaya', for being too concerned with conserving Japanese troops' lives in the Philippines, such that Yamashita was soon banished to training command in Manchuria, without even the opportunity to stop over and state his case in Tokyo. That he did not serve again until after Tojo fell in 1944 says much about the behind-the-scenes affiliations of Tsuji and his superior sponsors.

**

With Singapore now secure, Capt Iwasaki's Navy bombing unit now moved south and operated from the captured island.

**

On 9 March 1942 the Dutch Army unconditionally surrendered. Three days later the main body of the Guards landed at Labuhanruku. There was scarcely any resistance, so the important targets of Medan and Padang came under their control within five days.

Alice Loveday's brother, John, surrendered with the Royal Air Force in Java and taken PoW. Luckily his wife and daughter had evacuated from Singapore in time to return to North Shields. She would not know his fate until one year later. Norman Bryer would have been part of this Air Force cohort had he not been hospitalized earlier.

Pte Edwin Buffton, ex-32 Coy RAMC, had found his way to Sumatra and was initially reported as missing: 'After leaving Singapore, I was in Sumatra for approximately three weeks, and during that period I saw none of the personnel of 32 Company other than those who left at the same time as I did.'

By this time, Edith Stevenson had been travelling by night for nearly one month, hitchhiking her way across Sumatra, tending to the sick and wounded on her way. She'd reached the capital, Padang, and a week later, the Army sent her on her way to Bombay, luckily just ahead of the arrival of the invasion force.

And so, the perfect storm that had bought all participants in the massacres face-to-face, just as quickly dissipated and now – those lucky enough to escape with life and limb intact – scattered in all directions to face new challenges.

ROLLING ON TO RANGOON

'The most traumatic day of my whole life.'

23 February 1942. The Japanese juggernaut rolled on. Just eight days after the fall of Singapore, the IJA 15th Army invaded Burma, using overland routes from Indo-China through Thailand. Burma was another piece of prime colonial British real estate, having been a province of British India and then an independently administered colony.

A succession of Anglo-Burmese wars had resulted in British rule since 1824, giving the British access to the oil and teak wood that Burma was so rich in. Exactly the sort of thing Japan might need, of course, but another reason to despise the plundering colonialists and reclaim it as part of their 'Asia for Asians' posturing.

The now-legendary figure of Lt Gen Joseph 'Joe' Stillwell entered the fray, taking command of the China theatre as adviser to Chiang Kai Shek and – as commander of the India-Burma theatre – reporting to Admiral Louis Mountbatten. Fluent in Chinese, Stillwell would only add more quirky colour to the cast of leaders in Southeast Asia. Like Tsuji, he was rebellious and cared not much for correct process and ceremony when more expeditious military moves got the job done better. His acerbic manner earned him the nickname 'Vinegar Joe' but, unperturbed, he proudly pinned the cartoon which a subordinate had drawn of him – rising genie-like from a vinegar bottle – to his wall. On his desk, the New Yorker (whose 59th birthday would be in a few days' time) had a mock-Latin motto '*Illegitimi non carborundrum*' which roughly translated to: 'Don't let the bastards grind you down.'

By now Capt Roy Hudson of the Indian Army had shipped down with his Sappers and Miners. 'We got hold of a ship, from Calcutta to Rangoon, spent a night in the jail at Rangoon, they'd emptied out the jail because there was nowhere else for us to stay and then we went up north to a very, very nice part of Burma.' Their destination was about 600km due north: Taunggyi, capital of the

Shan States. 'I had a wind-up gramophone and played dance music. Eventually we arrived at a station called Kyaikto where we got off.'

The Japanese were in hot pursuit. Commanding the Allies' overall retreat was Brig Sir John Smyth, VC, who faced Hobson's Choice when the 1st Burma Division and 17th Indian Division reached the strategically significant Sittang Bridge: Destroy the bridge, stranding more than half of his own troops on the wrong side, or let the bridge stand and present the Japanese a clear march westward into the capital, Rangoon.

Roy fixed me with a long stare and sighed: 'Then the most traumatic day probably of my whole life was the following day.'

The situation was precariously poised. Of three brigades in the 17th Indian Division, only one had already crossed. '2nd Brigade had been cut during the night by the Japanese so they didn't get to the bridge. So we had a party defending the bridgehead hoping that the balance of the division, two brigades of men, a good number of men, eight battalions, could get through and get over the bridge before we blew it up.' Roy was assigned the detonator.

Field Marshal Slim would describe the next four days of action as 'the decisive battle of the first Burma campaign.' Immediately, though, Rangoon fell to the IJA 33rd Division on 4 March, and therefore the Japanese had effectively taken Burma.

**

Was it an omen that on 1 April 1942 – April Fool's Day – HQ IJA 18th Division embarked for Burma? Takeda, Noguchi, Arai, and the units who'd been so active around The Alex, all boarded, and started arriving in Rangoon by sea around 6 April. They advanced through Mandalay to Taunggyi, where Hudson and his men had previously camped out in the Shan States, where they spent around six months. Dr Suzuki was with them, and then he moved with HQ 18th Division to Maymyo. 18th Div then linked up with 55th Division to press the Chinese 5th Army north towards Mandalay. On a roll, they advanced all the way to Irawaddy when the Ava Bridge was blown in front of them, stopping them in their tracks. Slim called this 'a really brilliant example of rearguard work' by the Gurkhas. But, as in Malaya, there was no real stopping the overall momentum of the Japanese attack.

On 29 April, British and British Indian Armies were ordered back to India. The key Burma Road supply chain was severed, isolating China, apart from the hazardous air route – nicknamed 'The Hump' – that traversed the Himalayan foothills from northern Burma to western China.

Stillwell made his name as a leader here, walking out with his team, a rugged journey of a few weeks, to India. But, unlike Tsuji, he cared for his average foot soldier, many now preferring to call him 'Uncle Joe.'

**

The Japanese strategic team was hard at work as always. Operation 21 was on the drawing boards. This targetted the HQ city of Imphal, where essentially all Britain's supplies were stored, and would give them a powerful bastion from which to defend Burma and attack India. But this terrain represented some of the worst line-of-communication conditions in the world.

In July 1942 the Japanese scrubbed the operation for fear of over-extending resources.

For their part, the British masterminds had Operation Anakim in mind,

a joint full-scale invasion by British and Chinese forces. They called it off in January 1943.

But while the 18th Division sat relatively and uncharacteristically peacefully in the Shan States, many of the men and women they'd conquered in Singapore and Malaya were descending into ever-deeper levels of hell.

COULD THINGS GET ANY WORSE?

'There were many levels of hell under the Japanese.'

By May 1942, young Hector Rogers found himself in Melbourne. Having initially fetched up in Perth, where Shell had teed up some guardians for him, Hector then made his way to Melbourne. His mum, having disembarked the *Empire Star*, eventually finished up in India in March, and from there she was flown to Melbourne. 'That was the best time she and I ever had because it was just the two of us, we did develop bonds and ties.'

But then, devastating news regarding dad, Geoffrey Rogers, who'd been bayonetted outside the operating theatre: 'Well into 1942 mum had a notification from the War Office that my father was missing, presumed killed. It was the first time she knew he had not survived, had not become a prisoner of war. But we didn't know he was dead till my mum got this letter from Betty Webster, whose own husband (Maj Lyndsay Webster) had become a prisoner and was able to get a message to her that my father was dead and Betty Webster told my mother,' he inhaled deeply, 'he was dead, because Mr Webster was in the hospital as well.'

Hector sighed, then paused. 'My mother was very upset obviously, and I was upset because at the time she wouldn't talk to me. I was angry this had come between us. It's difficult to define. Rather than holding me close, she sort of pushed me away. She didn't want me to be part of her grief, I suppose. Of course that made me angry, that what had happened elsewhere had done this to her.'

It would be in December 1942 that Alice Griffin received a notification about her young husband, Lance Sergeant Oswald Griffin, who'd held up the Japanese invaders at the hospital to allow others to affect an escape. 'Missing in Action, Fall of Singapore,' is all it said. Which was perplexing, because she and all others assumed they'd deployed to North Africa. She had lost her father in the Somme, so it must've hit doubly hard. She showed it to Ossie's mum.

'Alice remarried very quickly during the war after he died,' said great-nephew Neil Storey, 'which was frowned on.'

**

All this time, Capt Soejima – who had been hit by flying shrapnel near the Normanton oil tanks – was laid up in No 1 Temporary Field Hospital (probably Singapore General Hospital) till May, before rejoining his unit in the Shan States, Burma, for six months then being posted back to Japan for rest of the war.

In June, the 'Tiger of Malaya' Yamashita finally left Singapore, heading to the Philippines, where he would remain for the rest of the war. Indeed his shortened life.

Lim (the brick-maker part of Loveday's Ring) set up the Sino-British guerrilla task force Force 136 with Capt John Davis of the Special Operations Executive (SOE). This unit would go on to become much-storied with their disruptive operations behind enemy lines in Malaya.

August 1942 saw Ito of the 55th Regiment transferred. 'In October I returned to Japan for a staff training course.' He was then promoted in March 1943 to lieutenant colonel, graduated from Military Academy in September and posted to staff HQ 60th Division in Soochow (Suzhou) as Staff Officer of Operations.

Tsuji meantime had turned his attention to masterminding other theatres, and insisted on visiting the frontline action at Kokoda, Papua. En route via destroyer, an Allied bomber unleashed its payload and a small shrapnel fragment caught him in the throat, causing only slight injury. But, despite his personal shows of bravery, the Japanese were turned around on Kokoda, and their Rabaul campaign was blunderous.

**

Tom Smiley worked for the first few years in the Robert Barracks, alongside his mentor Col Julian Taylor, the latter engaging in pioneering work designing and constructing artificial limbs, with engineer Capt Bradley, fashioning them from aluminium ceiling fans. 'No doubt there were very dark times and Tom like all of the FEPOW suffered from malnutrition, beatings and hard labour in the blazing heat,' explained daughter Fiona Smiley, 'but he considered himself as one of the lucky ones as he had his work, ambition and love of Elizabeth to keep him going. He was determined to keep himself as active as he could and was very much a part of the Changi University. He read medical books, learnt to speak German, played the violin, sang in the choir and spent time in the morgue studying anatomy. 'He became inseparable friends with Dr John Falk and they were known as the "surgical twins" and together they tried their hands at bee-keeping, hen rearing and vegetable growing in order to help the poor diet of their patients.'

Nearby, others knuckled down to their new reality in a different way. The indefatigable Ethel Mulvany was interned in Changi prison as a civilian. While enduring horrific conditions there, she came up with the idea of compiling the *Changi Jail Cook Book* as a means of getting the salivary glands of the prisoners working to prevent deaths by starvation. 'It would relieve our hunger,' Ethel wrote, 'to compile a recipe book. It seemed to help when we were most hungry. I made this collection when I weighed 85 pounds.' Sixty fellow inmates gladly contributed their favourite recipes, all jotted down in old ledger books kindly given to them by the guards. 'Of all the pains you have ever had in your life, there is nothing like that debilitating going-down-the valley-one-by-one pain of hunger. Nothing is stronger.'

They devised methods of getting letters and messages out and around Singapore. She wrote to husband Denis and was overjoyed to receive his response 10 days later. She wanted, *needed*, his hug. Which gave rise to her idea of stitching quilts with embedded secret messages to send out to the men in other camps, which became famous later as the 'Changi Quilts' project. She also initiated the Red Cross retreat room project in which a small room was constructed, replete with 'throne' of orange crates and canvas cushions, where inmates could go and have some quiet reflective time to themselves.

**

In the Dutch East Indies, the nursing PoWs were faring none too well. One of Sister Brenda Macduff's diary entries reads: 'Rats are a menace, they eat everything.' The prisoners were given one bar of soap a month and toilets were containers that needed to be emptied by hand. Dysentery, diphtheria, jaundice and malaria decimated them, with only glucose, salt and tea available as medicine.

In October 1942, the spirited sisters Mary Cooper, Margot Turner, Olga Neubronner and Macalister were sent to work in a native hospital. Then six months later they were suddenly interred by the Kempetai in a small cell in the local jail on suspicion of being spies. Turner lost a front tooth to an over-zealous guard. Those closest to Mary say she never fully recovered from that confinement ordeal, her irrepressible spirit clearly shattered, and sadly passed away in captivity in Muntok in June 1945.

Macduff was grateful she could keep working as a nurse: 'I wasn't just sitting in the camp and taking my tin plate and getting food. It was hard work looking after patients but I was young and strong and that was my job.'

She still knew nothing of the fate of her husband Ken, who'd been fighting with the Volunteers, but he had been taken PoW and sent up to the Thai Burma Railroad, of which she – and the rest of the Western world – knew nothing at that stage.

**

Sydney Hoskins' run of bad luck continued and the RAMC private was on the first mainland party train to Thailand on 20 June 1942. 'The scars on my wrists made by the rope with which I was tied up, remained visible twelve months after my escape,' he, one of the five outhouse survivors, said. Thereafter from Nong Pladuk, he was shuffled up and down the line to Tha Makham, Kanburi and other sites, remaining in Siam all the while.

'I will not dwell on our horrible conditions in the hospital,' wrote Sgt Jack Slater to his wife Anne when he was expecting to die on the Railway when cholera ripped through the northerly camps, and he was stricken. 'Suffice to say I will not forget them to my dying day.' Fortunately he rallied and pulled through.

Fergus Anckorn found himself slaving as a labourer on that infamous project, his nearly-severed hand having healed sufficiently: 'I built the Whampao viaduct,' he would tell me, of the most structurally significant section of the railway, hugging the cliffs as it does, just shy of what the world would one day know as 'Hellfire Pass'. The conditions were debilitating. 'At first I threw up from the stench of ulcers plus the latrine trenches. Then within three days I was sitting on their beds eating my rice. All my friends but one died foul deaths. I saw the worst deaths possible, 15 a day for months.' He irrepressibly entertained his camp-mates with his magic, and also helped sweeten the attitude of the guards who loved his conjuring tricks before their very eyes.

Dick Lee, the gunner-turned-dispatch rider, was himself dispatched to the work camps at Tarsao. 'You're watching people up there dying of all these bleedin' diseases and the suffering. I mean in the hospital in the early days you were getting supplies, you were getting injections, up there you couldn't get a bleedin' Aspro, you couldn't get a bandage, you couldn't get nothing. And you were watching human beings rotting away ...,' he said as the feelings welled up again inside him nearly 70 years after the fact. 'You're watching these people rotting away with these fuckin' ulcers in their legs, and the pain and suffering that they were going through with these legs. *That's* suffering.'

Dick got split up from his good friend Tony. 'Split up for six months. They had a tough, tough time people in Songkhla. And he came down. Somebody come to me and says, "Your pal Tony's just come in on this trainload". I never recognized him. They were filthy.'

'It was only by their voices that we often recognized the scarecrows that were our friends,' mirrored Capt Hugh Pilkington, after one chance encounter with Graham Henderson of Sungei Ujong Estate, who was a pre-war friend and fellow rubber planter in Seremban. 'Pilk' also shipped up to work on the Railway, his shoulder nowhere near in perfect working order. This attracted further unfortunate attention from the guards. 'One arm no good-ah! One arm no good-ah!' they'd shout while attempting to beat him into productivity. He spent time in camps like Kanyu, Malai Hamlet and Kanchanaburi.

George Britton was sent off to Chung Kai, Tha Markan, and even 62 Kilo camp in Burma. Stealing food from the guards for his comrades one time – perhaps in retribution for the bread loaves stolen by the Japanese in his makeshift ward in The Alex – he was caught in the act, a rifle butt smashing and fracturing his cheekbone.

Dr William Young, the founding general duties medical officer at The Alex was later awarded for his work in the dysentery wards in the camp hospitals around Kanchanaburi.

Len Knott of the RAMC found himself in Nong Pladuk (where his commander was the well-respected Lt Col Toosey, later portrayed in the film *Bridge on the River Kwai*) and he would also serve time under Lt Col Malcolm, RAMC, at Kanburi camp, the main Allied Hospital Camp along the river. Here he performed life-and-limb saving work scraping out tropical ulcers with a spoon, and introducing maggots to eat any remaining dead flesh, a procedure he repeated countless times. Part of his unpleasant task list was placing bodies of fellow PoWs in sacks in preparation for burial. The camp padre saw him doing this and said: 'You will get your reward in heaven, my son.'

Being a medic didn't exempt him from normal duties or beatings. He had his teeth knocked out by a Japanese rifle butt, and was forced to stand in a fast-moving river up to his armpits bashing in bamboo piles to create one bridge. Nearing the point of death himself one time, Len exchanged a gold ring for some eggs from a Thai trader. Thereafter he was sent off to the Ubon Camp ('a frightful dump') under Maj Smyth, whom he'd known as one of the senior medicos at The Alex. Smyth would remain as OC of that camp till war's end.

In the Malai camp, many of the bedraggled and beleaguered faces who had something to do with The Alex were otherwise familiar. That Indian Army man from the Officers' Ward, Capt Brown, was present and correct. Two of the outhouse escapees were corralled here too: Bryer and Waller. Capt Brown said he got to know 'the only survivor to the best of my knowledge' who escaped from the Sisters' Quarters incident there. This was Waller (who also spent time in Chung Kai, Nong Pladuk, Kanburi and Nakhon Nayok).

Brown heard Waller's escape story 'first hand', which went like this: 'As it was dark, he saw a 60-gallon oil drum with no top on it, and jumped into it. It was almost full of oil, and he kept just the top of his head above oil and he stayed in it nearly 24 hours, then he came out. Some Japanese soldiers saw him, but they just roared with laughter and brought him back to the hospital again.' This is an interesting point because it indicates different units were probably involved, with others uninformed or unaware of the extermination effort. Otherwise, aiding a known survivor, a witness no less, would not be countenanced.

'The fact that I could cook rice saved my life,' Malaya hand Bryer would tell his daughters, Lyn and Vicky. Apart from being a 'powder monkey' – carrying gelignite to the rock face – he was a designated cook, and also a designated pall-bearer when cholera struck. 'I was chosen as one of the people to carry the bodies to the fire.'

Of 32 Coy RAMC, Sutton – part of Smiley's operation theatre crew – QMS Lunt, and the dispenser Torbit were also here, as was Capt Constantine Petrovsky. The Russian exile had some extraordinary experiences on the Railway. 'Because he was big, being 90kg and six foot, and spoke Japanese, the Japanese officers would invite him in to drink alcohol,' his son, Nikolai, told me. 'They did this as a regular challenge to drink him under the table. "Drink to the Emperor!" "Drink to the King!" They'd get shitfaced. As long as he kept winning, the invitations kept coming. The extra calories from alcohol would be useful.'

Not all ended up in Siam. Others were shipped to Formosa (Taiwan) and Japan. The Engineer, Lt Frederick Croft, Loveday's underling, was shipped to Formosa in August 1942 then to Japan, finishing up in Sendai 8B Kosaka.

Camp life in Formosa claimed the life of Gunner Edward Furness, the appendectomy patient who'd managed to climb out of his ward window and scarper back to Allied lines. A fellow PoW would tell the family later: 'You would not have wanted him to come home because he had suffered terribly and was not the person you knew,' having been constantly tormented by Japanese and Korean guards.

Harry Saye, 32 Coy RAMC, was in Singapore until he, at which point he shipped to Chosan, Korea, in August 1942, where he spent the balance of the war. Daniel Fraser of the Royal Engineers shared exactly the same journey and duration.

Interestingly, though, their former victors from Singapore, IJA 18th Div, were now facing a rapidly turning tide in Burma. And soon, the memories of their victorious rampages through China and Malaya turned to similar hardships and deprivations that their vanquished PoWs were experiencing.

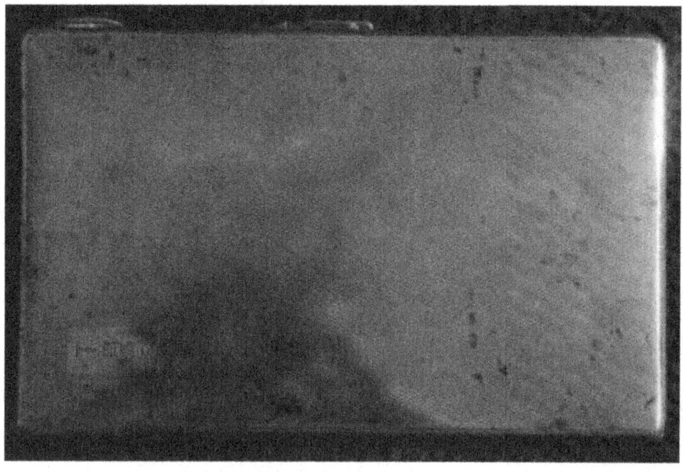

Above: The silver cigarette case that saved Capt Smiley's life (his initials 'TBS' can be seen lower left).
Below: The 'Oner' magazine published by the 198th Field Ambulance in Changi, 1942.

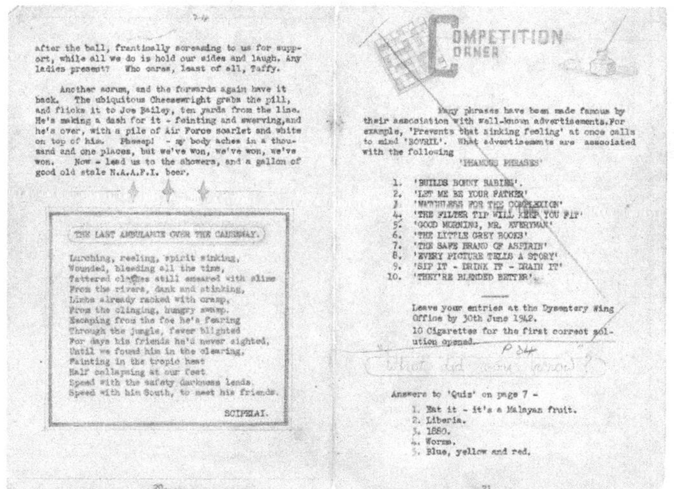

after the ball, frantically screaming to us for support, while all we do is hold our sides and laugh. Any ladies present? Who cares, least of all, Taffy.

Another scrum, and the forwards again have it back. The ubiquitous Cheesewright grabs the pill, and flicks it to Joe Bailey, ten yards from the line. He's making a dash for it - feinting and swerving, and he's over, with a pile of Air Force scarlet and white on top of him. Pheeep! - my body aches in a thousand and one places, but we've won, we've won, we've won. Now - lead us to the showers, and a gallon of good old stale N.A.A.F.I. beer.

THE LAST AMBULANCE OVER THE CAUSEWAY.

Lurching, reeling, spirit sinking,
Wounded, bleeding all the time,
Tattered clothes still smeared with slime
From the rivers, dank and stinking,
Limbs already racked with cramp,
From the clinging, hungry swamp.
Escaping from the foe he's fearing
Through the jungle, fever blighted
For days his friends he'd never sighted,
Until we found him in the clearing,
Fainting in the tropic heat
Half collapsing at our feet
Speed with the safety darkness lends
Speed with him South, to meet his friends.

SCIPELAI.

20.

COMPETITION CORNER

Many phrases have been made famous by their association with well-known advertisements. For example, 'Prevents that sinking feeling' at once calls to mind 'BOVRIL'. What advertisements are associated with the following

'FAMOUS PHRASES'

1. 'BUILDS BONNY BABIES'.
2. 'LET ME BE YOUR FATHER'
3. 'MATCHLESS FOR THE COMPLEXION'
4. 'THE FILTER TIP WILL KEEP YOU FIT'
5. 'GOOD MORNING, MR. EVERYMAN'
6. 'THE LITTLE GREY BOOKS'
7. 'THE SAFE BRAND OF ASPIRIN'
8. 'EVERY PICTURE TELLS A STORY'
9. 'SIP IT - DRINK IT - DRAIN IT'
10. 'THEY'RE BLENDED BETTER'.

Leave your entries at the Dysentery Wing Office by 30th June 1942.

10 Cigarettes for the first correct solution opened.

Answers to 'Quiz' on page 7 -

1. Eat it - it's a Malayan fruit.
2. Liberia.
3. 1880.
4. Worms.
5. Blue, yellow and red.

21.

The battered suitcase Ethel Mulvany took into Changi with her, and below, bowing to Japanese guards while in Sime Road civilian camp. Bottom: collection of cards Dick Lee received while in Changi PoW camp.

Above: Lt Gen Mutaguchi's star was rising when he was promoted to general in command, 15th Army, in early 1943. Meanwhile PoWs like Dick Lee and Bert Gurd were thankful for the occasional card or message they could send or receive.

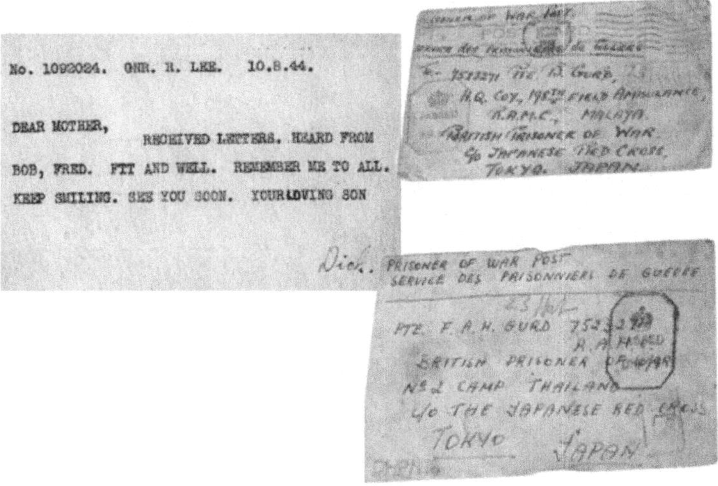

No. 1092024. GNR. R. LEE. 10.8.44.

DEAR MOTHER,
RECEIVED LETTERS. HEARD FROM BOB, FRED. FIT AND WELL. REMEMBER ME TO ALL. KEEP SMILING. SEE YOU SOON. YOUR LOVING SON

Dick.

PRISONER OF WAR POST
SERVICE DES PRISONNIERS DE GUERRE
PTE. F. A. H. GURD
BRITISH PRISONER OF WAR
Nº 2 CAMP THAILAND
c/o THE JAPANESE RED CROSS
TOKYO JAPAN

H.Q. COY, 198TH FIELD AMBULANCE,
R.A.M.C., MALAYA.
BRITISH PRISONER OF WAR
c/o JAPANESE RED CROSS,
TOKYO. JAPAN.

THE VICTORS BECOME VANQUISHED

'They'll be rats in a trap.'

March 1943. Occupying a now relatively quiet corner of Burma was not what Mutaguchi wanted, nor was suited to. It did not serve his lofty aims. He hated the Chinese more and more with each victory he dished out, and despised the British for how he had crushed them in Malaya and Singapore. He wanted and needed more vindication of himself as a great general.

That chance came when Mutaguchi was promoted to general in command of 15th Army, which consisted of 33rd Division and 55th Division, the original invaders of Burma. His beloved 18th Division conquerors now came under command of Lt Gen Tanaka Shinichi.

Meanwhile, Maj Fujiwara Iwaichi had been training up the 50,000 members of the Indian National Army, and had a wealth of knowledge from his pre-war immersion and current location in northern Burma. He fed much of this to the new commander, but Mutaguchi dismissed most of this collated intelligence.

Brig Orde Wingate's Long-Range Mission unit – the guerilla-styled Chindits – had penetrated deeply and disruptively across Burma by foot, which impressed Mutaguchi and set in motion his anti-British plan to do the same, only in the opposite direction. The spiritual-minded officer favoured the fact that *seisho* (spirit) would somehow divinely deliver a Japanese victory. But Stillwell had other ideas, sending his Chinese X Force into Burma from India that October and building up the opposition. Within a couple of months, Mutaguchi got into the ear of his super-supporter, Tojo, who was now a very handy sponsor, being the minister of war, supreme general, *and* prime minister all in one. Mutaguchi's idea was to essentially reboot Operation 21, a two-pronged pre-emptive attack leading to the occupation of India. An attack on the HQ city of Imphal would drive the Brits out of northeast India, and he would throw his three IJA divisions at it.

Time was of the essence here: they needed to do this before Slim launched his own invasion to retake Rangoon. But the savvy Slim had predicted this play exactly, and was happy to concede some easy territory to allow the Japanese to over-stretch their supply lines as they crossed the Burmese border into India. Obviously there was tons of resistance around the table to this notion of allowing easy entrance to the jewel of England's colonial collection.

Mutaguchi's masterplan included a simultaneous diversionary decoy, Operation Ha-Go in the Arakan, to distract and soak up Slim's resources there, with Operation U-Go being an offensive into Assam, a grandeloquent 'March on Delhi.' He haughtily put it down as a three-week plan to invade India. As usual they would travel light for speed and nimbleness, supplies carried by thousands of oxen.

Uproar! Most of the other Japanese officers favoured a defensive line. All his divisional commanders objected, some referring to him as a 'bully' and a 'blockhead.' Leveraging his Tojo connection, he submitted his own plan without prior approval of his immediate superior, Gen Kawabe Masakazu. The idea was a pre-emptive *blitzkrieg* on Imphal before Britain's counteroffensive could be organized, and to establish a Free India provisional government, all before the monsoon arrived. Rather ambitious. And completely contemptuous of the British' ability to fight and defend. Slim's 14th Army was a different animal to anything he'd faced in Malaya. Besides, winning the battles of Imphal and Kohima was not the same as gaining and holding all of India. That would've required a whole different level of logistics, materiel and manpower.

And yet Mutaguchi received orders to launch U-Go on 7 January 1944.

**

18th Division IJA were up the treacherous Ledo Road, opposing the Chinese in Yunnan province at this stage. Such mountainous terrain, with its precarious hairpin bends, were diagonally opposed to what they experienced in Malaya and Singapore. They faced the American-trained 22nd and 38th Chinese Divisions under Vinegar Joe, supplemented by the Long Range Penetration Regiment, which was a guerilla-style outfit nicknamed 'Merril's Marauders', run along the lines of Wingate's Chindits which had proved disruptive behind lines.

By now it was two years since their mighty and memorable victory in Singapore. Their designs on India seemed feasible and achievable. But they didn't realize they'd enjoyed all the 'easy' victories they would ever rack up, and completely failed to realize they were playing into Slim's carefully-set trap. Slim had successfully sucker-punched Mutaguchi ... encouraging him to over-extend his supply lines and critically weaken his army.

**

From 5 February for the next two and a half weeks, the 'Battle of the Admin Box' at Sinzweya raged viciously. Mutaguchi's 55th Division, under field commander Lt Gen Sakurai Shozo, featured in an eerily familiar scene as told by George MacDonald Fraser:

'Good god, they've gotten into the hospital!' British officer Adams said, hearing small arms fire coming from behind him. The hospital was just 300 yards from the British staff HQ. The Japanese surrounded the hospital and set up a defensive perimeter around it. 'Inside the Japanese were interrogating their prisoners, binding some of them by their hands and feet, and bayonetting others in their beds.'

The infirmary's Indian MO Lt Basu was pressured by Japs to hand over the hospital's drugs (morphine and quinine mainly). 'While other Japanese soldiers destroyed anything they couldn't use.'

Adams held fire on the facility overnight. But in the morning, patients were told to 'come and get treatment.' They led around 20 patients out behind the building. 'As prisoners were led to a dry creek bed just behind hospital, the Japanese troops sprayed machine gun volleys at them until all of the British had fallen.' Three soldiers, including Basu, played doggo, covering themselves in their comrades' blood, and lay among the pile of corpses for several hours before slipping away. The British later fired tank and artillery fire into the hospital before storming it, only to find most of the invaders had already fled in the night. 31 British and Indian soldier-patients' bodies were recovered, along with four doctors.

George MacDonald Fraser also pointed to another hospital-related atrocity, but this one perpetrated by the Allies: 'There was a village which contained a curious concrete building, about forty feet by twenty. Down the length of the floor ran a central trench, rather like a very big garage inspection pit. The building was used as a prison hospital for sick and wounded Japanese, who were laid on stretchers and palliasses down both sides, but not in the central trench. They were guarded day and night, by pickets drawn from various units. I was never on guard myself, but saw the Japanese, who may have numbered anything from 20 to 50. They were all in pretty poor shape. One morning after an Indian unit had been on guard, there were no Japanese to be seen in the building, and the central trench was full of rocks. The Japanese were found underneath them, dead. They had been thrown into the trench in the night, and the rocks hurled down on them. I am fairly sure that the section, myself included, could well be charged with war crimes. It seems to be established that knowing of a war crime, and winking at it, is to be guilty, at least as an accessory, or by association. I know the killing (or murder, which is what it was) of those Japanese was well beyond the civilized borderline.'

So the Japanese did not have a complete monopoly on atrocities.

**

Thus far, the Burma Campaign was a points-decision in favour of Japanese, tantalizingly 30 to 40 miles short of Imphal within days. Slim tenaciously held his metal. His army was compressing itself, forming a formidable defensive ring, as the Japs stretched and stretched, time and distance beginning to play their part on the invaders as predicted.

It was a decisively brave gambit by Slim because, while the mountain was hard to hold, it was imperative the rail line (especially the rail head at Dimapur) was held. Otherwise, disaster! The supply of 60,000 men in Imphal and Kohima would then have to rely on air supply, a logistical impossibility with unthinkable consequences.

The 33rd Division, under Lt Gen Yanagida Motozo, were

instrumental in taking and holding the key Tiddum Road. On 18 March they captured a supply post with enough Churchill Supplies to keep 33rd Div in food and ammo for a good couple of months. Again, the British had helped their enemy to fight against them.

From the south the IJA 18th Division pushed further and further north across the rugged jungle-covered mountains to cut off the Chindits' escape route to India. They were starting to play the Brits at their own game, offensively pushing through northern Burma towards Imphal. 'When I get to Imphal I'll have their supply base,' Mutaguchi said. 'They'll be rats in a trap.' This was to be his decisive battle.

Mutaguchi commandeered a suitable house in the picturesque colonial hill station of Maymyo (known today as Pyin Oo Lwin). He had a *shinto* spirit house built near his home, a square of white sand with bamboo poles marking each corner, where on a daily basis he would intone the gods.

In March 1944 he sat down and wrote in his diary: 'I started off the Marco Polo Incident which broadened out into the China Incident and then expanded until it turned into the Great Asian War. If I push into India now, by my own efforts and can exercise a decisive influence on the Great Asian War, I, who was the remote cause of the outbreak of the great war, will have justified myself in the eyes of our nation.'

Some might say he was becoming delusional about his own importance, and dangerously coming to believe his own spoutings.

But there were a couple of assumptions factored in to predicate his success. One was securing the Imphal dumps and all their invaluable 'Churchill Supplies' to sustain the onward effort. The second was that the British opposition would be of similar calibre to that they met with in Malaya.

It seems the Allies in Burma fought with greater tenacity and less 'withdrawal complex'. Perhaps news of the fate of PoWs in Singapore and elsewhere had hardened their resolve? Also, Mutaguchi had underestimated that, in the event of a retreat, getting back over the monsoon-ridden roads would be a nightmare of epic proportions. He had effectively already burned his bridges and his boats.

Furthermore, the biggest strategic miscalculation made was his assumption that any British reinforcements would take a while to arrive by river, road or rail. He completely overlooked the Allies' ability to use the air to fly in fresh boots on the ground.

**

Stillwell was now at Slim's HQ, poised – like a compressed spring – to push back the IJA 18th Div to Myitkyina, whose airfield would be a huge fillip to supplying China. Meanwhile, Wingate's brigades would be tasked with outflanking, disrupting and, by any other devious means, chipping away at the rear of the 18th Div. How the tables had turned!

Mutaguchi continued his chest-thumping on the eve of launching the U-Go attack: 'The Army has now reached the stage of invincibility – and the day when the Rising Sun shall proclaim our definite victory in India is not far off. We must sweep aside the paltry opposition we encounter and add lustre to army tradition by achieving a victory of annihilation. This operation will engage the attention of the whole world and is eagerly awaited by 100 million of our countrymen. By its very decisive nature, its success will have a profound effect on the course of the war and may even lead to its conclusion ...'

So confident was he of this invincibility, that comfort women – of which he was notoriously fond – were on standby to be flown into Imphal in just 10 days time as reward for he and his men.

At his command, 115,000 Japanese infantrymen and support crews headed into the mountains. 12,000 horses and mules, 30,000 oxen and over 1000 elephants did their heavy lifting.

**

And so they interlocked in East India: Slim's 14th Army vs Mutaguchi's 15th Army around Kohima. 40,000 Japanese meeting 30,000 British, of which only 3800 Allies were located in Kohima itself.

Quite an even match, as Mutaguchi had expected. But Slim bought in two more divisions, balancing the fight in favour of the

British. Further, the ox started to falter – they were used to pulling carts along streets, not being used as heavy-haulage pack animals in mountainous terrain. Alarmingly the oxen started collapsing from starvation and exhaustion, and his soldiers were only too happy to gobble them up to supplement their own meagre rations. The IJA were running low on supplies.

31st Division moved on Kohima in early April, but Mutaguchi's grand plan to pounce on the railhead at Dimapur was thwarted when Gen Kawabe nixed it as 'not within strategic objectives'. This was a costly error because of the physical and strategic value of Dimapur. Taking Dimapur would have been a — perhaps *the* — decisive hammer blow in their India aspirations. In retrospect this might have been the pivot point of the Burma campaign: a shot at goal not taken.

By May a frustrated despondency was setting in. Every one, including Mutaguchi in private reflective moments, realized they had a problem. But no one wanted to lose face by ordering a 'retreat', a word that had been actively expunged from the Japanese military manual in the mid-1930s. This refusal to consider even the outside possibility of defeat meant the mentality was one of throwing good money after bad. A sunk-cost fallacy.

The 33rd Division under Maj Gen Tanaka was withering away, but he rallied them with a serious and surprising call: 'Now is the time to capture Imphal. It must be expected that the division will be almost annihilated ... in order to keep the honour of his unit bright, a commander may have to use his sword as a weapon of punishment.'

**

Mid-May saw Stillwell's Chinese units pushing back the 18th Division, further and further back down the Hukawng Valley, while Merril's Marauders sniped at them, outflanked them, and finally took Myitkina airport. This allowed thousands of Chinese troop reinforcements to fly in, and facilitated an easier air-route to China. But fanatical Japanese defenders stoically stood their ground for three months.

When the Japanese had originally taken Myitkina, a dreadful episode had unfolded. 'The Japanese murdered all the wounded British soldiers they found as they entered Myitkyina,' according to Maj JCK Marshall, 'and then proceeded to behead a large proportion of the male population of the town on suspicion that they were British collaborators.'

All oxen had been eaten and bullets all but expended by late May. Mutaguchi's commanders of 15th and 33th Divisions implored him to issue a 'Withdraw to Burma' order, where they could get medical care and provisions and materiel, but Mutaguchi only ramped up his resolve.

Cracks and stress fractures appeared in the iron will of the Japanese invaders. On May 25, Sato Kotoku, the 51-year-old commander of 31st Division – with vast experience against the Russians – informed Mutaguchi that he was withdrawing from Kohima by 1 June. It was not a request! There had been bad blood along factional lines between these two since 1934, but this was a flagrant crossing of the line of the *bushido* code. Mutaguchi exploded, threatening a court-martial.

'Do what you please,' said Sato over the radio, 'I will bring you down with me.'

'He has lost the battle for me,' fumed Mutaguchi.

Sato sent off one last radio call to Imperial Army Command in Rangoon, saying, 'The tactical ability of the 15th Army staff lies below that of cadets.' With that he turned off his radio and ordered all of his division's radios turned off too, and they about-turned and retreated southwards. (Sato was relieved of command on 7 July, refused an invitation to commit *suppuku*, and had his day in court airing his grievances about the 'blockhead' Mutaguchi.)

The commanders of 15th and 33rd Divisions soon asked permission to withdraw. He summarily sacked them. His three-week campaign was drawing into its fourth month by now. A dismal failure by any measure.

His *shinto* incantations grew increasingly voluminous, and he cut a desperate pot-bellied figure in his *sarong* shouting to each and every one of the 800 gods to turn things around in his favour.

**

By late June 1944, Mutaguchi was clearly losing the plot and disconnected with his reality. An order of the day read: 'The struggle has developed into a fight between the material strength of the enemy and our spiritual strength. Continue in the task until all your ammunition is expended. If your hands are broken, fight with your feet. If your hands and feet are broken, fight with your teeth. If there is no breath left in your body, fight with your spirit. Lack of weapons is no excuse for defeat.' His beady black eyes burned with rage, frustration, desperation.

Increasingly his troops were feeling the pinch of over-extension. 'Our losses had been dreadful,' said Pte Wada Manabu of 138th Infantry Regiment. 'Our soldiers had no rations, no rifle or machine gun ammunition, no artillery shells for the guns to fire.' His regiment of 3800 was now reduced to 'just a few hundred.'

Between November 1943 and June 1944, the first major phase of this campaign, total Japanese casualties exceeded 100,000 men. 'The Japanese suffered their worst defeats of the war on land,' the *Straits Times would* later report. 'In 1943 battle casualties were in the proportion of one wounded to 120 sick.' The conditions were clearly debilitating.

The Kohima and Imphal campaigns alone – the largest defeats in Japanese history – were the opposite of Malaya and Singapore. Their 55,000 casualties included 13,500 dead. Many of those dead were not from enemy fire but sheer exhaustion, starvation, and disease. It had been an expensive six months.

It was easy pickings for the Allies now, with the Japanese being killed at a rate of at least four (possibly five) for each Allied soldier killed. 'If 500 Japanese were holding a position, you'd need to kill 495 of them before it was ours,' noted Slim of their tenacity, 'and then the last five killed themselves.'

Finally Mutaguchi understood his situation. On 7 July he radioed Rangoon for permission to pull back all three divisions. But this was refused by Gen Kawabe, who instead gave him firm orders to bat on. He went back to his hilltop shrine and chanted more *shinto* verses for help.

The very next day, a change of orders came through: the shattered and pummelled IJA would pull back from East India. Mutaguchi painfully and reluctantly accepted defeat.

According to a Japanese documentary, *Sekinin Naki Senjo 4*, made by a NHK Film Crew, 'When the situation of the Imphal campaign got disadvantageous, Mutaguchi spoke to Fujiawara Iwaichi, the staff officer of the Army and said: "In order to show my apology to His Majesty, I would like to kill myself." Then Fujiwara said: "I haven't heard anyone who claimed 'I would kill myself' and who already did. As one of your staff officers I am officially expected to stop you from killing yourself when you start saying such a thing. If you really feel responsible for this operation as the highest commander, then please do not inform me that you want to kill yourself. You can kill yourself silently and no one would stop you from doing that. You don't have to worry about anything and kill yourself. I believe the failure of this operation would be worth the responsible commander's suicide".' Tough words.

**

When the monsoon rains came, they were a metaphor for the Japanese aspirations. To put the Burmese monsoon into perspective a few numbers help to quantify it: 3,000 millimeters (118 inches) of rain fall per year in this part. However, there are heavy rainfalls from May to October, while the rest of the year is dry. So in just six months, typically around 20 inches of rain falls *per month*. London – which many consider to be a rain-bound capital – by comparison receives just over 22 inches of rain *annually*.

The decrepit state of 18th Division and Mutaguchi's other men is most graphically described in Louis Allen's *Burma: the Longest War 1941-45*: 'The tatterdemalion divisions staggered back along the mountain roads. Weapons gone, clutching a stick in one hand and a rice tin in the other, the Japanese stumbled painfully through the torrential rain. The pain from untended wounds, the frantic hunger, and the inward racking of malaria and dysentery pushed them inexorably to the moment when they would beg passers by for a hand-grenade with which to finish themselves off.'

At times the trail was just a metre or so wide, with elevation climbs and drops of over 1000 metres one after another. Japanese troops often just had the rice they carried in their belt bags, and the ammo they had with no chance of resupply here in the monsoonal mud. Their desperation led to them stealing supplies from other divisions and the 18th Div earned the nickname 'thief troopers'.

'The men were barefoot and ragged, and threw away everything except canes to help them walk,' said an embedded Japanese news correspondent. 'Japanese were reduced to boiling grass, eating slugs and leeches for protein. We fell amongst corpses again and again as we stumbled. Thousands and thousands of maggots crept out of the bodies.'

The Japanese were oozing south from Myitkina and into the central plains of the Irrawaddy. Some nicknamed this the 'Human Remains Highway'.

Mutaguchi had achieved his 'victory of annihilation'. Unfortunately it was over his *own* army. When a correspondent asked him about the defeat, he was contrite for once: 'I have killed thousands of my men.' He had lost 30,000 dead, many more wounded.

The once-mighty Mutaguchi was relieved of his command and sent to Singapore in disgrace in August 1944. The self-styled *bushido* warrior joined the General Staff. After six months there he laid down his sword and retired, before being recalled just one month later at the beginning of 1945 and appointed as superintendent of the Military Academy.

**

August 1944. Gen Katamura Shihachi replaced Mutaguchi commanding the 15th Army, and the 'God of Strategy' Tsuji was ominously posted to from Nanking to Rangoon at the same time, as a senior staff officer of the 33rd Army, to see if he could swing the momentum via his usual cunning and devious means. This would team him up with the 18th Division again, after their close co-operations back in Singapore.

In another game of musical chairs, a couple of months later, the charismatic Stillwell left the China-India-Burma theatre. Meanwhile, Slim's 14th Army pushed rapidly into northern Burma, enabled by overwhelming Allied air power, given that many of Japan's airmen – such as Capt Iwasaki – were now sucked into operations around the Pacific Islands.

But Tsuji was still swishing his sword. Or a piece of jagged bomb fragment to be exact. Because Tsuji's forward HQ in Mangshih, northern Burma, had been detected and selected for an air raid. The American 14th Air Force's 25th Fighter Squadron swooped in low, bombing and strafing. But return fire hit one of the American planes, and Lt Benjamin Parker bailed out. They captured him and now brought him before Tsuji. The latter struck Parker across the face with the shrapnel, causing a deep bloody gash, and ordered him publicly executed.

It took the executioner three swings with his blunt blade to kill Parker, after which Tsuji ordered him to slice the meat of the airman's thigh. This meat was preserved in salt, then cooked and shared among a few men to be eaten.

As war correspondents heard the story, it was actually the airman's liver, cut up and roasted on skewers. 'The more we consume,' Tsuji proclaimed, 'the more we shall be inspired by a hostile spirit towards the enemy.' Some officers toyed with their meals, some spat it out. Tsuji called them cowards and polished off his entire portion.

Shortly after this, Tsuji was awarded a citation of appreciation. Only one other officer besides Tsuji ever received this rare honour while they were still alive.

**

The IJA 18th Division was also caught up in musical chairs in early 1945, with their former commander Lt Gen Tanaka Shinichi – who'd led them in northern Burma – sent upstairs to become chief of staff to Kimura, while the incumbent, Lt Gen Naka Eitaro, was demoted following the Imphal implosion, and took over command of the 18th Division.

From January to March 1945, the savage battle for Meiktila

raged, 700km to the south of Mytkyina. 18th Division rushed down there from the north, with other IJA divisions also converging from all parts of Burma. Despite reinforcement by 119th Regiment, the 18th Division IJA were resoundingly thrashed in and around Meiktila, losing thousands of men on this battlefield alone.

The Allies had a highly efficient wire intercept service in place, meaning they could locate and target HQ units, wiping out not just their command structure but also their signals.

An episode here speaks much about the mentality and field service code under which the Japanese forces had trained and fought. 'In one hospital more than one hundred had committed suicide rather than be taken,' noted George Macdonald Fraser of its Japanese soldier-patients. 'It seemed incredible after the hammering he'd had at Imphal. They were hoping to hear of cases of surrender at this stage of the war but apparently there had been none.'

Senjinkun, suicide rather than surrender, was that specific code.

Before retreating, the Japanese soldiers had one last duty. 'Japanese hospitals and field aid stations were sometimes filled to the ceilings with the now-bloated bodies of men who had been wounded in battle, and were then shot in their beds by comrades sparing them the disgrace of becoming prisoners of war.'

'There were makeshift hospitals, the beds and stretchers filled with the dead, some with a bullet hole through the forehead,' noted Evans and Brett-James, the authors of *Imphal*. 'In one collection of huts, skeletons were sitting up in improvized beds, the bones picked clean by ants.'

By the end of March the last Japanese in Meiktila were eradicated. 6513 were killed and 6300 wounded or missing in this battle for central Burma.

The road to Rangoon was now open with Allies having full use of their armoured corps and air supremacy. The Thai-Burma Death Railway – conceived for the northward offensive – came in handy as a fast southbound withdrawal route. Ironic images come to mind of beleaguered Japanese infantry from 18th Division passing through the railway camps full of the very men they'd fought and tried to kill in Malaya, Singapore and especially the Alexandra

Hospital three years earlier. All parties were doubtless unrecognizable to each other.

**

Tsuji was in Pyawbwe in April 1945 when the HQ of 33rd Army – which had subsumed Mutaguchi's 15th Army's role in northern Burma – was surrounded. This included the 18th Div. While panic and fear gripped commander Lt Gen Honda Masaki and his men, Tsuji did something characteristically quirky to demonstrate his supposed bravery and lack of concern for his own life: he stripped off in full view of all his troops and treated himself to a leisurely bath. Somehow, he and the unit managed to escape successfully from that action.

On 2 May 1945, Slim re-entered Rangoon the hard way: overland. (The smart money on both sides were backing an amphibious operation.) By way of a sadly familiar parting shot before liberation, the Japanese blew up St Philomena's Convent, a makeshift hospital for wounded Japanese soldiers. 400 of their own helpless comrades were killed outright. 'The officers responsible told the mother superior that they could not take their patients with them and could not bear to see them fall into enemy hands.' Further evidence of their *senjinkun* mentality, and why they might have felt nothing in running their blades through enemy patients.

The city jail, which held Burmese prisoners of the Japanese, was also torched. Perhaps by way of retribution, the Burmese gave the Japanese a dose of similar medicine. 'A party of Japanese nurses were bayonetted and shot as they tried to flee the city.'

Tsuji retreated to the safety of Southern Army HQ in Singapore, and transferred to Bangkok around July 1945, where he found the garrison troops lethargic and somnolent. He set about a program of rapid reinforcement, including the airport and other key installations, against a British invasion.

But, for all his rallying enthusiasm, the steam had largely gone out of the Japanese overseas war effort. The Potsdam Declaration was issued on 26 July 1945, in which the USA, Britain and China outlined terms of surrender to Japan:

Failure to surrender would result in 'prompt and utter destruction.'

The Japanese had already experienced utter destruction in Burma. Of 305,000 Japanese soldiers in Burma, only 125,000 made it back out, an unconscionable attrition rate. As for the 18th Division, they ended the war in southern Burma. Of the 31,444 men sent to Burma, more than 20,000 – a full two thirds – never made it home to their mothers.

There would be a great percentage of Allied PoWs connected to The Alex in Japanese hands who were looking increasingly unlikely to make it home, either.

A DEADLY DIASPORA

'He was knelt down to have his head chopped off.'

Ethel Mulvany was faring very badly in Sime Road camp, Singapore, where most civilians had been holed up since May 1944 to make way for Death Railway PoWs returning to Changi. She had been mentally unhinged for some time but now she tipped right over the edge, rushing through the camp one day to attack a Japanese general. Japanese guards overpowered her, then got 10 Englishmen to restrain her by chaining her to a tabletop. The Japanese removed her Red Cross uniform and held her in a barred cage.

As part of the subsequent interrogation she had wisdom teeth removed without anesthetic and her prison ID number 2665 was branded into the flesh of her left forearm. She was held in solitary confinement from February to August 1945, where – completely out of her mind – she warbled *Rule Brittania* and other patriotic songs at the top of her voice. The cell was subsequently padded, and – clad in a sarong – all she was allowed to possess were a bible (she was ultra-religious), and a pencil. One day she ate the spine of her bible hoping there'd be valuable protein in the horse glue binding. She befriended two spiders in the cage, naming one Churchill and the other Tojo. And had time to count the 264 boils and three carbuncles that blotched her skin.

Also in Sime Road Camp was former surveyor and part-time pianist and fiddle-player, Robert Loveday, interned with the civilians, and keeping himself busy – and others entertained – with his frequent performances in the Camp Orchestra. These programs never failed to break the monotony of the prisoners' lives and bring them some temporary joy, even though he himself was enduring torturous treatment and was shedding weight perilously because the calories were simply nowhere near enough to sustain his once-imposing frame.

**

Meanwhile the IJA 38th Division kept moving with the Japanese front as it spread far and wide across the South Pacific. But as the tide of the war turned palpably following the pivotal Battle of Midway, so did the fortunes of the division.

A battalion of the murderous 229th Regiment set sail for the next epic battle on Guadalcanal, only to have 11 of their 14 ships blasted out of the water, at a cost of 1000 men. Those who did make the landing on Guadalcanal, invariably got thrown into the grand battle for Henderson Field, and few Japanese emerged alive from that.

Yet another battalion found itself in action at Buna-Gona, a battle which followed on from the signature scrap on Kokoda Track which turned the Japanese around for the first time. Buna-Gona pitched the Japanese against the 7th Division Australian Infantry Forces for three months from November 1942, decimating the Japanese with only 11 managing to escape that battle alive.

Later in June 1944, a third battalion were headed to the Japanese-held New Admiralty Islands. Half of the IJA battalion landed successfully but then was reported missing in action after a pitched battle with the Americans. While the other half were turned back and made for Rabaul – which had become a major Japanese base – instead. So the chances of any survivors among the 'grubby little men' who raped Hong Kong and the nurses on Bangka were very slim indeed.

**

And what of the men of 14th Independent Mortar Battalion, those troops among the closest to The Alex? After action in the Philippines they were needed to bolster the defences of Saipan. On 29 May 1944 they were split into two groups and boarded two ships of a nine-ship convoy. Her 12 officers, presumably including Maj Tanaka, and 313 enlisted men boarded the *Havre Maru*.

The other half of the battalion, 324 other ranks, embarked on the *Katsukawa Maru*, a newly built troop transporter. They slipped anchor at dawn, leaving the safe harbour of Tokyo. Four days later and less than 500 miles from Saipan they were intercepted by a US Navy submarine task group. Lt Cdr Edward Blakely on the *USS Shark* lined up the shot and released his torpedoes. The *Katsukawa Maru* was holed and sunk, dumping 2884 IJA soldiers into the South Pacific. Many were rescued by their fellow vessels and made it to Saipan (minus their mortars and other equipment), where subsequently half of all IJA troops were killed in action.

**

From April 1943, the Intelligence Officer and white flag carrier, Cyril Wild, was in Malai camp, too, among other camps with F Force all the way up to Three Pagodas Pass, helping out where he could with Japanese translation but not expecting – and certainly not receiving – any preferential treatment. The Japanese guards even had a nickname for him: '*Nemuranu Se No Takai Otoko*'. The Tall Man Who Never Sleeps. He called the building of the Railway 'one of the horrors of war.'

George Poole would doubtless agree. The medic found himself in camp at the Three Pagodas, too. 'The Japs were determined to give us hell on earth,' he said. 'Men were prodded with bayonets and if they still couldn't keep up they were left to die. I think only half arrived.' Caught operating a hidden radio, they marched him off and questioned him for two to three hours. 'I wouldn't say anything so they knocked me about, damaging the nerves in my spine. They put me in a bamboo cage which was built so I couldn't stand up or sit down, and it rained. They left me there for a fortnight with one bowl of rice a day. When they let me out I couldn't walk and my friends had to carry me back to the hut.' He couldn't get up for a further two weeks after that.

And Gunner Richard Gwillim, who'd narrowly escaped death on the floor of The Alex hospital's kitchen, was indented here, too. Aah, kitchens – a fond memory!

Food was scarcest in these northern reaches. 'There wasn't a cat or dog for miles around because we'd eaten them all.' He and his campmates would wake at 5am to ambush snails as they emerged from cracks in the ground. Although escape attempts were futile, one was attempted here. George knew the Japs would find out, so they needed to cover for the absentee. 'That night three of us got out of the compound, under the wire and went up the hill to the cemetery. We found a grave and dug with our hands till we came to the body. It was a hell of a job getting him out and back to camp. We put him in a hospital bed and covered him up. Next morning when the Japs came round counting, we told them a man had died of cholera. They didn't look.'

Cholera was a cruel cannibal: 'I've seen men of 10-stone go down to six stone by the next day and by the day after that they were dead.'

Wild was already taking on the role of collating the horror stories and abuses rained upon the PoWs on the railway, interviewing men, and noting their reports. But he needed somewhere to secure these documents. Enter Padre Noel Duckworth of 2nd Royal Cambridgeshires with this two attaché cases. He secreted Wild's incriminating papers that would prove invaluable after the war.

Also aiding and abetting Wild was 23-year-old Arthur Lane, who'd joined the Manchester Regiment seven years earlier, and already seen service in Egypt, Palestine and Malaya. As an Army musician, he was allowed to keep his bugle, and even had a pass which allowed him to travel between camps to play at funerals. This he did, using the opportunity to take note of the names of those who'd not died from natural causes. He passed these on to Wild.

Wild's inspirational conduct here was recommended for an award for his 'conspicuous and imperturbable courage, his intelligence and resource in handling the Japanese' by Lt Col Francis Dillon of 18th Div and Lt Col Stanley Harris, RA.

The Engineer who'd had such a rugged time behind the hospital, and later inspecting the carnage, Daniel Fraser, was in Malai (he would later ship out to Jinsen Camp, Chosan, working in a carbide factory). As was Sapper Cyril Lush, the son of Allen and Mary from Dover. His professionalism as a QMS on the construction site had been such a pain to Soh, that Soh had paid $2000 to Loveday to have him sidelined so that the corruption games could be played out.

He died here at the end of April 1944, not yet 28. Exactly the average age of death of all Railway PoWs.

**

Among the older men in PoW ranks were officers from the Indian Army. Lt Col Willis Southern of the 8th Punjabs who was 47, and Lt Col Louis Sobaux Ingle of the 14th Punjabs, 46.

But one poor chap, at least, celebrated his 50th birthday as a PoW: Brig George Ballentine, CO of the Indian 44th Regiment, who was shipped as part of a special party (containing all the most senior officers from Changi to separate them from the men) on the *England Maru 2* to Formosa on 16 August 1942. He spent the rest of the war in Mukden, Manchuria. He reportedly had a set of stones he used to suck on to allay hunger pangs. These were sucked into small smooth pebbles by the time of the Japanese surrender, and would later take them home to Ireland where he kept them in a drawer.

Also on board were Brig Stringer, DDMS, and Brig Newbigging, the other surrender-flag carrier with Wild.

**

The work of medicos on the Railway was legendary. But while the likes of Weary Dunlop have become canonized, there were many, many superhuman efforts overlooked. Hugh De Wardener of 4th Field Ambulance was one such stalwart. Poor Janet, pining at home, received notification that her husband was 'missing, believed dead.' But here he was saving lives from cholera and diphtheria in various camps, even though he himself developed the latter plus tuberculosis. Ever the academic, he made detailed notes on the cases with dysentery and Wernicke's encephalopathy, securing these in a four-gallon can, buried in a deep hole for security, which would form the basis of two seminal papers published in *The Lancet* in 1946-7.

In August 1944 Capt Petrovsky (along with fellow medic Capt Donald Longbottom) was among a group of around 750 men sent on a 'hell ship' from Singapore to Japan, via the Philippines and Formosa, where they were shipwrecked and beached by a typhoon.

They would spend the next year toiling at the Sanyo coal-mining camp just outside a place called Hiroshima.

In a series of low points, this was to produce the lowest point of his whole war. 'When he was knelt down to have his head chopped off,' his future wife, Dr Kathleen Petrovsky, would tell me. There are two theories as to why: one involved a Japanese interpreter who smuggled in food under her *kimono* for the sick prisoners. 'He was always very guilty about it.' Or perhaps it was the disagreement he had with guards over kitchen and cooking hygiene. 'They made him kneel down, put the sword on his neck, raised it to do the final *coupe de grace*. But someone called the camp commandant who came running and yelled, "Stop!" Because Constantine had taken out the commander's root abscess tooth and ever after that he couldn't do wrong as far as the commandant was concerned.' Petrovsky himself was down to about 45kg now, half his former bodyweight, and sporting a lush beard which he vowed not to shave off until Japan surrendered.

**

While it is generally well known that some prisoners spent their whole war on Singapore, others shipped off to Borneo, and most to Burma and Thailand, there were oddities which at least one RAMC man from The Alex team got caught up in.

18 October 1942 saw 600 men of the Royal Artillery shipped out to Rabaul in New Britain (Papua New Guinea) on the *Kenton Maru* 'hell ship'. Six men from the RAMC were selected to accompany this party known as 'Gunners 600' for medical support. Lord only knows why, given the Japanese apathy towards PoW health. Among these was young Pte Frank Hill, whose wife Nancy had heard nothing since his 'all's well' telegram in early February. The other RAMC men, according to the Roberts Hospital Singapore Daily Orders, were Sgt Leslie Knox, and Privates J Hoult, Percy Neaves, Charles Robinson and Kenneth Sharman (the latter three of the 198th Field Ambulance). Also in this was Gunner Francis Docketty. The party was soon trans-shipped to Ballale Island in the Solomons chain, to

build an airstrip for the enemy in conditions similar to those endured on the Railway.

On Ballale Island, American air raids included much 'collateral damage' (to use today's verbiage) of PoWs who were not allowed to dig trenches to take cover. 'The Japanese, believing that the island would be taken by the Americans, ordered all the remaining prisoners from the 'Gunners 600' Party, including the medics, to be shot,' said Brian Hill of events on 5 March 1943. One of those was his father Frank, just 23. 'This was an horrendous ending.'

Indeed. And fortunately for those who had survived thus far, the end of this sickening saga, the Second World War, was nigh.

Capt Constantine Petrovsky as a PoW in Hiroshima. He grew a beard and vowed not to shave it off until the Japanese surrendered. He watched the atom bomb drop from the Enola Gay on 6 August 1945, and was knocked off his feet *twice* by the blast waves.

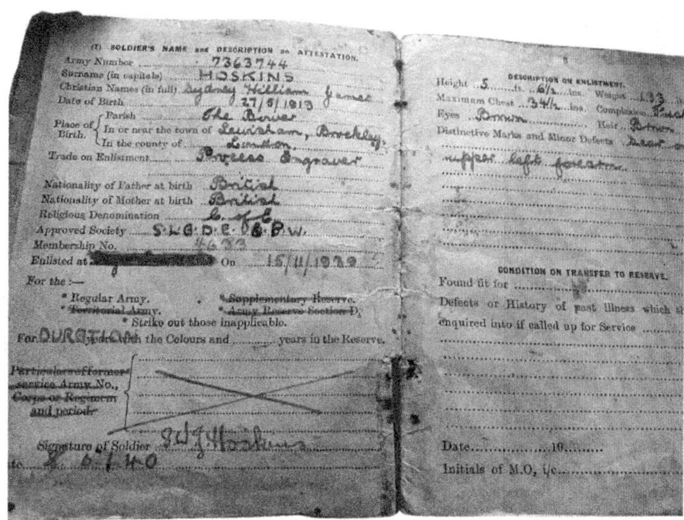

(1) SOLDIER'S NAME and DESCRIPTION on ATTESTATION.

Army Number 7363744
Surname (in capitals) HOSKINS
Christian Names (in full) Sydney William James
Date of Birth 27/8/1913
Place of Birth: Parish The Bower; In or near the town of Lewisham, Brockley; In the county of London
Trade on Enlistment Process Engraver

Nationality of Father at birth British
Nationality of Mother at birth British
Religious Denomination C of E
Approved Society S.L.G.D.E. & B.W.
Membership No. 4683
Enlisted at [redacted] On 15/11/1939
For the :—
* Regular Army. * ~~Supplementary Reserve.~~
* ~~Territorial Army.~~ * ~~Army Reserve Section D.~~
* Strike out those inapplicable.
For DURATION ~~years~~ with the Colours and ...... years in the Reserve.

~~Particulars of former service Army No., Corps or Regiment and period~~

Signature of Soldier S.W.J. Hoskins
to 2.6.40

DESCRIPTION ON ENLISTMENT.
Height 5 ft. 6½ ins. Weight 133
Maximum Chest 34½ ins. Complexion
Eyes Brown Hair Brown
Distinctive Marks and Minor Defects Scar on upper left forearm.

CONDITION ON TRANSFER TO RESERVE.
Found fit for ......
Defects or History of past illness which should be enquired into if called up for Service ......

Date............19.........
Initials of M.O. i/c......

Above: Sydney Hoskins' medical record.
Below: Capt Richard Waller's Japanese POW card.

収容所 Camp	泰	番號 No.	泰I 8459
姓名 Name	WALLER, Richard de Warrenne.	生年月日 Date of Birth	4th October 1915.
國籍 Nationality		所属部隊 Unit	No. 66005 H.Q. L of C area.
階級身分 Rank	Captain, ~~118 Field Regt., R.A.~~ ~~Ward Supervisor.~~		
捕獲場所 Place of Capture	SINGAPORE.	捕獲年月日 Date of Capture	昭和 17 年 2 月 15 日
父ノ名 Father's Name	Robert Studdert de Warrenne.	母ノ名 Mother's Name	Agnes Emily.
本籍地 Place of Origin	Zancor, India.	職業 Occupation	軍人
通報先 Destination of Report	Father, Mr. Waller, Nayland, Colchester, England.	特記事項 Remarks	

Part 3

POST-WAR

(Detail of memoir by Sgt Norman Bryer)

THE BEGINNING OF THE END

'This has been no picnic.'

6 August 1945. Twenty-five miles from Hiroshima, in Sanyo camp, the tall and now skinny and bearded Capt Petrovsky was outside one morning. 'He saw a plane, which was unusual,' Dr Kathleen Petrovsky would tell me. 'As he watched it, he saw something drop, then an almighty explosion – he was knocked to the ground by a seismic explosion, and rushed to the men in the huts, and was knocked to the ground again.' He had witnessed the atom bomb being dropped, although they initially thought an ammunition dump had been hit, triggering an earthquake. 'He was blinded from looking directly at the flash.'

Just over a week later Emperor Hirohito broadcast to his vanquished nation – once again in those delightfully oblique Japanese terms – the news that, 'The war had developed not necessarily to Japan's advantage.' Meaning total and unconditional surrender, of course.

One of the people listening in keenly was airman Capt Iwasaki, then on Formosa. 'Towards the end of war, my squadron was stuck in Taiwan and we couldn't even fly anywhere as there were always so many enemy planes flying over us. On 15 August 1945, everyone was ordered to gather one place at the airfield and we heard the radio message from the Emperor. Everyone got so upset or depressed so badly, and I didn't know what to do or how to live after that.'

In Sanyo camp, 44-gallon drums of supplies were being dropped, some of them sadly landing on and killing some local children. 'They dropped food, but also a white substance in syringes,' Kathleen Petrovsky said. 'But the prisoners didn't know what penicillin was.' It was only a very recent development, unknown to the captive medics. 'Still, the Japs didn't even tell them the war was over. The Japs were sitting around crying and said, "You very bad people" because they'd bombed Hiroshima. So they had to ask the guards, "Is the war ended?"'

The Allied Prisoners of War were no longer prisoners.

**

Craven and Lunt were among the luckier ones of the RAMC to serve their entire time as PoWs in Singapore where conditions were relatively better.

Smiley too had managed to be on Singapore island all along, moving in the latter stages to the hospital camp in Kranji, in the north of the island, to treat the sick survivors returning from the Thai-Burma Railway. By a strange quirk of fate, Smiley was liberated by fiancee Elizabeth's twin brother, Graham Mills, who was in the 14th Army serving under Gen Slim and had fought throughout the reconquest of Burma. Amazingly, they had never met before this moment, and Graham wrote off straightaway to Elizabeth:

'Tom looks reasonable but you must prepare yourself to find him very thin. The PoWs have been starved and badly treated but in comparison to some I've seen, Tom is well. The most characteristic thing about him is his tremendous heart. He is a very cheerful and optimistic man and has been happy in his surgery. He is obviously a first-class and highly respected surgeon. He and two others have performed over 1000 ops in the last years. He is not depressed at all. Thank God that he had his work and I'm sure it has been of inestimable value to his general well being.'

Others connected to The Alexandra Hospital were not so lucky.

Denis Mulvany wrote Ethel a letter which overjoyed the now-wretched woman who had watched the Union Jack flag-raising with a strong sense of revenge. With food 'that didn't induce more attraction than a pig's trough' she'd plummeted from 148 pounds to just 108. 'Darling husband,' she replied. 'It is so wonderful that you are coming to get me for keeps. Bless you darling this has been no picnic, but I will be fine as soon as we are together again. I shall be happy as a sand-boy when I see you and there is much that we can do together. Come as soon as possible, my darling, my love.' He was aware of her breakdown and had sequestered her medical record which stated she was 'very sick and required sedation to control her moods.' Other key words in her record were 'violent, abusive, dirty, self-harming, confused.' She dreamed of returning to Pulau Shorga to relive the pre-war idyll but alas that world didn't exist anymore for them.

Instead they sat on the doorstep of her cell relishing the moment of reunion, which brought her bliss akin to her wedding day, 'sitting there with that cell behind you and everything ahead of you.'

Her local newspaper on Manitoulin blared: **'Mulvany's are Freed from Japs!'** with Ethel adding, 'We are free! After a long and terrible nightmare. None can imagine, who has not been a prisoner of war, just what joy it is to be alive after these gruelling times.'

Ethel was stretchered out of Sime Road camp, and taken via ambulance to the SS *Rajula* hospital ship. As the band struck up *When You Come to the End of a Perfect Day,* she was carried up the gangplank. Lady Mountbatten, elegantly dressed in her St John Ambulance uniform, leaned over and thanked her for the sterling work done for the Red Cross. The ship docked in Madras, where they disembarked and boarded a Bangalore-bound hospital train.

She wanted to remain in India, while Denis wanted to return to the UK. After checking her stability with her doctor, he caught a flight on 25 November to attend his father's funeral. Three days later she was back in hospital. Denis returned just after New Year and found her to be a broken woman again, with medicos recommending she return to the UK and be placed in care indefinitely.

Denis believed she was certifiable and committed her to the Bethlem Royal Hospital, nicknamed 'The Madhouse of Bedlam'. Soon she was receiving shock treatment therapy for mania, and insulin coma therapy. She wrote loving letters to Denis daily.

By July it was agreed she was well enough to leave, but Denis – who'd had a tough time of his own as a PoW – was emotionally depleted. Ethel boarded the *Queen Mary* for Halifax alone and, looking less than elegant in a blue jacket fashioned from an old blanket, was a far cry from her glamorous musk furs and pearls of yesteryear.

Staying on in the RAMC, Denis was soon promoted to lieutenant colonel, and wrote to her with a simple announcement ending their 13-year union: 'I want to be free.' The words hammered her, like a shell from an 15-inch gun. As would the news that Denis had met and professed love for a medical student, Eileen, 21-years his junior. 'Well, I think when he saw what I was like after liberation, and saw what others were around him, that even he couldn't stand it,' she said, harbouring anger and bitterness that never abated until after he'd started his new family, when she finally agreed to a divorce. A melancholic sadness would haunt her the rest of her days.

**

Robert Loveday, the corrupt construction surveyor, found himself in the Sime Road camp upon the surrender. His condition was shocking. "It was apparent that he had been badly treated and tortured by the Japanese," his grandson Phil Loveday (son of Loveday's son Donald), would tell me after discussing this with his mum, Donald's widow, Norma. "He was less than seven stone and suffered traumatic life-changing injuries." That's a 193cm man reduced to less than 45kg, which is half of what is considered a healthy BMI for that height.

He was repatriated on the Dutch vessel seconded by the Royal Navy and used as a hospital ship, *HMS Tegelberg*. They arrived at the Princess Dock, Liverpool, five years – nearly to the day – after he'd been sentenced. He then headed straight to North Shields, where Alice's family was from and where they had married 27 years earlier. The quiet coastal village of North Shields was characterized by red-brick semi-detached houses, rather a come down from the splendour of their colonial bungalow in Singapore. Also, because he was captured as a civilian after being cashiered, there would be no Army backpay.

On the upside, daughter Dorothy, 25, a sergeant in the Auxilliary Territory Service, had recently married a warrant officer in the Royal Signals Corp, and soon made Robert and Alice grandparents to kickstart their next chapter in life.

**

Medic George Poole had been returned from Three Pagodas to Woodlands camp, Singapore. He was placed on a medical detail to treat Japanese soldiers with VD and left unsupervised to get on with it. Knowing these men would return to the combat front once cured, George hatched his own white-anting plan. 'Every Jap that came in to see me got a tap water injection instead of drugs. I used to take the food and drugs they gave me back to the camp for our men.'

But there was still more in store, placed in a 'hell ship' bound for Nagasaki. But his ship was bombed by the Americans, and he was only one of five survivors from 300 starters who made it to shore, where the Japanese picked them up and returned them to camp in Singapore. The once-solid footballer was now down around six stone and apathetic about whether he lived or died. Then one day the Gurkhas arrived into his camp and they were free. 'The Gurkhas were asking which Japs had beaten us up. In the night I heard rifle shots as the Gurkhas started bumping them off. I didn't agree with this.'

He returned home to Sheffield only to find his wife Lottie had started drawing a widow's pension. She'd assumed he was dead having received just the one card from him since 1942.

**

Sydney Hoskins, upon the surrender, was recovered from Ubon in the dry central northeast of Thailand. He flew back to the UK because each plane of repatriated soldiers had to have a medical orderly in attendance. 'The plane before him crashed, and the plane after him crashed,' is how grand-daughter Jo Walker remembered the story told.

Len Knott was also recovered from Siam. 'For years I haven't known the day or date,' Len wrote in a letter home to Joan, 'the days have passed in a miasma, one similar to the other. Your letters burst from the box in which I keep them, became torn, dirty, indecipherable, and I had to burn them. But I still have some pages with a few stained photographs and they are all you: at Tunbridge, that very sweet one at Brighton beneath the Black Rock, and a very dim misty one of you standing on the bank of a river. I always had to hide these in the ground, the Japs had an incredible desire to get hold of photos of English girls and they would have inevitably stolen them.'

Apart from Joan he had clearly been doing much thinking about the big things in life, too. 'I ponder the fact that I've left the poverty of a Nip camp but I'm going home to a slum, I'm changing one type of barrack for another,' he wrote. But one thing was the weather in Asia. 'I want to get a job here somewhere, where the sun shines and where there is something which, once experienced, never leaves one. Heavens, the thought of an English winter after these years of sunshine freezes me and I have less fat now than I ever had before. I'm revelling in the comfort of civilization: I look around and wonder, feel awed when I strike a match and amazed that I haven't lost the knack of using a fork and knife. I savour all these things with profound pleasure, especially the cleanliness, dear God, everything's clean, clean, clean.'

Capt Richard Waller of 118th Field Regt, RA, had been in Thailand since November 1942, and was recovered in Nakhon Nayok, mountainous terrain north of Bangkok. It seems his family never knew until the very end of the war that he had in fact survived it.

Bert Gurd of 198th Field Ambulance had been sent to Thailand at the same time and the war's end found him in Nakhon Pathom, just 12 miles to the east of the Death Railway jump-off point in Bang Pong, west of Bangkok.

James Torbit, the quick-thinking dispenser of RAMC 32 Coy, found himself on the 9th train of F Force bound for Thailand in April 1943. He survived the rigours of the railway, returned to Singapore before being shipped to work in Hiroshima. In the northbound train just behind his, was young George Johnson RAMC 32 Coy. He also made it back to Singapore.

Norman Bryer, the planter-turned-RAF man, was dispatched on the fifth train constituting H Force to the railway in mid-May 1943, the height of the manic and murderous 'speedo' period. He made it back to spend the rest of the war in Singapore, suggesting he was in very poor shape and of no more labouring value. 'He was skin and bone in a loincloth,' his daughter Vicky would say. 'He came out at 45kg,' confirmed daughter Lyn. Upon his release, he bumped into his former boss from Malaya who advised him to return to UK to get demobbed, then get permission to get back to the coconut estate again, which he did.

Brig Charles Stringer, RAMC, the Deputy Director of Medical Services of Malaya Command Headquarters was recovered from Mukden, Manchuria.

**

1 September 1945. Canadian Lt Col Arthur Stewart headed a small group of commandos, and liberated the PoWs from Changi in Singapore. How sturdy and strong this well-fed man seemed compared to the emaciated inmates.

Stewart was the highest ranking non-PoW Allied officer on the island. With the Japanese now stripped of power and position, this made Stewart literally the replacement for Percival, indeed, the replacement for Shenton Thomas, the pre-war Governor of Singapore, too.

Cyril Wild spent a couple of days with Stewart, debriefing him on all the ungodly goings on since 15 February 1942. A lifetime ago. It was decided that Wild should set up a War Crimes Investigation Unit, and on 5 September this came into being, with two British officers from the Malaya police force and a British officer from the Federated Malay States Volunteer Force assigned to assist Wild, who now effectively became their top detective in the Far East.

Seventeen investigation teams would be established throughout Asia, each comprising around 15 team members, typically led by a lieutenant colonel, and intended to contain a legally trained member, if and where available. Wild was neither.

The War Crimes Coordination Unit – jointly under the Adjutant General's Branch and the Deputy Judge Advocate General's office, as though the lessons on bloated bureaucracies of the pre-war had never been learned – set themselves up at the Goodwood Park Hotel. This hotel, designed by the same architect as The Raffles, had endured see-sawing fortunes. In the First World War it was seized because it was a German asset, having started life as The Teutonia, the German expats' club. Then in the recent few years the Imperial Japanese Army had fancied it for themselves. It was now in British hands.

Wild's unit's first action was to exhume buried reports, interview witnesses, and try to identify any Japanese suspects. With their shingle now up above the door officially, their 'to do' list exploded exponentially.

The Japanese on the other hand had issued orders for all records and potential evidence of War Crimes to be systematically and comprehensively destroyed.

'On my release as a PoW I handed my copy of the detailed report on the overrunning of The Alex to the War Crimes Investigation Commission at Changi Gaol, Singapore,' Craven said. He had previously given one copy to Brig Stringer in May 1942.

British War Crimes investigators approached their American counterparts in Tokyo, with entreaties to arrest any suspected war criminals who'd made it home to occupied Japan. But it seemed that Britain was not really set on prosecuting anything that did not involve British military personnel directly, and the Japanese defence teams set to play off the Americans versus the British to divide, conquer and delay where they could.

**

A 30-year-old rustbucket, the P&O Liner *Karapara,* docked in Singapore in early September. 'The most dreadful ship I've ever seen in my life, the rats were running around,' said Lt Nora Irvin of the 69th Indian Base General Hospital. It had been fitted out as a 500-bed hospital ship, paid for by British India. Irvin and her cohort had been mobilized in India then sailed down to Burma where they lay at anchor in Rangoon 'for I can't tell you how long. They recruited us for the invasion of Malaya, but they don't tell you anything when you're in the Army. My first impression of Singapore was leaning over the railing of the ship, observing the prisoners of war walking by in the most aimless fashion. We were really horrified by these people.'

She and the 69th IBGH team were transferred to the The

Alex. 'Some of the Japanese were still there. All the Japanese medical staff had cleared out when we came.' And Irshad Ali was still working there, switching across from the Japanese to the Indian Army without missing a beat.

'It didn't strike me as being very dirty,' but getting the hospital in full working order was first priority, and then accommodation came next. At first she stayed in the hospital itself, on the second floor, then a little later moved over to a house 'now a boarding school run by Shears. We shared about three to a room.' There was no airconditioning 'but there was a defiling fan.' As for the food? 'Very poor ... army rations in a box for a short time.'

The advance team also included its new CO: Col Paddy Stokes, RAMC, effectively Craven's replacement, was a Normandy veteran. 'He still wore his Tank Corp beret, it was very funny,' said Irvin. 'Our Lt Col was James Lusk and surgeon Lt Col Harry Graham, all international rugby players.' Scotsman Douglas Banker was one of the doctors in that advance batch. He could be seen cycling across to Singapore General Hospital several days a week.

There were no *amahs* (maids) so all work was undertaken by military personnel. 'We just had the privates and the corporals.' Many of the orderlies were Indian. Plus of course the QA Sisters – but naturally none with prior experience in Singapore.

Irvin's next task was to set up a blood transfusion department.

But they didn't have PoWs as patients. 'Any POWs that were fit enough to be drafted went to Raffles Hotel. We looked after civilians who were not well enough to travel.'

Once they got on top of the initial demands, there was time to explore the neighbourhood around Ayer Rajah Road (which she described as 'a dirt track, a very small road'. Just outside the hospital gate was a shopping area called The Dip. 'There were cleaners and tailors and shoe cleaners, the *dhobi* laundry, he was there the longest. A shop on the corner used to sell beer where the boys from the barracks used to drink too much sometimes,' she laughed.

They didn't venture into Singapore city very much, 'apart from shopping once a week – Wednesday maybe – into Raffles Square for a couple of hours. No one knew I had a car.'

Despite the obvious physical damage to the infrastructure of Singapore, Irvin says they never spoke about the war in their free time. 'We wondered what happened to Singapore but we didn't realize till it was all over that people started writing books about the terrible debacle of the whole campaign. It was such an awful badly disorganized disaster.'

And were whispers of the massacre doing the rounds in the hallowed hallways? 'No, not immediately,' Irvin confirmed, 'sometime later. But in the particular room where I worked apparently some atrocities were alleged to have happened because a lot of photogaphers came in and a lot of press people, mainly Australians.'

Irvin was aware of the Sisters' Quarters servants block in which the men were held overnight. 'We did hear, there were rumours, some terrible things happened in the Servants' Quarters at the back. Then someone said that was a lot of nonsense, all the massacres happened at Alexandra Park where there is a mass grave of, I've heard, a figure of 400 who were buried. They made a mass grave and were buried.' So lots of conflicting information, even at that stage. But perhaps the following anecdotes more clearly points to where their mood and interests lay:

'Later, one funny thing we learned was that there were lots of crates of whisky alleged to have been buried in the grounds in February 1942, and we were all jokingly looking for a whisky diviner! But I don't think anyone ever found those crates.'

After a year she and many other of that QA batch were drafted back to the UK.

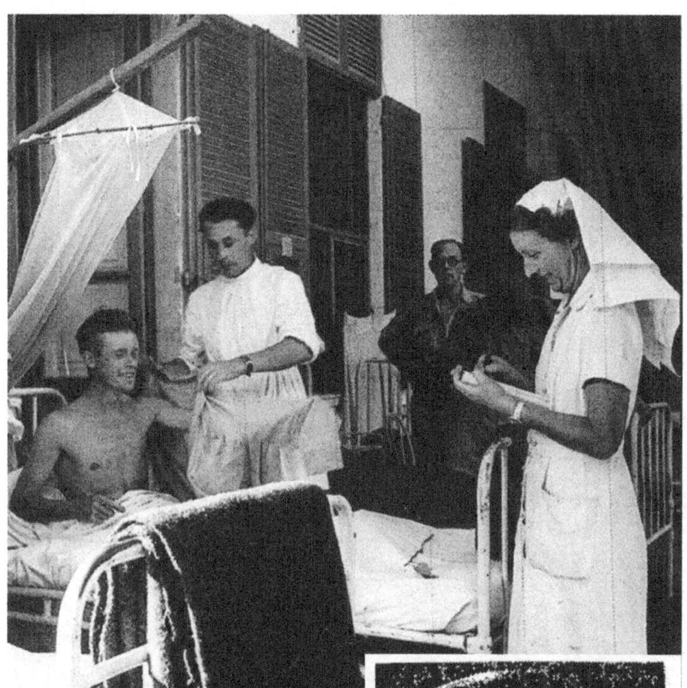

In September 1945, the 69th Indian Base General Hospital took over running the hospital under CO Col Paddy Stokes. His predecessor Col Joseph Craven (right) was reported as returning home after the war.

LT.-COL. J. W. CRAVEN, medical superintendent of the Auckland Hospital, who was a passenger in the Sydney-Auckland plane this

The headstone of Cpl Robert 'Bob' Veitch of the Federated Malay States Volunteer Force. The 28-year-old was a mining engineer in Malaya, and injured in the foot after a bomb blast in his armoured car. He was on the operating theatre table when the third wave attacked.

**

Over in the Philippines the US Army had arrested Yamashita, the much-fabled 'Tiger of Malaya', after he surrendered himself on 3 September 1945. Yamashita's trial by the Americans was fast-tracked to start on October 29.

Knowing how central he was to the British cases, it was decided that they should interview him post-haste, otherwise it might be too late and he might take secrets to the grave, if indeed that is where he was imminently headed. Lord Louis Mountbatten himself underlined the importance of this instant access by sending an urgent telegram to the Commander of Armed Forces, Western Pacific, one Lt Gen Wilhelm Styer.

Wild's 'special knowledge of the case' (whatever that was) was noted, yet Mountbatten was diplomatic enough to request the interview be 'at such a time and such a manner as not to interfere with the trial.'

That interview nearly didn't happen because, when he arrived, much squabbling was put forward by Yamashita's American defence counsel, George Guy. That Wild was not a trained lawyer perturbed many, and put noses out of joint. Who the hell did this interloper think he was? By what right?

Finally, he was granted one precious hour with Yamashita, and started by reminding him they'd met across the table at the surrender of Singapore. An hour was scarcely enough time to go into any detail of one let alone the nine atrocities on his list simply titled: 'Atrocities Committed in Malaya and on Singapore Island During Action 1942.'

The fourth item on the list was 'Alexandra Hosp.'

a/ Murder of MDs, orderlies and wounded inside hospital on occupation by the Jap forces.

b/ Murder of large number of MDs, orderlies and wounded taken from hospital as prisoners. (Total approx. 20 MDs, 80 orderlies and 100 wounded.)

'Yamashita disclaimed all previous knowledge of each of these atrocities, as I recounted them in detail,' said Wild. He had been warned as much. 'He took notes, including the names of some witnesses. He did not question any of the evidence. On several occasions he condemned perpetrators in fairly strong terms.' Such as with The Alexandra Massacres.

But there was something about his temperament that made Wild feel that possibly, just *possibly*, Yamashita was as ignorant of the actions of his underlings as he made out. 'Yamashita gave the impression of speaking the truth when he disclaimed previous knowledge of these Malayan atrocities.'

It was a pattern that Yamashita would carry forward unsuccessfully into his trial.

After his hour was up, Wild typed up his report and lodged it with Allied Land Forces Southeast Asia. The signals between Singapore and London indicated the interrogation as 'exceeding expectations'. One of his key action points was a request that the Americans arrest Mutaguchi. He was hoping to get Yamashita to request Mutaguchi's co-operation in writing, but time – and Yamashita's defence counsel – was against him and this didn't happen.

Wild filed three reports to HQ in Singapore based on that hour's discussion. Curiously, he also sent copies of these reports to his family members in the UK. Whether these were intended for the attention of his brother, Reverend John (who'd meantime become the chief historian of the USAF) is not known.

Wild also created the first of his 'most wanted' lists, with all ordered to be arrested immediately. Col Sugita Ichiji was #2 for his possible role in the Singapore *Sook Ching* civilian massacres. They had met previously – Sugita had led the British surrender party to the Ford Factory.

'Sugita was an intelligence officer, and by this time a full colonel,' said Miyazaki Mamoru, who was now assisting the British Field Security Service (yes, the same man who'd been arrested on espionage charges by the British, shared a cell with Loveday, had been Advisor to IJA Defence HQ during the Occupation, been a 'Japanese Oskar Schindler' during the Chinese civilian clean-up, and finally the British had welcomed him aboard their team after the Japanese surrender.

'Col Sugita was the only staff officer attached to 25th Army HQ left,' explained Miyazaki. 'Tsuji had disappeared, Hayashi killed in an air crash, Asayeda died in action.'

**

Tsuji was readying to escape because he felt he would be on the British 'most wanted' list. He made contact with intelligence agents in Chunking, China, sure that the Nationalists would want his strategic expertise against the Communists. They did. Tsuji disappeared from Bangkok, slinking surreptitiously out of the Japanese HQ building in Buddhist robes in September 1945. He headed for Nanking where he was afforded protection by Chiang Kai Shek's Chinese Nationalists for four years.

Another who was serving in China at the time of surrender was Ito, who'd led his battalion alongside The Alex Hospital at the time of attack.

**

Tom Smiley boarded the Holland America liner *SS Nieuw Amsterdam* in September and set sail with a full load of PoWs returning to England.

'My Darling Sweetheart, Here I am on my way to you at last! We have been at sea for two days – two days of tense excitement and novelty – good food, good living conditions, clean sheets, clean clothes and a good toothbrush. It is almost unbelievable for us all after so long and so much suffering but not nearly so difficult to appreciate the fact that soon I shall have you in my arms! Oh my darling Beth – so many times I have dreamed of it.

'What a wonderful girl you have been darling being so good, faithful and comforting. I shall never be able to tell you just what a comfort and anchor your love has been to me during this interminable separation, soon now to end ...

'I'm afraid, I've seen the very best and the very worst of mankind during my time of captivity. I've seen great acts of kindness and then at times I've seen complete disregard for human suffering. Many of the poor prisoners who survived the railway were barely alive and yet there were people, often officers, who were only out to look after themselves with no concern for their fellow men.

'We have a lot of internees including some women. Some of these poor creatures have taken their incarceration much worse than me and look very old, tired and unwell, especially the women. As for my plans, well dearest it is very difficult to say until I see you, but one thing for certain is that I'm going to take my FRCS and become a practising surgeon. Col Taylor thinks very highly of me (I'm still frightfully modest!) – and I think he will be a great help.'

After a few more days' sailing, he penned an update:

'Hullo my Darling, the only definite thing I can tell you about arrangements is that we arrive at Liverpool on the 16/10 at approx 8am. The next time you hear me dear, will be when I'm really near to you. Oh blessed thought – how I love you. At last we will be TOGETHER for the rest of our lives.'

Capt Elizabeth Mills, RAMC, was indeed waiting at the Liverpool Docks, five and a half years since she had farewelled her Tom at the Belfast docks. She too had been amidst the horrors of war, based in London, and lost dear friends, but her love had stayed strong. Despite family reservations, Smiley and Elizabeth married within two weeks of the boat docking, with his 'surgical twin', Capt John Falk, his best man.

**

After five weeks of Yamashita sitting in full regalia on a single chair on a tiny podium backed by map enlargements, and cramped by prosecutors, defence, translators and stenographers, the stubby-fingered general's trial wrapped on 7 December. His case hinged on culpability and accountability. The khaki-clad American prosecution argued that Yamashita must have 'willfully permitted ' or 'secretly ordered' the widespread atrocities of his army. His defence did not hold. It was deemed that an officer of his commanding rank 'must have known about them, or if he did not know of them he should have known of them.' This became a precedent in legal circles, known as 'The Yamashita Standard of Strict Liability.'

Guilty, and sentenced to die by hanging. The British were wildly optimistic that the Americans would delay the execution because Yamashita might be useful in witness trials for Malayan war crimes. But the sooner the 'Tiger of Malaya' swung, the better the American PR machine would play.

The arrest of Mutaguchi would happen on 12 December 1945, albeit with none of the drama of Tojo who had shot himself (though not fatally) as the arresting officers moved in. Other officers in the prison had items removed with which they might commit *hari kiri*. It is noteworthy that of the officers who preached *bushido*-ism fervently, precisely *none* followed their own entreaties of death before dishonour.

Mutaguchi was checked into Sugamo at 2:20pm that chilly afternoon, the temperature hovering about the six degree Celsius mark. Would Mutaguchi be held to the same standard as a commanding officer? The ALFSEA prosecution was not united on the 'strict liability' angle.

Wild was completely exhausted, and returned home to Oxford for Christmas, thankful for the first time he'd had with Celia and his siblings in five long eventful years.

**

Meanwhile, statements and evidence were being proferred by those wanting to vent their experiences or exact revenge, and hunted down from those who might have something valuable to share and contribute to a prosecution.

The Alexandra Hospital's Official War Diary, signed off by Percival, stated as follows: 'It is difficult to understand the reason for this barbaric attack on this hospital and investigations were carried out to discover a possible explanation. Rumour has it that the Indians caused it. But enquiries revealed that five or six Indian Sappers and Miners digging a tunnel at the rear of the hospital had presumably made a run for it when the Japanese advanced, and passed through the building.'

Christmas over, QMS Edward Lunt made a statement in Lancaster. 'All round the ground floor of the hospital there was a blast wall and I do not think it was possible that any firing could have gone on from the ground floor, and the Japanese did not go upstairs until 15 Feb when they went to loot extensively.

'I do not think that any firing could have gone on from the hospital, as I have never heard it mentioned by anyone who was in the hospital at the time. So far as as I know the troops in the neighbourhood were the Loyal Regiment, the Bedfordshire and Hertfordshire Regt, and some Ordnance Depot Staff.

'The only Indians, other than patients, attached to the hospital were about six or eight Sappers and Miners who had been engaged during the previous months in making an underground emergency operating theatre. They were unarmed.

'I had however been confined to the hospital for several days and knew very little of what was going on outside.'

The last one is a valid point. Many patients were bed-ridden with no view or perspective beyond the nearest wall, and we must be meticulous in weeding out hearsay and conjecture.

On this point, Capt Brown – of the Punjabs himself – added: 'I heard later on some soldiers had come up onto the balcony of the floor where I was, but I never saw them, and they fired from there. The Japanese said they didn't know it was a hospital as they were being fired on and they came into the hospital.'

Ironically, it could've have been men from his very own regiment or battalion, whose discipline and formations had collapsed in the face of the onslaught. 'Once I got to the Alexandra I had no word of the unit – had not the slightest idea where my own battalion was – until ... we just heard they'd been sent down to Changi.'

But more than likely the retreating Indians were not the 6/1 Punjabs, at least not en masse, because 'as I learned later on they were at Buona Vista when the surrender came, in Duff Cooper's house, so when they left the house they took some very good silver with them,' he laughed. Duff Cooper was the Minister Resident who'd formed the War Cabinet there. 'So we had very good cutlery for a time anyway.'

Speaking of cutlery, Brown was on the end of a bayonet threat in the hospital when they took his Rolex: 'I can still feel that bayonet pushing into my throat,' he said many decades later.

A couple of weeks later, Capt Richard Waller – a survivor of the outhouse incident – followed suit. 'My conjecture is that the Japanese carried out a massacre of the prisoners because they were angry about the noise in the huts during the night, and were inflamed by the whisky which had been carried away from the Sisters' Mess.'

On 4 February 1946, Sydney Hoskins alerted authorities to the fact that he survived the massacre. The War Crimes office keenly took his statement and forwarded a minute sheet to ALFSEA in Singapore, which listed British prisoners of war taken out of the hospital 'who were believed to have been massacred':

He listed only Bryer, Johnson and Gurd as fellow survivors.

'We have not yet been able to trace any witnesses who can state that he saw these people being killed, the two survivors so far interviewed merely state that they never saw any of these men again and that the common belief at the hospital was that they had been massacred,' read the minute sheet.

'Pte Hoskins tells me that the wives of several British PoWs have enquired during last week as to the fate of their husbands and that he has so far expressed no opinion.' Sydney Hoskins, then 28, would marry Pat the following year and they honeymooned on the Isle of Wight. 'They lived in very modest housing, lived a very simple life, with occasional caravanning holidays,' his grand-daughter Lauren Lloyd would tell me. 'They had the most beautiful relationship and marriage. Not so much passionate, just a very respectful and amicable partnership.'

Four years to the day since the hospital was over-run, Cpl George Johnson was having having to relive the horrors of the Sisters' Quarters incident in making his own sworn statement in the County of York. 'I was told by Col Craven that there was a rumour that Indian troops had fired on the Japanese from the verandah of the hospital, but he himself said he had no grounds for believing it, and I know of nothing to suggest that it was true.'

Craven, we should bear in mind, was holed up upstairs for the duration of the initial invasions.

Bert Gurd made a sworn statement in Westminster, on 21 February 1946, one week after his 40th birthday.

**

Among the towering Corinthian columns of the Supreme Court, Singapore, the first British War Crimes trials started on 21 January 1946, less than four months since it had been used to stage the Japanese surrender ceremony.

News cameramen, reporters from Allied countries, Allied observers, and members of the public jostled each other for better vantage points to catch a glimpse of the 10 Japanese prisoners – each with a number from 1 to 10 pinned to their plain khaki shirts – as they were marched into court under armed guard.

They bowed and entered the dock, awaiting the arrival of the three British military judges who would decide their fate 'in accordance with the principles of British justice.'

In terms of context, these military courts could pass a sentence of anything from a fine, or imprisonment, upto and including a death sentence.

The 1945 Royal Warrant Courts were run on a common law adversarial process, with the prisoners allowed to have defence counsel from Japanese or British legal advisors. But the trials and processes were not as rigorous nor as formal as one might expect in, say, the case of a court martial.

ALFSEA Instruction No 1 said it all, emphasizing the 'summary nature of trials,' and exhorting that 'justice be administered promptly and efficiently.' Expediting the case was to take priority over a formal approach to witnesses and evidence. If calling a witness meant postponement of a trial, the judge often denied it.

In other words: *Get on with it*! The shortest trial lasted one day; the average six days; the longest 31 days.

Regulation 8 (ii) of the Royal Warrant was pivotal. It leant heavily towards employing the concept of organizational membership. Meaning, if you were a member of a body of men, such as a platoon, if evidence against one member could be found, this was *prima facie* evidence of the responsibility, complicity, and participation of all platoon members in that crime.

Most Japanese used the 'superior orders' defence ploy, meaning: within the hierarchy of the Japanese Army I was ordered to do it, which is to be carried out absolutely. As recently as 1929, the British Manual of Military Law recognized this defence, although it was not formally a source of law and a subsequent tweak to the manual in 1944 meant that it did not automatically confer immunity.

130 trials – involving over 400 accused – would follow in Singapore over the next 26 months. Most of these would be of low military rank: sergeants were the most prosecuted ranks, then lieutenants and captains. One fifth would be for crimes committed in Singapore, while nearly one third would be for crimes committed in Thailand and Burma.

89 percent would be found guilty. Not good odds if you were accused. But there were grumblings that British courts were overly vindicative judging by the ratio of 'sentenced to hang' verdicts they were getting. The military argued it was down to better preparation and evidence. But in reality, cases that wouldn't return a death sentence, or at least a seven-year jail term, were not vigorously pursued and often thrown out.

**

By February 1946 Wild was well-rested and ready to return to the fray, perhaps buoyed by his negotiated promotion to colonel (to be on a rank par with his US counterparts), plus an official title that befitted his work: War Crimes Liaison Officer Malaya and Singapore. He'd also successfully negotiated that Celia join him on this tour of duty in the chaos of post-war Singapore, which had been under the administration of the British Military Administration (BMA) for the past five months. The BMA, nicknamed the 'Black Market Administration' by some for its corrupt practices, was due to hand control back to the British government the following month.

They enjoyed the six-day Sunderland flying boat journey back to the Far East, and ensconced themselves as residents at the Raffles Hotel. Almost simultaneously the news came through that Yamashita had hanged.

**

From this point on, there were endless internal and external correspondences as the grieved and berieved tried to make sense of the losses that were now confirmed by returning friends and members of their relatives' regiments.

One example was Conrad Hayes who wrote upon hearing of his dentist brother Lloyd Hayes' death and burial in the hospital grounds from Willard. He wanted to know if he could arrange a suitable headstone to be erected. It was nearly three months before the wheels turned on this incident sufficiently to warrant a response: 'All graves in the Alexandra Hospital area will be concentrated in the Kranji Military Cemetery shortly,' said the note. 'They will in due course receive IWGC headstones.

Brig Stringer had typed up his atrocity report in Hoten Camp, Mukden, Manchukuo in August 1945 based on information from his campmates there, Pte Luniffe and Pte Benjamin Seals, both RAMC, plus a private of the Loyals Regt, who were in The Alex at the time of the attack. On 25 February 1946, at Westminster, he added an 'Exhibit A' to it:

'Total hospital staff murdered by Japanese: Officers = 14, Other ranks = 81. The rest of the party [of prisoners taken to the Sisters' Mess] were butchered and are believed to be buried in a long trench at the back of the hospital where excavation should reveal their remains.'

In 1946, all known graves were exhumed from around the hospital and re-buried in the war cemetery at Kranji. Hayes was subsequently buried in the Singapore Memorial section of the Kranji War Cemetery for those whose bodies were never recovered. One wonders how Willard might have located his body specifically, given that Hayes was in the Sisters' Quarters outhouse incident, which were technically not in the hospital grounds, but over the road. Was it a fanciful construct to appease Hayes' family which then took on a life of its own? Or had he, as a final act of mercy, separated out his friend's body from the mass grave trenches, and given him a final bit of dignity?

**

In 2020, an archeological dig was arranged, ahead of an extension of the hospital's footprint. 'The open area behind the main buildings is thought to conceal the remains of about 200 victims,' reported the Livescience website. Tan DinXiang, the strategic communications manager for the hospital added: 'We identified two areas of interest. One being the football field, and the other encompasses a patch of land behind Elizabeth House (Block 19). We're still making sense of the data collected and in due time ISEAS will report their findings to us and the National Hospital Board.'

As a very interesting aside, a paranormal group in Singapore, writing under the moniker GlobalSoundis, studied the area a few years back and reported 'paranormal activity extra at secondary forest site of oil tanks, more even than in the hospital.' They posed the question: Why is a huge expanse of forested land undeveloped more than 80 years after the war in land-scarce Singapore? Perhaps George Poole's macabre observation of outhouse inmates being walked into the blazing tank fires was the awkward truth after all.

**

Toward the end of February 1946, Capt Tom Smiley, then just 28, made his statement under oath in Northern Ireland.

'I am totally unable to give any information regarding the names and description of the Japanese Army Unit responsible for the atrocities. I saw no Indian troops but the conduct of the Indian troops who, I understand were near the hospital, was to my knowledge investigated by a Brigadier of the Royal Engineers. I was informed by one of the patients who had his leg amputated that he had seen Indian soldiers running into the hospital on 14th Feb and that they were not carrying arms.'

**

Meanwhile March 1946 saw the start of the Hong Kong War Crimes trials. Lt Gen Tanaka Hisokazu, former governor of Hong Kong, had fled to Tokyo, and was later shot by firing squad in Canton. On the eve of his execution he grumbled: 'We'll see who is calling the shots in East Asia in ten years time.'

Col Tanaka Ryozaburo, commander of 229th Regiment, was charged with war crimes, including the St Stephen's hospital incident, and other incidents such as that of the Bangka Island nurses. He was found guilty and sentenced to just 20 years even though the court was satisfied 'the whole route of this man's battalion was littered with the corpses of murdered men who'd been bayonetted and shot.'

Capt Masaru Orita gave himself up at the end of hostilities, and was held by the Russians as a PoW before he was arrested and transferred to Sugamo Prison, Tokyo, awaiting trial on his involvement in St Stephen's and Bangka Island. He committed suicide days before his matters came to court.

**

Back in the UK, on 8 April 1946, Edward Lunt added to his affidavit he'd made in January about the divisional commander: 'I have been shown two photographs and ... I recognize these as being photographs of the said divisional commander who arrived at the Alexandra Hospital on 16 Feb 1942 and who apologized for what had happened.'

Within four days a 'CONFIDENTIAL' letter from office of The Judge Advocate General, London was forwarded to ALFSEA.

'Mr Lunt recognizes Mutaguchi as the person to whom he refers in his previous affidavit. Captain R de W Waller was not certain that the photographs were of the officer who he saw at Alexandra Hospital just after the massacre.'

The evidence was beginning to pile up. Wild and team laboured tirelessly around the clock. An Evidence Sheet, written probably by Maj MGA Watson, in spidery fountain pen, read as follows:

<u>*Evidence:*</u>
Craven – good, and identifies Mutaguchi. Where is his other statement?
Lunt – first class and identifies Mutaguchi.
Smiley
Hoskins
Warrene Waller
Bryer
Dickinson
Gurd
Stringer
Johnson
Bull
'Good stuff' had been scribbled as a general comment near the top of the page.

Despite this, Col Frederick Kerin of Legal Staff – a long-standing member of the British Indian Army, and experienced Judge Advocate – penned a note on 17 April to Col Wild re the Alexandra case:

1. In my opinion there is no evidence in this case which will enable proceedings to be taken.
2. It is clear from affidavit evidence that Japanese troops forced an entry into the hospital on 14 Feb 1942 and that patients and hospital staff were indiscriminately massacred; then during the same day a number of patients and hospital staff were led away to an adjoining bungalow and that at about mid-day on 15 Feb a large proportion of these were taken away in pairs and bayonetted to death. There is no evidence by any person who saw death inflicted on 15 Feb but there is evidence on affidavit to show that these persons were in fact massacred.
3. The case falls to the ground however as there is no evidence identifying the criminals.
4. It is said there is presumptive evidence of responsibility against the Japanese Comd 18 Div. As the facts stand at the

moment there is nothing to support this. There is evidence to show that Indian troops were firing from the hospital buildings which at the material times lay between the lines of the opposing forces. The massacres were committed in the heat of battle and I do not see how responsibility can be attached to a senior officer who was not present unless it can be shown that he had some cognizance of what took place.

5. Stress is laid on the fact that Senior Japanese officers, variously described as GOC Singapore – presumably Comd 18 Japanese Div – and as the Jap equivalent of DDMS – inspected the hospital on the evening of 16 Feb 1942, that there were dead bodies lying about, victims of the massacre, and that he expressed regret at the sufferings of those in the hospital. The result of his visit was that Japanese guards were put in the hospital and looting ceased.

6. Photographs of the Comd 18 Div have been forwarded to War Officer for identification but unless witnesses can connect this officer more closely with crimes committed in the heat of battle, particularly in the light of evidence that most unfortunately firing came from the hospital directed at the Japanese forces, I do not see that a case can be made against him. Of the identity of the actual perpetrators there is no evidence.'

Signed: FCA Kerin, Col Legal Staff, for Allied Land Forces, SEA.

One might imagine the frustration that Wild might have felt on receiving this missive punching large holes below the waterline of his accusations. It took him over three weeks to get around to composing and delivering his retort:

This is a case which should not have been passed to your department until investigation was complete.

I entirely agree that in its present uncompleted form it falls to the ground, as we have neither arrested nor even identified any of the criminals.

I shall be grateful, therefore, if you will return the file to me, and I shall not return it unless I have made of it a case fit to go before the war crimes court.

I give below an outline of past and proposed investigations:

a/ in October 45 I narrated the story of this massacre to Gen Yamashita at Manila. Remarking 'the fools to have done this brutal and senseless thing,' he urged me to interrogate Lt Gen Mutaguchi, GOC (Jap) 18 Div, to find out from him the names of subordinate officers responsible.

b/Yamashita himself said that whether it was Lt Gen Mutaguchi or a senior officer of his staff who inspected the hospital on the day following the massacre, Mutaguchi must *have been informed of it.*

c/ If any of your witnesses in England or New Zealand can positively identify Mutaguchi's photographs as that of the inspecting officer I shall be on even stronger ground.

d/ But even without (c) I shall have an excellent starting point in (a) and (b) for my interrogation of Mutaguchi, and I have little doubt that his replies will carry this investigation a long way further.

Even should the case not come to trial, I still feel most strongly that I should continue enquiries, in order at least to demand good explanation from the Japanese for the killing of 20 medical officers, 60 medical orderlies and 150 wounded men (figures from memory), most of them in cold blood on the day after_*the over-running of the hospital.*

Wonderful English understatement. Let's back up to point (c). Lunt had identified him as early as 12 April in the 'Confidential' letter on this sent to DJAG, HQ, ALFSEA, nearly one month earlier. Had this not been brought to Wild's attention yet? If not, why not?

**

Meanwhile, the International Military Tribunal for the Far East (IMFTE), also known as Tokyo War Crimes Trial, began 3 May 1946 and would continue until 1948. The capacious and curtained War Ministry Hall in Tokyo was decorated with flags of all the countries signatory to the surrender, adding a somewhat festive atmosphere, yet helmeted MPs stood ready to quell any attempt of escape or violent overspill.

Proceedings covered the Nanking Massacre, Japanese medical experiments on captives, the Bataan Death March, the Thai-

Burma Death Railway, and countless other episodes, eagerly listened into by all attendees with headphones such that they could hear the translation. Often, people removed them, not being able to bear anymore the horrific and graphic descriptions of the alleged crimes.

**

Back in Singapore, the case-load was at peak frenzy. Eight court locations were in use (plus one each in Kuala Lumpur, Rangoon, Hong Kong and Borneo). Not all were as grand as the Supreme Court. One was a tent set up in the grounds of the Goodwood, while six pre-fab hutments had been set up around Changi Gaol. The tropical heat was somewhat abated by use of Japanese prisoners serving as *punkahs*, pulling on ropes which swished the fans around.

But the terrier work continued apace, despite the heat, despite the delays to travel schedules caused by monsoons, and despite the overflowing inboxes. The co-ordinating secretary had sent out a note: 'What news of the arrival of Mutaguchi and the other two Div Comds?' Scrawled in the margin: 'Col Wild told 10/5/46'. Another note read: 'AAG. I have asked SACSEA to send another hastener to UKLIM re Mutaguchi. Col Wild informed 11/5.'

Cyril was anxious, agitated, frustrated. He wanted Mutaguchi badly. Interestingly, the sneaky Tsuji had only just appeared on the Allies' radar, and the British formally approached the Americans in Tokyo to help track him down. As far as the Japanese were concerned he was listed at their HQ as 'missing'.

On 23 May, Wild penned his most passionate letter yet to War Crimes Co-Ord, referencing their letter of a couple of days' prior.

Lt Gen Mutaguchi's photograph has now been positively identified by two witnesses.

I have therefore every confidence that I shall bring this case to a successful conclusion as soon as Mutaguchi is brought to Singapore.

I cannot emphasize too strongly that until Mutaguchi and the other two Div Comdrs are produced, not one case of the well-documented atrocities committed during action in Malaya in 1941-42, whether against British and Australian troops, or the civilian population, can be solved.

In addition to the two Alexandra files, WCI teams and I have anything up to 40 files of evidence, not one of which can be taken further until I can get at these three generals; and my successful interrogation of General Yamashita last October remains completely wasted, seven months later.

It will be a disgrace if we have to confess ourselves beaten in this most important and promising field of War Crimes in which so much work has already been expended, simply because we were incapable of transferring three generals from Allied-occupied territories to Singapore!

I shall be only too willing to take this up with SACSEA if you will let me see the previous correspondence.

Signed: Col Wild.

One can imagine this landing with a heavy thud when it was passed on to AAG on 25 May. And, pray tell, why was he not privy to the 'previous correspondence'?

Just three days later, Wild's poison pen was out again, this time to War Crimes Co-ord Sec, referring to their signal of the previous day.

Total British casualties were nearly 300, including approximately 20 MO's and 60 orderlies, the remainder being British wounded removed by the Japanese from their beds in the wards.

No further progress can be made in this case, or in about 40 other cases, comprising all known atrocities in 1941-42 committed during or immediately after action, against British and Australian troops and British-protected subjects, until SACSEA succeed in bringing to Singapore not only Lt Gen Mutaguchi (18 Div) but also Lt Gen Nishimura Takewa (Konoye Div) and Lt Gen Matsui Takura (5 Div), not necessarily as prospective war criminals, but as essential links in the chain of investigation.

Until this is done, all past work on this most important aspect of War Crimes is wasted: and we are limited to the investigation of atrocities committed during the occupation only.

Signed: Cyril Wild.

It was June before Lloyd Hayes' brother in Nigeria would receive a response, from Brig MB Dowse, to his enquiry:

Progress in bringing the perpetrators of these crimes to justice is as follows ... all necessary affidavits obtained. Perpetrators not yet been identified because no witness has been able to give any evidence at all on that point.

We have, however, just discovered the identity of the Senior Japanese officer who came to the hospital the next day. He is now in Japan but we are in process of finding out from him the names of the Japanese responsible. Steps will then be taken to bring them to Singapore for trial. Investigations in cases of this sort are difficult and take time. Hundreds of suspects will have to be photographed and their photographs then sent to the United Kingdom to be identified by our ex PW witnesses before the case can be completed.

It is being pursued, however, with utmost zeal.

**

After all those years in the balmy tropics, one wonders how Col Joseph Craven felt back in the nine-degree Celsius June mornings in Auckland, where he had resumed his pre-war position of Medical Superintendent of the Auckland Public Hospital. On 12 June he made sworn statement:

'I have been shown a photograph by Det Jones and I identified it as being Lt Gen Renya Mutaguchi who was the Japanese General Officer Commanding referred to in my report which I made in May 1942.'

Craven was forced to make this statement by the detective. It was not voluntary. Craven had undergone a change, as many did, upon release. Or even before then. He certainly appeared to want to distance himself from all these nasty events. Hardly surprising. But digging deeper, one could possibly surmise that perhaps reflecting on his performance as CO, he knew or now felt that enough reasons had been given on his watch to justify the Japanese attack of the hospital as a legitimate target. Witness: allowing ack-ack guns to be placed and operated from within in the grounds, not enough effort had been made to ensure troops did not withdraw through the grounds and use the hospital as cover, weapons stockpiled in the reception area, and so on.

Added together, this could be seen to justify or at least significantly mitigate the Japanese attack. Hence his generally evasive 'No more to add' nature and posture. He would resign from the Auckland Hospital for health reasons in 1949, aged 60, and move down to Rotorua.

Still, he'd now finally added the positive identification Wild and team wanted and needed so badly to place Mutaguchi at the scene of the crime.

THE SUGAMO SHOWDOWN

'This horrible and senseless thing.'

9 September 1946. Three figures gathered awkwardly in a central interrogation room in the drab tan-concrete confines of Sugamo Prison. It was a crisp autumn Tokyo day, around 23 degrees.

The 50-year-old utilitarian building had emerged amazingly unscathed from the intense incendiary bombing which reduced the surrounding northwestern suburbs to cinders and ash. So the fences of the outer compound were just as much to keep the inmates – including notables such as Gen Tojo Hideki and Iva 'Tokyo Rose' Toguri – in, as to keep the hungry foraging locals out. No chances were being taken, with the 10-foot 14-strand barbed wire deemed enough to consider it escape-proof. Just in case, the ratio of guards for its 1073 inmates was one to every three.

Two officers faced off. The trim, beak-nosed, smartly uniformed figure was Col Cyril Wild, war crimes liaison officer. The other was a prisoner brought down from Red East, Block 4, Tier A, Cell 17: Mutaguchi Renya, a vanquished yet proudly defiant *bushido* warrior, who cut a conceited but concerned figure in his plain khaki prisoner's tunic.

The entire discussion was conducted in Japanese, with Wild then translating the questions and answers to his assistant, Miss Constance Rolfe, a translator with the International Prosecution Section (British Division), who furiously scribbled her transcript of proceedings in shorthand into a notebook with a carbon copy.

The record started with the standard housekeeping questions of name and rank. Mutaguchi, just short of his 58th birthday, answered: 'Formerly lieutenant general.'

'What was your position during the Malayan Campaign?' asked Wild.

'I was in command of the 18th Division,' replied the seasoned combat veteran who entered the military academy the same year his interrogator was born, and is coming off eight years of see-sawing fighting fortunes which left his features of high forehead on a round head, bushy eyebrows and brush-like moustache, now looking beleaguered and gravity-affected. Gone were the avuncular crinkles around his eyes that once appeared readily in moments of humour.

The interrogation was very matter of fact. But Mutaguchi occasionally asked questions of Wild, trying to understand his own involvement and movements within the theatre, or perhaps trying to cultivate some engagement and curry some positive, favourable relationship. Wild politely and pithily answered, but then dived headlong into the next question he had lined up.

Wild was on an urgent mission, one which he approached with a terrier-like missionary zeal, perhaps not surprising given he was, after all, the son of a vicar. He was making it his life's work to bring war criminals to justice. He had solemnly promised fellow PoWs that he would 'pursue to the ends of the Earth' those Japanese responsible. Literally as though to impress the metaphor, the sleeves of his epaulletted army shirt were neatly rolled up above the elbow. With his nine years of living in Japan, plus time in captivity, he understood the Japanese psyche and could work it well.

Nearly one year later after his release, Wild had regained much of his prior weight, but still cut a rather gaunt figure with big eyes and sharp features, a military-issue pencil moustache, head topped by a foppish mop of dark brown hair. 'And the 18th Division under your command took part in the assault on the island?'

'Yes, on the west of the island,' replied Mutaguchi.

'So your division was on the Japanese right for this attack?'

'Yes.'

Wild was warming up now, probably literally, because Sugamo's ventilation systems were notoriously inadequate, zeroing in to the real core of that day's meeting. 'And in the final assault on the inner perimeter around Singapore, how were the divisions disposed?'

'On the Japanese left, the Konoye Division under Lt Gen Nishimura.' The Imperial Guards. 'In the centre the 5th Division under Lt Gen Matsui, and on the right (ie, the west of Singapore), the 18th Division under myself.'

'What was the divisional boundary?'

'My front was from the coast to a point west of the Bukit Timah Road,' he said, referring to the Malacca Straits and the central arterial road that runs north-south through the island.

One can imagine that Wild's pulse might have quickened as he came to his next pivotal question. 'Do you know Alexandra Hospital, the big hospital on the hill west of Singapore City?'

'Yes, I know it,' confirmed Mutaguchi.

'Do you know that the troops of 18th Division captured Alexandra Hospital?'

'Singapore had surrendered on 15 February 1942, before they entered.'

Wild didn't take a backward step: 'On the contrary, troops of the 18th Division entered Alexandra Hospital on 12 February 1942.'

'Is that so?' countered Mutaguchi.

Wrong date, Colonel Wild! The date was 14 February, but the fact remains it was *before* the capitulation.

'Early on 12 February, or on the evening before, our troops withdrew on the west of the city and left Alexandra Hospital in no-man's land. The hospital was therefore now in an undefended locality and the British line was a long way behind it.'

Perhaps Wild felt emotionally wound up now, because instead of asking another question, he charged into a lengthy overview of the massacres.

'The troops of the 18th Division entered the hospital and started shooting and bayonetting everyone in sight. In the operating theatre they bayonetted a patient on the operating table and the surgeon who was operating on him. They killed both these, and wounded another medical officer and a medical orderly. After killing a lot more medical personnel and wounded, they collected over 200 as prisoners from the hospital and took them half a mile away, where they locked them up in some very small rooms. The next day they took them and machine gunned or bayonetted all but five, who escaped and became prisoners of war. The total number murdered in this hospital was over 20 medical officers, over 60 medical orderlies, and over 200 wounded.'

Once again, Wild's numbers were wrong, unfortunately erring on the low side, but they are the facts he was playing with at that time.

Mutaguchi's response was telling. 'Are you sure it was the 18th Division?' is the best he could muster.

'Yes, I am.'

'Is that so? I never heard of it until today.'

'Well, last October I flew to Manila and told this story to Gen Yamashita. He told me that it must have been men of the 18th Division who did what he called "this horrible and senseless thing". He said that you must have heard of a massacre on such a scale as this, and he himself advised me to ask for your explanation of it.'

'I never heard of it until now. I am astonished to hear it.'

One thing Wild had noted with interest was that the long-tradition of personal loyalty to senior officers and subordinates in the Japanese military had quickly been shed out of self-interest and preservation. 'This is one of their most striking proofs of awareness of defeat,' he noted. This was generally making his work easier, but Mutaguchi was a stubborn subject.

'Yamashita himself said that, whether it was Lt Gen Mutaguchi or a senior officer of his staff who inspected on the day following the massacre, Mutaguchi *must* have been informed of it.'

So this was Wild's direct challenge. 'The senior officer, a major general or lieutenant general, went into the hospital the next day and told Col Craven that he was sorry about what had happened. In fact, he made some sort of apology and said, "Some of our men have no sense". He also said that Col Craven should regard his visit as an honour, as he was the representative of the Emperor of Japan. Was that you?'

'I never heard of it. I am surprised if Japanese soldiers did this.'

Clearly, with such stone-walling, it was game on. Just the sort of challenge Wild relished. 'The threat of putting [them] on trial as war criminals will probably make them talk,' he'd written earlier to colleagues. But he was up against a formidable foe here. Mutaguchi had embraced *bushido* culture more than most officers. He actually *loved* fighting. He'd earned a reputation for bravery in the line of fire. He'd personally put his sword through the body of many enemy. And he'd bullied to the point where he was more hated than loved by all he came across. But, make no mistake, he was respected. Which is how he made major general by the age of 30. What he didn't need was Wild's pesky meddling.

Wild figured he had gone as far as he could for the day, and he was due back in Singapore for two major trials starting imminently – those of his own F Force on the Thai-Burma Railway, and the Outram Road Gaol – for which there were 65 defendants, all of whom he'd personally arrested in Johor.

While Lt Gen Nishimura Takuma, commander of the Imperial Guards' Konoye Division, was in Wild's sights as one of his 'most wanted' suspects across the board, Mutaguchi's sketchy answers and mendacious manner just elevated him in Wild's mind.

He took the original top copy of the four-page interrogation transcription and slid it into his ubiquitous bulging leather briefcase, beside the sworn affidavits from Col Craven and QMS Edward Lunt who had both positively identified Mutaguchi as *that* visiting senior officer.

Mutaguchi was returned ignominiously to one of Sugamo's 700 cells, where the doors had been removed, with a guard posted outside each, to ensure no *hara kiri* suicidal acts were carried out.

Miss Rolfe kept her signed carbon copy separately, and they headed out of the arched gateway of Sugamo Prison, back to Wild's office overlooking the Imperial Palace from a medium-rise block in central Tokyo.

Within two weeks, one of these key figures would be dead. Yet another mystery within the greater puzzle of the Alexandra Hospital Massacres.

Sugamo Prison in the outskirts of Tokyo. Former Lt Gen Mutaguchi was held here, and interrogated by Col Cyril Wild in September 1946. Other inmates included Gen Tojo Hideki and propaganda queen 'Tokyo Rose'.

THE CASE THAT CRASH-LANDED

'Wild was then ordered to cancel any further work in this direction.'

September 1946. Wild's office was neatly stacked with much of his incriminating research and assiduously compiled papers, and 12-to-15-hour marathon days were not unusual for he and his team here.

There was much to do, such as helping his Tokyo team – headed by former Artillery man, Lt Col Nicholas Read-Collins, aided by Capt Richard Crewdson – examine Japanese documents. He also had discussions on improving interrogation techniques in the field and Singapore-Tokyo information sharing, which he promised to remedy on return. Plus, in the next couple of days, he would start giving trial testimony on the Singapore *'Sook Ching'* Chinese massacres, the Selarang Incident, Parit Sulong, and several other PoW camp atrocities.

It was becoming apparent that the common architect in most of these matters was Tsuji. He was at that stage implicated in the Chinese massacres and the Alexandra massacres. But he was still at large.

Wild was slotted into the Tokyo War Crimes Trials, out of order, because he was to urgently return to Singapore in the next few days to take on the commencement of two of his biggest trials: that of F Force horrors on the Railway, causing 1200 deaths under Lt Abe Horishi, and that of the outrages in Outram Road jail, where over 1000 deaths had occurred on the watch of Capt Koshiro Mikizawa.

In all, these War Crime testimonies at the War Ministry Building – in the same Tokyo neighborhood where he and Celia had enjoyed their spell together 10 years ago now – took him a week.

As expected, his horrific revelations were front-page news:

'Singapore Terror Described In Tokyo' blared the *Straits Times* on 12 September 1946.

'Col Cyril Wild, continuing his evidence before the War Crimes Tribunal today, described the massacre of patients by Japanese

soldiers, who ran berserk through the rooms of the Alexandra Military hospital at Singapore, bayonetting and shooting everything they saw.

Col Wild said they bayonetted and killed the patients on the operating table and the surgeon who was carrying out the operation. The Japanese slaughtered 20 medical officers, killed 60 medical orderlies and many patients. Two hundred others were wounded.

'The rooms and corridors were littered with the dead bodies of medical personnel and patients,' Wild said.

He added more than 100 patients were ordered from their beds and marched to small houses, one and a half miles from the hospital, where they were crowded into a few rooms so tightly that five died of suffocation during the night. Later, they were taken from the houses in parties of five and shot or bayonetted outside.'

Of course it should be noted that Wild was in the Battlebox command bunker at Fort Canning, nowhere near the hospital, so his 'testimony' was often second- or third-hand curation of evidence and witness reports. Primarily those from Bull (mixing up Smiley and Allardyce's fortunes), plus some others he'd spoken with in PoW camps. But he had begun to gather a bit of a super-star aura around his tireless work and his depositions were accepted by Sir William Webb who presided over proceedings.

**

Some say Wild was also summoned back to Singapore by MacArthur, because – with Wild's customary transparency – he'd just dropped a bombshell by declaring he had evidence directly linking Emperor Hirohito to a number of atrocities, including the Unit 731 Laboratory in Chunking, China, at which Japanese medicos and scientists had conducted unspeakable biological warfare experiments on Chinese prisoner and civilian inmates.

Of course, through the Japanese Prince's direct praise of the Nanking Massacre, there were fingerprints of royal complicity easily visible to the naked eye, to those who chose to see them. Additionally Hirohito himself was a trained scientist with published papers in academic journals, and had expressed interest as early as the 1920s in chemical and biological warfare. Further, Hirohito had bestowed a meritorious citation on the unit's leader, Maj Ishii Shiro, in 1939. The Emperor's own brother had visited the facility and been photographed outside its main gate.

Hirohito, to his credit, was willing to fall on his sword, face trial, and accept ultimate 'sole responsibility for every political and military decision made and action taken by my people in the conduct of the war.'

Such accountability is at the very heart of the Alexandra Massacres story. At which point up the hierarchy, does it or *should* it, stop? An infinitely huge debate in itself, but one seemingly settled by Yamashita's guilty verdict: The Yamashita Standard of Strict Liability. How neat and tidy that would have been. By accepting accountability and guilt, it would mean that all other accused and defendants would have, by definition, to be let off. No more War Crimes trials. Job done. Move on.

But Macarthur was not happy with this solution and outcome. Because in the post-war climate, the USA needed to side with Japan in order to take on the blustery Cold War foe of Communism. And killing their dear Emperor was not the way to the hearts of minds of the people. Entreaties had been made to the British Ministry of Defence to call off its attack dog, one Maj Cyril Wild.

He received a 'cease and desist' notice and was further instructed he'd be taking his orders from the commander of the occupation of Japan, Gen Douglas Macarthur. The conscientious Wild didn't think much of that idea.

Arthur Lane, a former bugler and campmate of Wild's on the Railway, was now manning the switchboard which carried all signals between Britain and the Far East. As such he was privy to otherwise confidential conversations. 'Wild was then ordered to cancel any further work in this direction and to hand over all the documentation he had so far accumulated.'

**

Wild was due back to Singapore, so he – together with Spencer Davies who'd also been involved in the Tokyo trials as part of the

Judge's Advocates Department – hopped aboard a flight to Hong Kong, because seats from Tokyo to Singapore were notoriously hard to come by, what with wanted criminals and witnesses like Sugita being rushed to Singapore at this time.

Seats from Hong Kong to Singapore turned out equally scarce, they found out. Wild and Davies dined at Victoria Barracks on the evening of 24 September with Col James Crossley, RA – a former PoW, too – and Jack Edwards, who were involved in the administration of War Crimes for Hong Kong, Taiwan, and Shanghai. As they enjoyed their after-dinner coffee in the buildings overlooking the Royal Naval Dockyard and the harbour, an orderly arrived.

'Urgent message, sir.' It was for Wild and Davies. Wild read with delight the note indicating they had seats on an RAF plane to Singapore leaving at 9:30 the very next morning. Wild was a trifle surprised because he'd made enquiries earlier that day and was told no flights were available the following day. But he would be glad to get back to his ever-patient wife Celia, awaiting faithfully for him in Singapore.

What Wild didn't know at that stage was that two civilians had been removed from the passenger list to make way for them.

September is typically the best time to be in Hong Kong, because the mid-Autumn festival is in full swing, the sea is warm for bathing, and while the weather is still humid, rain only falls less than once than every two days, averagely dropping about an inch of rain each time.

That's *typically*. But Wednesday 25 September 1946 dawned blustery. Wild might have noted the choppy waters whipped up on Victoria Harbour, and a typhoon warning was posted. Wild and Davies made their way to Kai Tak airport – which looked like an ugly scar carved into the foothills of Kowloon despite having been in situ for 20 years already – with clusters of medium-rise housing pressing right up to its very perimeter.

On the runway, against the grey-green hills, stood a grey-green Dakota with the markings of 110th Squadron RAF. Perhaps the more nervous passengers that day were feeling a bit grey-green themselves?

The plane had just been returned to service from repair, so – apart from pilots Warrant Officers Alistair Christie, 22, and Rex Blackmore, 24 – three more Flight Sergeants were on board: John Hazeldene (a pilot), John Holden (navigator), and Richard Bond (wireless operator). A total of five crew left room for 14 passengers, including a number of Royal Army Service Corps personnel, a Navy signaller, and an Artillery gunner.

Several representatives from the Yick Wah Trading company in Hong Kong, one with her son, and a lone American press reporter boarded with Wild, his bulging attaché case as ever by his side, for some in-flight reading and preparation. At 9:39am, Christie gunned the twin Pratt and Whitney Wasp engines of Dakota KN414. They thundered northwest up Runway 31, the twin propellors getting them airborne with a wobble caused by 25 knot crosswinds.

Up, over the apartments, 200 feet, up, there's the harbour, 500 feet, up to 700 feet then ...

BANG!!!

A flash was seen by two Chinese ground-crew workers. The Dakota yawed hard to port, leaning over, over, *over*, flames trailing, and speared into the rocky slopes between Lion Rock and Beacon Hill. Fire soon engulfed the crash scene, with all passengers and crew dead. Wild's original evidence reports and affidavits went up in smoke with it.

Air Commodore Webster rushed to the scene just over two miles from Kai Tak, but all was lost. About 20 feet from the charred debris was the only sign that this had been an aeroplane – a large chunk of wing. The wreckage smouldered for a couple of days.

Fortunately it missed the densely populated urban area of Kowloon Tong by about 500 yards, but it was still the colony's worst air tragedy in its history.

**

That evening at their adopted home, the Raffles Hotel, Celia Wild sat down to catch up on the news of the day. A headline caught her attention: **'AIR DISASTER: 19 KILLED IN DAKOTA CRASH AT KOWLOON.'** All those on board were listed. And that, tragically, is how she came to know of the fate of her diligent and dedicated husband, Cyril.

**

Webster promised an enquiry and it was duly conducted by RAF investigators, and the Air Accident Report tabled.

As to the pilots, Christie was relatively experienced for his age, with 489 hours flying time, of which 389 was on Dakotas. Blackmore was vastly more experienced with 1352 hours of which 427 was on Dakotas, and acting as screening captain on this flight: meaning, he was there to monitor Christie's performance.

It claimed the aircraft 'dropped out of control ... because the plane met turbulence from the foothills caused by a 20-30 degree crosswind of 15 to 25 knots as it became airborne.' It further claimed 'the pilot failed to realize the dangers of turbulence over the foothills and crashed in stall.'

The engines and the air-frame were rated 'E', meaning totally written off, but no specific statement on the condition of the engines was made.

Arthur Lane was not at all happy nor satisfied with these findings. Lane also found it odd that it burst into flames, or was indeed seen to have fire, before it impacted, as seen by the local Chinese witnesses. 'The only Dakota to have burst into flames after crashing during the whole of the Second World War and since,' he claimed, basing his claim on what the RAF accident investigation team had experienced.

Then he fired his own incendiary round: 'I believe the aircraft was sabotaged on the orders of the American security services,' said Lane. 'It is my opinion that a small bomb or inflammatory device was put on the plane.' He believed the motivating factor was the USA's desire to rid themselves of Wild's nuisance value. 'The real reason for the murder of Col Wild was not only to silence him, but also to destroy the evidence which he had accumulated.'

Everyone loves a good conspiracy theory. But was this justified? A number of experts weighed in on the possibilities and probabilities of this.

The Dakota is known by pilots to be a very forgiving craft to fly. But Kai Tak was a notoriously difficult airport to land and take-off on.

'Re-examined by today's Accident Bureau I am informed that a novice pilot could have maneuvered the crosswinds of less than 30 mph,' said Lane. Some pilots would say that those conditions would affect a loaded plane more in the moment of becoming airborne, than being aloft. Also, how could it stall – a term which implies zero airflow over the wings – given that there were known winds on the day?

Pilots talk deferentially of 'the clutching hand', the catastrophic turbulence phenomenon created in the lee of winds blowing over hills, such as can be found in Kowloon. But these were experienced pilots, who'd had a wind warning issued to prepare for such eventuality.

What might cause such a turning to port? Perhaps the plane commenced its turn and was caught by crosswinds, especially as it was operating at the peak strain of its performance envelope at that very moment.

But again Lane believed differently. 'If the aircraft was in a climbing turn to port for instance, and it suddenly lost the port engine, the power from the starboard engine would spin it into the ground. My suspicions are that a small explosive had been attached to one of the engines.'

Indeed, the OSS (a forerunner to the CIA) had been experimenting with altitude-triggered bombs, called anerometers, although typically these set off around 5000 feet. They were easily attached to an engine or a tail.

Kuo Min Tang Intelligence Chief Lt Gen Tai Li, known as the 'Himmler of China', had met a very similar fate only six months earlier, after he'd become seen as a liability to Chiang Kai Shek's operation. The KMT were very much in league with the US as their anti-Communist friends, and several once-insiders of the OSS have claimed most of these bombs were shipped to the China theatre and Tai Li's downing was their handiwork.

'I knew Wild and I know he would never depart leaving a mystery,' said Lane of his former campmate. 'From the beginning to the end, I believe that the British authorities have covered this incident up.' Alas, in this case, the mystery endures.

**

Upon hearing of Wild's sad demise, a close companion, fellow ex-PoW and war crimes investigator, Capt James Godwin, hastened to Wild's Tokyo office. Godwin was particularly interested in safeguarding the information and notes Wild had accumulated against Hirohito.

But the cupboard was bare. Someone had beaten him to it. Who and why?

**

Only one of Wild's original files ever resurfaced (that of Abe Horishi) and, one week later, Godwin – who had personal investment in this matter by virtue of being sunk by the Japanese, taken prisoner in Java, threatened with execution and beaten while kneeling on tacks, then transferred to labour in Japan – received a clear message: 'Cease all further investigations forthwith'.

Godwin, a 24-year old New Zealander, was a pilot in the Royal Fleet Air Arm had acquired a smattering of Japanese while in captivity, and post-war became a captain in the Australian Army. He was appointed an investigator with the Second Australian War Crimes Section in Tokyo in July 1947. He investigated a wide range of Japanese war crimes, including mass killings of prisoners of war, with a zealous passion similar to Wild's because he too had been on the receiving end of Japanese treatment, and hated the political 'whitewashing' of war crimes that was clearly afoot.

'At this time I also received a letter informing me that the cases I was involved in would cost too much money and therefore the matters had been taken out of circulation,' said Arthur Lane. 'Hundreds of Japanese being held pending trial for war crimes were released and given varying sums of money to enable them to return to Japan.'

**

But the untimely demise of Wild – shrouded now as it was then, in mystery and conspiracy – didn't completely derail his dedicated detective work from being brought into effect against those accused of War Crimes.

Just two days after Wild's death, Mutaguchi's transfer from Sugamo to Singapore was ordered. He left the prison just after darkness had fallen on 29 September. Suspects were shipped to Hong Kong and Singapore via troop ships such as the *Devonshire* or via P&O liners such as the *Strathnave*r, but higher-ranked officers were typically flown by military aircraft.

The next day, Wild's interpreter assistant, Constance Rolfe turned up with her carbon copy of their four-page interrogation of Mutaguchi. The Tall Man Who Never Sleeps would now be at rest eternally in the civilian Happy Valley Cemetery, Hong Kong. But it seemed he would continue to talk from beyond the grave.

A memorial service for Col Cyril Hugh Dalrymple Wild was staged at St George's Garrison Church, Tanglin – about one minute from Loveday's former stately bungalow, and adjacent the Tanglin Barracks Hospital where Smiley and 32 Coy RAMC had operated – on the afternoon of 3 October. The church itself had suffered minor damage from four bomb and shrapnel incidents in the fierce final fighting in that area, and was missing its famed ornamental stained-glass windows.

The torrential rain pouring down through *The Last Post* played by Cpl Mortimore of 1st Devons might have disguised some of Celia's many tears for her 38-year-old husband.

TRIAL AND ERRORS

'As soldiers receiving orders, they were no more human.'

September 1946. Through all of this, one man remained free: Col Tsuji. Tsuji was squarely in the frame on three charges: the genocidal Chinese '*Sook Ching*' Massacres, the Alexandra Hospital Massacres, and an internment camp case in Burma. But no-one had yet connected him with the execution and cannibalism of the pilot, Parker, in Burma.

But in Tokyo, an American, Col Carpenter had come to the British War Crimes Office to break the news: 'It appears our friend, Col Tsuji, has joined Gen Chiang Kai-shek in the fight against the Communists in China. In the circumstances, Gen Willoughby asks that the United Kingdom drops her efforts to trace this officer and, in addition, all plans to prosecute him.'

Capt Crewdson was gob-smacked. 'They can't do this!' stormed Read-Collins. Apparently they could. Within 24 hours Singapore had come back agreeing to the request.

**

6 November 1946. Maj MGA Watson, Commanding No 7 War Crimes Investigation Team, who had become the lead investigator on the Alexandra Massacres case, arrived at the much-storied Changi Prison. Watson had been accused by some, such as Lt Col Oishi of the Kempeitai, most ironically, for torturing and coercing confessions, including kicking some subjects. A stain on the English reputation for justice and fairness.

On Watson's to-do list that day was an interrogation of Mutaguchi who had arrived at Changi smartly uniformed with his cap unable to hide his still steely determined gaze. His statement was made under oath, before Watson, and translated:

'I wish to state voluntarily that – I did visit the Alexandra Hospital though I cannot be sure of the date. I think it was 16 Feb 1942.

My visit was one of goodwill and I took with me my chief of staff, my senior medical officer, and other medical officers. I discovered that the hospital was in good order and there did not appear to be any trouble. I never had the slightest knowledge of the bayonettings and massacre to which you refer.

I wish to add that I never found any necessity to apologize for anything to the patients in the hospital, on the other hand I did express in a polite Japanese way my regrets for any possible inconveniences which they may have experienced.'

How Cyril Wild would have loved to pick up on this change of tune.

The flip-flopping astonishment of 'Is that so? I never heard of it until today' which Mutaguchi told Wild in Sugamo just short of two months earlier, now to this admission of being *that* visiting officer.

'The above statement has been read over to me by an interpreter,' said Mutaguchi, 'and is a true and correct transcript of what I have said, to the whole of which statement I now append my signature.' Mutaguchi's signature was a clear, proud flourish in black fountain pen.

True and correct *to what he said*, perhaps, but was it true and correct *per se*? Also, it's not a full admission. On the contrary it is still full of apparent denials, such as the hospital being 'in good order.'

Compare this to Bull's statement that, 'He could not have avoided seeing the corpses of the British medical officers which were still lying in the corridors.'

Then there is the typical soft-soap language of the Japanese: 'Any possible inconveniences,' to summarily describe the massacre of over 200 humans. Other euphemistic phrases such as 'strictly punished' or 'disposed' or 'mopped up' all meant one thing to the Japanese: to be killed. Such generic phrases are typical of many Asian languages – which lack the endless nuanced shades of specificity that English language enjoys – and allow wiggle room for everyone involved.

But Watson was buoyed by this admission and spent the next few days summarizing his case against Mutaguchi. Victims were '200-300 persons of various nationalities, predominantly British.' It outlined the massacre, adding that, 'the hospital was clearly marked by Red Crosses. No resistance was made by the inmates.'

We now know that this last part is slightly erroneous or disingenuous, because some inmates indeed resisted, and the hospital in general could have been seen to be used to resist with fighting soldiers using its infrastructure as protection (which in itself can be construed as a war crime, according to international law specialist scholar, Tom Stanley-Davies).

As for Witnesses and Summary of Evidence: 'Lt Col Sugita Ichiji will state that 18th Div troops were advancing over the sector of the island which contains the hospital, that these troops reached the hospital area on 14 or 15 Feb 42 that he is aware, that shooting took place at the hospital at this time and that 18th Div troops were responsible.'

It pointed to the affidavits of Craven and Lunt stating they identify Mutaguchi from the photographs. It also pointed to the affidavits of Bryer, Smiley, Hoskins, Waller, Gurd, Johnson and Bull. The summary highlighted that Bull's affidavit 'mentions the visit of a high-ranking Jap MO who, he states, obviously saw the carnage surrounding him. Mutaguchi says in his statement that his senior medical officers accompanied him.'

Watson's summary continued: 'Col CH Stringer was DDMS Malaya Command and as a PoW recorded and collated reports of survivors from the hospital. He confirms that the hospital offered NO resistance and this is a strong point made in the majority of individual affidavits which are forwarded.'

Highlighted under the 'Accused Statements' are:

a/ Mutaguchi in his statement to Col Wild 'knew nothing about anything.'

b/ In his second statement he does admit his visit to the hospital with a senior staff officer and medical officers. He thinks this was on the 16th Feb.'

On 25 November, the original manuscript and typed translation of Mutaguchi's voluntary statement was forwarded to the War Crimes Legal Section. Maybe *this* time their case would find favour with prosecutors?

They would know in just over one week when a letter came back from HQ, South East Land Forces, addressed to the War Crimes Section and received by Watson's investigation team on 6 December 1946.

Subject: War Crimes: Alexandria [sic] Military hospital:

'Apart from the interrogation of Lt Gen Mutaguchi Renya which do not carry the case much further, there is really no additional evidence which would justify the trial of this Japanese officer in respect of the massacre at the above named hospital.

There is abundant evidence that shortly after 1430 hours on 14 February 1942 Japanese troops entered the hospital, which was then in 'No-man's Land' between the opposing forces, and killed several Medical Officers and patients. At the same time they rounded up about 200 of the staff and patients and brought them to a Company or Batallion headquarters. This party was then locked up in the godowns of the Sisters' mess and in another bungalow and left there all night under the most appalling conditions. On the following day, whilst hostilities were still continuing in the area this party was massacred with the exception of a few who escaped when the doors and the windows of the room in which they were confined were blown in by shell blast.

There is not a shadow of evidence to show that Lt Gen Mutaguchi was aware of this incident at the time or that as Divisional Commander he would be in such close touch with his forward troops that he could not be unaware of it. Furthermore even if he knew that the massacre had taken place would he be in a position to take any steps to investigate the matter at a time when the troops who had committed it were amongst the forward troops in the Battle for Singapore?

In my opinion it is not possible to hold that Mutaguchi had a general responsibility for an isolated transaction in which there is no evidence that he was an aider and abetter. When, in addition, there is evidence that on the very first occasion he inspected the hospital, ie on 16th February, he put guards on it, resulting in an immediate improvement in the situation the whole case against him falls to the ground.

I do not consider it necessary to examine at this stage the possibility of Indian troops having fired from the top story of the hospital. I am inclined to think that such was not the case. If however it is a fact it would merely go to show that the attack on the hospital was unpremeditated and without orders from Mutaguchi.

I have seen the report by Lt Col Craven referred to in his affidavit of 12 June 1946, several times, and am well aware of its contents.

In conclusion I have no alternative but to advise that the case against Lt General Mutaguchi be dropped.'

Signed: FCA Kerin, Col, Legal Staff, SEA Land Forces.

Had he been around to receive this news, it would have hit Wild in the guts with the approximate force of a lusty blow from a heavyweight boxer. All that work ... all that sleuthing ... all those colleagues to vindicate.

How could Kerin be so superficial in his treatment of the evidence: 'I am inclined to think' which dismisses the strength and veracity of many witnesses. The point is also that the guard was seemingly put around the hospital by Mutaguchi's medical officers, not by Mutaguchi himself.

But the Legal Staff and Investigations teams seem to be flying at very different altitudes, if not attitudes, on this case.

John Pritchard, PhD, editor of *Tokyo Major War Crimes Trial the Complete Transcripts of the Proceedings of the International Military Tribunal for the Far East,* generally considered this a consistent pre-ruling by Kerin. 'Courts scrupulously adhered to the principle that an accused must be freed unless he can be proved beyond a reasonable doubt to be guilty of a specific, individual (as opposed to collective) offense,' he said. 'Mere membership in a platoon which participated in systematic murder was not regarded as suffficent proof of a soldier's complicity for war crimes.'

We can assume much. There were plenty of smoking guns, so to speak, but where was the direct evidence, Mutaguchi's fingerprints? Watson was not deterred and ploughed on. If Mutaguchi couldn't be held responsible, then surely someone not far under him could.

Within a couple of weeks, just a few days before Christmas, Watson was back face-to-face with Mutaguchi. Knowing, or perhaps sensing, that he was near to being off the hook, Mutaguchi now started singing freely, pointing fingers at all those below him in his command structure. After all, The Alex was only one part of his possible woes. He was also a key person of interest in the '*Sook Ching*' massacres in which up to 50,000 Singapore Chinese – deemed to be anti-Japanese or persons of questionable repute by whatever subjective measure such as tattoos – had been systematically slaughtered.

He mapped out the command structure of his 18th Division IJA as it was in February 1942, and outlined the major movements and positions of same.

Col Koba, OC 55th Inf Regt, was believed to be stationed in Keijo, Korea. Maj Ito, who he had as 1/55th commander, was in fact 2nd Bn, and was known to have gone to Burma and later to have returned to Japan. Maj Koda, vice versa, he had down as 2/55th commander instead of 1st. As for 3rd Bn Commander ... incredibly, the name and details were not remembered by Mutaguchi. It was Maj Tsugawa Naoshi.

And then more detailed discussions on battalion movements around the hospital on the 14 and 15 February 1942:

'From discussions and unbiased diagrams of the campaign produced by Mutaguchi, there seems little doubt that the hospital fell into 55th Inf Regt's sector,' wrote Watson. 'It will be noted that 55 Inf Rgt's axis of advance was through trig points 156 and 150. The hospital will be seen to lie roughly between these two points.'

Mutaguchi sketched out a rough map of the movements.

'Mutaguchi does not guarantee that his diagram is 100% accurate. He recommends it be checked with particular reference to the hospital sector, with his Chief of Staff, Lt Gen Takeda Ju. He states Takeda would be able in any case to produce a more accurate diagram as he was directly in charge of operations at this stage.'

Note the subtle distancing of himself here by Mutaguchi, with the additional feigned altruism of 'Takeda can definitely be located through Lt Gen Nukada Tadashi of the Japanese Demobilization Centre.'

'It is worth bearing in mind that Col Noda was in charge of Medical Services in 18th Div,' said Watson. 'He visited the hospital with Mutaguchi, who does not know where he is now but thinks that Takeda will.'

May these [trace map of Singapore] be forwarded to UKLIN for interrogation of Lt Gen Takeda and subsequent apprehension of the individuals involved.'

Signed: Maj GWA Watson.

A check of the handwritten Operation Record of 55th Infantry Regiment written by their commander Koba 'makes no mention of Alexandra Hospital at all,' Japanese military historian, Hajime Marutani, told me.

**

March 1947 saw the start of another big trial in Singapore. 'The centre of attraction was the War Crime, held in Victoria Memorial Hall,' reported the Straits Times, of the venue where Bill Frankland had operated his makeshift General Hospital just five years earlier.

'Six Japanese including two generals will be brought before the war crimes tribunal at the Victoria Memorial hall on March 10 for events connected with the massacre of several thousand Chinese just after the Japanese capturing of Singapore,' reported the Straits Times on 2 March. This was the Sook Ching 'ethnic cleansing' massacre of the Chinese population.

'The accused are Lt Gen Nishimura (commander Imperial Guards), Lt Gen Kawamura (commander Kempeitai, Town Division), Lt Col Oishi (commander Kempeitai Military Police), Lt Col Yokata, Maj Onishi, and Capt Hisamatsu (all sector commanders under Oishi).' These lieutenant generals –being the second-highest rank achievable in Japanese wartime military – were the highest-ranking suspects to be tried in Singapore. Some sources include Mutaguchi and Mitsui (the other Lt Gen divisional commanders) as being accused here too but the balance of evidence seems not to have them in this court on these charges.

The first witness called was ironically the man who had been #2 on Wild's most wanted list, Col Sugita Ichiji. His neck still sported heavy bandaging from when he'd plunged a stainless steel knife into his own throat when housed at the Field Security Service building.

He was sharing a room with Mamoru Miyazaki, when Nishimura – the man he was to testify against – had arrived and was incredibly housed in the same building (something to do with the strength of the case evidence not enough to warrant sending him to Changi directly).

'It was very upsetting for Sugita,' said Miyazaki. 'He didn't eat anything for a few days, only thinking about the fate of the general.' One morning, two or three days later, Miyazaki awoke to find Sugita's bed empty and a note on his desk: 'I cannot stand to be a prosecution witness against my senior officer – it is better for me to die. Best regards to our British friends.'

'I looked around and there in the backyard I found him sitting facing the northeast. He had already cut his neck and there was so much blood. He was trying to cut himself more and more. I quickly sprang at him and took the knife from his hand. If it was a Japanese sword he would have been finished. He had cut his windpipe and a faint breathing sound "peep, peep, peep" was coming out. I quickly reported to the officer on duty, Sgt Phillip, and we got Sugita into a jeep and he was rushed to Alexandra Military Hospital.'

At the hospital, Phillip gave his blood for transfusion to Sugita, and they were told to wait three days for a condition report. 'Sugita was treated for a long time in Alexandra Military Hospital,' said Miyozaki.

So finally here he was now giving evidence. 'The feelings of the audience were very hot against the accused,' recalled Miyozaki, who was the second witness called. He saluted the accused.

Nishimura defended his actions vigorously as simply obeying orders. 'I have not for a moment thought of obeying or disobeying orders,' said the Lt Gen in a telling statement of the Japanese military mind. 'If supposing I disobeyed orders, I would be charged with insubordination and, being on a battlefield, I would be shot. To obey an order is, to the Japanese soldier, greater than life and this is the resolution held by we Japanese soldiers.'

'As individual friends, they were warm and friendly,' said Miyozaki of the accused Japanese officers, most of whom he knew well. 'But as soldiers receiving orders, their character changed, they were no more human, they became like cold machines who could kill easily with no feelings.'

Most telling of the predominant mindset inculcated by IJA's *Military Manual* came from Maj Ito Toichi: 'It was war, hostilities meant just that. Prisoners required guarding and tied down our soldiers in non-combatant duties. We did not consider the disposal of prisoners as murder. What the Allies thought was of no concern. We expected at first to win the war, but then as fortunes changed, we felt sure of an armistice and with it, not enquiries into how we waged war.'

Another statement, by the Japanese defence counselor Kurosei, sheds similar light on expectation when he quoted a proverb: 'The necessity of war overrules the manners of warfare.'

**

Investigations still went on in Japan, and the matter of The Alex was still in the frame. On 4 April 1947, Maj Gen Takeda Hisashi ('Ju'), Chief of Staff of Mutaguchi's 18th Division, made a sworn statement and the Alexandra incident was recounted to him at that point. 'I think that Mutaguchi's diagram is slightly incorrect in showing troops advancing east of the railway line,' he said. 'As far as I remember no troops of 18th Div advanced beyond the railway line.'

Clearly they did – many had already placed themselves *northeast* of the oil tanks in accounting for their actions, and the railway line itself was a handy marching route.

'I have never heard of Alexandra Hospital by name until now,' Takeda added, perhaps not surprising because it was all part of the Keppel military complex as far as they were concerned. 'Secondly, at time of operation I did not know there was a hospital in the location indicated on the map. It was only several days after the capitulation of Singapore that we began to discover what various buildings had previously been used for: which were barracks, which were hospitals, etc. The only place that stands clear in my memory is Keppel Barracks. I never visited any hospitals on Singapore Island.

'I have not until now, ever heard of the incident you have described and I find it very difficult to imagine that any of the troops of 18th Div could have been involved in such an act against patients and defenceless hospital staff,' he said, mimicking Mutaguchi's defence almost verbatim. '18th Division holds a good record in China, Malaya and Burma. However, as there seems to be no doubt that this act was committed within 18th Division's perimeter, I cannot state definitely that it was not committed by 18th Div troops.'

What he said next might have momentous weight in implicating the real villains: 'On or about 14 February there were several other units within the area occupied by our forward troops, mostly directly under command of HQ 25th Army. They included a mortar unit and a tank unit. The fighting on the 14th was extremely confused and that co-ordination of the movements of various units was not well in hand on account of the heavy British shelling and bad intercommunications.'

'HQ 25th Army' points again to that man Tsuji and his headquarters henchmen. As no survivors and witnesses mention tanks, we can discount the involvement of an HQ tank unit. But that brings the HQ Mortar units under Takeda and the Mountain Artillery battalion under Kusido into the cross-hairs. But let Takeda finish first ...

'The troops who committed this atrocity could have belonged either to 55th Regiment or to the battalion of 56th Regiment which by error had advanced with 55th Regiment on the morning, or to other troops directly under Army command. It seems improbable that troops of 114th Regiment or of the main force of 56th Regiment were involved, though on account of the confused nature of the fighting, it is not possible to state with certainty that some elements of these regiments were not in 55th Regiment's area also.'

A telegraph also went out from British Minor War Crimes Tokyo to South East Asia Land Forces: 'Takeda repeat Takeda COS 18th Div interrogated confirms Alexandra Hospital in 55th Regiment area. Endeavouring trace 55th Regt personalities and others.'

Those others included Suzuki and Noda. Col Suzuki was senior medical officer of HQ 18th Division and investigators felt he too may be able to give some valuable information. You may remember he visited the hospital with Mutaguchi. Following a stint in Burma he was transferred to Manchuria in April 1943 as Chief Department HQ Defence Army, and promoted to maj general in August 1944. They wanted to know what he knew.

Colonel Noda was OC 18th Division medical unit, and was in Kinshu (Manchuria) at the time of the Japanese surrender. Within a few weeks, in late May 1947, Col (now Maj Gen) Nasu Yoshio, former OC 56th Regiment who went on to serve under Mutaguchi in Burma as his deputy chief of staff, made a sworn statement:

'I have read of the massacre which took place at Alexandra hospital before the fall of Singapore in an article in the Japanese press. This article appeared in autumn 1946 and was a report of evidence submitted by the prosecution at the Major War Crimes Trial. This was the first I had ever heard of the massacres. At the time I wondered which hospital in Singapore was Alexandra Hospital, where it was situated, and what unit would most likely have been responsible. Now that you have shown me this hospital on the map, I realize that during the fighting I came very near to it myself and that my 1st Battalion probably passed in front of it and came nearest to it. I did see the hospital myself on two occasions. Once was on the 16th when I passed near it without knowing that it was a hospital, and once again about the 21st when I was on my way to take my leave of the divisional commander before flying to Burma.

'On this occasion I saw Europeans and Indian patients at the windows of the building and realized that the building must have been an evacuation centre or casualty post. During the fighting I did not know what the various buildings along our route were. I certainly did not know this was a hospital. I have never received any report of any of my troops or any other troops having committed such atrocities as you may have described. If there had been any such conduct in my regiment I think I would have heard of it.

'As our regiment was in second-line reserve that day, all our troops were concentrated and well in hand. I don't think any party even smaller than a platoon could have drifted away from the main body either of the 1st Battalion. I know that no party from the rest of the regiment could have reached the hospital on that day.'

Well clearly, they could have, if they ran up the back of 55th Regiment on the railway line, at the same time when the attacking troops were seen coming by those in the hospital.

Read-Collins once again forwarded his original interrogation notes from Tokyo to Singapore: 'Nasu's account of his regiment's advance through Singapore corroborates the account given by ex-Lt Gen Takeda, Chief of Staff 18th Div, during this period. From Nasu's account it becomes increasingly evident that either 55th Regt and/or 1/56th Regt were in the immediate vicinity of Alexandra Hospital on the afternoon of 14 Feb 1942.'

Around this same time, Soejima Yoshito, OC Machine Gun Company, 56th Regiment, made an undated sworn statement, unsigned by the translator:

'I neither knew at the time or subsequently that there was a hospital in the vicinity of the oil tanks. I have never heard of Alexandra Hospital by name. I have never heard of any incident occurring in that or any other hospital involving Japanese soldiers on or about 14 Feb 42. I did not read any account of the atrocities committed in Alexandra Hospital in the press. This is the first time I've ever heard of it. As I was wounded and evacuated on the 15th Feb and did not rejoin my unit until June, when it had already fought through its first Burma campaign, I did not have an opportunity of getting any full report of the events of the 14th and 15th Feb 1942.'

So he was personally off the hook. The common thread from all of these statements is that the name 'Alexandra Hospital' was obviously not used by the Japanese. But their intelligence pre-war must have had it noted as a significant building within the Keppel/Alexandra area, and each interview was narrowing down which IJA units were closest to the hospital at the crucial time on 14 February. Provided of course the truth was being told.

**

But then on 5 June 1947 a letter was written to the British Minor War Crimes Section, Tokyo, and copied to War Crimes Section Alexandra Hospital Massacre Case File:

Legal section is of the opinion that, judging from the evidence at present available here, it is extremely unlikely that the Alexandra Hospital case will ever come to anything.

Even if we can establish what troops and officers were responsible for the affair (a very difficult matter as it took place in the heat of battle) the case would be still a weak one as there was undoubtedly firing by our own men from the hospital buildings. Moreover, more than one year has passed since General Mutaguchi's photograph was sent to England for identification by witnesses as the general who visited the hospital soon after the surrender, and no identification has been forthcoming.

Therefore, unless you are achieving any outstanding success and obtaining positive results in your investigations among ex-officers of 18 Div now in Japan, I propose, with Legal Section's approval, to drop the case and recommend General Mutaguchi's release.

I should be grateful if you would signal your views.

(signed) PGP, Major, Commanding No 7 War Crimes Investigation Team.

What about the positive identifications from Craven and Lunt made in June 1946, exactly one year earlier? Perhaps they felt that positive results were being gained, and the local ploughed on regardless.

In any case, Mutaguchi was released from Singapore but then immediately held in Hong Kong by the British who still felt he had cases to answer for in relation to massacres of natives in Malaya.

**

Just a few days later 47-year-old Major (now Lt Col) Tsugawa Naoshi swore before Intelligence Capt Newington in Tokyo. Although he conceded he was OC 3/55th Regt and had seen it 'from afar' he said: 'I have not heard that any incident ever occurred in the hospital.'

The very next day Dr Suzuki Susumu, then 58, gave a sworn statement as chief of medical department, 18th Division. 'I had not heard of any atrocities committed in Alexandra Hospital until the time of this interrogation.' Copies of his interrogation were sent off to War Crimes Section, in Singapore a few days later by Read-Collins:

It will be noted that Suzuki states clearly that Lt Gen Mutaguchi visited Alexandra Hospital about 20 Feb. In an interrogation sent under cover our letter 5 Oct 46 Lt Gen Mutaguchi denied all knowledge of this.

This about-turn must have convinced them that Mutaguchi had something to cover up. On 20 June 47 Capt Newington's to-do list included the examination and sworn statement of Maj Ito Kojiro, OC 2/55th Regiment:

I had not heard till now that Japanese soldiers had entered the hospital on the afternoon of 14 Feb 42. I only remember two big hospitals in the Singapore area, this one and the big hospital at Johor Bahru. If Japanese troops entered the hospital between 1400 and 1500 hours I think by that time my whole battalion was already in position fighting.

Two companies on the hill, to the right of the road and one company on the main road. I saw the corpse of a machine gun platoon commander and judging from what I saw I think that the firing there on the main road was so close that no part of that company would have been able to stray as far left of the company as the hospital. As regards the two companies on the hill, not one of their men could have crossed over the road in the direction of the hospital.

If there had been any information concerning the hospital from any of my men, or if any of them had been there, I think the matter would have been reported to me either officially, unofficially, directly or indirectly, but I swear that I have heard nothing of any troops entering the hospital either on, before, or after 14 Feb 1942.

Well, well, well. His battle report of 15 February sees the fighting going till 'after noon' then by the time they realize the enemy has withdrawn and order an advance it's already nightfall and the surrender has been called. There appear to be big gaps in this story's timeline: half a day to be precise. He was, circumstantially, the first in line of the Japanese troops ... Johnny on the Spot, so to speak. Straying left was easier because the hospital buildings would increasingly shadow them from the Allies' line of sight and fire.

51-year-old Maj Gen Nasu Yoshio (Commander 56th Regiment during Malayan Campaign), Capt Soejima Yoshito (OC

Machine Gun Coy 1/56th Regt), and Col Suzuki Susumu (Chief Medical Dept HQ 18th Div) to share what they knew, and their three interrogation reports were sent south on the next plane.

Read-Williams was still furiously on the scent, and dispatched interrogations of Capt Umemoto (Adj HQ 55th Regt), Capt Noguchi (OC MG Coy 55th Rgt) and Maj Tsugawa (OC 3/55th Regt) to Singapore. The latter, the battalion commander whom Mutaguchi could not remember, had placed himself at the oil tanks at the time they went up.

Capt Umemoto, adjutant of 55th Regiment HQ, 46, had a busy war, moving with the 18th Division on to Burma, including its retreat to the Shan States, before being promoted to major then returned to Tokyo to take up position in Iwakuni Army Fuel Depot. 'I never went into the hospital myself, nor did I receive any report that any of the men of our regiment had entered it either. Furthermore I did not hear any rumours to the effect that any Japanese soldiers ever entered the hospital.' This, despite the fact that he admitted being at the oil tanks, and seeing the hospital on the east of the road and the Sisters' Quarters on the west.

Read-Williams also sent off a letter to War Crimes Section, SEALF, attaching original and copies of Ito's interrogation plus five pairs of photos ('full face and profile') of Ito.

Did Read-Williams feel he was closer to finding his man?

'In endeavouring to trace the perpetrators of this massacre we have so far worked downwards from HQ 18th Division to the battalion commanders of 55th and 56th Infantry Regiments,' he wrote. 'Though it is still possible that the direct responsibility lies with forward elements of 56th Regiment, this first interrogation of a former officer of 55th Regiment gives indications that stray elements of the first or second battalion of 55th Regt might have been responsible. Divisional Mountain Artillery and Army Heavy Mortar Units were also within the Alexandra Hospital Area on 14 Feb 1942.'

So the 25th Army Mountain Artillery, under Lt Col Kusido, and Mortar Unit, under Lt Col Tanaka, came back into the frame. But it seems they were never hauled onto Read-Collins', nor anyone else's, mat for a 'please explain'. Odd, given that they were the easterly-most troops. But there seemed to be a myopic fixation on the 18th Division (especially 55th and 56th Regiments), to which they were only on temporary assignment at the crucial moment.

The postal routes between Tokyo and Singapore continued to run full as the half-way point of summer 1947 came and went.

And then ...

Singapore Investigation Section File number 717/111 labelled 'Alexandra Hospital Singapore - Affidavits' had large capital letters scrawled across the bottom in pencil: **'CASE DROPPED 23.7.47.'** This note was signed with an illegible signature.

**

Suddenly a few months later, in March 1948, Singapore cabled Read-Collins: Britain's Southeast Asian war crimes unit was to be wound down. Drop all cases, release all 50 prisoners, close the office. No correspondence to be entered into. Just like that.

The *Malaya Tribune* carried the sensational news on 8 April 1948 that Mutaguchi 'has been released by British authorities in Hong Kong and repatriated to Japan.' It went on to say he was released 'because of insufficient evidence to support charges of the Command's responsibility ... allegedly allowing the massacre of hundreds of Malayan natives.'

Mutaguchi returned to Tokyo a free man albeit one with wounded pride, and probably harbouring a sense of failure because he'd never got to ride his stallion into Delhi as the conquering war hero he saw himself as. He'd not restored the family name to national greatness as he obsessively and single-mindedly had set out to do. Instead he'd had demotions and those ignominious two and a quarter years in prison in three different countries.

By late May, eight weeks after the order to close, Read-Collins, Crewdson and team left Tokyo.

**

Three days later, Tsuji sidled quietly into Japan, disguised as a Chinese university professor. A gifted linguist, he could speak Chinese and Russian in addition to his native language, but never mastered English. Possibly his hatred of the West dictated his unwillingness to dedicate himself to that difficult pursuit.

On New Year's Day 1950, Tsuji – who was holed up writing his memoirs in a wooden house in Tokyo, harboured by former IJA Academy classmates – was officially removed from 'war criminal' status by MacArthur and the Americans. He maintained his 'period of penance' as a robed monk meant he had absolved his sins, and resurfaced a free man.

Not only that, but according to a 2007 report by Associated Press, a recently declassified file shows that the CIA incredulously attempted to recruit Tsuji as an intelligence agent. But the move proved futile with the CIA concluding: 'In either politics or intelligence work, he is hopelessly lost both by reason of personality and lack of experience.' But further down the record is an interesting summary of the man: 'Tsuji is the type of man who, given the chance, would start World War 111 without any misgivings.'

**

17 February 1950. Exactly eight years following the fall of Singapore, the Supreme Commander for Allied Powers reduced the sentences of around 120 Japanese prisoners in Singapore, and they were all transferred by ship to Sugamo to complete their lightened penalties.

Among these was Lt Gen Nishimura Takuma, commander of the Imperial Guards Division, who had completed just five years of his life sentence. But when the ship docked en route in Hong Kong, the Australian military authorities seized him, transferred him to the SS Changte, and sent him off to face further Australian War Crimes trials in Manus.

Investigator Capt James Godwin built up the case that Nishimura had ordered the shootings at Parit Sulong and the destruction of bodies he and his Imperial Guards had committed in January 1942 in southernmost Malaya. Nishimura was found guilty of ordering the mass execution and cremation of 155 wounded Australian and Indian soldiers at Parit Sulong, and hung on 11 June 1951. As The Alex case had been scrapped, it will never be known whether he had any complicity in the Sisters' Quarters atrocity which bore identical trademarks, or in the hospital massacre itself, where so many eyewitnesses talked of the Imperial Guards being there.

Were the Imperial Guards involved at all in the Alexandra Massacres, then their commander got his come-uppance by swinging.

**

To Godwin's point of 'whitewashing', the 2.5 years' duration of the Tokyo War Crimes trials made it the longest war crimes trial in history, earning the sobriquet of 'the other Nuremburg'. The transcripts generated 49,000 pages, filled with 10 million words, and 779 affidavits. 419 witnesses were called. Yet only 28 Japanese military and political figures were prosecuted.

Cyril Wild's War Crimes Investigation Unit scored a better ratio, causing 400 war crimes cases to be brought, resulting in over one hundred death sentences and 150 prison sentences.

And yet, the longest sentence any Japanese war criminal *actually* served was less than 13 years. No Japanese war criminal was still behind bars beyond 1958.

**

The Alexandra Hospital Massacres case was on the drawing board for prosecution for nearly three years before being dumped due to lack of evidence. Incredulously, it *never* had its day in court.

...orn statement by Lt Gen MUTAGUCHI Renya

I, MUTAGUCHI make oath and say as follows :-

I have been duly warned that I am not obliged to make any statemen[t] but that whatever I say will be taken down in writing and may be u[sed] in evidence.

I wish to state voluntarily that :-

I did visit the Alexandra Hospital though I cannot be sure of the date. I think it was the 14th of February 1942.
My visit was one of goodwill and I took with me my chief of staff, my medical officer and other medical officers. R.M.
I discovered that the hospital was in good order and there did not appear to be any trouble.
I never had any slightest knowledge of the bayonetings and massacre to which you refer.
I wish to add that I never found any necessity to apologise for anything to the patients in the hospital, on the other hand I did express in a polite Japanese way my regrets for any possible inconveniences which they may have experienced.

Renya Mutaguchi

After being transferred to Changi Gaol, Mutaguchi changed his tune. His November 1946 statement admitted he *did* visit the hospital. The investigating team felt their mounting evidence was 'good stuff'.

Evidence

[illegible] – Good & identifies MUTAGUCHI. Where is his other evidence?

[illegible] – first class & identifies MUTAGUCHI

SMILEY
HOSKINS
WARRENNE WALKER.
BRYER
DICKINSON
GURD
STRINGER
JOHNSON
BUCK

Good stuff.

350 [illegible]

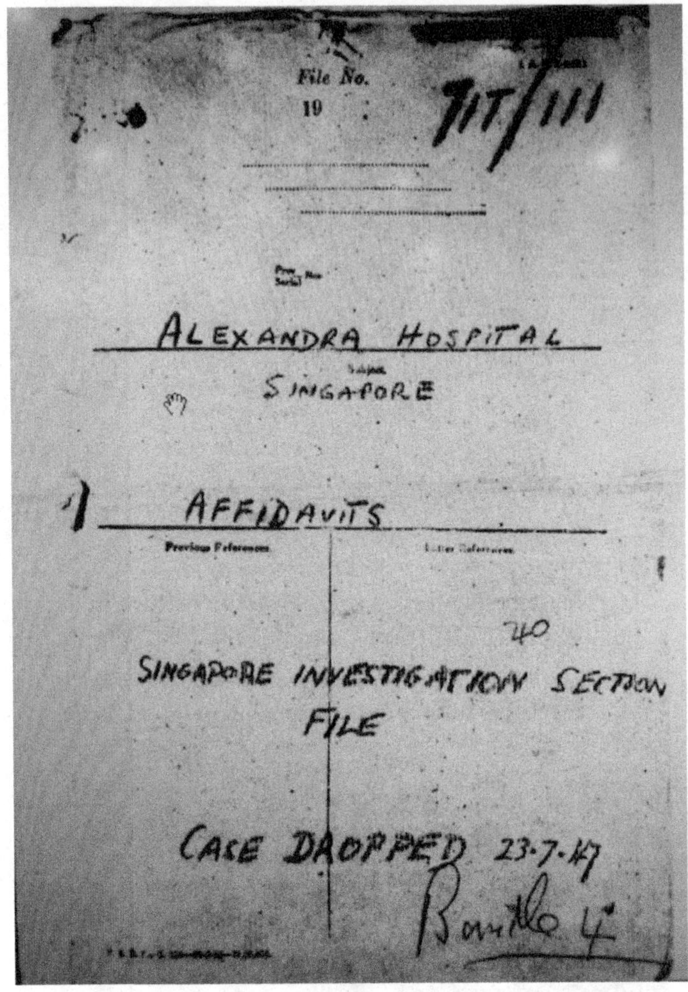

File No.
19 JIT/111

ALEXANDRA HOSPITAL
SINGAPORE

AFFIDAVITS

Previous References | Later References

40

SINGAPORE INVESTIGATION SECTION FILE

CASE DROPPED 23-7-47

A devastating blow to the investigation team and to all connected to The Alex when the case was dropped in July 1947. A few months later, Britain's Southeast Asian war crimes unit was wound down and all cases dropped.

A BELATED BOMBSHELL

'You ... were the planner, instigator and executioner of the massacre.'

At a distance of 80 years, we now have the benefit of hindsight simultaneously coupled with the disadvantage of that gap, the latter being that witnesses and perpetrators are no longer alive to cross-examine deeper to clarify and question and fill in some of the now more-obvious blanks.

One critical piece of the puzzle is that forward 'company or battalion HQ' with the unidentified officer of some rank and importance, where orderlies and soldier-patients were marched past en route the Sisters' Quarters on 14 February 1942.

Here's the real bombshell ...

Could that officer have been none other than Col Tsuji Masonobu, the bloodthirsty director of strategy for the 25th Army's Malayan campaign?

**

Post-war Tsuji led a very public life back in Japan, even entering local and national politics, using his signature cunning to attract votes and deflect criticism and attention when it suited. Still very much the 'god of strategy' especially when it came to self-promotion and advancement.

But by 1959 it became too much for some when he ran third in the national House of Councillors' elections.

The retired Lt Gen Kawaguchi Kiyotake wanted the world to know who this man *really* was. He documented Tsuji's wartime atrocities in a several-page dossier, wrote an open letter to the elected councillor, and demanded Tsuji's resignation plus an apology for his shameful wartime behaviour. The US Embassy in Tokyo hastily sent full translations of his documents to Washington. But as we now know, there was little value in alienating Japan by continuing trials and enquiries while the USA was trying to strengthen alliances with them against a new common foe, Communist China.

You can imagine the stink this would have raised in that precarious post-war period. So what was incendiary about his damning document?

'You, Mr Tsuji, were the planner, instigator and executor, of the massacre of Singapore Chinese merchants, the Bataan Death March, the massacre of doctors and nurses at Alexandra Military hospital in Singapore, and the atrocious murder of the leading Philippine government official, Jose Abad Santos, and many other terrible acts.'

Bang – take that! Kawaguchi laid bare Tsuji's meticulous planning of all of these atrocities, collectively yet conservatively totalling around 75,000 deaths.

He insisted Tsuji had arranged the hospital massacres in retribution for the heavy casualties inflicted on the Japanese by British Artillery in the immediate area. Tsuji's response to this was that the hospital gave protection to British gunners.

So Tsuji did not deny it: rather, he proffered an excuse for it. This on top of the fact that there was tacit acceptance that he was well-versed on the specifics of the local battle, and he personally spoke of the Keppel Barracks which was adjacently west (no more than 500 metres) from the hospital.

Further, Kawaguchi claimed that, 'it can be proved conclusively that Tsuji was at the forward headquarters of the Japanese unit responsible for the attack on the hospital, and just three hundred yards from the massacre scene, when the killing began.'

Indeed, when I triangulated what we now know about the specific movements of forward elements of the 18th Division, such as Koba's 55th Regiment, and overlaid it with Tsuji's first-hand account in his own words, a very clear picture emerged.

Ito's 2/55th Battalion position 15 February 1942 (drawing by Ito).

So desperate was Tsuji to paint a picture of himself as the leading-from-the-front warrior-leader, I believe he hung himself with his own words. Sometimes in what he said, but also by what he *didn't* say. For example there appear to be no accounts of his movements on 13 and 14 February. He skips from Thursday 12 February to Sunday 15 February, missing two surely most-crucial days of intense battle for the island.

**

As for Sunday 15 February Tsuji claimed to have been at his own HQ – Trig point 120 along Buona Vista Rd – and took a call from Staff Officer Hashimoto, officer in charge of operations for 18th Division. 'Today, the division will attack with its full strength towards Keppel Barracks. Will you be good enough to look in at our position?' Tsuji claimed to have not yet been to the 18th Division area – even though his HQ was well within their divisional boundary – and set out in a car with his orderly towards West Coast Road, 'moving in the intervals between shellfire.'

His intention was to call in person at 18th Division HQ and presumably meet with Mutaguchi. This would seem a normal, sensible, starting point to gain an overview and battlefield briefing. 'Changing the plan, however, we drove straight through to the frontline headquarters of the Koba Regiment which overlooked the enemy position.' Tsuji put this as being 'two or three hundred yards from the enemy frontline'. So he drove down Ayer Rajah Rd towards, and probably past, the oil tanks. Tsuji parked his car under the shade of a tree and walked forward. I calculated this path would have taken him past the Sisters' Quarters to his right (either in his car or likely on foot).

Koba had his 55th Regimental HQ position sheltered in a firing trench (actually an octopus trap) from which he could see the enemy in Alexandra and Gillman Barracks, but the enemy could also observe him, 'so that the movement of even one Japanese soldier brought down concentrated shellfire on the position.'

Koba's plan was to attack at 2pm while Ito indicated his battalion was in situ at 13:00. They of course had been there since the previous afternoon, Saturday 14.

Ito launched his battalion's attack, their rising from their trenches attracting an immediate response from British guns. 'It seemed as if everyone on the battlefield would be suffocated by the dust and smoke from the burning shells,' recalled Tsuji. 'Arms and legs were flying through the air and heads scattered everywhere.' Takeda, 18th Division chief of staff directing the attack, called it off as impossible and unviable.

Tsuji, Koba, and cohort took their regimental colours, evacuated their trench and sought shelter behind the blasted brick wall of a nearby house. As they clung tightly there, 'a soldier beside me had his head blown off, and blood was scattered everywhere.' Tsuji went on to say 'in all probability they were soldiers of the Ito battalion.' So he was in the trenches directly alongside them until 4pm when the bombardment eased off, and the guns trained their attention elsewhere.

Tsuji and his orderly moved 'tired and heavy-footed' back along the road they'd arrived on that morning (meaning the Ayer Rajah Road) only to find his car had been blasted to smithereens. It was the third time his personal vehicle had been destroyed by shellfire in the Malayan campaign. So they proceeded *on foot* to the 18th Division HQ, back on Hill 110. (That distance would averagely take someone around 90 minutes.) There he gave Mutaguchi a strategic debriefing, and it was there that they had the exchange about Tsuji not wanting Mutaguchi to visit the frontlines, the former using very deferential language such as 'Your Excellency' and 'Sir.'

**

The question is only whether it was the killing in the hospital, or the killing at the Sisters' Quarters, that Tsuji masterminded? Or *both*?

The outhouse massacre certainly fits the grisly undertaking the *bushido*-brandishing and *shensei*-singing Tsuji took delight in, along the lines of the Parit Sulong massacres. And it makes sense of the reports of that senior officer sighted so far forward at a 'company or battalion HQ.'

Although, critically, it must be conceded that Kawaguchi himself was not in-country at the time and had a grudge to bear with Tsuji, too, over how he was portrayed in Tsuji's book, *Guadalcanal*. The reason for the friction was that Tsuji ordered Kawaguchi to shoot Santos, the Philippine politician, which Kawaguchi refused to do. Santos was then transported elsewhere, where someone else did the dirty deed. But Kawaguchi was found guilty anyway, and imprisoned at Sugamo Prison from 1946 until 1953.

In July 1960, Mutaguchi and Tsuji – by now a member of the Japanese upper house – invited Lt Gen Gordon Bennett (the Australian senior-ranking officer who controversially escaped Singapore at capitulation) as guest of honour at a farewell dinner in Tokyo, while Bennett was holidaying with his wife in Japan. For former enemies to meet and shake hands post-hostilities is not unheard of, but to dine with our two prime suspects is unthinkable and at very least a massive slap in the face – or kick in the groin with an army boot – to Bennett's own men and all other Allied soldiers and PoWs.

One can only wonder at the tone of the meeting, and the conversation topics. Only one topic we can say for sure was Tsuji's book, *Singapore: The Japanese Version – Japan's Greatest Victory, Britain's Worst Defeat.* After all, Bennett wrote the introduction for the English edition when it was published that same year, praising Tsuji as 'a master planner and an outstanding field officer,' all the while acknowledging how he'd stayed away from Japan until all charges were cleared.

The fact remains that Tsuji was never once questioned by anyone – not one single investigator from any Allied nation, about *any* of the allegations of his involvement in, or knowledge of, any atrocities.

Tsuji for his part wrote of finding a way to 'lead away from domination by force to alliances based on moral principles and sincerity' and hoping his book 'should be read by all the peoples who long for peace beyond past vengeance.'

While complete validation of Kawaguchi's claims is not possible, and he passed away in 1961, the claims seem to have met with general tacit acceptance of being majorly true. And, perhaps most tellingly, were *not* denied by Tsuji.

So, we have our mastermind. But he was way too smart to leave his fingerprints on the dirty work itself. He clearly left the heavy-lifting to his heinous henchmen. But who were they?

**

Several theories and suspects can be shortlisted:

One: Mutaguchi himself.

Two: Imperial Guards Division. This is circumstantial, based purely on what some of the witnessing patients and solders described them as, based on their size and uniform.

Three: Elements of 25th Army attached to 18th Division. 'On or about 14 February there were several other units occupied by our forward troops,' said Maj Gen Takeda 'Ju' Hisashi, chief of staff of Mutaguchi's 18th Division. They included a mortar unit and a tank unit.'

Four: Kagawa's 1/55th Battalion.

Five: Ito's 2/55th Battalion. Tsuji was *in* their forward HQ.

Six: Koba's 55th Regimental HQ unit.

Seven: Matoba's 1/56th Battalion HQ and Soejima Yoshito's errant 1/56th Machine Gun Battalion, who advanced 'mistakenly' with the 55th, and supposedly dug in for the night 'northeast of the oil tanks'.

Let's deal with each of these in turn.

**

Though Mutaguchi was evasive and contradictory in his bumbled defence, I net out in the position that he was aware that it happened but he himself had not ordered them nor participated in the massacres. Back on Hill 110 he could be considered relatively too far removed from the battlefield. In my opinion he was generally trying to run interference, obfuscate, deflect any possible involvement and loss of personal reputation, because he realized his division was implicated and therefore they could saddle him with ultimate responsibility.

Any junior officers of the 18th Division who were summarily executed at the hospital most likely came from the 55th or 56th Regiment, because it would be the 18th Division disciplining its own. It also implies that Mutaguchi was not the mastermind because otherwise such disciplinary action would not have been taken had he made the orders.

The Imperial Guards. While they had form of a very similar nature, and many witness accounts refer to them by name, I remain unconvinced that they would be operating so far from their eastern divisional area. I believe most Allies were just generally surprised by the size and skill of the Japanese troops, and misattributed or mistook them for the Guards. Additionally, the experience of the 13th Australian General Hospital on the east coast with the Imperial Guards was exemplary. Rather, I believe their modus operandi from Parit Sulong was merely mimicked under the orders of Tsuji.

The IJA 25th Army 1st Mountain Artillery Battalion under Lt Col Kusido, and the 14th Independent Mortar Battalion under Lt Col Tanaka. Both units were recently assigned to 18th Div and specifically mentioned in battle reports on the west coast by Koba's 55th Regiment as part of their 'left wing unit'. This would make them the most easterly of all 18th Div troops, importantly on or to the *east* of the railway line, where the hospital lies. Movement to their left, eastward to the hospital, would be unimpeded by opposing infantry (there were none left in the area, bar retreating Indian troops) and place them increasingly in the protective shadow of the hospital's buildings, restricting line-of-sight from any Allied troops on the Singapore side of the hospital. Maj Gen Takeda, 18th Div chief of staff, said they were 'mostly directly under command of HQ 25th Army.' As Tsuji was 25th Army HQ, he could have easily brought his influence to bear on these men, but they were probably too busy pouring fire over the hospital onto Allied lines beyond.

Kagawa and his 1/55th Battalion were conspicuously off the radar. The battle order said it 'was to be ready to move to the left side of 2nd Bn if necessary.' Given the 2/55th under Ito were *on* the railway line and on Ayer Rajah Rd, anyone left of there had no physical choice but to be *in* the hospital grounds. But as there was no subsequent mention of this unit after they took Hill 130 due north of the hospital, where the hell were they? This also tallies with the second wave coming from the *north* of the hospital. But no-one from 1/55th was ever summonsed and questioned. Fertile avenues of enquiry unexplored.

Ito's 2/55th Battalion was in action immediately west, adjacent the hospital, he himself placing his 5th Coy at the intersection of Ayer Rajah Road and Alexandra Roads. The entire battalion had marched down 'the main road' to Singapore, around the oil tanks, to regain the road, with the hospital to their left and the Sisters' Quarters somewhere to their right. The timelines are contradictory – on the one hand he talked of 10 minutes detouring the tanks and regaining the road, on the other hand it was around two to three hours to regain the road, leaving a gaping hole in his defence, at the precise time of the initial hospital attacks. I suspect their involvement very strongly in the initial pursuit of retreating Indians and the Saturday hospital massacre because they were the frontliners. Additionally, Tsuji has placed himself in the 2/55th Battalion headquarters. The 29-year-old commanding officer 2nd Bn Machine Gun Coy, Noguchi Akisumi, had been hit in the leg shortly after landing in Singapore, and hospitalized in Johor ever since, so he can not be personally implicated. Perhaps in his absence this lends further credence to the 'very junior officers' that were summarily executed for their role. Possible. But I believe they were too engaged in fierce fighting at close-quarters near Alexandra Barracks and Gillman Barracks on the Sunday to be implicated in the Sisters' Quarters atrocities.

Koba and Ito were operating shoulder-to-shoulder, and dug-in along the Ayer Rajah Road, adjacent the northwest edge of the hospital. This would enable them to roam (as Tsuji did) anywhere behind them, which made the Sister's Quarters – directly adjacent or behind them by my reckoning – easily accessible. If not, how would the Sister's Quarters be known of as being there and being suitable for their dastardly purpose? The fact that Tsuji shared Koba and Ito's trench on 15 February paints a strongly compelling picture of complicity.

Either Koba's HQ team played henchmen around the outhouse, or less engaged units – such as Tsugawa's 3/55th slightly behind the frontlines – lent a heinous hand.

Soejima's location was just too proximate to the path taken over the railway line by the chaingang of orderlies to ignore. Not making any progress, they dug in there for the night of Saturday 14. 'We were out of touch with the main strength of the regiment behind us and the Battalion HQ ahead of us,' he said. If this was his own 1/56th HQ, then its commander, Matoba, would most likely have been that unidentified officer that harangued the prisoners en route. But Matoba was never questioned, unless he had already been taken out of the equation in that 'kangaroo court' clean-out of 18th Div junior officers responsible? Matoba's 1/56th and Matsuoka's 3/56th had recently teamed with the 1st Mountain Artillery and 14th Mortar units in the battle for Hill 270. So why wouldn't they be teamed up again, operating as the eastern-most units? Yet these units seemed to have slipped under the radar in the wash-up, and nothing is known about Matoba. Soejima's machine gun battalion had been hammered severely, so they would have been feeling very sore and retributive. (He himself was wounded on Sunday 15 at this very place, and sent behind lines for treatment.) Besides, Nasu of the 56th talked about going in pursuit of retreating troops – most likely the 44th Indians –

who possibly coaxed them unwittingly into the hospital. If the 1/56th had moved east towards and beyond the hospital it would make sense of the vacated space some of the outhouse escapees found to hide out on the afternoon of 15 February, and of some of the patrols encountered near the Thye Hong biscuit factory late on the Sunday afternoon.

In general, the investigators' myopic fixation on the 55th Regiment resulted in failure to adequately interrogate potential protagonists of the 56th who were generally behind the 55th but certainly moving on a more easterly bearing, bringing them directly in line with the railway and the hospital. As the odd-ones-out (not being a 55th Regiment unit), could it be that they were deliberately assigned to deal with the hospital while Koba's 55th units focussed on the frontline battle?

**

In summary, for the Saturday hospital massacre, I believe the weight of evidence falls heaviest on Ito's 2/55th and Matoba's 1/56th, with Kagawa's 1/55th responsible specifically for the second wave coming in from the north. Ito's 2/55th timeline discrepancy made them well-positioned (as the leading unit) and motivated for the first wave, too, especially when lured into the chase in the heat of battle by retreating Indian units.

As for the outhouse massacre on Sunday, Koba's HQ men had the motivation and means to carry out the outhouse massacres under the masterminding guidance of Tsuji, doubtlessly encouraging them to ever-increasing evilness to carry out those senseless acts. They were battle-fatigued, angry and frustrated, but mostly, *they were there.*

What did they achieve by all these murders? Strategically and tactically, *nothing.* The massacres were a purely wasteful exercise, happening as they did between 36 and six hours before Singapore capitulated. The medical staff and patients would have become prisoners of war anyway. One can only surmise that the perpetrators wanted to guarantee their victims, especially the valuable RAMC personnel, would or could play no further part in the

Allied effort.

But perhaps, just *perhaps*, it hints at doubt – even in Tsuji's mind – that the Japanese would secure the victory, because the Allied pushback intensified at exactly the wrong time in exactly the wrong place. Creating the perfect storm.

Weddings happened quickly for many reunited couples. Tom and Elizabeth Smiley married within two weeks of his return. Below: Bert and Rosa Gurd late 1946. Bottom: Sydney Hoskins and Pat married in 1947.

Capt Dick Waller, RA, stayed on in the Army for a few years before switching to missile guidance systems. Below: Norman Bryer met future wife Annie in a store in Malaya, and went on to retirement in Western Australia.

Sydney Hoskins often enjoyed a 'cheeky pint' down the club. At his grand-daughter Lauren Lloyd's wedding. Below: Sister Brenda Macduff on her 100th birthday.

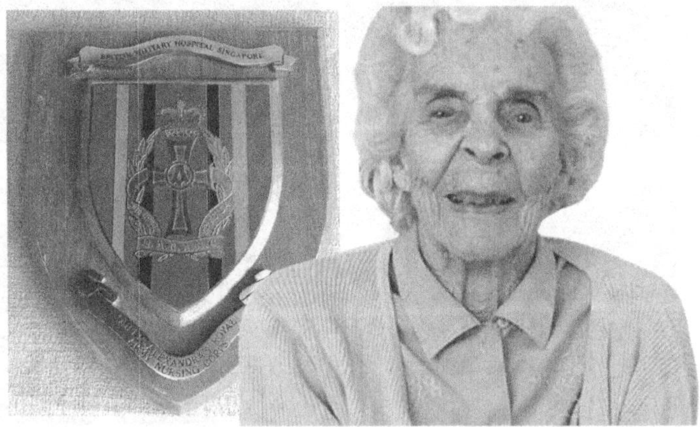

Col Tsuji Masonobu went on to a career in politics, before mysteriously vanishing in 1961. The 'god of strategy' is venerated in his hometown of Kaga.

MAKING SENSE OF THAT SENSELESS THING

'It chokes me now to talk about it.'

Most of the men – soldiers, patients and medical staff – were just in their twenties at the time of these massacres in 1942. Survivors then wasted three-and-a-half years as PoWs before returning home late 1945 or early 1946. Meaning they were mostly still aged younger than 30 when their post-war 'normality' resumed.

Leaving them up to 70 years in some cases to deal with those memories, and make sense of 'that senseless thing', as Yamashita had called the massacres.

What did post-war life hold for them and what, if any, life lessons had survivors, relatives, and those touched directly or indirectly by these events, learned? I was interested in those reflections, both of the survivors as well as their nearest and dearest. Let's start with the medical team in the hospital.

**

Tom Smiley lived off Elizabeth's savings whilst he set about studying for his FRCS. He spent a year as resident surgical officer under Sir Clement Price Thomas at the Brompton Hospital, London, and continued to develop his interest in thoracic surgery. He returned to Belfast and passed his FRCS in 1948.

'Tom would speak rarely about his time as a prisoner and occasionally related stories about eating rats and snakes and using bamboo for many uses in surgical procedures,' recalled one of Capt Smiley's four children, Fiona. 'However, despite the hardship his experience as a FEPOW was one that he never regretted and he never held any grudge against his captors. He made lifelong friends and saw the very best of human courage and tenacity and it shaped his life from then on.'

As Tom was at the very epicentre of the massacre, and perhaps one of its most storied participants, how did he fare post-war as a functioning human being and parent?

'He was compassionate, fun, and enjoyed life and people and particularly children,' she said. 'He could not bear any hypocrisy and was forthright and often could be very blunt and told people exactly how he felt. He held high ideals and expectations for himself and his family which, as his children, we all felt hard to live up to, however we knew that he would always be there for us.'

I asked her if there was any residual scarring on the body of Smiley from his ordeal? 'Yes, my father did have bayonet scars on his hand, body and groin.'

Tom was particularly interested in pioneering heart surgery. In the 1960s, together with John Bingham, he established the cardio-thoracic unit in the Royal Victoria and he instituted the open-heart surgical programme. During the late 1960's, Northern Ireland began the period known as 'The Troubles'. This was to dominate much of the activity in the Royal Victoria Hospital. 'Tom found the violence abhorrent. The Troubles continued throughout the '70s and Tom would be called out at all times after a horrific bomb attack; a sniper bullet wounding a soldier or saving the life of one of the infamous IRA bombers,' said Fiona.

In 1968, Irwin reached out to Smiley, who replied in a letter: 'It is so long ago that I'm afraid that my memory for other than the main events is sketchy. I wish I could see Alexandra Hospital again – in spite of it all I have happy memories.' He tried to organize a lecture tour to sponsor his visit to Singapore but it seems not to have eventuated.

At the age of 60, Smiley retired and Elizabeth and he embarked on yet another project of restoring an old farmhouse with 20 acres in Norfolk, England, so he could further indulge his passions for horses, farming, and gardening.

'It was with a certain surprise when he announced that he had accepted a visiting professorship at the University of Malaya, Kuala Lumpur in 1980,' according to Fiona, who herself lived in Borneo for a period. 'He would be demonstrating operations and examining final year medical students but most of all he would be returning with Elizabeth to show her the Malaysia that he always held dear to his heart. Tom was thrilled to be back in Malaysia and to be operating again. He was able to show Elizabeth places he had visited before 1942 and to once again be amongst the lovely people of Malaysia.' Before long he was back into full time surgery there.

Their two sons meantime became doctors.

The news that Elizabeth's twin brother's (who had retired as Maj Gen Graham Mills, CBE) beloved wife was dying of cancer shortened their stay and they returned to the UK in July 1981. 'Tom finished reading the lesson in the village church and, just as he was returning to his seat, he had a fatal heart attack in front of Elizabeth and the congregation,' Fiona related. 'The ambulance arrived too late and Tom died at the age of 64.' After all he had lived through, with the compounding irony of he himself being a respected heart surgeon.

Elizabeth lived until the age of 91. 'The letters that Tom had written to her were found in a plastic bag in her wardrobe after her funeral and the silver cigarette case was also found safely in her care,' said Fiona.

Fiona was privileged to attend the 70th anniversary of the Fall of Singapore in Smiley's honour. During that visit she donated the famed silver cigarette case and Smiley's Military Cross to the Changi Museum for permanent display.

While admitting that 'I knew so little about those dark years of your life' in a letter-style blog to her father, Fiona was deeply affected by her visits to the Changi museum. 'I don't think any of the family will forget how affected I was. But the emotional key was unlocked and the tears flowed. The story of how you were saved by the cigarette case given to you by mummy is actually one of those stories that is recounted and known by many in association with the Alexandra Hospital Massacre, which will probably seem strange to you after so many years. Maybe the romantic element has captured the imagination of people.' Not maybe, Fiona – *definitely*!

'I am still very proud to be known as "Tom Smiley's daughter",' she said of the way she was introduced around everywhere.

Of the other medicos in The Alex's orbit, Hugh De Wardener went on to become an expert in treatment of kidney disease, pioneered dialysis techniques, and was the first surgeon to perform renal biopsies. He was made an OBE in 1946 for his sterling support as a physician to his fellow PoWs, and again in 1981 for his contributions to nephrology.

As professor emeritus at University of London and Charing Cross Hospital, he was known as 'charming and charismatic' by colleagues, 'and his dedication to his patients' welfare was exemplary.'

Perhaps those at home saw a very different side of the man – he married four times. He died in 2013 one week short of his 98th birthday in a hospital ward aptly named after himself.

Post-war, he and Dr Constantine Petrovsky continued their firm friendship. 'My husband loved to travel, and when we travelled we had to call on his favourites, his PoW friends,' Dr Kathleen Petrovsky told me. 'They all became professors.' His two favourites were De Wardener and Dr Hugh Henderson, former registrar at The Alex and professor of pathology at Newcastle. When son Nikolai went to London for his attachment there, his father Constantine said: '"Stay with De Wardener, he's my old PoW mate". All my father's records, Hugh published them under his own name. But they remained great friends.' Interestingly, whenever they stopped over in Auckland, Craven was not on their to-do list. They also travelled to Singapore and Thailand but Petrovsky never visited any of his former camp sites or war locales.

Immediately post-war though, Petrovsky was accepted into the permanent army sent back to Occupied Japan. 'He fell in love with the place. He wanted to spend the rest of his life there,' said Nikolai. 'But it was handed back to Japan and he declined to sit a Japanese registration exam.' Next it was off to the Malayan Emergency, where he had a narrow escape when his convoy was ambushed by Communist Terrorists. 'The bullet would have killed him if it had been further over,' said wife Kathleen of the graze which left a scar on his wrist.

After briefly joining the International Refugee Organisation in Germany, he wrote to his Army and PoW mates and – as Australia accepted his British degree – he found a position in Tasmania as the General Superintendent, Launceston General Hospital in 1952. It was here that he met wife-to-be Kathleen, when he recruited her as an intern. 'He was a good-looking man, a bit stiff and arrogant,' were her first impressions. They would go on to have five children, two of whom became doctors, one who became a nurse.

It is interesting to get their perspectives, as medical people, on Petrovsky's post-war disposition. 'The influence of the war years he kept under very tight control,' said Nikolai, now a leading vaccine researcher and university professor. 'But when he was drunk he probably had flashbacks – we got the most out of him when he was very drunk,' he laughed.

'I don't think anyone can go to a war and see a fraction of what he saw and not be affected,' said Kathleen, adding symptoms of PTSD 'were obvious. I could never wake him up suddenly – he'd come up fighting. Or if he'd too much to drink, as if he had hallucinations and was fighting again. I'd have to be very careful. Some of his friends ... you just had to speak of the Japanese and it was toxic. They were traumatized. But he didn't have that hatred. He had a calm acceptance of what had happened.' He passed away in 1990. Kathleen is now 92 and still a registered general practitioner in Tasmania.

Petrovsky had the unusual distinction of having witnessed the atom bomb. Pte Roy Temple of the 198th Field Ambulance also defended the use of nuclear bombs. 'The atomic bombs undoubtedly saved our lives and also thousands more of Allied soldiers, had the invasion gone on and had the war proceeded indefinitely. That is why I defend to this day the dropping of the atomic bombs after all the inhumane treatments meted out to my fellow prisoners and subsequent torture and death of them. I think in all my war years and captivity I must've had a "guardian angel" watching over me as I was close to death many times and I am still around sixty years on.'

Dr William Young returned from London in 1947 to become a radiologist at Tan Tok Seng and Singapore General Hospitals, then became a consultant radiologist in in KL in the 1950s and was in the Dept of Radiology at the KL University Hospital until the mid-70s.

Medic Cpl George Poole returned home with the illicit camp radio that'd nearly cost him his life. He would later become an electrician, and subsequently donated that radio to the Imperial War Museum. 'If anybody had given me rice pudding when I came back, I would've thrown it at him,' he said. Time has not diminished the horrors of his experiences. Holding a cup of tea is sometimes too difficult because of his hands trembling. 'Sometimes I go to bed and Lottie thinks I'm right as rain. But before I go to sleep I'm not there any longer – I'm in that prison camp or on the Burma Railway. I have dreams today of that march,' he said, talking of the 90-mile mountainous trek up to the Three Pagodas. 'The misery and suffering of the absolute hopelessness in which comradeship was just not enough.'

He summed up that hellish period, saying: 'They broke our bodies but they couldn't break our spirits.'

**

Evacuated nurse, Edith Stevenson, had fetched up in Bombay in April 1942, where she met her future husband, a field ambulance officer. They married and had four children. They settled in Dumfries, Scotland, and Edith typically kept herself active. At 76, she clinched an honours degree and was amazingly still teaching the piano at 90.

About apportioning blame for the incident she made an interesting observation: 'There was a Bofors gun near the Sisters' Mess which may have led the enemy to think it was a legitimate target. A large Red Cross was laid on the hospital lawn for bombing planes to see, but because we were near the ammunition depot, the planes had an excuse to bomb the hospital.'

'I look back and the memories are as vivid as ever,' she told *The Free Library* of her six weeks at The Alex which must've seemed an eternity. 'I just think I was jolly lucky to live.' She passed away in hospital aged 93.

The equally irrepressible Ethel Mulvany, returned to her native Canada after the war with just $14 in her pocket and those ledger books chock-full of prisoners' dream recipes. She selflessly sold copies of her *Changi Cookbook* to raise money to send oranges (the fruit of her dreams while in captivity), tea and cigarettes to former PoWs in the UK. Typically, she eschewed use of her name on the cover, using her initials of 'ERM' only. In all she raised $18,000 (equivalent to $200,000 in today's money) from sales of 20,000 books. She also went on to develop a social enterprise importing exotic artifacts into Canada, that turned over nearly $1,000,000 per annum at its peak. She built a well for a village in Hoskote, southern India, with some of the proceeds.

She had her prisoner number burned off her forearm using caustic chemicals in a final attempt to rid herself of that mental yoke. 'I was kind of a number until I did. If you call a person Mary, they become Mary. But if you call yourself Billy, you're Billy. Well if you call yourself 2665 and you were willing to live under it, then you're 2665.'

Her biographer Dr Suzanne Evans noted that her hatred of Japanese 'saturated her waking hours.' A surprising step on her road to forgiveness was sponsoring a financially-strapped Japanese man to bring his wife out to Canada. (Generously she also allowed them to sleep in her bedroom for three months, while she slept on the couch.) But while temporarily soothing, her warped mind ensured the hatred of all things Japanese consumed her. She suffered from what we now call bi-polar disorder, describing herself as a 'triad of shadows' made up of herself pre-war, in prison, and present, which couldn't be integrated.

Ethel died aged 87. Two of her nieces followed her footsteps into nursing, and her cookbook was repackaged and reprinted as recently as 2013, with a biography about her life published in 2020.

Tragically, Dr Denis Mulvany took his own life on his 67th birthday, apparently unable to bear the lingering pain from repeated surgeries since the war. Pulau Shorga has reverted to its original name of Pulau Hantau and is a thriving dive site, popular with day-trippers.

Sister Brenda Macduff and cohort flew back from the Dutch East Indies to Singapore in September 1945, and were billeted at the Raffles, while waiting for onward passage to UK, Australia and so on. 'Here we heard for the first time what had happened at the Alexandra Hospital after we left.' But no word yet about husband

Ken (a private who'd also been captured). They were reunited in Liverpool in 1946, moved back out to Ipoh in 1950 then emigrated to New Zealand in 1955. Brenda enjoyed 'a long life, richly and generously lived' as a grandmother of seven and great-grandmother of 10, before passing away peacefully aged 105.

Dame Margot Turner, Royal Red Cross Medal, OBE, was also at the Raffles. She wrote home: 'Thank you so much for the helpful postcards which came in with great regularity, at least as many as the Japs would allow in. I am coming home to England soon, but meanwhile I am waiting on here as long as I can bear it, hanging on to the 1% hope I still have that Pen may have been picked up at sea and taken to some unknown camp.' She would devote a huge proportion of her life to the Queen Alexandra Royal Army Nursing Corps, ultimately rising to the rank of colonel commandant, the highest ranking military nurse. She passed away aged 83, but not before she had been celebrated on *This Is Your Life* to her initial objections.

Vivien Bullwinkel, MBE, AM, won the Florence Nightingale Medal. She married late (aged 62). She returned to Banka Island in 1992 to unveil a shrine to the nurses who, unlike her, had not survived the war. She would finally unburden herself of the secret, that all the nurses including her were raped, before dying. 'She was ordered when she was still in the Army not to include these details in her depositions to the Tokyo War Crimes Tribunal,' forensic historian Lynette Silver told me.

**

I called up Fergus Anckorn one day in 2015. 'Anckorn,' answered the voice on the other end, in a tone so spritely I was unsure if I was talking to the 97-year-old former gunner, his son, or perhaps even his grandson. 'Most people say I look 70 but they are just flattering me,' he laughed.

At the beginning of the war he was the youngest member of Britain's Magic Circle club of magicians. Now he was the oldest (Fergus sadly passed away from cancer in 2018).

He remembered Capt Smiley, who looked after him in The

Alex: 'I would have been sorry to find out he didn't survive the war. Regrettably, I never saw Dr Smiley, but over the years, I have often thought of him. I found out that after the war, he was in a hospital in Ireland. He got the Military Cross. I think VC would have been a more correct honour.'

He's visited Singapore and the Death Railway in Thailand three times since. 'With my son and daughters. Just a feeling of wonder. I went to the Alexandra Hospital with my daughter. They wouldn't let us go in. "You can't come in, it's a hospital." Reason: the local people think the place is haunted and don't want that reputation. The second time we had a doctor with us, well connected, and she arranged a full conducted tour.'

I was intrigued by what flashbacks or feelings that might elicit? 'It didn't register going back because I was unconscious going in, and unconscious going out. Like a dream sequence.' True, Fergus was there for an inordinately short time, and probably out of it on morphine for the duration anyway. 'It's been rebuilt and it's a completely different ward. I said to the nurse, "This is where the massacre took place." She said, "No, there were no beds here." I said, "You see that window there? A shell came through the window and I was lying here." She didn't believe me, she didn't *want* to believe me.'

Fergus was once asked on the BBC show *HardTalk* does he hate the Japanese? 'No, I hate the war. If there had been no war I'd never have seen a Japanese.' He wasted no time in getting to the point with me on where he stands on forgiveness. 'The Japanese and Koreans were absolute bastards to us, couldn't stop bashing us even as we were working. I was just thinking I don't mind if he breaks my arm, but I just hope he doesn't kill me. When we were freed, I thought, Now I can say "No", that was so important.'

He wrote to his mum: 'I am free – free – free! After three and a half years.' His feeling was, 'I was going home to mum and put the whole thing behind me. First thing I did was learn Japanese. If there was to be another war I would be the interpreter,' he laughed. 'I've always been interested in learning foreign languages. I've learned French, Latin, at school. Went to learn Greek in PoW camp, but the captain died a month later. Then we had a lot of Dutch prisoners of war, so I went on Dutch-only working parties. When I got home I thought I could not make any sense of Japanese language – it sounded like you were being sick. So I went to night classes. The Japanese teacher's name was Yoko Harmer,' he laughed. 'She'd married a British chap.'

He mentioned a friend of his was throwing a reconciliation party with one of his Japanese guards in June 2015. 'I've seen the Jap on TV. He said he's sorry, there was nothing they could do for us because he had orders. They and we had no say in it at all.'

His first trip to Japan was around 1950. 'Went free of charge on Japan Airlines with the British Legion. I jumped at the chance. I travelled to Japan and spoke at a couple of schools. They were all in tears when I told them what went on. And I did my magic all in Japanese,' he added, reciting a few phrases.

'I didn't forgive or unforgive but I'll never forget it. Of the veterans I know, about a 50/50 split between those who will never have something Japanese in their house. The others, let bygones ... Japs are taught to be absolutely brutal with no kind thoughts of all. Everything that gets in the way of the Emperor you kill them or eat them, it's in their genes.'

I wonder if there was any difference or distinction between the Death Railway and The Massacres? 'It's all the same. I just took it as something happening over which I had no control at all. I just hoped that at the end of it I would be alive. It was just our life – being beaten, being in the full sun. No one complained. We were like animals. '

He clearly took pride in his resilience. 'Four times I've said, "I'm dead". Within four seconds of being dead. All I was trying to do was be alive each evening. We just took it as we came.'

His badly injured hand, the reason why he ended up in The Alex, was clearly a handicap for a professional magician specializing in sleight of hand tricks. 'I didn't have use of my hand for seven years, so was practicing magic left-handed. I met the surgeon from the Fullerton Building, met him seven years after the war at a magic show. He tapped me on the arm and said, "How's your arm?"'

'Who are you?

'I'm the one who left your hand on.'

His energy remained positively irrepressible to the end. 'I've had a wonderful life. District commander of district police, been to Buckingham Palace three or four times, all over the country giving talks.' And, perhaps one of the highlights, he was honoured in 2016 by being involved in the finals act of magician Lance Cpl Richard Jones, who won *Britain's Got Talent* that year.

Signaller Cpl Bill Cowan spent the rest of the war as a PoW in Malai 1 Camp on the Death Railway. On his release and return to Britain, he wrote to Dorothy Young, sister of Signaller Hal Hart in December 1945, to break the news of Hart's death, describing the berserk Japanese rampaging through the hospital. 'But that is enough of that, Dorothy, perhaps I have said more than I should,' wrote the butcher. 'There is one consolation. I am positive that if Hal met his end in the hospital he would've gone down fighting and that he would've taken at least one yellow rat with him. The fellows who died as PoWs didn't have that chance to go out fighting. Hal's death would be clean, theirs was a miserable end.'

Dick Lee saw it through the same lens. 'You're watching these people rotting away with these fuckin' ulcers in their legs, and the pain and suffering that they were going through with these legs, and you couldn't get an Aspirin, couldn't get a jab,' he said of the Railway PoW experience. '*That's* suffering. My language will start coming out in a minute. I never saw that suffering in Alexandra, what I saw there was that bit of a massacre for a couple of days. It's a different thing entirely.'

Dick Lee's normally effusive Cockney voice dropped to a lower hushed tone: 'It chokes me now to talk about it. Never in a million years will you ever see the same bleedin' things in normal peace times as we had to see and suffer. Them *bastards*!'

But perhaps some small consolation can be had that those who met their end in their hospital beds or in the outhouse quarters experienced a sudden and swift death with no lingering suffering.

Dick returned home after the war only to find that his sweetheart had given up on him, presumed dead, and got hitched to another fellow. 'I was a bit down in the dumps when I first came home,' he told me on the phone from his semi-detached house in Glasgow. 'I found it hard to mix with people, especially women because they was difficult. I wasn't too bad with my brothers. For a few weeks I couldn't get comfortable in a bed, I slept on the floor. So strange everything. For a few months I'd wake up in a bleedin' sweat. I had some right doings,' he said of nightmares that initially haunted him. 'But then you gradually get back in to the swing of things.'

Dick was paid £200 backpay, 'a small fortune' which went on a new motorbike, of course. People fussed over him, and his neighbour Peggy took him to the cinema. They were married in 1946, while he worked doing deliveries for a bakery. Dick and Peggy produced two 'lovely' daughters, and drove deliveries to a market each weekend in Scotland. 'I didn't want to work inside, as I was out in the open all that time as a PoW.' As a result he started up his own market stalls in Glasgow's Barrowlands district, selling 'anything and everything' and over the years his garage became the proud home of Jaguars and Mercedes Benzes.

'Of all the Scots I knew up here, the Argylls, I can't pick up the phone to anyone here or down in London, they've all passed on now.'

Dick passed away aged 88, not long after our most recent email correspondence, from tuberculosis, which – it is suspected – possibly lay dormant in him for all those years after being exposed to it in a Railway camp.

Oddly, East Surreyman John Wyatt was not even sure what he'd actually experienced until he found out he'd been part of something so hugely and heinously horrific, many decades later. 'It was not until many years after the war that I knew I had the very dubious privilege of being in the Alexandria (sic) Military Hospital Singapore during what was one of the worst and little known cold-blooded massacres of Allied soldiers during the Second World War.' The catalyst was being contacted by Peter Bruton in 1989 who was researching his uncle, RAMC Cpl John Bruton's, death in the hospital.

Cowan made another interesting observation: 'The Alex Hospital was never bombed by Jap airmen, who, right till the end, recognized it as a military hospital. They had that much decency, which may seem strange, comparing their chivalry with that of the Japanese fighting forces.'

Indeed a few I've interviewed make the distinction between the IJA and their Naval and Air Force counterparts, the latter two services being more worldly.

Dr Constantine Petrovsky agreed: 'One thing I must say about the Japanese – they did not drop a single bomb on Alexandra Military Hospital. Nearby, yes.' Remember of course he'd been transferred away at the beginning of February. 'It's the situation of the hospital which we didn't like so much. It was near the railway line. An Ordnance Depot was just across the road. They bombed the Ordnance Depot but they didn't bomb the hospital at that time.'

OK, perhaps the Air Force *did* recognize and respect the Red Cross: but what of those incidents around Bangka?

'According to our Navy airmanship tradition, we never attacked civilian targets and we never shot wounded enemy soldiers,' Capt Iwasaki told me through translator Hajime. 'None of us has ever thought of killing wounded survivors in the sea. We never did such a thing.'

Clearly *someone* did because many civilians and nurses met a miserable and messy end this way.

Australian Pte Alex Drummond had been reported KIA on 20 January 1942. But later his family was advised he was actually a PoW! He worked pre- and post-war for *The Truth*, Melbourne, in charge of the publishing department. 'Let's analyze civilized society and their approach to killing in various aspects. A man becomes a soldier with the future task of killing as many of the enemy as he is capable of, he is highly trained in the most skilled methods of performing this objective, their killing condoned by the Powers That Be is quite legal.

'If at anytime the section of society of which your designated enemy is a member changes its alliance on the individual concerned from disloyalty, cowardice or some other second thought does so, he is no longer the enemy, he is friend, and to kill him is not only no longer legal but murder. If through cowardice, injury or betrayal of his command the enemy becomes your PoW, the changed status of the enemy makes it no longer legal to kill even though he still remains the enemy.

'Cold-blooded killing as we accept it, killing while the emotions are at fever heat is condoned if the victim is classified enemy but cold-blooded killing the same enemy under most circumstances is murder.'

'As far as we knew it was an international rule that you avoided hospitals so I doubt there were any soldiers in there,' said Danny Fraser, the sapper stationed with the 36th Engineers right out the back of the hospital. 'They wouldn't have been allowed. Maybe wounded soldiers yes but not the likes of our troops who were fit and well, going in there and using the balconies to fire at Japanese. No way.

'The only consolation we have as far as that incident was the ones who went through the hospital came out the back and come over this hill. And we sincerely hoped at that time that we got every one of them but there was about 100 more Japanese soldiers. Very few got back. But we didn't know at that time what they had done. We didn't know the Japanese were going to go to the extent they did. We even got an apology from Tojo [sic]. His excuse was that they managed to get hold of some alcohol, like bottles of whisky, and they were drunk, and there's nothing worse than a drunk soldier. In war you have that feeling it's going to be your last minute, your last second, anytime. And you come across that drink and stuff, it gives you false courage, no two ways about it.'

So for those perhaps seeking solace in the fact that justice was immediately served to the perpetrators within the hospital, perhaps Fraser's comments above contain it. They got decimated coming out the back after their rampage.

'There was no daring to fire bullets at the Japanese so there was no reason to attack it. Yet if we went over first to protect then that might give the Japanese the authority to attack. So when you think you're doing the right thing, you think you're doing the wrong thing.

'My honest opinion is that if we did know what was going on we wouldn't have remained in the same position, we would have made every effort to try to go in, but then it would become a battlefield in the hospital. So you were sorta ... One way international law, the other side doesn't obey international law ...' A silent, reflective pause hung in the air.

Hector Rogers was interviewed extensively on a visit to Singapore a full 62 years after his family received the dreadful letter informing of his father's death, and was still clearly troubled by it.

'The fact that Maj Webster knew ... whether he had seen my father was dead, or was told, I don't know. It must have been pretty confusing to be honest. It must've been an awful situation going on. Certainly, reading the account, reading between the lines, it must've been pretty close to mayhem in that hospital. I don't know ... difficult to understand.' He inhaled, regathered himself, then weighed in. 'There's one account where the senior officers in the hospital were having a discussion of what to do next, when already outside the hospital there was a battle going on, even before the Japanese came into it. Discussing what to do next. It struck me as being not really on top of things. I am sorry that I never had the chance to develop a relationship with my natural father. Next question!' He obviously never quite found the closure he was looking for.

Hector's mother adjusted slowly to life post-war. 'All her original hopes and aspirations had gone out the window. Her dreams of being the wife of a successful country GP, gone. But she did remarry another professional man, a geologist, who was not unknown to us when we were in Miri. He gave us a sort of stability and home life that the war had taken away from us.'

As an adult, Hector became an archeologist. 'Archeology shows you that people have been killing each other for thousands of years. War is to my mind a most unsatisfactory way or resolving any sort of dispute. Why we have to resolve our disputes in that way I don't know. It comes down to respect and humanity.'

The war, that episode, the what ifs of life, weighed on the back of his mind for most of his adult life. 'But it was only in my late sixties that I needed to bury my ghosts. I became involved in that war only through accident, just by being born when I was born, an accident of time if you like. What happened to my father, and the experiences of what I went through as a result of it, to visit his grave, visit the hospital where he was killed. Mum was witheringly scathing about it. And having done that – I knew Singapore had changed – and that's it, I don't plan to come back again. As far as I'm concerned, mission accomplished, I've laid my ghosts.'

Another son, Brian Hill of Bournemouth, reflected on the story he inherited, having also lost his father (Pte Frank Hill, RAMC) when Brian was just three. 'When I was a schoolboy, my grandad and grandma Hill would never talk about my father or the war therefore I have little 'home' knowledge.

'My father was reported missing after the Fall of Singapore,' he told me. 'My mother received a certificate of death from the War Office in February 1946 certifying that my father was presumably killed in action on 14 February 1942 while serving in the Far East.' The next part is unfathomable. 'I did not know until 40 years after WW2 that my father is commemorated in Singapore. And another 25 years before I found out that he survived the massacre at Singapore and taken as a PoW. And another 10 years before knowing he was put on a "hell ship" which sailed from Singapore to Rabaul in October 1942. And then some confusion whether he finished up on Ballale Island or Borneo.' Tireless detective work by himself, his wife, and son-in-law Col (Ret'd) Marty Slade, RAMC, finally pieced it all together. One of the pieces of evidence was a copy of the *Oner* pamphlet from Changi camp in mid-1942. 'Amongst them can clearly be seen my father's signature! It was unbelievable to find my father had been held as a PoW.' So much for the accuracy of the death certificate.

'I saw my father's commemoration in Singapore for the first time in 1987, which was an enlightening experience. I visited again in 1989 with my wife to celebrate my 50th birthday. When I was 80 I visited the Alexandra Hospital with my eldest daughter and son-in-law, and was shown around the hospital and the Japanese point of entry.'

WW2 names were only added to his local Kirkburton Church Cemetery and Gardens cenotaph in 2009. 'It is uplifting to know after all these years that my father is remembered there, and all the good and caring work they are doing. It is delightful to see. Many missed opportunities to visit Kirkburton, had I known.'

On his return home, Pte Len Knott would marry Joan, then moved to New Zealand, and became a pharmacist (spawning a few pharmacists among his offspring). They were married for 50 years and died within six weeks of each other. 'Yes the letters are beautiful,' said his daughter Kathy Knott. 'But believe me, Len could be a difficult man, deeply scarred by his experiences, and the 51 years my mother spent with him, before they died a few weeks apart, were not easy at times. Likewise as a father.'

On pharmacists, Cpl James Torbit, the quick-thinking dispenser in The Alex, stayed on in the RAMC after the war, making captain in 1950 and finally major.

**

And what of the five known survivors of the Sisters' Quarters outhouse incident? Richard 'Dick' Waller's family had presumed he was longsince dead in the absence of any news. But he returned to England. 'He came back to Victoria Station, and our grandmother went to meet him,' his daughter Louise Kidd told me, 'but for some reason he was on a different train.' Her brother Rob picked up the story. 'So he'd gone up to the house, but they weren't there because they'd moved. Granny told the story of how, unaware there was rationing for civilians back in Britain, on his return he'd spread the whole week's butter ration on one piece of toast.'

Dick, still a captain, soon took a job in the War Office, while his colleagues and contemporaries who had been in action throughout the war emerged as colonels or even brigadiers via battlefield promotions. At a party one night, he met Cynthia, a former ATS ambulance driver who was now working as a typist in London. Although her first impression was of a 'shy, withdrawn army officer', they hit it off. 'Her sister was JRR Tolkien's typist. He was completely unknown at that time,' Louise said. Soon they were enjoying walks in the park together and even dancing. 'Apparently Dick was a tremendous dancer.' A waltzer of note. But he had some stiff competition. \

While he had been a prisoner of the Japanese, Cynthia's other suitor had earned a DFC for skill and valour in attacking Japanese troops in Burma. While he would take her to the local Lyon's Corner House, (later Sir) Anthony Montague Browne, KCMG, CBE, DFC – a dashing former fighter pilot who'd seen action over the Middle East and Burma – would try and impress her with dinner dates at The Ivy. But sensing he was 'too smooth and simply not a keeper' she sympathized with the slight man from the War Office, and selected

Dick instead. She dodged a bullet: Montague Browne went on to become Winston Churchill's personal secretary, and – apart from being twice-married – bedded one of Churchill's other secretaries, resulting in an illegitimate child who would go on to become the Archbishop of Canterbury (paternity proven by DNA after Montague Browne's death).

In 1949, with lingering troubles around India's Partition, Dick worried that he might be posted over there. 'He rang Cynthia up one day and said, "We need to get married, I might get sent out to India." He proposed on the telephone.' She accepted, they married and set about creating a family. With the Army continually moving them around, Dick found this increasingly annoying and unsettling. 'He realized he needed to get out of the army.' Especially as promotion prospects were low. With a baby and toddler disrupting the domestic peace, he rented a room in a pub so he could get some quiet time to study at the Royal Military College of Science, and for the mathematics exam required to join Sperry Gyroscope, who hired him in 1956 as an engineer working on missile guidance systems. 'Still artillery then,' said his son, Robert. 'He spent time working at a job that he never really wanted to do, and had quite a depressing time being the breadwinner.'

Dick would sit in his chair and listen to music. 'He bought a decent Sony kit and would sit upstairs with a huge collection, particularly of Mozart, and listened all day with headphones,' Robert noted. 'And cut himself off from the family in doing that.' He wouldn't do much else, and didn't show a lot of interest in much else. If he had been a keen rugby player pre-war, there was no sign of that now. No interest in rugby nor cricket. 'He was a terrible loser. We played tennis, and if he lost ...'

Apart from this, he seemed characterized by an inability to show affection. And even then, his family never knew he'd spent time on the Death Railway. 'He told Cynthia (mum) that he was about to be shipped to the Burma Railway when the war ended,' Robert said.

Amazingly Robert and his family did not know of Dick's amazing derring-do survival until after a discussion at his funeral, when a friend 'googled' him and shared his story with the family. Furthermore, he didn't know of Dick's time in Thailand Railway camps until around 2015. 'He never spoke of his experience,' said Robert. 'And we didn't ask. In retrospect I wonder if we should have done, but there never seemed to be the right moment and we wanted to respect his apparent wish not to share it.'

'Why on earth did *we* not Google him?' Louise asked herself. 'The feelings it's engendered in me is, not necessarily anger, but just sort of despair that we didn't know. It sheds an enormous amount of light on how our parents' marriage functioned, how we functioned as children, and the damage that the internment has caused to the next generation.'

Robert described his father's general demeanour as 'quite withdrawn, and sometimes impatient and difficult, although his sister said he'd always been like that as a child. His character might also have been formed by the childhood experience of growing up in the empire,' he said of his father's birth and formative years in India due to his grandfather being in the Indian Army, and years in the English public boarding school system.

'Like other former PoWs, he never talked about his experiences, particularly to his loved ones. Even to our mother. None of us managed to glean more than tiny pieces of his experience as a PoW. His mother remarked to mum that the man returned from the war was not the Dick she had known. 'Of course, the mental scars were as obvious to his family as the physical ones,' Robert said. Apart from a couple of bullet wounds and a scar to the thigh still visible, 'there was some shrapnel in his foot which every few years would move around and cause him problems.'

This adds to the incredible feat of his escape, given he was partly incapacitated in the leg. Additionally, Robert noted another injury he carried: 'His two little fingers were both crippled and I assumed the suspicious symmetry must have been the result of torture of some kind.' Probably sustained while working on the Railway in Thailand.

They both painted a picture of Dick being a spiritual person and a lifelong learner who studied maths, and even programmed computers into his eighties.

The only other known non-RAMC survivor from the Sisters' Quarters incident was Norman Bryer, the Air Force pilot. Post-war he returned to Perak to ply his trade at the Bagan Pasir estate. He continued to enjoy his beloved golf and tennis.

One day he bumped into a teenaged girl, Annie. 'A local girl, whose mum – from Phuket – owned a shop. Once he saw her, that was it,' his daughter Lyn, now a schoolteacher in Canada, would relate to me. They married when she was 19, Norman being 20 years her senior. 'Annie's mum was like, "What are you guys doing?"' Life in Malaya appealed to Norman, who loved the jungle and the adventures it promised, as well as places like Penang. 'He fell in love with Penang, describing it as "the most beautiful paradise, the pearl of the Orient",' said Vicky, his second child, born in quick succession. Norman and Annie would go on to have six children.

'Norman's mum was quite a character and quite strong so I think she would disapprove of his marriage,' ventured grand-nephew Justin Parsons. 'Christmas cards would arrive each year, gradually revealing his wife Annie, then his six children.'

Despite a Malayan childhood 'full of lively memories and very joyful' as Vicky recalled it, they found themselves caught up in the violence and vagary of the Malayan Emergency. Annie and the children moved off the exposed estate, to live with her mum in the town of Taiping. Norman continued to be involved in the Rotary Club, and as a cub-scout master, earning him the Perak Meritorious Service Medal, bestowed by the Sultan of Perak. In the mid-Sixties, with Malaysia adrift, they emigrated to Western Australia. As a parting gift, he gave his loyal cook, Supramaniam – who'd served him for almost 25 years – a parcel of land.

'My dad made a big impression on my life,' said Vicky, still living in Western Australia. 'He encouraged me to read Somerset Maugham – one thing, never drop your standards, forgetting that you're a British colonial representing the empire. He didn't go out to conquer and plunder. He never failed to empathize with others – he could feel at home sitting on the floor with workers, or with the Sultan.' Having retired from the plantation business, he became a very devoted father and husband. 'He was a larger than life personality – he was my hero. A great humanitarian, a man of his word. Very upright, intelligent.' Daughter Lyn saw him the same way: 'Constantly reading.' He borrowed just about every book available from his local libraries, and immersed himself in Greek mythology, Tolstoy, the classics and poetry, Robbie Burns being a favourite: '"Man's inhumanity to man makes countless millions mourn" was a quote he oft repeated,' said Vicky, inadvertently albeit accurately amplifying the original quote. 'You couldn't believe he never went to university.' And in the background, always classic music and opera. Perhaps this was his own therapy to make sense of the atrocities he'd suffered and witnessed, because he didn't believe in psychiatrists, and yet seemed to have found peace in himself and with the world.

'All the time growing up, he'd talk about it intermittently,' said Vicky, ' a ... debriefing – I think you had to bring it out or it would drive you mad.' He was always a moderate drinker, never drinking to excess: '"May I offer you a sherry?"' was his typically old English welcome. 'He was English to the core, and a gentleman to the core.' Sherry and whisky sat in decanters on the shelf.

Like Capt Smiley, he never revisited the sites of the war. 'Who would want to go back there and relive all that?' he would say. His great camp-mate from the Railway, Peter Peacock, remained a great close friend post-war. 'But when Peacock went up to revisit it, he was really badly affected,' said Lyn, 'and didn't live long after that. "Part of me died with him", dad said.'

But he didn't seem to bear a grudge. 'He always said self-pity is the worst thing for a human being to have,' said Lyn. 'If you had self-pity you would just crumble.' But he didn't and couldn't ignore his experiences, because there were physical reminders. 'He had a huge scar down his right side. As I kid I'd say, "What is that?" and he'd say, "It's where I got hurt". It was around six-inches long, from the bayonetting he received. But if you didn't know he'd been through it, you wouldn't have guessed. He held it together, never lost his temper. I had a very good relationship with my father. A really great dad, supportive. The way he parented, he obviously had thought about the important things in life.'

'He showed us the cuts on his back,' recalled Vicky. 'And when he'd go for an X-ray the doctors would always say, "There's a bullet inside you!" and he'd say, "Oh, that's my souvenir from the war". But it caused him no discomfort.'

'We had Japanese cars," laughed Lyn, as evidence that Norman bore no grudges. 'Also, they had exchange students and had a couple of Japanese students. He was very fond of them, and never said anything bad about the Japanese.' Vicky has visited the Death Railway, when her husband was working in Thailand. 'This hit me very hard when I walked the war cemetery ... thousands of crosses with names and ages as young as 17 years old.' Her son worked in Japan. 'He speaks Japanese fluently, and my grand-children speak Japanese. It shows the capacity of humans to forgive and forget. I think my dad would not like us to hold a grudge. War to my father was a sign of man's failure to keep his eyes on the purpose of his existence which is love for God and for his fellow man and the desire to make this world and leave it in a better state for future generations.'

And yet the tendrils of February 1942 still reach deeply into the 21st century. It turned out Norman had penned his memoirs which Lyn keeps in a safe in her home. 'I have never read them from front to back. After he passed I couldn't bring myself to do it. It's very emotional, because he had distinctive handwriting.' She very generously agreed to scan the relevant pages regarding the Alexandra Hospital and sent them to me. I trembled as I read them. Indeed, it felt like a very clear voice from beyond the grave to glean, for the very first time, what it really *felt* like moments before, and during, the massacre in the Sister's Quarters outhouse.

The thoughts. The confusion. The tension. The desperation. The horror.

'You can't imagine that happening in a hospital,' Lyn reflected. 'Such a war crime.' Yet, knowing the heroic survival story of her father didn't surprise her: 'Yes, it matches with him,' she said. 'Stoic.'

Norman died in Perth aged 89. 'When we collected his ashes, the Japanese bullet was still in there. As we sprinkled his ashes into the Swan River, it went "clink" and sunk down into the water.'

Bert Gurd returned from the war, but not before he'd gone on leave overseas first to recuperate. He finally married his long-time sweetheart Rosa late in 1946. They soon added a daughter, Maureen, and a son, Stephen. I was disappointed to learn that Bert's dream of living a simple life back on the farm – articulated to his pals in those early days of captivity in Changi – hadn't come to pass. 'I think the three boys were all reluctant farmers,' explained Maureen of Bert and his two brothers. 'So he worked in an infirmary, but the hours were unsociable. I remember going to the infirmary when I was a small child on Christmas Day. I think he used to work a half day on Christmas Day.'

'It wasn't earning enough money,' surmised Stephen, adding that Bert then went to work at Wellworthy's, the local Lymington car parts factory, manufacturing piston rings. 'He did it because he had to, but he didn't enjoy it.' There were a couple of ironies there: one is that Bert never owned a car, preferring to ride a bicycle or walk everywhere. The other was the factory eventually merged when most jobs were lost to the burgeoning low-cost automotive manufacturing centre of Japan.

'I had a Japanese car,' said Stephen, living in Birmingham. 'Dad would be mortified! He didn't hate them, but ...'

'Just couldn't reconciliate with them,' clarified Maureen. 'Not bitter. He wasn't that sort of man.' Which got me wondering, what kind of father was Bert, who was in his early 40s by the time she was born? 'Kind, caring, interested in people. He just wanted to forget about the war and lead a normal life. He was "Uncle Bert" to everyone, very popular. And my mum was a popular auntie.' Family holidays were scarce, and usually involved time with Rosa's family in Watford, or family coming to stay with them in Lymington, where the nearby ocean and the New Forest were local attractions.

'He was a good dad, a good guy,' agreed Stephen. 'He wasn't abusive. He was deeply religious – his Roman Catholic faith got him through a lot. I don't know why he joined the Army and went to war. Before the war he was with St John Ambulance. He didn't want to go to war with a gun and shoot people. And he was in a reserved occupation as a farmer. He went because of his care for other people.'

'A very caring person,' nodded Maureen from her home in Ireland. Jointly they paint a picture of a contented man living a humble family life. 'Dad was a quiet, caring man who led a simple life. Perhaps after all the horror and trauma of the war years he was happy to settle for just that.' And a centrepiece of that life was the traditional Sunday lunch, replete with a roast. 'Sunday lunch was one o'clock on the dot,' according to Maureen who noted Bert's good appetite, and a particular soft spot for lashings of cream.

'But he'd get quite cranky if you played with your food. And one thing he'd never eat was "dirty, filthy rice".'

'Yes, kind, and a gentleman, but strict,' added Stephen. 'He didn't like blasphemy.'

'And disciplined, quite Victorian in his outlook,' reflected Maureen. 'I never heard him swear, not even a mild swear word. I mean, when he was in the war, they must've swore like troopers, like all the time.' We all laughed at the literal accuracy of that statement. And not outgoing, often preferring the company of a good book such as *Tennyson's Poetical Works* or *The Story of Lord Kitchener*. He also enjoyed music, singing in the local choir for a time. 'My grandmother had an old windup gramophone on which we played 78s, and one of Dad's favourites was *Swedish Rhapsody*, and he loved the voice of John McCormack, the Irish tenor.' Often he'd be found doing crossword puzzles and playing word games, at which he was particularly adept, once winning a competition in 1959 and buying the family a TV with his £25 winnings. He also tried to supplement his wages with a win in the football pools. 'We always had to keep quiet while he filled in his results in the newspaper from Sports Report on the radio at 5pm on a Saturday afternoon.'

So how did his heroic deeds around the hospital and escaping the massacre site square away with the man they knew? 'No,' said Stephen emphatically. 'Almost like a completely different person.' Maureen tried to reconcile the rather sturdy man she knew zig-zagging his way, dodging machine gun fire and grenades. 'Doesn't really match him at all. He said in his memoir "I ran like I never ran before" ... haha!' He was a walker, but never sporty.'

They never really spoke openly with Bert on those events. 'Maybe Dad wanted to protect us from all that rubbish,' ventured Maureen. 'They were not encouraged to talk about it. We can only imagine the horror! I suppose they just didn't want to keep on reliving it, perhaps.'

Bert never attended a local ceremony on Remembrance Day, and only kept in touch with a couple of his wartime pals, one being Ralph Day another being 'someone Earley'. 'I don't know why, but he used to watch the Cenotaph service on TV and get very emotional about watching that,' added Stephen. But generally otherwise he seemed to have kept his emotions in check, and was 'comparatively fine' post-war. 'He didn't have a tropical illness or anything like that,' said Maureen.

'There will not, I fancy, be many to envy my position,' wrote Bert in his personal memoir of the massacres, 'but I was there.' Bert lived until he was 74 and was sorely missed thereafter. In 2006 the siblings planted an oak tree (now 25-feet tall) at the National Memorial Arboretum in Staffordshire in his memory. There, a replica of the Changi Prison gate dominates the area. 'His plaque says: "Kind, and a friend to everbody who knew him." Every person he met, he was kind, friendly, generous,' said Stephen, who visits the site regularly.

'A lovely tribute,' said Maureen as her eyes welled up. 'I'm very proud of him, and I'm glad he's getting the recognition.' She and husband Don went to Singapore in the early 2000s. 'We saw where the hospital was, very poignant. I was quite emotional, just to think he was there and that's where it all kicked off.' Their son – Duncan, who was in the Navy – visited the memorial fountain at the hospital.

'To survive that ... and then three years on the Railway ..." Stephen trailed off.

'I don't know how the people at home coped,' said Maureen, thinking of her mum, Rosa, and the families of the FEPOWs. 'It was absolute torture. It must've been tough not knowing all that time. Oh, it must've been terrible.'

Sydney Hoskins returned to his pre-war trade of printing, and had two children with Pat. 'He had his own printing business in the 70s and 80s,' grand-daughter Lauren Lloyd (no relation) told me. 'Then his son Peter took on the business, and Sydney became a driver for the business.' She described a 'very funny man with an extremely dry sense of humour' who would daily say 'I'm just popping to the shops' and then head down to his local Legion club in Burgess Hill for a 'cheeky pint' or several. 'Sometimes grandmother would have to call up the Legion to find out where he was,' she laughed.

Interestingly he seemed to have avoided talking to his PoW mates: rather he sought out company around his own age. 'He was often contacted to go to reunions,' noted Jo Walker, another granddaughter, 'and he said, "Why would I want to remember that?"' She described him as someone always smiling and 'his sense of humour shone through'. Lauren saw him as 'very introverted, very quiet' although – as the CEO of a voluntary organization with a career in many philanthropic foundations – she was clearly fond of him. 'Granddad didn't want to talk about his experiences, he was *adamant* about that.' He did obviously share some things with wife, Pat. 'But she didn't want to betray his confidence by sharing that thing we don't speak of.' Lauren's sister, nurse Selena, remembered one thing he did reflect on though: 'He always laughed at the fact that if he hadn't decided to go travelling he would've had a completely different experience. He got that wrong!'

If there were children in the house, he'd leave and sit in a separate room to quietly smoke his pipe. 'And he would leave a room if a Japanese car ad came on the TV,' said Jo. One thing Lauren did notice: he wore long sleeves 'all the time', and one wonders whether it was to cover up the scars from the wrist bindings that cut into his flesh when he was rounded up?

'I think he truly just blocked it all out,' said Jo. 'He just wanted to live a normal life of family, pints, and caravan.'

Sydney's son, Peter (Lauren's father), was tragically killed in a car crash in his mid-thirties. 'He had to bury his son. That was a huge trauma. He never recovered from that. That's an injustice. He was a shell of a man. We knew he'd witnessed horrific experiences. He'd been a prisoner of war, that's all we knew, but I didn't know that that meant.'

So I shared Sydney's experiences in The Alex and his dramatic escape from the outhouse with them. 'Mindblowing!' she said. 'Absolutely fascinating and incredible to hear granddad's story, how lucky, but also how much personal grit informs whether you survive something or not. I always wondered where I got my tenacity.'

Jo added: 'I wish I'd known when I was in Singapore two years ago, I would've gone to see the hospital.' Sydney passed away aged 86.

George Johnson's parents had received news in May 1943 that he was a prisoner of war, held at Malai camp. This bittersweet news made the local paper. Upon return he was discharged from the RAMC with an exemplary record, and was placed on a pension for 'a nervous disability'. Fully understandable. He wasted no time marrying local lass Mary Waterson, and a couple of children soon followed. But he remained clearly troubled because in 1951, the 33-year-old father of two was found by police trying to get into a shop in Lynn Street via its backyard. That shop was Lipton's, the same store where'd he'd worked as a young lad. He was put before the court where his solicitor said: 'He can give no explanation except that he was drunk.' Upon considering his service record and PoW experience, he was given a conditional discharge and behavioural bond for one year. He and Mary appear to not have had children, and he lived till 88.

**

Of others in the hospital, time often did nothing to dull the pain and impact of February 1942.

'There's a part of my grandmother that's never been closed on the death of her brother, Oswald Griffin,' great-nephew, Neil Storey, told me. 'She was sad every February. She thought maybe he was still out there somewhere, in a village in Malaya or something. Declaring someone dead is not the same as someone *being* dead. I want my great uncle to have a full honours funeral because he died for his mates. Not for me but for my grandmother,' he grew misty-eyed. 'Even if not in my lifetime. I have a son, and a grandchild ...' he tailed off, openly weeping. 'It's a legacy I've been given. It's not mine but it's to be shared.'

Capt Hugh Pilkington returned home to meet his son, Paul, who was born around the day the 6th Royal Norfolks headed up-country to the Malayan battlefields. Pilk had recurrences of malaria throughout his life, and his shoulder continued to plague him, requiring further operations. Pilkington apparently cooked up a mean curry, a legacy of his time pre-war as a planter. He regained most of the five stone he'd lost during the war.

'In those days the attitude was, "Bad luck, you survived the war, now get on with your life"," Paul told me. "I thought *everybody's* Dad went to Changi. I thought it was normal.' Pilkington then set about his post-war life with Phyllis and two children, including Paul's newly-arrived brother, Rupert. 'He set up this business renting out agricultural machinery. He was contracted to mow Air Force bases, etc.' He increasingly 'enjoyed a drink' and was an emotionally unavailable father, sometimes withdrawing or totally disappearing for a few days at a time. 'Not a day went by that he didn't mention the camps. "The Japanese this, or Changi that." But he would never *really* talk about it ... never said anything, right till the end.

The war was obviously never far from his mind as in 1949 he typed up all his letters and diaries, calling the result, *The Missing Years* (which I subsequently turned into a war history travelogue, retracing his steps with Paul). 'This record of the years 1941-1945 will, I hope, be of interest to you and the children,' he wrote. Pilk lived to the age of 77.

**

One of the most contentious issues is whether there was provocation and mitigation of the Japanese attack due to withdrawal of Indians through the hospital and 'double dipping' by using the Red Cross as protection and insurance?

'Their officers must have known their own plans,' contended Danny Fraser of the Japanese. 'Sometimes I think about it and sometimes I wonder why such a waste. The patients were a mixture of soldiers and civilians. There were very few soldiers in there but the Japanese said they threw back the clothing and found soldiers lying there with rifles beside them, and that was the reason they made sure by butchering everybody.

Second Lt John Wilson, the Kiwi with the Indian Army agreed: 'Absolutely ... an horrific action,' he sighed. 'One for which I've never forgiven the Japanese. I cannot forgive or forget. The

Japanese were a very capable race and when they became aggressive and decided to dominate the Far East with their military machine, they then allowed nothing to stand in their way. They abandoned all pretence at humanity and the troops in the front line acted without regard to the Geneva Conventions. I am not talking about the prisoners of war, I'm talking about their actions in the battlefield. Nothing would stop them and if anybody was in their road, if they were inconvenienced, they would shoot them.

'And in a case like this where they alleged there had been some firing, whereas we who were there, were quite convinced this is not the case, as they would have to pass up through the wards and up on the balconies, and no-one up there saw them, but they insisted.

'And, as a reprisal, which is completely against the rules laid down by the Geneva Convention, they massacred all those who were on the ground floor. Unforgivable!'

'Customary international law – the law of accepted practice by civilized nations – demands that all non-combatants, whether captured soldiers or medical personnel, be treated with a basic level of dignity and humanity,' international law specialist and scholar, Tom Stanley-Davies, told me. 'The actions of these Japanese forces ignored all this. Several of those acts surely amount to war crimes.' However, he went on to explain *jus in bello,* the law of warfare, regarding the Indians' use of hospital buildings as firing stations. 'Such behaviour recklessly and thoughtlessly placed those patients in harm's way, effectively making the hospital a legitimate target for approaching Japanese forces. Whether the Japanese attack was proportional and measured is difficult to say. However, once inside, several atrocities began to take shape. The indiscriminate killing of medical staff and wounded does not appear to be motivated by anything resembling military necessity. The capture, treatment, and extra-judicial killing of prisoners over the following days was in complete contravention of fundamental international law, and an affront to human conscience.'

Amazingly, some of the patients who survived did *not* hold the Japanese to blame for attacking the hospital, rather they held some Allied officers responsible. Capt Pilkington kicked off: 'It has never been established who the officer was who gave the order to withdraw under cover of the hospital, but whoever he was broke the first and greatest rule of the Geneva Convention. No blame in my opinion can be attached to the Japanese for the deaths of medical staff and patients during this period of battle.' Note, he seemed to be emphasizing the *battle* part. Not the aftermath.

Gunner Fergus Anckorn supported his view of the attack on the hospital: 'I think it could be justified,' he told me. 'Somebody fired a revolver from the balcony of the hospital. If you go into hospital armed, you must get rid of all your arms. If it happened, the Japanese would just rush in. If somebody actually did that, they brought it on themselves.'

Lt TR Bond of the Loyals was familiar with the area from personal observations while having to attend the hospital to collect fellows from his company, or equipment in The Alex area: 'The incident is supposed to have occurred as a result of Indians firing from within the hospital grounds and from the balconies of the hospital building during a withdrawal through the area. Although the building and area was obviously marked as a hospital site, there was a very heavy pall of smoke from the burning oil tanks nearby and visibility was poor at times. The Indian troops could, I suppose, be blamed for withdrawing through this area, but three points should be considered:

'Firstly, the chaotic conditions on the island at that point in time. The defence perimeter had by then been reduced to the outskirts of the city – from Alexandra and Gillman Barracks to the west, Tanglin Barracks to the north, and Kallang Airport to the east – and within this perimeter was a civilian population greatly increased by refugees. In addition a large number of troops – many from the base units whose workshops, storage depots, etc in the Changi, Seletar, Kranji and Alexandra (Pasir Pajang Ridge) areas had been overrun and were in this area.

'Secondly, many of the Indian units fighting in the area had by that time been reduced to a cadre of trained soldiers and had only recently been reinforced with recruits newly arrived from India and virtually untrained.

'Thirdly, the main points of the Japanese attack were from the west (along the coast road) and northwest (from Bukit Timah towards Alexandra and Gillman Barracks).

'Whilst the heat of battle, the presence of guns and mortars in the Alexandra area, and the use of small arms weapons from the hospital grounds, *might* provide some excuse for the initial reaction of the Japanese troops, there can, in my opinion, be no justification whatsoever for their behaviour once inside the hospital – as it was very apparent that only patients and medical personnel were there, grossly overcrowded as it was with injured troops.'

Brig George Ballentine, as CO of those retreating Indians, should ultimately cop the main flak, but his three commanding officers – Sainter, Southern and Ingle – were in better positions to stem or guide the flow. Incidentally, Weary Dunlop the eminent Australian surgeon on the Railway did not rate Sainter at all. In one famous confrontation at Nakhon Pathom, the former international rugby player shirt-fronted Sainter: 'There are several things I do not like about you. I do not like your manners, which are revolting, your discourse which is disgusting, your reputation which is repulsive ... or your appearance. If you ever come to my section of the camp making trouble again, I shall seize you by your dirty neck and the seat of your pants and throw you out.'

Ballentine retired in 1946, returned to Ireland and settled with Margaret. Their daughter married a major in the 14th Punjab regiment that same year, continuing a family tradition of Indian Army connection, especially as their son-in-law's family (on both maternal and paternal sides) had served with it, too. George served as the High Sheriff in County Tyrone over the next decade. They decamped to Belfast where he later died at the age of 81.

**

The happy youngster, Pte George Britton, was a changed man (all of 24) by the time he returned home. 'Cantankerous,' was how sister Elsie described him post-war, although he remained essentially 'very kind and thoughtful'. He married Barbara two years after returning to England, and worked as a draughtsman while studying at night for a mechanical degree, plus adding two children to the family. After he graduated, he worked for the London Hospital Board. He never spoke about the war, never attended any memorial parades, and shied away from any emotion. Only when his daughter and son-in law were working in Singapore did he travel there, and up to Thailand, not saying much, but sharing snippets of his shocking experiences over the years with his sister, Elsie.

'They didn't like us very much,' was how Punjab's Capt Robert Brown summed up the Japanese view towards them. 'Reason is Japanese have no time at all for sickness and anyone who is wounded or sick is of no further use to them, they may as well be dead. They didn't have big field hospitals like we did, and as I found out later on in Thailand, they despised anyone who was sick or wounded because he couldn't fight. '

How did a man of the cloth look at the incident? 'Terrible business,' Father Brendan Rogers summarized, laconically. 'That was a bad show. I think the Japs themselves were upset when that happened.' As for his own treatment as a PoW: 'We were the bottom of the list, and we got it from just ordinary soldiers. I got my face slapped a number of times, back and forth. By a *corporal*! They'd beat you up for not understanding. Incredible! I didn't know a single word of Japanese and was told I should learn.'

Pte Stan Sharpley made it home at the end of 1945 – albeit blind in one eye from catching diphtheria in Changi – and married Jean in 1946. They had three children who, in turn, gave them seven grandchildren and nine great grandchildren. I met Stan in 2005 in Singapore where he'd come to commemorate the 60th anniversary of the Fall of Singapore, with one of his grandchildren in tow. I asked him what he felt when he hears the Last Post? 'Oh, me mates, the lads from the regiment. We'll hear it tomorrow at Kranji.' He was sombre for a moment, lost in that mental distance, then took a sip of his gin-and-tonic, and was back reminiscing fondly of Singapore again as the sun set on the lawn of the British ambassador's rather splendid residence, Eton Hall, where the Union Jack still flew proudly.

Stan passed away at the grand age of 96 and was given a guard of honour comprising soldiers of the Duke of Lancaster's Regiment (a successor to his beloved Loyal Lancashires). The vicar described him as a 'friendly outgoing man who would get on with anyone.' I concur wholeheartedly.

Upon the end of the war, Danny Fraser, just 25 when his Royal Engineers were dug in immediately behind The Alex on that fateful weekend, went down to convalesce with relatives in Australia, before finally making it home to his clan in Motherwell early 1946. He stayed on with the Army and was promoted later that year, and married his sweetheart, with a daughter following the next year, plus a son the year after that.

'When he was discharged from the Army,' his grandson Mark Dalton told me, 'he qualified as a gas fitter, was a school janitor, taught plumbing in St Andrew's school in Shannon, was a pest control officer at the Faslane Naval Base, before becoming a caretaker at the army camp in Garelochead.' This is near the Clyde River in Scotland.

'He went to an art club in Garelochhead in his later years and painted as a way of dealing with his time as a PoW. He never could stand hot days and it was the only time we'd see him grumpy. He used to annoy my Gran when he made a Malay curry as it would stink the house out, and she never liked curry!'

Clearly he had a lot playing on his mind, inerasable, indelibly stamped memories of the incident at the hospital, a full half-century earlier.

'Sometimes I wake up through the night, dreaming about the hospital,' said Danny. 'It's like a game you play with yourself. Should I have done this? Should I have gone over and helped? Should I have stayed back or should I have charged over to the hospital? And it's a thing that will never be answered. That's all the regrets I have, but ... what I saw there I will never forget,' he sighed.

**

Interestingly, many of the expatriate men living in Singapore and Malaya pre-war (many serving with the FMS Volunteers) who survived the Alexandra Massacre, returned to Southeast Asia soon post-war. Partly, it was economic necessity to re-establish the mining and rubber industries, partly to escape a rather moribund post-war Britain, and partly perhaps to 'get back on the horse' after their ordeals in war and captivity. Afterall, Malaya was in the blood of many of these men and their families.

Among those who did were three from the armoured car blast in which Veitch was a part. Cpl David Alexander went to work with Guthrie's in Singapore again from 1946-51. The Aussie mining engineer Jack Slater returned for another few years before heading back to Australia. And the towering presence of that rubber man, Peter Lucy, and wife, Tommy. Post-war he was back on the estates, and became an honorary Inspector in the Auxiliary Police as the Communist threat stepped up. He adapted their family cars into makeshift armoured vehicles for they were often under attack by guerillas, and he won the Colonial Police Medal in 1952 before heading off to plant in East Africa instead. Their adventures were captured in Noel Barber's evocative book on the Malayan Emergency, *War of the Running Dogs*.

South African-born Lt Jack 'Hugo' Hughes had been an assistant planter in Malaya. Despite his amputated leg, lost in the battle around Pasir Panjang, he returned to KL in 1969 as Director of Malayan Estates.

The larger-than-life Philip Paxton Harding spent a further six years in Malaya at the Strathairlie Estate in Sungei Buloh, and later continued life as a visiting agent.

The tennis-and-cricket-mad Charles Mounsey also returned in 1946, sans family after his marriage dissolved, and stayed on into the fifties.

**

And what befell the other characters and bit-part players in this drama?

Robert Loveday, the central figure in The Alex construction corruption scandal, was never to experience such wealth again. His mother Fanny passed away in December 1946, leaving him a share of her meagre £296 estate. By then he was again practicing as an architect and surveyor, which he continued to do until his death at the age of 68 in Devon. His probate amount to Alice was just £400, and she passed away nine years later.

Their daughter Dorothy, married to RSM Derek Crosby, lived a typically itinerant army life with postings with the British Military Attache in Norway, Germany and Hong Kong among others. Youngest daughter, Pamela – described in a newspaper report as an "attractive brunette" – was a keen motorcyclist, mixing it up with the men of the motorcycle clubs in the Newcastle area. As for Loveday's son, Donald, he somewhat ironically became a policeman. In turn, Donald's son Phil also appears to have been a policeman for decades before becoming a forensic manager chasing down money launderers and tracing corporate fraud. He's also a keen musician (with a performing party band) and had no idea of his grandfather's musical prowess.

When I contacted Phil to discuss Robert and Alice's time in Singapore, he told me: 'Until now, I was never aware of this, as it had never been discussed or brought to my attention. I met my grandfather maybe twice as a young child and I have no real memory of him.' He indicated his keenness to help and even find some photos of the couple in Singapore. The reaction from his mother, Norma (the widow of Donald), was diagonally different. 'Mentioning this scenario was a bit of a shock to her, and brought back some bad memories which she doesn't want revived.'

After presumably doing some rummaging around himself and learning more about his grandfather, Phil apparently ghosted me, and my further emails went unanswered. A chance for a family redemption story lost, I felt, especially after Robert's positive and earnest start.

Capt Robert Loveday's local co-conspirator in The Ring, Lim Bo Seng, left a more positive legacy. Having been instrumental in Force 136 behind enemy lines, the 35-year-old brick and biscuit maker was in killed in 1944. A 1954 memorial plinth at Esplanade Park lauds him as a war hero and loyal Chinese patriot, and he even has a street named after him in modern-day Singapore.

Charles Withers-Payne, who presided over Loveday's court-martial, ended up being sued by OCBC Bank in 1959 for bankruptcy due to an outstanding loan of $504,000 (around $4.5m in today's money). This was served on him and his company in Singapore and at his chambers in London. As a result he was disgraced and ended up relocating to Tanzania, East Africa, where he was still able to practice, advising farmers, and driving a monstrous Chevvy called the *Queen Mary* around. His work in advising farmers and representing them against an increasingly nationalistic government earned him an OBE.

Vaux, the prosecutor of the case, post-war became the president of the Singapore Chess League and continued playing competitively for many contented years.

**

The adage that 'the victors write history' is largely true. Many of the Japanese soldiers returned home and got on with life best as they could, keeping a low profile, possibly harbouring doubts and shame over some of their actions and involvements, but naturally over the defeat itself.

Because their military code essentially called for them to not return if they were not victorious.

But they had regimental associations just like their Allied counterparts did. Places where they could go for empathy and brotherhood. For who else could possibly understand some of the actions and activities they'd been involved in?

In the process of my detective work for this book I was preparing to fly to Japan and go and knock on some doors of the shortlisted suspected battalion associations just when Covid shutdowns struck. I just wanted to meet *one* Japanese soldier who admitted he was in The Alexandra Hospital on 14-15 February 1942. So I could ask the question: 'What were you thinking?'

Alas that opportunity was kyboshed and at 80 years' distance now the chance of finding someone alive and coherent enough is sadly infinitesimally small. But quite a few of the Japanese protagonists in The Alexandra Hospital Massacres had their say, albeit nobody ever admitted to the massacres per se.

In terms of sentiment perhaps Pte Miyake Genjiro of IJA 5th Division, who was ordered to carry out bayonet killings of 400

Chinese near KL, gets closest to the essence I imagine. 'As a human being, I don't want to talk,' said the veteran soldier-turned-carpenter to academic researcher Henry Frei. 'Why? Because of shame. Our shame. It is too difficult to talk about. But I can testify to it in my own person.' He did speak out in a documentary *Aggression on the Malayan Peninsula: The War They Did Not Teach Us About* to awaken the world and explain the realities of war. His orders were simple: 'Now by the order of His Imperial Majesty, kill them.' The situation he reluctantly found himself in, was that 'if the godlike Japanese Emperor ordered you to perform a task, however terrible, there was no choice but to obey.'

Dr Suzuki Susumu, the head medical man for 18th Division through Singapore and Burma until April 1943, transferred to Manchuria in April 1943 as Chief of Medical Section Kanto HQ Defence Army, promoted to major general in August 1944, moved to Tokai (Nagoya where there were many PoW camps), and ended the war looking after the medical affairs of the last-ditch 13th Area Army, defending that area of the homeland in preparation for the Allied invasion.

Interrogated to make a statement in 1947 he was less than totally forthcoming, given his denial of any wrongdoings and atrocities at the hospital, something which was abundantly obvious to all others given the state of the place. Or perhaps he was just toeing the party line of his then-boss, Mutaguchi, with whom he visited the hospital.

Mutaguchi penned a memoir of sorts in 1954. It turned out it was never published and the manuscript, scrawled in Japanese *kanji* , sits in original draft form at the National Institute of Defense Studies in Tokyo. While illuminating, it is totally self-serving.

'I always blamed myself because I couldn't appropriately manage the Peiping/Wanping Bridge incident and caused a lot of troubles to the country and the Army, and that was why I insisted to attack Assam,' he wrote. 'I later discovered that it was done by a group of young officers from the Chinese 29th Army who didn't like the ceasefire agreement with the Japanese. In my diary I wrote that it took more than 25 years where the truth of the history (that we

Japanese did not start it) was revealed.' This despite the fact that he openly boasted several times of starting the whole fracas.

'I strongly believed that to complete the offensive mission in Burma with victory would be the only way to prove my faith to the country.' However, his insistence was dismissed by the Army and, instead, the Imphal Campaign was ordered for the 'passive strategic purpose to defend Burma.' The remains of around 20,000 of his Japanese soldiers still lie scattered in the hills of Manipur and Nagaland to what was arguably Japan's greatest defeat following on from their greatest success in Singapore. Those looking for justice in any of this, might find solace in that fact.

All of this clearly continued to weigh heavily on Mutaguchi's mind. When his disobedient commander Sato died in 1959, Mutaguchi attended his funeral, taking the opportunity to print up leaflets denouncing Sato for failing to move on Dimapur. Four years later a study claimed that Imphal had failed because of this lack of initiative. Of course, Mutaguchi came out with the Japanese equivalent of 'I told you so' to anyone who would listen.

According to Hajime there is no mention in his memoir of his time in Sugamo or Singapore jail on the war crimes raps. I was especially keen to know his feelings of being released from Changi and imprisonment in general. 'I couldn't find any related statements in his diary.' Selective, self-serving.

This is equally applicable to his possible involvement in The Alexandra Hospital Massacres.

Here is the key paragraph from his handwritten manuscript, written in 1954, and translated directly into English by Hajime for me: 'I had never heard of the massacre at the British hospital till when Col Wild of the British Army visited me in Sugamo Prison in Tokyo and told me about it on 9 September 1946. It was first time for me to hear such a story. It seemed the British misunderstood that I apologized about what happened at this hospital because I visited the hospital next day after it was believed to happen. But I didn't mean to apologize because I didn't receive any of such reports till after the war.'

Mutaguchi seemed to guard his private life zealously, although he did have a son who co-operated with his father's biographer to give us a better understanding of the man. Mutaguchi died aged 78 in Tokyo in 1966.

Warrant Officer Arai Mitsuo of 114th Regiment published a memoir of his wartime experiences. He was one of the frontline officers closest in combat to The Alex. But I did not consider him a suspect because they were working their way across from the west coast and didn't cross Ayer Rajah Road. We learned that after fighting in Singapore then Burma, his term of military service expired in July 1942. He returned to Japan. However he was later re-drafted and sent to north China until war's end. In February 1946 he was repatriated to Japan.

'It's difficult to evaluate those years,' he said. 'Were they good or bad years? It was all fate. Our fate. When I look back now that I've reached 80 and I don't know how many years I've got left, when I come to think about death, I think I might have been better off to die together with those people who fell one after another around me at that time in the battle for Singapore. One has to die anyway. Is it not better to die at the time one is required to die?' Reading between the lines there is clearly survivor guilt at play, and perhaps the mental anguish of living with the horrors he witnessed.

Capt Yoshiaki Iwasaki, the pilot, also had a hell of a war by anyone's standards but lived to tell his tale. 'After the Fall of Singapore, I flew from Manila, Davao, Java, Borneo, Indian Ocean, Paramushir Island near Russia, Marshall Islands, Rabaul, Guadalcanal, Buna, Taiwan, Hainan Island, and Okinawa,' he said, essentially tracing the arc of the dynamic frontline and America's intervention in the South Pacific. 'I didn't have any idea how long the war would continue.' But as depressed as he was by the surrender and the end of the war, he went on to live a long life, still active when I interviewed him in 2018.

After the war he became a rescue helicopter pilot, and also became a pilot for transporting Prime Minister, Takeo Fukuda. As his fortuneteller had predicted, during and after the war, he crashed his planes – sometimes coming precariously close to causing a serious accident – but he never got seriously wounded. 'In Okinawa, toward the end of war, I was bombed by an American bomber and a piece of bomb fragment hit my body and it is still in my body today,' he told me.

Tsuji, as we've seen, returned to Japan when all war crimes charges against him – a disgustingly extensive list – were astonishingly dropped due to American political motivations.

But Tsuji did give us some insights into his mindset in his memoir: 'Battlefield mentality is very strange. When you see the blood of a friend or comrade or subordinate, at that moment you just go crazy ... you go off the rails. Afterwards, when you cool down, you understand what you did was wrong.' Could this be construed as a very veiled admission or apology of sorts?

'The numerous and disgusting later breaches of military discipline must be considered in comparison with the far more numerous fine and noble actions of the battlefield. Beside them any discreditable actions will in time be swept into oblivion.' Indeed you are wrong, sir! Eighty years on these atrocities still disgust as unfathomably and strongly as ever.

With a failing political career, he applied for 40 day's leave from the Diet (Japanese parliament) to go on an 'inspection tour of Southeast Asia' – taking in Singapore, Burma, Thailand, South Vietnam, Laos and Cambodia – and intending to return on 13 May 1961.

He boarded an Air France plane in Haneda, bound for Bangkok. Ten days later he was seen with his old acquaintance, Col Ito Chikashi (*not* Ito Kojiro of 55th Div), a defence attaché from the embassy in Bangkok, together in Vientiane, Laos, where he converted enough local currency for two or three days' stay. He asked Ito to send his briefcase back to Japan, requesting specifically for it to be held at the Japan Airlines office in Tokyo with a note: 'I am to return about 10 May.'

That case turned out to contain no more than dirty underwear and some gifts of silver plates and dishes.

He sent a postcard to his family (his son Toru, 30, was then a student at Tokyo University) indicating he'd met two high-ranking officers in Thailand's defence force and saying, 'I am going to teach at the Military Academy' while indicating the same return date.

But 10 May came and went, his leave of absence expiring. His wife made enquiries with the Foreign Ministry and the Upper House secretariat.

There were all sorts of reported red herrings over the next few months: he was in Indonesia where he had received three billion Yen for his activities, he was 'getting along fine' in Nepal, he'd 'died in Jail' in Cambodia, he was 'with Ho Chi Minh's Army' having smuggled himself into Viet Nam, and so on. One of the wilder theories was that he was on the trail of the so-called 'Yamashita's Gold' of treasures looted by the IJA, worth an estimated 17 trillion Yen and stockpiled in Singapore, but these were never shipped back as intended to Japan.

His wife received a mysterious call from a Chinese person at the end of July informing her that Tsuji was shot to death by a Chicom police officer in Kirin, China, where he was apparently lecturing students from North Vietnam, Indonesia and North Korea in guerilla tactics. It was felt that the Communist Chinese disliked the fact that he was publicizing their support with operational funds.

And his disappearance became headline news in Japan and across Southeast Asia. The CIA kept an active dossier on all his reported movements but had no firm grip on his status or whereabouts. An envelope dated 8 August 1962 was subjected to handwriting analysis by the CIA and deemed conclusively to be his handwriting. His son planned to fly to South Vietnam to get some definitive answers, but none were ever forthcoming.

In July 1968 he was formally declared 'presumed dead'. A statue in Kaga, in the prefecture of his birth, commemorates this famous yet infamous figure.

Like the demise of Cyril Wild, the disappearance of Tsuji is yet another enigma within the greater puzzle, destined to shroud the secrets of the Alexandra Hospital Massacres in perpetual mystery.

**

To date, no Japanese on his deathbed has ever made a confession of involvement. To the contrary, it has stoically been deny, deny, deny.

So I put this question to Fergus Anckorn: What message

would he send to any Japanese soldier involved in the massacres if he ever met one? 'If someone said they had done it, I'd say if he had orders to go in, I'd understand it. He might be a nice chap in other circumstances. You could just say, "I was there". It was a nasty part of the history of the world and I am glad you got away with it, and glad I got away with it.'

**

'Reflecting on this, my most traumatic experience, it is not the terror that overshadows all else in my memory,' wrote Norman Bryer in his hand-scrawled unpublished memoir. 'What I can recall of my emotions, the strongest were depression, sadness and regret. I suppose I had a heightened awareness of what was happening around and to me, and a readiness to adjust as necessary. I did not expect to survive but I had a faint hope of doing so but, if and when I had to die, I thought I might as well die with courage and dignity as shamelessly pleading and grovelling. But if survival depended upon grovelling and pleading, I might have done so.

'Although I did save my life by my initiative, not forgetting the Madras Sapper and Miner, I didn't really think I could escape my awful plight, but I didn't want to be slaughtered like a sheep, as I saw the poor fellows through the crack in the door being treated. It was worse than any nightmare I ever had and worse than the most fearful ordeal I had ever imagined could happen.'

Fully understandable, for what was seen could never possibly be unseen. And he spoke for all those unfortunates directly and indirectly involved. The British Military Hospital Singapore was indeed – for those two days of February 1942 and in the living memory beyond – a bleeding slaughterhouse.

– The End –

If you are a relative of someone involved in The Alex's history, the author would love you to contact him to join our community, keep the conversation going, and meet with other relatives you have a common touchpoint with.
Email stulloyd.worldsmith@gmail.com and introduce yourself.
Thanks!

Acknowledgments

First and foremost, thank you to all the ladies and gentlemen who served their countries. Lest we forget your bravery, hardships and sacrifices.

The scope and scale of this was brought home to me by interviewing two survivors of the massacres, Gunner Dick Lee (RIP) and Gunner Fergus Anckorn (RIP). Speaking with someone who was there, lived to tell the tale, and is describing their survival experiences to you, is something indescribably humbling. I am also indebted for the generous time and insights given to me by WW2 veterans Dr Bill Frankland, Maj (ret'd) Roy Hudson (RIP), Pte Stan Sharpley (RIP) and Capt Iwasaki Yoshiaki. The ability to ask them specific questions that could fill in blanks of my knowledge or comprehension was invaluable. And civilian Sion Abraham kindly shared his memories of growing up as a child in pre-war and wartime Singapore.

The next best thing was speaking to the relatives of veterans, who added depth and texture and invaluable tracking of personal documents, diaries and photos to flesh out the characters, as well as lend an understanding of the often residual effects of such a traumatic series of events on the protagonists and their families. Among these generous sharers who allowed me to intrude repeatedly into their lives are siblings, sons and daughters, sons- and daughters-in-law, nieces and nephews, and grandsons. Mark Dalton; Elsie Britton Douglas and Beth Steiner Jones; Stephen Gurd, Maureen Lane and Don Lane; Brian Hill; Kathy Knott; Lauren Lloyd, Selena Hoskins and Jo Walker; Phil Loveday and Norma Loveday; Justin Parsons, Denise Bryer, Lyn Bryer and Vicky Kingsbury; Dr Nikolai Petrovsky, Sharen Pringle and Dr Kathleen Petrovsky; Paul Pilkington; Mike Poole; Vickie Quinn; Fiona Smiley; Neil Storey; Robert Waller and Louise Kidd. It was a particular delight to deal with Elsie (I don't receive many facebook friendship requests from centenarians!). But each of these allowed me to probe into deeply personal areas, often even when it was clearly uncomfortable for them, to gain a clearer understanding, or in some cases for me to help them gain closure by sharing what I knew.

Col (ret'd) Marty Slade, RAMC, is the son-in-law of Brian Hill, and I especially thank him for his interest and keenness to pen the Foreword to this book, a suitable tribute to the men and women of the Royal Army Medical Corps, who figured so proudly and prominently in this episode, and – true to their motto – gave so much amid startling adversity.

When I started researching this book in 2008, and approached the Alexandra Hospital, I was entertained kindly and professionally by the PR team. But my incessant demands possibly had the irritant value of a mosquito at a garden party. It was not until the management of the hospital came under the National University Hospital of Singapore (and CEO, associate professor Jason Phua) that I made a truly valuable ally in Tan DinXiang, now the assistant manager. I found someone whose passion for the history of the hospital matched my own, and who worked tirelessly to ferret out archival materials, put me in touch with valuable co-conspirators, or even double-check on Japanese translations (he's a multi-linguist). I've also seen him give endlessly to other PoW's relatives seeking information in social media forums, and help to build a community of those touched by their involvement with The Alex.

On the note of forums, gosh, where would we be without the Herculean and unstinting efforts of Ronnie Taylor and his FEPOW family /COFEPOW website and facebook pages, and Michael Pether and his Malayan Volunteers Group website?

My amateurish genealogical search for the Loveday clan led me to contact Kim Crosby, who turned out not to be a related grand-daughter at all, but she did put me in touch with super-sleuth genealogist, Dr Jane Cavell, who turned out to be an absolute terrier and went way beyond my brief to help me track down living relatives of many of the key characters of the cast. I would highly recommend her to anyone wanting to pull together family tree information.

Hajime Marutani was a pleasure to work with in seeking answers from long-lost Japanese veterans and neglected documents in archival storage in Japan.

Jonathan Moffatt, an author himself, was incredibly generous in sharing his knowledge of all things Malaya, especially related to the Federated Malay States Volunteer Force. Another author, Cecil Lowry, also over-shared his knowledge and research of The Alex, while forensic historian Lynette Silver was a willing sounding-board on areas such as the Bangka and Parit Sulong massacres, and Dr Toby Norways shared his knowledge of regimental actions around the hospital. Other subject-matter experts I tapped included Commander Jim Macmahon of the NSW Fire & Rescue Service, Takayuki Shiraishi about Japanese regional diets and nutrition, Lynette Ramsay Silver, AOM, on the Bangka massacres, and Tom Stanley-Davies about international law.

Thanks to the following institutions and the wonderful people within them, who helped me to finger what I needed from them more efficiently and effectively: Australian War Memorial, Central West Libraries (especially Jasmine Vidler and Sean Brady), Imperial War Museum, Museum of Military Medicine (for *Oner* magazine), National Archives of the United Kingdom (especially Katie Fox), National Army Museum, UK (especially Justin Saddington), Reflections at Bukit Chandu (especially Nicholas Charles), Royal Engineers Museum (especially Rebecca Blackburn), Singapore National Archives (especially Hanif), Singapore National Library (especially Irfanya), Singapore Tourism Board, Thai Burma Railway Centre (especially Andrew Snow), Wellington College (especially archivist Caroline Jones).

And to the following who also played their part in helping me get nearer the truth in some way: Rehman Aziz-ur, Sharon Court, Paul Gilbert, Ann Hacke, Anthony Hallam, Martin Heyes, Andre Langlois (*North Devon Gazette*), Lim Shao Bin, Dick Lindsay, Jasmine Lloyd, Justin Lloyd, Mark Moore, Martin Morland, Angus Robertson, John Robbins, Matt Stanyard, Hal Suzuki, Soko Tomita, and Sandy Wilson.

The book you have in your hand (or on your screen) now went through several metamorphoses. I am hugely indebted to the following publishing industry figures who showed interest in this topic, and invested their time to read and critique my manuscript: Michael Leventhal, Peter Schoppert, and Brig Henry Wilson. Rod Eime, Paul Pilkington, and Stephen 'Scotty' McKenzie also helped me to carve this rock into a better shape.

With thousands of data points included, alas, any errors of detail are entirely of my own making and remain mine to lament. Because I am acutely aware that with military history I am playing with the legacy of real people who put their lives on the line and deserve total respect accordingly. Lest we forget.

Bibliography and Sources

Primary research interviews/ correspondence undertaken by Stuart Lloyd:

Sion Abraham, interview, 08/10/2019
Gunner Fergus Anckorn, 55th Div, RA, interview, 11/06/2015
Mark Dalton, email correspondence 18/02/2021
Elsie Britton Douglas, email correspondence 23-28/02/2021
Capt Bill Frankland, RAMC, interview, 12/09/2005
Sgt William Hook, US Marines, 25/04/2019
Selena Hoskins, email correspondence 15/09/2021
Maj (ret'd) Roy Hudson, Royal Engineers, interviews, July 2009
Kathy Knott, email correspondence 16/2/2021
Gunner Dick Lee, RA, 11th Division, interviews, September 2015
Lauren Lloyd, interview 10/9/2021
Phil Loveday, email correspondence 28/8/2021
Nick 'Albert' Mitchell, 5th Royal Norfolks, interview, 12/09/2005
Pte Stan Sharpley, 2nd Loyals, interview, 12/09/2005
Lynette Ramsay Silver, interview 27/03/2019
Fiona Smiley, email correspondence, June 2021
Neil Storey, interview 03/03/2021
Rob Waller and Louise Kidd, interview 25/08/2021 and emails
Capt Iwasaki Yoshiaki, IJNAS, interview, 30/06/2018
Dr Nikolai Petrovsky, interview 26/08/2021
Dr Kathleen Petrovsky, interview 31/08/2021
Sharen Pringle, email correspondence, September 2021
Lyn Bryer, interview 05/10/2021 and emails
Vicky Kingsbury interview, 17/10/21 and emails
Maureen Lane, Don Lane, Stephen Gurd, interview 04/11/2021

Primary Research Sources:

Private Papers:

Richard de Warrenne Waller - *Some words on the occasion of his funeral*, Robert Waller 10/9/2010.
Tom Smiley, various letters to fiancee, 1940-41.
Thomas Boyd Smiley 1917-1981, biography by Fiona Smiley.
'A Most Splendid Soldier': The Life of My Great-Grandfather Major General George Bruce, Orson Fry
Military Cross presentation speech to Tom Smiley, 29/8/45
Walter Salmon letter to Jonathan Moffat
Henry Francis de Camborne Lucy account
Capt Hugh Pikington diaries, 1945
Dr Constantine Petrovsky – undated book manuscript draft
Francis Herbert Gurd – memoir: *I Was There*, 1942.
Norman Bryer – memoir, undated.

Oral History Recordings by National Archives of Singapore:

Dr Robert Brown, Stanley Bryant-Smith, Dr Benjamin Chew, Marie Cockburn (nee de Souza), Francis Docketty, Daniel Fraser, Irshad Ali Khan, Lee Koon Choy, Nora Irvin, Matthew Jubang, Dr Constantine Petrovsky, Father Brendan Rogers, Hector Rogers, Lt Vine, RAMC, Prof Hugh de Waardener, John Wilson, Dr Yeoh San Aun.

Imperial War Museum:

IWM 87/50/1 Maj JWD Bull, plus Annexed notes.
Private Papers of Col LE Vine Object 1030015510

Australian War Memorial:

AWM 54/1010/4/38 Craven War Crimes Trial Statement
MSS 1530 recollection by Alex Hatton Drummond 2/29th AIF
MSS 1583 Eyewitness account by Robert Mutton
MSS1548 The Matter of a Massacre, Peter Bruton

National Archives of Singapore:

100045 MD/JAG/FS/JC/ 10/ 4A Affidavit Francis Arthur Herbert Gurd, 21/2/46

100045 WCLS Alexandra Mil Hospital Case, Col Kerin 17/4/46
100045 WCLS War Crimes: Alexandra Military Hospital, Col Kerin 3/12/46
100045 WCLS War Crimes: Alexandria Military Hospital, 3/12/46
10045 MD/JAG/FS/JC/10/4A Affidavit George William Johnson 14/2/46
4507/BMWC Interrogation of Col Ito Kojiro 24/6/47
4507/BMWC Interrogation of Itami Tadao, 16/6/47
4507/BMWC Interrogation of Takeda Hisashi (Ju) 21/4/47
4507/BMWG Alexandra Hospital massare – interrogation of Nasu Yoshio
7IT/111/16 Alexandra Hospital Massacre Case
7IT/111/16 Alexandra Hospital Massacre Case, 5/6/47
7IT/68/106 Report on Massacre at Alexandra Hospital, 11/11/46
7IT/68/122 Lt Gen Mutaguchi Interrogation at Changi 21/12/46
Affidavit Joseph Wilfred Craven, 12/6/46
Affidavit Thomas Boyd Smiley, 26/2/46
AG/WCS/50568 Interrogation of Mutaguchi Renya by Cyril Wild, 9/9/46
BM/WCS/50668 Alexander Hospital Massacre Interrogation reports of Nasu, Soejima, Suzuki, 8/7/46
Certificate of warning Mutaguchi by Watson 6/11/46
Examination summary of Nasu Yoshio, 26/5/47
Examination summary of Soejima Yoshito (undated) 1947
Examination summary of Suzuki Susumu, 11/6/47
Examination summary of Takeda Hisashi 11/4/47
Examination summary of Umemoto Togoro, 11/7/47
Exhibit A of affidavit of Brigadier Stringer, 23/8/45
Identification of Mutaguchi by Craven 12/6/46
Japanese Atrocities – exhibit A, Stringer 23/8/45
Letter from Conrad Hayes to C-in-C British Forces, Singapore, 23/2/46
Letter from GL Peet to Col Irwin 9/10/68
Letter from GMG Atkins to Col Irwin 22/8/1968
Letter from HE Sayle to Col Irwin 8/9/68

Letter from Isobel Macfarlane to HA Dawkins 11 April 1942
Letter from Maj (ret'd) CF Jackman to Col Irwin 1968
Letter from Maj LEC Davies to GHQ India 8 April 1943
Letter from Major James Bull to father of Hugh Mitchell 29/9/45
Letter from SG Upperton to Col Irwin 10/9/68
Letter from Tom Smiley to Col Irwin 1968
Letter from TR Bond to Col Irwin 1968
Letter Pte E Varney to Mrs Lewis 4/12/45
Letter to Bill Davidson from Sir Ian Fraser, 6/11/68
MD/ JAG/FS/10/4A Affidavit of Cedric Norman Claude Bryer 14/2/46
MD/JAG/FS/10/4A Affidavit and annexe of Edward Lunt, 15/1/46 and 8/4/46
MD/JAG/FS/JC/10/4A Affidavit of Charles Herbert Stringer, 25/2/46
MD/JAG/FS/JC/10/4A Affidavit of Frederick William Bales, 5/4/46
MD/JAG/FS/JC/10/4A Affidavit of Richard de Warrenne Waller, 1/2/46
MD/JAG/FS/JC/10/4A Affidavit Sydney William James Hoskins (undated)
MD/JAG/FS/JC/10/4A Japanese War Crimes identification of Mutaguchi 12/4/46
MO 10 'Note on Singapore Fortress' 21/1/42
MO 10/00/BM/258 Loose Minute 'Approximate strength of Singapore Garrison' 18/2/42
NAB 1192 IWM87/50/1 Cyril Wild War Crimes investigation
Recollection by Brenda Macduff, QAIMNS/R, undated.
Statement BMH Singapore by Major Torbit (undated)
Summary of examination of Noguchi Akisumi 11/7/47
Summary of examination of Tsugawa Hiroshi 11/7/47
Sworn Statement by Lt Gen Mutaguchi Renya 6/11/46
Sworn Statement by Lt Gen Mutaguchi Renya, 6/11/46
Telegram to South East Asia Land Forces re Takeda interrogation (undated)
The Alexandra Outrage 13 February 1942, Col WJ Irwin
WCLO/21/148 to War Crimes Co-Ord Sec from Cyril Wild

WCLO/21/115 to War Crimes Legal from Cyril Wild
WCLO/4/167 to War Crimes Co-Ord Sec from Cyril Wild
WO 32/3624 Normanton Oil Tanks 1922
WO 361/1416 Survivors names from Japanese Massacre from Pte SWJ Hoskin
WO 361/293: Malaya: 32nd Company, Royal Army Medical Corps; missing personnel
WO 361/752 Alexandra Hospital Singapore recollection from Mr DF Carse
WO 361/752 11678 Letter to Dorothy Young from Bill Cowan 48DONR section 3/12/45
WO 361/770 Letter from Major Bull to father of Hugh Mitchell, 29/9/45
WO 361/770 Stringer recollections, October 1945.
WO361/770 Report by Brig Stringer, DDMS Malaya, October 1945.
WO361/770 Statement by CFE Mounsey, 22/9/45

Secondary Sources:

Newspapers:

Straits Times, various issues, August 1940
The Times, 3 March 1938
Singapore Free Press 10 March 1947
Sydney Morning Herald, 8 May 2019
Post Magazine, 9 August 2014.
Daily Express, 14 August 2008, True Horror of the Singapore Massacre
Manawatu Times, 11 September 1937
Ashburton Guardian, 22 April 1936
The Sheffield Star, 20 April 1973

Museums:

Bukit Chandu Museum: Various exhibits
Nanjing Massacre Memorial Museum, Nanjing, China: Various exhibits
Yasukuni Shrine, Tokyo, Japan: Various exhibits.

Communiques and Papers:
Alexandra Hospital War Diary
An Overview Of The Singapore War Crimes Trials (1946–1948): Prosecuting Lower-Level Accused, Cheah W L
Federated Malay States, Medical Department, Annual Report 1930
Instructions from Japanese High Command 16 Feb 1942, TSW Thomas
Interrogation Form (1) TB Smiley 19/12/1945
John Pritchard, PhD, editor of *Tokyo Major War Crimes Trial the Complete Transcripts of the Proceedings of the International Military Tribunal for the Far East*
My Wartime Experiences in Singapore, Mamoru Shinzaki interviewed by Lim Yoon Lim, Institute of Southeast Asian Studies, 1973.
National Probate Calendar, England and Wales, 1947.
The Defence of Hong Kong, December 1941, Terry Copp
The Story of 13th Australian General Hospital 8th Division 2nd AIF 1941–1945, Lex Arthurson.

Published Sources/Books and Suggested Reading:
44 Days, 75 Squadron and the Fight for Australia, Michael Veitch.
A Hell of a Licking, The Retreat from Burma 1941-2, James Lunt.
Alexandra Hospital: From British Military to Civilian Institution 1938-1998, Jeff Partridge.
Cyril Wild: The Tall Man Who Never Slept, James Bradley.
Faithful in Adversity, the Royal Army Medical Corps in the Second World War, John Broom.
Forgotten Armies: The *Fall of British Asia, 1941-1945*, Christopher Bayly, Timothy Harper
Four Samurai, A Quartet of Japanese Army Commanders in the Second World War, Arthur Swinson
From Hell Island to Hay Fever: The life story of Dr Bill Frankland, Paul Watkins
Grunt, The Curious Science of Humans at War, Mary Roach.
Hellfire, The Story of Australia, Japan and the Prisoners of War, Cameron Forbes.

Hong Kong Internment, 1942-1945, Life in the Japanese Civilian Camp at Stanley, Geoffrey Charles Emerson.
Japan's Greatest Victory, Britain's Worst Defeat from the Japanese Perspective: The Capture of Singapore 1942, Col Masanobu Tsuji.
Japanese Army in World War Two, Conquest of the Pacific 1931-45 (2), Dr Duncan Anderson
Japanese Army in World War Two, Conquest of the Pacific 1941-2, Dr Duncan Anderson.
No Better Friend: One Man, One Dog, and Their Extraordinary Story of Courage, Robert Weintraub
No Mercy From the Japanese: A Survivor's Account of the Death Railway and the Hellships 1942-45, John Wyatt and Cec Lowry.
Nursing History for Contemporary Role Development,
On Radji Beach, The Story of the Australian Nurses after the fall of Singapore, Ian Shaw.
Orders of Battle, Second World War 1939-1945, Lt HF Joslen.
Prisoner of the Turnip Heads: Horror, Hunger and Humour in Hong Kong 1941-1945, George Wright-Nooth
Quiet Heroines: Nurses of the Second World War, Brenda McBryde
Roll On: a Changi PoW Remembers. The Secret Diary Kept by Corporal Joseph Nutter, RAMC, Joseph Nutter.
Sepoys Against the Rising Sun – The Indian Army in Far East and South-East Asia, Kaushik Roy.
Seventy Days to Singapore, The Malayan Campaign 1941-42, Stanley L Falk.
Shanghai and Nanjing 1937: Massacre on the Yangtze, Benjamin Lai and Giuseppi Rava
Sisters In Arms: British Army Nurses Tell Their Story, Nicola Tyrer
Slim: The Standardbearer, Ronald Lewin.
Spitting on a Soldier's Grave: Court Martialed After Death, the Story of the Forgotten Irish and British Soldiers, Robert Widders.
Sugamo Prison, Tokyo – an account of the trial and sentencing of Japanese War Criminals in 1948 by a US Participant, John L Ginn
The Battle for Hong Kong 1941-45, Hostage to Fortune, Oliver Lyndsay

The Brave Japanese, Kenneth Harrison.
The Bridge at Parit Sulong: An Investigation of Mass Murder, Malaya 1942, Lynette Ramsay Silver.
The Hunting of Force Z – The Sinking of the Prince of Wales and the Repulse, Richard Hough.
The Japanese Thrust, L Wigmore
The Kempeitai in Java and Sumatra, Barbara Gifford Shimer
The Last Lap, Edith Stevenson.
The Men Who Lost Singapore 1938-1942, Ronald McCrum.
The Rape of Nanking, Iris Chang.
The Taste of Longing, Suzanne Evans.
The Two Beginnings, A History of St George's Church, Tanglin, John B Hattendorf.
They Were in Nanjing: The Nanjing Massacre Witnessed by American and British Nationals, Suping Lu
To Singapore and Beyond: Story of the 4th, 5th and 6th Battalions, Royal Norfolk Regiment, 1939-45, Neil R Storey

For full list and links to websites consulted, please visit catmatdog.com/ableedingslaughterhouse

About Stuart Lloyd

Stuart has worked as a professional storyteller – in advertising, radio, newspapers, the corporate world, and military history tour guiding – for 30 years. His books have sold over 100,000 copies around the world, topping best-seller lists in three countries and topping five separate Amazon charts, too.

His writing has featured everywhere from *National Geographic Traveler, Sydney Morning Herald, The Australian,* to the *South China Morning Post,* among many others.

The Telegraph, UK, called him 'the perfect storyteller' which Stuart says just goes to show you can't believe everything you read in the papers.

Stuart is passionate about motorcycle touring and enjoys seeing the world on two wheels. When not writing or riding, you'll find him listening to Latin reggae music or African jazz (oh, he's a fourth generation Rhodesian -- born in what is now Zimbabwe – and has lived in nine countries, including 25 years in Southeast Asia.)

Praise for Stuart Lloyd's war history writing:

'Absolutely compelling.' – John Kerr, Radio 2UE, Sydney.

'An amazing read ... a historical document which Stu Lloyd has done an amazing job on.' – Simon Owen, Radio 3 AW, Melbourne.

'We are in the hands of a truly professional wordsmith ... I am lost for words.' Rear Admiral (ret'd) Ian Richards, Royal Australian Navy.

See more of Stuart's titles at amazon.com/author/StuLloyd

Made in the USA
Monee, IL
04 October 2025

31337898R00312